Mechanical Engineering Craft Theory and related subjects Volume 1

Mechanical Engineering Craft Theory and related subjects
Volume 1

R.L. Timings and O. Alabi

**Pearson Education Limited
Edinburgh Gate, Harlow,
Essex CM20 2JE, England
and Associated Companies throughout
the World**

© Longman Group UK Limited 1983

All rights reserved; no part of this publication may be reproduced, stored in a retrieval system, or transmitted in any form or by any means, electronic, mechanical, photocopying, recording, or otherwise, without the prior permission of the copyright owner.

First published 1983
Thirteenth impression 2011

ISBN 978-0-582-65801-1

Printed in Malaysia, PPSB

British Library Cataloguing in Publication Data

Timings, R.L.
   Mechanical engineering craft theory. -
   (Longman international technical texts)
   Vol.1
   1. Mechanical engineering
   I. Title   II. Alabi, O.
   621   TJ145

ISBN 0-582-65801-2

Library of Congress Cataloging in Publication Data

Timings, R.L. (Roger Leslie)
   Mechanical engineering craft theory.
   (Longman international technical texts)
   Includes indexes.
   1. Mechanical engineering.   I. Alabi, O.
II. Title.   III. Series.
TJ146. T45   1983   621   82-14909
ISBN 0-582-65801-2 (v. 1)
ISBN 0-582-65802-0 (v. 2)

Acknowledgements

The publishers are grateful to the author for permission to reproduce photographs in the text with the exception of the photos appearing on page 98 which were supplied by J. Allan Cash Limited and those on page 317 which were supplied by Joseph Such Associates Limited.

Contents

1
Workshop calculations *1*
The need for calculations, Fractions, Vulgar fractions – manipulation, Cancelling, Decimal fractions, Percentage, Average, Ratio, Proportion, Formulae, Angular notation, Angular measurement, Angular conversion, Squares and square roots, The right-angled triangle, Exercises.

2
Engineering science *26*
Basic units, Heat, Expansion of metals, Transfer of heat energy, Quantity of heat, Sensible heat and latent heat, Specific heat capacity, Temperature, Workshop estimation of temperatures, Temperatures associated with forging, with heat treatment and with soldering, Melting points of the more common metals, Force, Principle of moments, Exercises.

3
Engineering drawing *48*
Introduction to projection, Orthographic projection, Conventions, Dimensioning, Duplication and selection of dimensions, Auxilliary dimensions, Dimensioning from a datum, Tolerancing, Sectioning, Screwed connections, Screwed thread conventions, Rivets, Simple geometrical drawing, Development, Sketching, Exercises.

4
Engineering materials and heat treatment *91*
Properties of materials, Engineering materials, Hot and cold working processes, Common forms of supply, Ferrous metals, Non-ferrous metals, Non-ferrous alloys, Particular uses of copper and aluminium, The workshop identification of common metals and alloys, Heat treatment, Quench-hardening plain carbon steels, Tempering plain carbon steels, Case-hardening plain carbon steels, Annealing plain carbon steels, Normalising plain carbon steels, Annealing non-ferrous metals, Hardening faults, Exercises.

5
Safety *120*
The need for safety, Causes of accidents, Legislation, Behaviour, Personal safety, Safety rules for particular tools, machine tools and processes, The safe way to work, Exercises.

6
Engineering measurement *129*
Standard of length, Measuring with the rule, The construction and use of calipers, Transfer calipers, Telescopic gauge, The micrometer caliper, Care of the micrometer, Reading the metric micrometer, The vernier caliper, Measurement of angles, The surface plate, Feeler gauges, Radius gauges, Gauging, Ring gauges, Exercises.

7
Marking out *147*
The need for marking out, Preparation for marking out, The scribed line, Sharpening scribing instruments, Setting scribing instruments, The combination set, Use of templates, Datum lines and edges, The centre line datum, The edge datum, The datum surface, The use of vee-blocks, Exercises.

8
Forging *163*
Principles of hot forging, The hearth, The anvil, Work holding,

Contents

Hammers, Forming tools, Basic forging operations, Exercises.

9
Metal cutting 174
Clearance angle, Tool angle, Rake angle, Chip formation, The chip breaker, Application of cutting angles, Tool life, Cutting speed, Cutting fluids, Sheet metal cutting principles, The off-hand grinding machine, Re-sharpening cutting tools, Exercises.

10
Fitting 194
Fitter's bench, Vice, Cold chisel, file, Hacksaw, Use of hand tools, Screwed fastenings, Locking devices, Use of screwed fastenings, Screw thread taps and dies, Screw thread tables, Exercises.

11
Sheet metal working 215
Cutting tools, Hand forming tools, Forming machines, Simple operations, Simple bend allowance, Self-secured joints, Riveted joints, Types of rivet and rivet-head, Defects in riveted joints, Soft soldering, Soldering fluxes, Types of soldered joints, Exercises.

12
Drills, drilling machines and drilling 234
Types of drill, Twist drill cutting angles, Twist drill cutting speeds and feeds, Types of twist drill, Twist drill failures and faults, Blind hole drilling, Reamers and reaming, Miscellaneous operations, Basic alignments of the drilling machine, The bench drilling machine, The pillar drilling machine, The column type drilling machine, The radial arm drilling machine, Holding the drill in the drilling machine, Work holding, Drilling thin plate, Drilling plastic materials, Exercises.

13
The centre lathe and turning 261
Construction features, Basic alignments and movements, Work-holding on the centre lathe, Concentricity, Tool height, Types of turning tool, Boring on the lathe, Speeds and feeds, Exercises.

14
The shaping machine and shaping 286
Generation of a plane surface, Construction of the shaping machine, Basic geometrical alignments, Slotted link quick return mechanism, Work holding, Tools and tool-holding, Shaping machine application, Exercises.

15
The milling machine and milling 302
Types of milling machine, Milling cutters, The mounting of milling cutters, The cutting action, Speeds and feeds, Milling applications, Safety, Exercises.

1. Workshop calculations

The need for calculations

A knowledge of basic calculations can be very useful in the workshop.
1 To check dimensions on a drawing.
2 To calculate additional dimensions for marking out, setting up, or checking a finished component.
3 To calculate the correct feeds and cutting speeds for a machining operation.
4 To check your pay slip. (A very important calculation!)

Fractions

A fraction merely means 'part of the whole'. There are various sorts of fractions as shown in Fig. 1.1.

Vulgar fractions – manipulation

Table 1.1 will remind you of the techniques used in adding, subtracting, multiplying and dividing vulgar fractions and mixed numbers.

Note how the calculations are laid out in logical steps with all the 'equal' signs under each other. The usual reason for getting calculations wrong is bad layout.

Figure 1.2 shows a workshop application of the *addition* and *subtraction* of vulgar fractions and mixed numbers.

Figure 1.3 shows a workshop application of the *multiplication* of vulgar fractions and mixed numbers.

The manipulation of vulgar fractions becomes more complicated when there is a mixture of signs in the same problem, or when brackets are introduced into a problem. It is only by strict observance of the rules governing

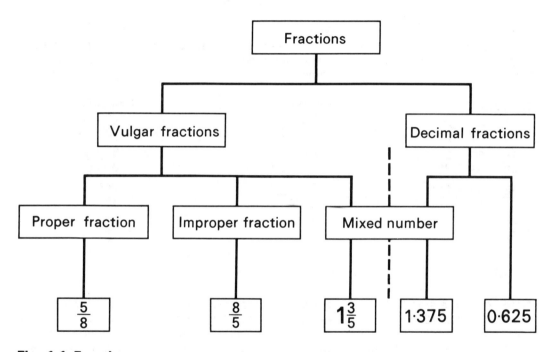

Fig. 1.1 Fractions

Table 1.1 *Manipulation of vulgar fractions and mixed numbers*

ADDITION	SUBTRACTION	MULTIPLICATION	DIVISION
Rule To add vulgar fractions make all the denominators the same.	**Rule** To subtract vulgar fractions make all the denominators the same.	**Rule** To multiply vulgar fractions make all mixed numbers into improper fractions.	**Rule** To divide vulgar fractions invert the divisor and multiply.
Example $$\frac{3}{8} + \frac{5}{12} + \frac{7}{16}$$ $$= \frac{18}{48} + \frac{20}{48} + \frac{21}{48}$$ $$= \frac{18 + 20 + 21}{48}$$ $$= \frac{59}{48}$$ $$= 1\frac{11}{48}$$	**Example** $$\frac{7}{8} - \frac{5}{12}$$ $$= \frac{21}{24} - \frac{10}{24}$$ $$= \frac{21 - 10}{24}$$ $$= \frac{11}{24}$$	**Example** $$2\frac{2}{3} \times \frac{3}{5}$$ $$= \frac{8}{3} \times \frac{3}{5}$$ $$= \frac{24^8}{15_5}$$ $$= 1\frac{3}{5}$$	**Example** $$2\frac{2}{3} \div \frac{3}{5}$$ $$= 2\frac{2}{3} \times \frac{5}{3}$$ $$= \frac{8}{3} \times \frac{5}{3}$$ $$= \frac{40}{9}$$ $$= 4\frac{4}{9}$$
Note: 48 is the smallest number that 8, 12, 16 will divide into exactly. It is called the **lowest common multiple**	**Note**: 24 is the smallest number that 8, 12 will divide into exactly. It is called the **lowest common multiple**	**Note**: The word 'of' can also be used in place of the multiplication sign. $$2\frac{2}{3} \times \frac{3}{5} = \frac{3}{5} \text{ of } 2\frac{2}{3}$$	**Note**: 1. The number following the ÷ sign is the divisor. 2. The problem could have been written $$\frac{2\frac{2}{3}}{\frac{3}{5}}$$

Table 1.2 *Order of operations*

| MIXED SIGNS | BRACKETS |

MIXED SIGNS

Rule

× ÷ are strong signs, **calculate first**.
+ − are weak signs, **calculate last**.

Example 1

$$\frac{3}{4} + \frac{5}{12} \times \frac{3}{5} - \frac{1}{8}$$

$$= \frac{3}{4} + \frac{5 \times 3}{12 \times 5} - \frac{1}{8}$$

$$= \frac{3}{4} + \frac{\cancel{15}^{1}}{\cancel{60}_{4}} - \frac{1}{8}$$

$$= \frac{3}{4} + \frac{1}{4} - \frac{1}{8}$$

$$= \frac{6 + 2 - 1}{8}$$

$$= \underline{\frac{7}{8}}$$

Example 2

$$\frac{3}{4} + \frac{5}{12} \times \frac{3}{5} \div \frac{3}{8}$$

$$= \frac{3}{4} + \frac{5}{12} \times \frac{3}{5} \times \frac{8}{3}$$

$$= \frac{3}{4} + \frac{\cancel{5}}{\cancel{12}_{3}} \times \frac{\cancel{3}}{\cancel{5}} \times \frac{\cancel{8}^{2}}{\cancel{3}}$$

$$= \frac{3}{4} + \frac{2}{3}$$

$$= \frac{9 + 8}{12}$$

$$= \frac{17}{12}$$

$$= \underline{1\frac{5}{12}}$$

BRACKETS

Rule

1. Irrespective of the rule for mixed signs, make the calculation in the bracket first.
2. If the signs **in the bracket** are mixed, the rule for mixed signs applies.

Example 1

$$\frac{3}{4} \times \left(\frac{1}{4} + \frac{1}{2} \right)$$

$$= \frac{3}{4} \times \left(\frac{1}{4} + \frac{2}{4} \right)$$

$$= \frac{3}{4} \times \left(\frac{3}{4} \right)$$

$$= \frac{3}{4} \times \frac{3}{4}$$

$$= \underline{\frac{9}{16}}$$

Note:

$$\frac{3}{4} \left(- - - \right)$$

is the same as

$$\frac{3}{4} \times \left(- - - \right)$$

Example 2

$$\frac{3}{4} \left\{ 2\frac{1}{2} - \left(\frac{3}{4} + \frac{1}{2} \div \frac{3}{8} \right) \right\}$$

$$= \frac{3}{4} \left\{ 2\frac{1}{2} - \left(\frac{3}{4} + \frac{1}{2} \times \frac{8}{3} \right) \right\}$$

$$= \frac{3}{4} \left\{ 2\frac{1}{2} - \left(\frac{3}{4} + \frac{8}{6} \right) \right\}$$

$$= \frac{3}{4} \left\{ 2\frac{1}{2} - \left(\frac{9 + 16}{12} \right) \right\}$$

$$= \frac{3}{4} \left\{ 2\frac{1}{2} - \left(\frac{25}{12} \right) \right\}$$

$$= \frac{3}{4} \left\{ 2\frac{1}{2} - \left(2\frac{1}{12} \right) \right\}$$

$$= \frac{3}{4} \left\{ \frac{1}{2} - \frac{1}{12} \right\}$$

$$= \frac{3}{4} \left\{ \frac{6 - 1}{12} \right\}$$

$$= \frac{\cancel{3}^{1}}{4} \times \frac{5}{\cancel{12}_{4}}$$

$$= \underline{\frac{5}{16}}$$

Table 1.3 *Cancelling*

WRONG	CORRECT
$\frac{3}{\cancel{4}} + \frac{\cancel{4}}{7} = \frac{3}{7}$ ✗	$\frac{3}{\cancel{4}} \times \frac{\cancel{4}}{7} = \frac{3}{7}$ ✓
This is **wrong** because numbers added or subtracted are NEVER cancelled as it gives the wrong answer	This is **correct** because numbers that are multiplied or divided can be cancelled and still give the correct answer
$\frac{3}{4} + \frac{4}{7}$	$\frac{3}{4} \times \frac{4}{7}$
$= \frac{21}{28} + \frac{16}{28}$	$= \frac{3 \times 4}{4 \times 7}$
$= \frac{37}{28}$	$= \frac{\cancel{12}^{3}}{\cancel{28}_{7}}$
$= 1\frac{9}{28}$	$= \frac{3}{7}$
Note: $1\frac{9}{28} \neq \frac{3}{7}$ ($\neq$ means 'not equal to')	

Table 1.4 *Decimal fractions – some facts*

TRUE

It is true that for many calculations decimal fractions are more convenient.

Only decimal fractions can be used with such aids to calculation as:
1. The slide rule.
2. Mathematical tables such as logarithms, powers, roots and reciprocals.
3. Tables of trigonometrical ratios.
4. Mechanical and electronic calculators.
5. Computers.

UNTRUE

It is not true that decimal fractions are more accurate than vulgar fractions.
1. 0·25 is equal to ¼ and no more or no less accurate.
2. 0·3 is less accurate than ⅓ to which it approximates. 0·333 is a closer approximation to ⅓, but no matter how many decimal places are taken the **exact number** ⅓ can **never** be exactly represented as a decimal fraction.

the order of operation that the correct answer can be obtained.

Table 1.2 shows the correct order of operation.

Cancelling

If in doubt, do not cancel. Many mistakes are made through cancelling the wrong terms in a problem. Table 1.3 shows what happens when cancelling is correctly and incorrectly applied (page 4).

Decimal fractions

With the adoption of the metric system of weights and measures, the use of decimal fractions is rapidly increasing. Table 1.4 is included on page 4 to remove some of the mystery that always seems to surround decimal fractions.

It can be seen from Table 1.4 that often it is not convenient or possible to represent a vulgar fraction as an exact decimal quantity.

The mathematical quantity π is often written as 3·1416, 3·142, or 3·14 depending upon the accuracy of the calculation in which it is used.

1 The number 3·1416 is reduced to 3·142 because the fourth decimal place (6) lies between 5 and 9 inclusive.

2 The number 3·142 is reduced to 3·14 because the third decimal place (2) lies between 1 and 4 inclusive.

Therefore, when the last number of a decimal fraction lies between 0 and 4 inclusive it is *rounded down*, and when it lies between 5 and 9 inclusive it is *rounded up*.

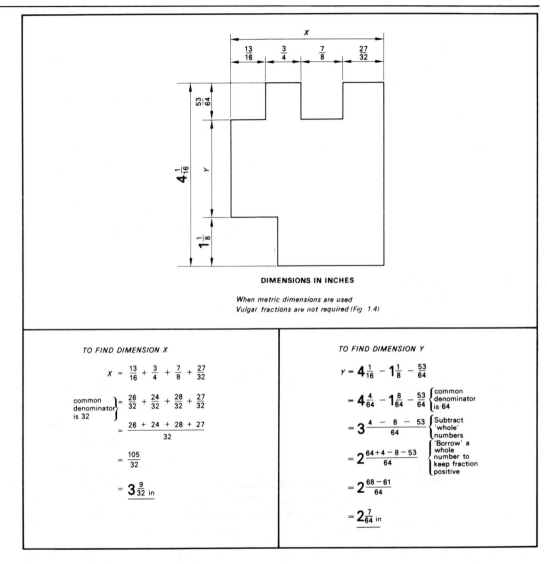

Fig. 1.2 **A workshop application of the addition and subtraction of vulgar fractions and mixed numbers**

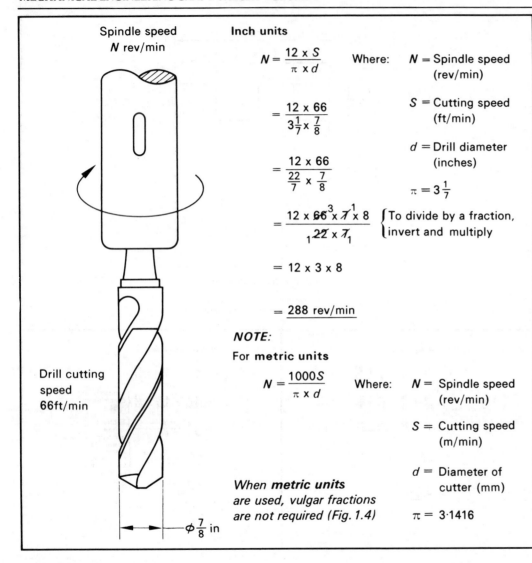

Fig. 1.3 A workshop application of the multiplication and division of mixed numbers and vulgar fractions

When a decimal fraction will not resolve into a figure of reasonable length, it is better to give an approximation and state the accuracy. There are two ways of doing this, as shown in Table 1.6 (page 8).

Decimal fractions – manipulation

The greatest difficulty for most people, when calculating decimal quantities, is deciding where to put the decimal point in the answer. Tables 1.5 (a) and 1.5 (b) show how decimal quantities are added, subtracted, multiplied and divided.
Note: where mixed signs and brackets are involved in a decimal calculation, the rules shown in Table 1.2 should be applied.

Figure 1.4 on page 8 shows the application of decimal fractions to workshop calculations.

It is sometimes necessary to convert from decimal fractions to vulgar fractions, and vice versa. This is quite a simple operation, as is shown in Table 1.7 on page 9.

Percentage

The word 'cent' means hundred. Thus 'per cent' means *per hundred*, or a fraction expressed with 100 for the denominator:

$$\frac{1}{2} = \frac{50}{100} = 50 \text{ per cent (\%)}$$

Table 1.5 Decimal fractions – calculations

A) ADDITION AND SUBTRACTION	B) MULTIPLICATION	C) DIVISION

Rule
Arrange the numbers in columns with the decimal points placed under one another.
  Add up or subtract as for ordinary whole numbers.
	Rule
	Ignore the decimal point during multiplication.
	  Fix decimal point in the answer by adding the total number of decimal places.
		Rule
		Make the divisor a whole number by moving the decimal point the same number of places in both the divisor and the number being divided.

Example *Add*: 120·13, 0·062, 79·931 $\qquad$ 120·13 $\qquad\ \ \ $ 0·062 $\qquad\ $ 79·931 $\qquad$ 200·123 **Example** *Subtract*: 28·816 from 412·715 $\quad$ 412·715 – – – (i) $\quad\ \ $ 28·816 – – – (ii) $\quad$ 383·899 – – – (iii) *Check* Line (ii) × Line (iii) should equal Line (i) $\qquad\ $ 383·899 $\qquad\ \ \ $ 28·816 $\qquad\ $ 412·715 $\qquad\qquad$ **correct**	**Example** *Multiply* 7·375 by 15·3 $\qquad\qquad$ 7 375 $\qquad\qquad\ \ \ $ 153 $\qquad\qquad$ 22 125 $\qquad\quad$ 368 750 $\qquad\quad$ 737 500 $\qquad\quad$ 1128 375 $\qquad\ $ 1 2 3 $\quad$ 1 $\qquad\ $ 7· 3 7 5 × 15·3 Total number of decimal places = 3 + 1 = 4 $\qquad\qquad\qquad$ 4 3 2 1 $\qquad\qquad\ $ 112· 8 3 7 5 *Answer*: $\qquad$ <u>112·837 5</u>	**Example** *Divide* 73·275 by 0·25 $\qquad\qquad \dfrac{73·275}{0·25}$ $\qquad\qquad = \dfrac{7327·5}{25·0}$ $\qquad\quad\ \ $ 293·1 $\qquad\quad $ 25)7327·5 $\qquad\qquad\ \ $ 50 $\qquad\qquad\ \ $ 232 $\qquad\qquad\ \ $ 225 $\qquad\qquad\quad\ $ 77 $\qquad\qquad\quad\ $ 75 $\qquad\qquad\quad\ $ 25 $\qquad\qquad\quad\ $ 25 $\qquad\qquad\quad\ $ .. *Answer*: $\qquad$ 293·1

Table 1.6 Order of accuracy

DECIMAL PLACES

237·3762 is correct to 4 dec. places
237·376 is correct to 3 dec. places
237·38   is correct to 2 dec. places
237·4   is correct to 1 dec. place

When the accuracy is to a 'number of decimal places', no further reduction can take place.

SIGNIFICANT FIGURES

237·3762 is correct to 7 sig. fig.
237·376   ,,   ,,   ,, 6 ,,   ,,
237·38   ,,   ,,   ,, 5 ,,   ,,
237·4   ,,   ,,   ,, 4 ,,   ,,
237   ,,   ,,   ,, 3 ,,   ,,
240   ,,   ,,   ,, 2 ,,   ,,
200   ,,   ,,   ,, 1 ,,   ,,

and there we must stop.

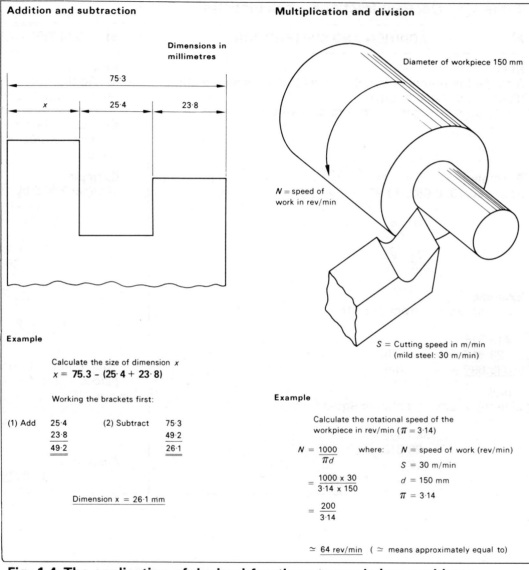

Addition and subtraction

Dimensions in millimetres

Example

Calculate the size of dimension x

$x = 75.3 - (25.4 + 23.8)$

Working the brackets first:

(1) Add   25·4   (2) Subtract   75·3
          23·8   49·2
          ────   ────
          49·2   26·1
          ════   ════

Dimension $x = 26.1$ mm

Multiplication and division

Diameter of workpiece 150 mm

N = speed of work in rev/min

S = Cutting speed in m/min (mild steel: 30 m/min)

Example

Calculate the rotational speed of the workpiece in rev/min ($\pi = 3.14$)

$N = \dfrac{1000}{\pi d}$ where: N = speed of work (rev/min)
                                    S = 30 m/min
$= \dfrac{1000 \times 30}{3.14 \times 150}$ d = 150 mm
                                              π = 3.14
$= \dfrac{200}{3.14}$

$\simeq$ 64 rev/min ($\simeq$ means approximately equal to)

Fig. 1.4 The application of decimal fractions to workshop problems

WORKSHOP CALCULATIONS

Table 1.7 *Decimal fraction/vulgar fraction conversion*

DECIMAL FRACTION → VULGAR FRACTION

Rule:
1. The decimal fraction forms the numerator of the vulgar fraction.
2. The denominator of the vulgar fraction is formed by placing a 1 under the decimal point and a 0 under each significant figure.

VULGAR FRACTION → DECIMAL FRACTION

Rule:
Divide the denominator of the vulgar fraction into the numerator

EXAMPLE 1

Express 0·025 as a vulgar fraction

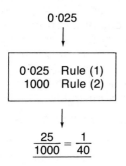

EXAMPLE 2

Express 2·3 as a mixed number

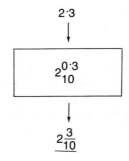

EXAMPLE 3

Express $\frac{3}{4}$ as a decimal fraction.

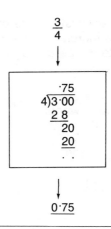

Example 1.1 A brass alloy consists of 70 per cent copper and 30 per cent zinc. Calculate the quantity of copper in 50 kg of the alloy.

Solution The copper represents 70 per cent, or $\frac{70}{100}$ of the whole.

The 'whole' in this example is 50 kg. Therefore the copper is

$$\frac{70}{100} \text{ of the whole}$$

or $\frac{70}{100}$ of 50 kg

$$= \frac{70 \times 50}{100}$$

$$= \underline{35 \text{ kg}}$$

Example 1.2 A machinist's wage of ₦40.00 per week is increased to ₦45.00 per week. Calculate the percentage rise.

Solution

Percentage rise $= \dfrac{\text{increase}}{\text{original wage}} \times 100$

$= \dfrac{(45 - 40) \times 100}{40}$

$= \dfrac{5 \times 100}{40}$

$= \underline{12 \cdot 5\%}$

Average

The average is the arithmetical mean of a set of quantities. It is calculated by summing (adding up) the set of quantities, and dividing by the number of items in the set.

Example 1.3 Find the average weight of four castings that have individual weights of 20 N, 18 N, 16 N, 22 N. (N = newton, the SI metric unit of weight.)

Solution

Sum of individual weights $= 20 + 18 + 16 + 22$
$= 76 \text{ N}$

Number of individual weights $= 4$

Average weight $= \dfrac{\text{sum of individual weights}}{\text{number of individual weights}}$

$= \dfrac{76}{4}$

$= \underline{19 \text{ N}}$

Ratio

Ratio is a relationship between two or more quantities expressed in a way that allows easy comparison of their magnitudes. There are several different ways of expressing a ratio and these are shown in Table 1.8.

Proportion

Quantity A is said to vary in *direct proportion* to quantity B if, when A is increased or decreased in a given ratio, B increases or decreases in the same ratio. This is shown in Fig. 1.5 (page 12).

The statement, *A is directly proportional to B*, is written as A :: B or as A ∝ B.

Figure 1.5 shows the relationship between the distance travelled and the time taken by a motor cycle to travel the distance at a constant speed.

1 For any distance s travelled, a certain time t will be taken. This time will depend upon the speed of the motor cycle.

2 It will be seen that for any increase in distance travelled (d) there is a corresponding increase in the time taken.

3 It can be said that any increase in t is in proportion to the increase in s.

4 Writing the above statement using mathematical symbols:
$$t :: s$$

5 Because the graph is a straight line, and because it rises from left to right, t gets bigger when s gets bigger, so it is said that t is directly proportional to s.

However, quantity A is said to vary in *inverse proportion* to quantity B if, when B is increased in a given ratio, A decreases in the same ratio.

The statement, *A is inversely proportional to B*, is written A :: $\frac{1}{B}$.

Figure 1.6 shows the relationship between the diameter of a milling cutter and the spindle speed of a milling machine in order to maintain a constant cutting speed. (See Chapter 8).

1 For any diameter of cutter d there is a corresponding spindle speed S. This spindle speed will depend upon the cutting speed chosen.

2 It will be seen that for any increase in diameter d of the cutter, there is a corresponding decrease in spindle speed S.

Table 1.8 Ratio

a : b reads as, a to b	a : b	1 : b	a : 1	$\dfrac{a}{b}$
Gear teeth: 100T (a), 20T (b)	Ratio of the gear teeth is: 100 : 20	$\dfrac{100}{100} : \dfrac{20}{100}$ $= 1 : \dfrac{1}{5}$ OR $= 1 : 0\cdot 2$	$\dfrac{100}{20} : \dfrac{20}{20}$ $= 5 : 1$	$\dfrac{100}{20}$ $= \dfrac{5}{1}$
A brass contains 70% Copper & 30% Zinc	Ratio of copper (a) to tin (b) is: 70 : 30 $= 7 : 3$	$\dfrac{70}{70} : \dfrac{30}{70}$ $= 1 : \dfrac{3}{7}$	$\dfrac{70}{30} : \dfrac{30}{30}$ $= 2\dfrac{1}{3} : 1$	$\dfrac{70}{30}$ $= \dfrac{7}{3}$
Circumference (a) = 220 mm Diameter (b) = 70 mm	Ratio of circumference (a) to diameter (b) is: 220 : 70 22 : 7	$\dfrac{220}{220} : \dfrac{70}{220}$ $= 1 : \dfrac{7}{22}$	$\dfrac{220}{70} : \dfrac{70}{70}$ $= \dfrac{22}{7} : 1$ $= 3\dfrac{1}{7} : 1$	$\dfrac{220}{70}$ $= \dfrac{22}{7}$ $\simeq 3\cdot 142\ (\pi)$
180°F (a) 100°C (b)	Ratio of degrees Fahrenheit (a) to degrees Celsius (b) is: 180 : 100 $= 9 : 5$	$\dfrac{180}{180} : \dfrac{100}{180}$ $= 1 : \dfrac{5}{9}$	$\dfrac{180}{100} : \dfrac{100}{100}$ $= \dfrac{9}{5} : 1$	$\dfrac{180}{100}$ $= \dfrac{9}{5}$
Triangle sides a, b, c	Ratio of the lengths of sides of a triangle is: a : b : c			

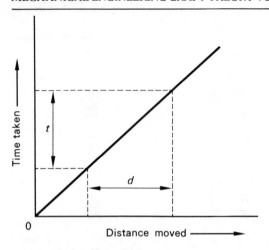

Fig. 1.5 Direct proportion

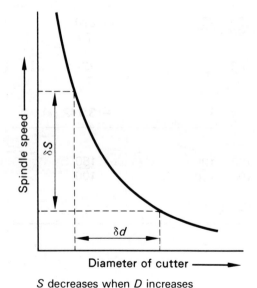

S decreases when D increases

Fig. 1.6 Inverse proportion

Table 1.9 Examples of proportionality

DIRECT PROPORTION

Example 1
100 kg of cartridge brass contains 70 kg of copper. How much copper is there in 250 kg of the brass?

$$250 : 100 :: \text{quantity of copper} : 70$$
$$\frac{250}{100} :: \frac{\text{quantity of copper}}{70}$$
$$\therefore \text{weight of copper} = \frac{250}{100} \times 70$$
$$= \underline{175 \text{ kg}}$$

Example 2
The resistance of 750 m of wire is 15 ohms. What is the resistance of 250 m of the wire?

$$250 : 750 :: \text{resistance} : 15$$
$$\frac{250}{750} :: \frac{\text{resistance}}{15}$$
$$\therefore \text{resistance of wire} = \frac{250}{750} \times 15$$
$$= \underline{5 \text{ ohm } (\Omega)}$$

INVERSE PROPORTION

Example 1
The spindle speed of a lathe is 80 rev/min when turning a bar 125 mm diam. What is the spindle speed for a bar 500 mm diam.?

$$125 : 500 :: 80 : \frac{1}{\text{speed}}$$
$$\frac{125}{500} :: \frac{1}{80} :: \frac{\text{speed}}{80}$$
$$\text{spindle speed} = \frac{125}{500} \times 80$$
$$= \underline{20 \text{ rev/min.}}$$

Example 2
The resistance of a wire of cross-section 0·25 mm² is 100 ohm. What is the resistance of a similar wire of cross-section 0·1 mm²?

$$0{\cdot}25 : 0{\cdot}1 :: \frac{1}{100} : \text{resistance}$$
$$\frac{0{\cdot}25}{0{\cdot}1} :: \frac{1}{100} :: \frac{\text{resistance}}{100}$$
$$\frac{0{\cdot}25}{0{\cdot}1} \times 100 = \text{resistance of wire}$$
$$\underline{250 \text{ ohm } (\Omega)} = \text{resistance of wire.}$$

3   Because any increase in cutter diameter results in a corresponding decrease in spindle speed, it can be said that any change in S is inversely proportional to any change in d.

4   Writing the above statement using mathematical symbols:

$$S :: \frac{1}{d}$$

5   For example, it will be seen that the spindle speed is halved if the cutter diameter is doubled.

Some examples of calculations involving direct and inverse proportion are given in Table 1.9.

Formulae

To find the circumference of a circle of diameter 20 mm:

Circumference $= 20 \times 3{\cdot}142 = 62{\cdot}84$ mm

The above information is useful if all one has to remember is the circumference of a 20 mm diameter circle. However, the craftsman has to calculate the circumferences of many circles, and he requires an easy expression that he can use on all occasions, such as:

$$\text{Circumference} = \pi d$$

where π is the constant, $3{\cdot}142$ (or $\frac{22}{7}$) and d is the diameter of the circle. The mathematical expression quoted above is called a *formula* (plural: *formulae*).

Very often formulae have to be changed around or *transposed* in order to find the required information. This

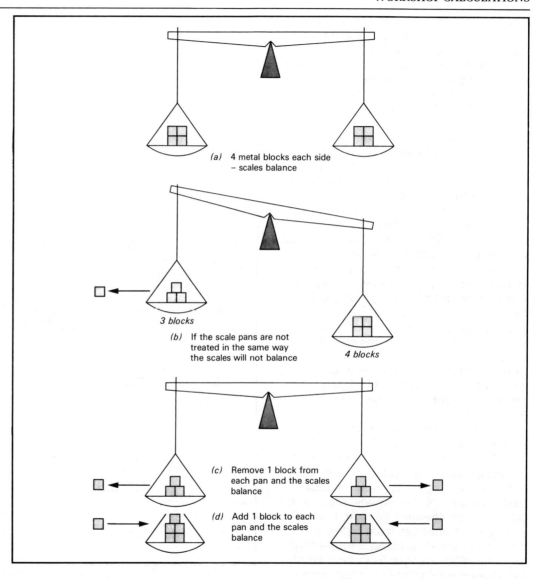

Fig. 1.7 Maintaining the balance

often causes much difficulty, so the principles of transposition will now be considered in some detail.

Figure 1.7 shows a pair of scales with four identical blocks of metal on each pan. If one or more blocks are taken away from the left hand pan, then a similar number of blocks must be removed from the right hand pan to keep the scales balanced. Similarly, if more blocks are added to one of the pans, the same number of blocks must be added to the other.

In Fig. 1.8 the blocks have been replaced by a simple formula. The 'equals' sign is the point of balance and what ever happens to one side must happen to the other side to keep the scales balanced. The aim is to leave S standing by itself. That is, to make S the *subject* of the formula.

First, divide *both sides* by 1000 and second, multiply *both sides* by πd as shown in Fig. 1.8.

After cancelling, it will be found that both sides still balance, but S has become the subject of the formula instead of N.

Now it might be felt that this is a rather laborious way of dealing with the problem but it does indicate one rather important fact. That fact is that when each element of the formula changes from one side of the 'equals' sign to the other, it also changes its sign. For example πd changes from being a denominator ($\div$) to being a numerator ($\times$). The 1000 changes from a numerator ($\times$) to a denominator ($\div$). Thus, when transposing formulae the rule is **when changing side : change the sign**.

Table 1.10 summarises some formulae used by engineers and shows how the rules for both methods of transposition are applied.

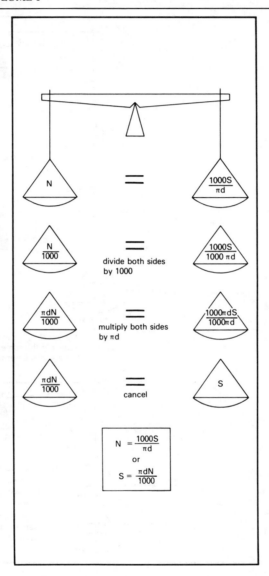

Fig. 1.8 Transposing a formula

Angular notation

If a line starts in the position OA and rotates about O in an anti-clockwise direction to the position OB, the amount through which the line has rotated is measured by the angle AOB. This is shown in Fig. 1.9a). The angle AOB is called an *acute angle*. Other kinds of angles are also shown in Fig. 1.9. Angles are measured in *degrees of arc*. The symbol for degrees is °.

1 A *right-angle* = ¼ turn or 90°. The lines of the angle are at right angles or perpendicular to each other as shown in Fig. 1.9b).

2 A *straight angle* = ½ turn or 180°. The lines of the angle make a continuous straight line as shown in Fig. 1.9c).

3 An *obtuse angle* is any angle which is greater than a right angle but less than 180°, as shown in Fig. 1.9d).

4 A *reflex angle* is any angle which is greater than 180° as shown in Fig. 1.9 e). If the line OA makes a complete revolution and returns to its starting position, it turns through 360°. A degree is $\frac{1}{360}$ of a complete revolution. An angle is measured as a fraction of a complete turn, with 360 as the denominator. Thus, if the line OA makes

Table 1.10 Transposition of formulae

FORMULA	TRANSPOSITION (Method 1)	TRANSPOSITION (Method 2)
$N = \dfrac{1000S}{\pi D}$	**1** Divide both sides by 1000 $\dfrac{N}{1000} = \dfrac{1000S}{1000\,\pi D} = \dfrac{S}{\pi D}$ **2** Multiply both sides by πD $\dfrac{\pi DN}{1000} = \dfrac{S\pi D}{\pi D} = S$ $S = \dfrac{\pi DN}{1000}$ S has now been made the subject of the formula.	**1** Transfer the 1000 $\dfrac{N}{1000} = \dfrac{S}{\pi D}$ (1000 × changing sides changes sign and becomes ÷ 1000) **2** Transfer the πD $\dfrac{\pi DN}{1000} = S$ (÷ πD changing sides changes sign and becomes × πD)
$R = \dfrac{V}{I}$	Multiply both sides by I. $IR = \dfrac{VI}{I} = V$ V has now been made the subject of the formula.	Transfer I $IR = V$ (÷ I changing sides changes sign and becomes × I)
$V = u + at$	**1** Subtract u from both sides $V - u = \not{u} - \not{u} + at = at$ **2** Divide both sides by t $\dfrac{V - u}{t} = a$ a has now been made the subject of the formula.	**1** Transfer the 'u' $V - u = at$ (+ u changing sides changes sign and becomes $-u$) **2** Transfer t $\dfrac{V - u}{t} = a$ (×t changing sides changes sign and becomes ÷t)

$\frac{1}{12}$ of a complete turn to the position

OB, it turns through $\frac{30}{360}$ of a revolution, or 30°.

For greater accuracy, a degree is divided into smaller parts called *minutes of arc*. A minute is $\frac{1}{60}$ of a degree and is written as 1'. An angle of 25 degrees 36 minutes would be written as 25° 36'. For even greater accuracy, a minute can be divided into 60 parts, each part called a *second of arc*, written as 1''. An angle of 32 degrees 17 minutes and 22 seconds is written 32° 17' 22''.

Summarising:
1 complete circle   360°
½ a circle   180°
¼ of a circle (right angle) 90°

1° = 60 minutes of arc (')
1' = 60 seconds of arc ('')

Angular measurement

A protractor or an adjustable set square is used to draw angles accurately. Examples of these are shown in Fig. 1.10. The protractors used for marking out metal components are constructed differently but are the same in principle and examples are shown in Chapter 7. *Vernier protractors* are used for more precise angular measurement and these are considered in *Mechanical Engineering Craft Theory and Related Subjects: Volume 2*.

Figure 1.10b) shows how a simple protractor is used to measure an angle.

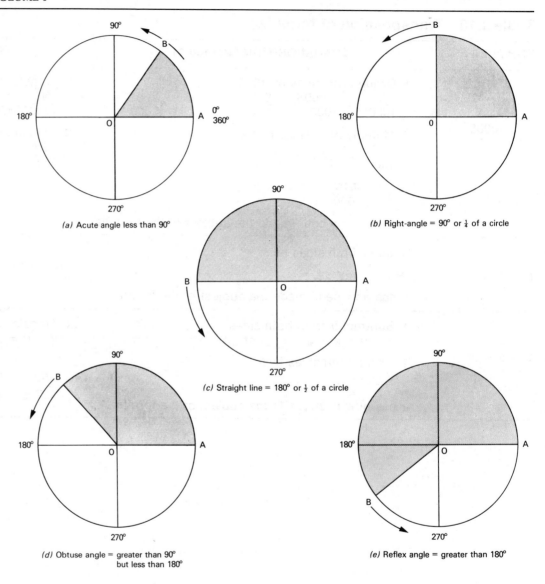

(a) Acute angle less than 90°

(b) Right-angle = 90° or ¼ of a circle

(c) Straight line = 180° or ½ of a circle

(d) Obtuse angle = greater than 90° but less than 180°

(e) Reflex angle = greater than 180°

Fig. 1.9 Types of angles

WORKSHOP CALCULATIONS

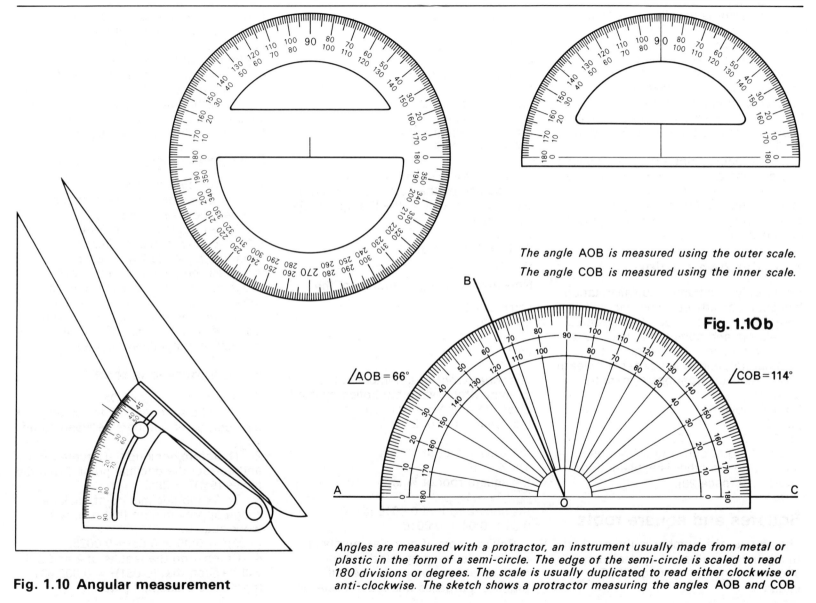

The angle AOB is measured using the outer scale.
The angle COB is measured using the inner scale.

Fig. 1.10b

∠AOB = 66°   ∠COB = 114°

Fig. 1.10 Angular measurement

Angles are measured with a protractor, an instrument usually made from metal or plastic in the form of a semi-circle. The edge of the semi-circle is scaled to read 180 divisions or degrees. The scale is usually duplicated to read either clockwise or anti-clockwise. The sketch shows a protractor measuring the angles AOB and COB

17

A protractor is usually made from metal or plastic in the form of a semi-circle. The curved edge of the semi-circle is scaled to read 180 divisions or degrees. The scale is usually duplicated to read either clockwise or anti-clockwise. Figure 1.10b) shows a protractor being used to measure the angles AOB and COB.

When adding, subtracting, multiplying and dividing angles, care must be taken to remember that 60 seconds equal 1 minute, and that 60 minutes equal 1 degree. Table 1.11 shows some typical examples.

Angular conversion

So far only traditional angular notation has been considered. However, with greater use being made of electronic calculators and computors, there is a growing tendency to change to a decimal notation. It is advisable to learn how to convert from one system to another.
For example:
16° 30′   = 16·5°
16° 30′ 18″ = 16·505°
The method of converting from one notation to the other is explained in Table 1.12 (page 20).

Squares and square roots

The *square* of a number is the product of a number multiplied by itself, as shown in Fig. 1.11 on page 20. For example:

9 is the square of 3
$3 \times 3 = 9$
64 is the square of 8
$8 \times 8 = 64$
¼ is the square of ½
$½ \times ½ = ¼$
$⁹⁄₆₄$ is the square of ⅜
$⅜ \times ⅜ = ⁹⁄₆₄$
0·49 is the square of 0·7
$0·7 \times 0·7 = 0·49$

A number to be squared can be represented by the number followed by the figure 2 placed at the top right of the number. Thus:
$9^2 = 9 \times 9$
$1·37^2 = 1·37 \times 1·37$
$(⅞)^2 = ⅞ \times ⅞$
Note that $7^{2}⁄_{8} = \dfrac{7 \times 7}{8}$ and is not the same as $(⅞)^2$
Similarly:
$3^4 = 3 \times 3 \times 3 \times 3$
$(⅖)^3 = ⅖ \times ⅖ \times ⅖$

The *square root* of a number is the quantity which when multiplied by itself gives the number. For example:
the square root of 25 is 5
$5 \times 5 = 25$
the square root of 16 is 4
$4 \times 4 = 16$
the square root of ¼ is ½
$½ \times ½ = ¼$
the square root of 0·0016 is 0·04
$0·04 \times 0·04 = 0·0016$

Square roots of complex numbers can be calculated by hand but the method takes a long time. For all practical purposes it is much easier to find the squares and square roots of numbers by using the tables provided in engineers' pocket books and sets of mathematical tables. The following examples are based on standard *four figure* mathematical tables.

The method of using tables to find the square of numbers lying between 1 and 10 is shown in Fig. 1.12 (page 21).

For numbers greater than 10·0

To find the square of 52·4.
1   The tables only list the squares of numbers between 1 and 10.
2   Therefore, look up the square for 5·24 and correct the decimal point. From the tables $(5·24)^2 = 27·46$.
3   To fix the decimal point, make a rough approximation that is easy to work out, i.e. $(50)^2 = 50 \times 50 = 2500$.
4   Comparing the results of (2) and (3) it will be seen that $(52·4)^2 = 2746$ (correct to 4 significant figures).

For numbers less than 1·0

To find the square of 0·051.
1   It will be seen that the tables only list the squares of numbers between 1 and 10.
2   Therefore, look up the square for 5·1 and correct the decimal point. From the tables $(5·1)^2 = 26·01$.
3   To fix the decimal point, make a rough approximation that is easy to work out, i.e.
$(0·05)^2 = 0·05 \times 0·05 = 0·0025$.
4   Comparing the results of 2 and 3 it will be seen that $(0·051)^2 = 0·002\ 601$ (correct to 6 decimal places).

ADDITION	SUBTRACTION	MULTIPLICATION	DIVISION

1   17°   15′ +
     28°   35′
     12°   20′
     ────────
     57°   70′
 	
 But 70′ = 1° 10′
 	
 Therefore 57° 70′
         = 58° 10′
 	
 2   30°   57′   32″ +
      0°   22′   30″
     62°   0′   12″
     ───────────────
     92°   79′   74″
 	
 But 74″ = 1′ 14″
 	
 Therefore 92° 79′ 74″
         = 92° 80′ 14″
 	
 But 80′ = 1° 20″
 	
 Therefore 92° 80′ 14″
         = 93° 20′ 14″
	1 60° 54′ −
	     20° 30′
	     ────────
	     40° 24′
	
	 2 30° 47′ −
	      0° 57′
	
	 Re-write as:
	
	     29° 107′ −
	      0° 57′
	     ─────────
	     29° 50′
	
	 3 32° 15′ 57″ −
	     10° 30′ 30″
	
	 Re-write as:
	
	     31° 75′ 57″ −
	     10° 30′ 30″
	     ───────────────
	     21° 45′ 27″
		1 60° 54′ ×
		            3
		     ────────
		     182° 42′
		      2° 60)162
		     180° 2° + 42′
		     ────
		     182°
		
		 Ans: 182° 42′
		
		     20° 24′ 32″ ×
		                      4
		     ───────────────
		     81° 38′ 8″
		      1° 2′ 60)128″
		     80° 96′ 2′ + 8″
		     ──── 60)98′
		     81°
		           1° + 38′
		
		 Ans: 81′ 38′ 8″
			1 28° 45′ ÷ 3
			
			      9° 35′
			     3)28° 45′
			      27°
			     ────
			       1°
			     × 60
			     ────
			      60′
			      45′
			     3)105′
			      105′
			      ──
			
			 Ans: 9° 35′
			
			 2 27° 30′ 44″ ÷ 4
			
			      6° 52′ 41″
			     4)27° 30′ 44″
			      24
			     ────
			       3
			     × 60
			     ────
			      180
			       30
			     4)210′
			      208
			     ────
			       2′
			     × 60
			     ────
			      120
			       44
			     4)164
			      164
			      ──
			
			 Ans: 6° 52′ 41″

Table 1.11 *Addition, subtraction, multiplication and division of angles.*

MECHANICAL ENGINEERING CRAFT THEORY VOLUME 1

Table 1.12 Angular conversion
1 degree of arc (1°) = 60 minutes (60'):
1 minute of arc = 60 seconds (60'')

Conversion of minutes and seconds to a decimal fraction of a degree.

Rule
Minutes of arc ÷ 60 = decimal fraction of a **degree**.
Seconds of arc ÷ 60 = decimal fraction of a **minute**.

Example
To convert 45°41'24'' into degrees and decimal of a degree.
Stage 1
24'' ÷ 60 = 0·4'

Stage 2
(41' + 0·4') ÷ 60 = 0·69°
  Thus: 45°41'24'' = 45·69°

Conversion of a decimal of a degree to minutes and seconds of arc.

Rule
Minutes of arc = decimal fraction of a **degree** × 60.
Seconds of arc = decimal fraction of a **minute** × 60.

Example
To convert 54·615° to degrees, minutes and seconds of arc.

Stage 1
0·615 × 60 = 36·9'

Stage 2
To remove the decimal from the minutes (0·9') multiply the 0·9' by 60.
0·9' × 60 = 54''
  Thus: 54·615° = 54°36'54''

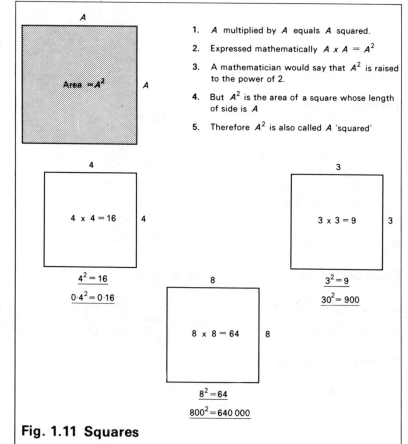

1. A multiplied by A equals A squared.
2. Expressed mathematically $A \times A = A^2$
3. A mathematician would say that A^2 is raised to the power of 2.
4. But A^2 is the area of a square whose length of side is A
5. Therefore A^2 is also called A 'squared'

Fig. 1.11 Squares

WORKSHOP CALCULATIONS

Fig. 1.12 Tables of squares

For numbers between 1 and 10

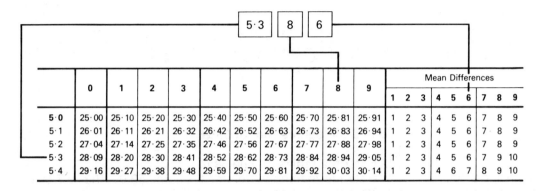

	0	1	2	3	4	5	6	7	8	9	Mean Differences								
											1	2	3	4	5	6	7	8	9
5·0	25·00	25·10	25·20	25·30	25·40	25·50	25·60	25·70	25·81	25·91	1	2	3	4	5	6	7	8	9
5·1	26·01	26·11	26·21	26·32	26·42	26·52	26·63	26·73	26·83	26·94	1	2	3	4	5	6	7	8	9
5·2	27·04	27·14	27·25	27·35	27·46	27·56	27·67	27·77	27·88	27·98	1	2	3	4	5	6	7	8	9
5·3	28·09	28·20	28·30	28·41	28·52	28·62	28·73	28·84	28·94	29·05	1	2	3	4	5	6	7	9	10
5·4	29·16	29·27	29·38	29·48	29·59	29·70	29·81	29·92	30·03	30·14	1	2	3	4	6	7	8	9	10

To find the square of 5·386

1. Enter the tables along line 5·3
2. Note the reading in column 8 on line 5·3, this is 28·94
3. Note the reading in the **mean differences column** 6 on line 5·3, this is '6'
4. The two readings are added together thus: 28·94 + 0·06 = 29·00
5. Therefore, correct to 4 significant figures, (5·386)² = 29·00

Table 1.13 Square roots

4 × 4 = 16, therefore 4 is the square root of 16, expressed: 4 = √16
3 × 3 = 9, therefore 3 is the square root of 9, expressed: 3 = √9
5 × 5 = 25, therefore 5 is the square root of 25, expressed: 5 = √25
0·8 × 0·8 = 0·64, therefore 0·8 is the square root of 0·64 expressed: 0·8 = √0·64
Thus √ ‾ is the square root sign alternatively √( ) is used.

MECHANICAL ENGINEERING CRAFT THEORY VOLUME 1

											Mean Differences		
	0	1	2	3	4	5	6	7	8	9			
											1 2 3	4 5 6	7 8 9
5·5	2·345	2·347	2·349	2·352	2·354	2·356	2·358	2·360	2·362	2·364	0 0 1	1 1 1	1 2 2
5·6	2·366	2·369	2·371	2·373	2·375	2·377	2·379	2·381	2·383	2·385	0 0 1	1 1 1	1 2 2
5·7	2·387	2·390	2·392	2·394	2·396	2·398	2·400	2·402	2·404	2·406	0 0 1	1 1 1	1 2 2
5·8	2·408	2·410	2·412	2·415	2·417	2·419	2·421	2·423	2·425	2·427	0 0 1	1 1 1	1 2 2
5·9	2·429	2·431	2·433	2·435	2·437	2·439	2·441	2·443	2·445	2·447	0 0 1	1 1 1	1 2 2

FOR NUMBERS BETWEEN 1 AND 10

To find the square root of 5·768

1. Enter the tables on line 5·7.
2. Note the reading in column 6 on line 5·7, this is 2·400.
3. Note the reading in the **mean differences column** 8 on line 5·7, this is '2'.
4. The two readings are added together thus: 2·400 + 0·002 = 2·402.
5. Therefore, correct to 4 significant figures, $\sqrt{(5·768)} = 2·402$.

This table can also be used for finding the square roots of numbers between:

　　　　0·0001 to 0·001　　　　100 to　　1 000
　　　　0·01 to 0·1　　　　　　10 000 to 100 000

The decimal point being fixed by approximation as previously explained.

FOR NUMBERS BETWEEN 10 AND 100

											Mean Differences		
	0	1	2	3	4	5	6	7	8	9			
											1 2 3	4 5 6	7 8 9
55	7·416	7·423	7·430	7·436	7·443	7·450	7·457	7·463	7·470	7·477	1 1 2	3 3 4	5 5 6
56	7·483	7·490	7·497	7·503	7·510	7·517	7·523	7·530	7·537	7·543	1 1 2	3 3 4	5 5 6
57	7·550	7·556	7·563	7·570	7·576	7·583	7·589	7·596	7·603	7·609	1 1 2	3 3 4	5 5 6
58	7·616	7·622	7·629	7·635	7·642	7·649	7·655	7·662	7·668	7·675	1 1 2	3 3 4	5 5 6
59	7·681	7·688	7·694	7·701	7·707	7·714	7·720	7·727	7·733	7·740	1 1 2	3 3 4	4 5 6

To find the square root of 59·25

1. Enter the tables on line 59·0.
2. Note the reading in column 2 on line 59·0 – this is 7·694.
3. Note the reading in the **mean differences column** 5 on line 59·0, this is '3'.
4. The two readings are added together thus: 7·694 + 0·003 = 7·697.
5. Therefore, correct to 4 significant figures, $\sqrt{(59·25)} = 7·697$.

This table can also be used for finding the square roots of numbers between:

　　　　0·001 to 0·01　　　　1 000 to　10 000
　　　　0·1 to 1·00　　　　　1000 000 to 1 000 000

The decimal point being fixed by approximation as previously explained.

Fig. 1.13 Tables of square roots

WORKSHOP CALCULATIONS

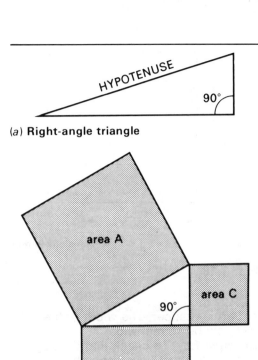

(a) Right-angle triangle

(b) Theorem of Pythagoras

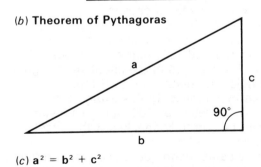

(c) $a^2 = b^2 + c^2$

Fig. 1.14 Right-angled triangle

A square root is the opposite of a square. That is, the square root of a number is the quantity which, when multiplied by itself, gives the number required, as shown in Table 1.14.

Square roots can also be found by using square root tables. Two sets of tables are provided and it is essential to use the correct table for any given number. One set is for numbers between 1 and 10, the other set is for numbers between 10 and 100. The reason for this is:
$$\sqrt{4} = 2$$
but $\sqrt{40}$ is 6·325 *not* 20.
The correct method of using square root tables is shown in Fig. 1.13.

The right-angled triangle

Figure 1.14(a) shows a right-angled triangle. The long side, opposite the right-angle, is called the *hypotenuse*.

An ancient Greek mathematician called Pythagoras noticed a special relationship between the sides of a right-angled triangle. In honour of his discovery, this relationship is called the **Theorem of Pythagoras**. Figure 1.14(b) shows this relationship. On each side of the triangle a square is drawn with length of side equal to the side of the triangle on which it is drawn. Pythagoras then found that the area of the square drawn on side 'B' *plus* the area of the square drawn on side 'C' equals the area of the square drawn on side 'A'. This he summarised in the statement: *The square on the hypotenuse of a right-angled triangle is equal to the sum of the squares on the other two sides*.

Expressed mathematically, with reference to Fig. 1.14(c), this becomes:
$$a^2 = b^2 + c^2$$
Thus, given the length of any two sides of a right-angled triangle, the third side can always be found.
$$a = \sqrt{b^2 + c^2}$$
$$b = \sqrt{a^2 - c^2}$$
$$c = \sqrt{a^2 - b^2}$$
Some standard right-angled triangles have sides in the ratio of:

a	:	b	:	c
5	:	4	:	3
13	:	12	:	5
17	:	15	:	8
25	:	24	:	7

Example 1.5 Figure 1.15 shows a triangle with one side of length 8 mm and another of length 6 mm. Find the length of the hypotenuse.
Solution
$$a^2 = 6^2 + 8^2$$
$$= 36 + 64$$
$$= 100$$
Thus $a = \sqrt{100}$
$$= \underline{10}$$

Example 1.6 Given the length of the hypotenuse as 6 mm and one other side 5 mm, as shown in Fig. 1.16, calculate the length of the remaining side.
Solution
$$c^2 = 6^2 - 5^2$$
$$= 36 - 25$$
$$= 11$$
Thus $c = \sqrt{11}$
$$= \underline{3·317} \text{ (from the square root tables)}$$

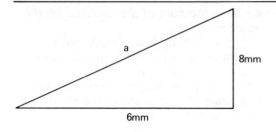

Fig. 1.15 Example 1.5

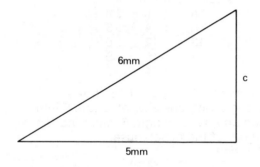

Fig. 1.16 Example 1.6

Example 1.7 Figure 1.17(a) shows a shaft which has to have a flat 18 mm wide machined upon it. Since it is impossible to measure the 18 mm width with a micrometer or a vernier caliper, the checking dimension x has to be calculated as this can be measured accurately.

Figure 1.17(b) shows the triangle that is used as a basis for the calculation of x, since x = length of side 'a' of the triangle plus the radius of the shaft (15 mm).

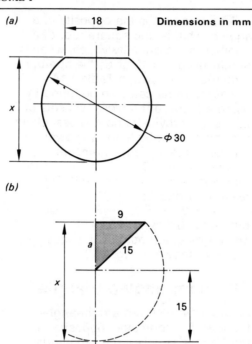

Fig. 1.17 Example 1.7

Solution
In the triangle:
$$a^2 = 15^2 - 9^2$$
$$= 225 - 81$$
$$= 144$$
$$\therefore a = \sqrt{144}$$
$$= 12 \text{ mm}$$
But $x = a + 15$ mm
$$= 12 \text{ mm} + 15 \text{ mm}$$
$$= \underline{27 \text{ mm}}$$

Therefore the flat is machined down until the dimension x is 27 mm as measured accurately with a micrometer

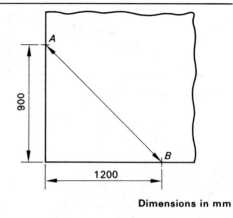

Fig. 1.18

or vernier caliper. The width of the flat will now be 18 mm wide.

Example 1.8 To check that the edges of a metal sheet have been sheared at right angles to each other as shown in Fig. 1.18.

Solution
1 Select a suitable 'standard' right triangle. (For this example a 3 : 4 : 5 triangle has been chosen.)
2 Mark off A and B in the ratio of 3 : 4 as far apart as possible. In this example 900 mm and 1200 mm were suitable.
3 If the edges of the sheet are at right angles the distance A to B represents the hypotenuse. In this example it should measure 1500 mm. This distance can be carefully checked with a steel tape.

This same technique is used for marking out sports fields and setting out the foundations of buildings.

Exercises

1. Complete the following:
   a) $\frac{1}{2} + \frac{3}{4} + \frac{5}{12} =$
   b) $\frac{17}{32} - \frac{3}{8} =$
   c) $\frac{3}{8} \times \frac{2}{3} \div \frac{3}{4} =$
   d) $2\frac{1}{2} + 1\frac{3}{8} \times 2\frac{1}{3} =$
   e) $\frac{1}{2} + \frac{1}{3}(1\frac{1}{2} + \frac{7}{12}) =$

2. With reference to Fig. 1.19, calculate the distance AB and the distance CD.

3. Sketch Fig. 1.19 and re-dimension it after converting the fractional sizes into decimal sizes of an inch.

4. Figure 1.20 shows the cutting angles of a cold chisel. With reference to the figure complete the following table:

A	B	C	D
15°		7°	
	62° 12'	5° 30'	
		5°	35°
		7° 12'	40°
18			

5. Convert the following to degrees and decimal fractions of a degree.
   a) 15° 48'
   b) 0° 18'
   c) 57° 15' 36''
   d) 0° 28' 48''
   e) 32° 0' 24''
   Convert the following to degrees, minutes and seconds of arc.
   f) 7·6°
   g) 22·8°
   h) 0·65°
   i) 48·51°
   j) 72·255°

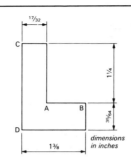

Fig. 1.19

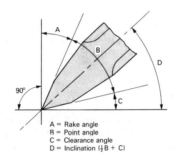

A = Rake angle
B = Point angle
C = Clearance angle
D = Inclination ($\frac{1}{2}$B + C)

Fig. 1.20

6. a) Draw a right-angled triangle, label the right angle C and label the hypotenuse AB.
   b) State Pythagoras's theorem.
   c) Using the triangle you have drawn, complete the following table. All the dimensions are in centimetres.

side AB	side BC	side AC
	3	4
13		5
	5	6
7·8	6	
	8·64	12·75

7. a) Calculate the average of the following dimensions:
   25·64 mm; 25·61 mm; 25·66 mm; 25·65 mm.
   b) 6 castings have a mass of 12 kg each, and 12 castings have a mass of 15 kg each. What is the average mass of the castings?

8. a) Calculate the spindle speed of a lathe when turning a 49 mm diameter component at a cutting speed of 33 m/min. ($\pi = \frac{22}{7}$)
   b) Calculate the time required to counterbore a hole 18·5 mm in diameter and 35 mm deep if the cutting speed is 1850 mm/min and the feed rate is 0·55 mm/revolution.
   (*WAEC* 1974)

9. a) A bronze alloy consists of copper, tin and zinc mixed in the ratio of 44 : 5 : 1. Calculate the mass of each alloying element in 1500 kg of the bronze.
   b) 2 kg of silver solder consists of 800 g silver, 740 g copper and the remainder zinc. Calculate the ratio of the alloying elements in the solder.

10. a) If it takes 120 seconds to turn a component 0·15 m long, calculate the time to turn components:
    (i) 125 mm long
    (ii) 300 mm long
    (iii) 25 mm long
    and the length of component that can be turned in:
    (i) 64 s (ii) 800 s (iii) 1·6 s.

2. Engineering science

Basic units

Most countries have now adopted the SI units of weights and measures. SI is short for Systeme International d'Unites (International System of Units) and was introduced by a general, international conference in 1960.

SI is based upon seven base units.

Quantity	Unit	Symbol
Mass	kilogramme	kg
Length	metre	m
Time	second	s
Temperature	kelvin	K
Electric current	ampere	A
Luminous intensity	candela	cd
Amount of substance	mole	mol

Mass

This is the quantity of matter in a body and is a constant quantity if the body is not changed.

An astronaut has the same mass on the earth as he has on the moon. However his *weight* is far less on the moon than on the earth. This is because weight is the effect of the *force of gravity* acting on a mass, and the gravitational force of the moon is a great deal less than that of the earth.

Weight (N) = Mass (kg) × 9·81 (m/s^2)

The unit of weight is the *newton* (N) which is the same as the unit of force. 9·81 m/s^2 is the acceleration of a body being pulled to earth by gravity. It varies slightly from place to place on the earth but 9·81 is the accepted average value.

For most practical purposes a factor of 10 is good enough.

Length

Although the *metre* is the basic standard of length, most engineering drawings are measured in millimetres. Longer distances are expressed in kilometres.
1000 millimetres (mm)
= 1 metre (m)
1000 metres (m)
= 1 kilometre (km).

Time

The basic unit is the second, but for practical purposes the minute and the hour are also used in some measurements, for example:
Rotational speeds of machines in *revolutions per minute* (rev/min).
Cutting speeds in *metres per minute* (m/min).
Vehicle speeds in *kilometres per hour* (km/h).

Temperature

Although the kelvin (K) is the basic unit, it is rarely used except by thermo-dynamicists (people who design heat engines, refrigerators, furnaces, etc.) The more usual scale for everyday purposes is the celsius scale (°C).

Freezing point of water	273 K	0°C
Boiling point of water	373 K	100°C

The units of electric current, luminous intensity and amount of substance are not immediately important to the mechanical engineering craftsman and will not be considered here.

Heat

Heat is a form of energy and when applied to a body it causes the temperature of that body to rise. For example, a block of metal placed in a hot furnace.

When heat is taken from a body the temperature falls. For example, when something warm is placed in a refrigerator.

Some of the more important effects of heat energy are listed below.
1 Most substances expand when

heated and contract when cooled. Water is a notable exception to this rule as it expands when cooled between the temperatures of 4°C and 0°C. However, it acts as other substances do for most of the time.

2   Some substances have a change of state when heated or cooled, for example, ice can be turned into water, and water into steam by the addition of heat.

3   Many substances have a change in composition when heated. This is particularly noticeable when wood is heated and changes by burning into charcoal or carbon. It should be noticed that this change is not reversible, as wood cannot be obtained from charcoal by cooling.

4   Heat can cause an electric current to flow. If two dissimilar metals such as copper and iron are joined together and heated, a small electric current is generated which can be measured by a sensitive galvanometer. The name given to the junction of the two metals is a *thermocouple*. Thermocouples are used in the measurement of high temperatures.

5   Heat applied to a substance can cause it to change colour; for example, iron glows red when heated.

Expansion of metals

All metals expand when heated and contract when cooled. This fact can be illustrated by the ring and ball shown in Fig. 2.1. The ball will drop through the ring when the ring and ball are at ordinary room temperature. If the ball is heated it will expand and will not pass through the ring. If the hot ball is placed upon the ring it will cool and contract. Some of the heat energy in the ball will be transferred to the ring which will expand. Soon, the contraction of the ball and the expansion of the ring will allow the ball to drop through the ring.

Some metals expand more than others with the same rise in temperature. This can be shown by uniformly heating the bi-metal strip shown in Fig. 2.2. Here a copper strip and a mild steel strip have been riveted together. The copper expands more than the mild steel and the strip bends as illustrated. Bi-metal strips are used extensively in such devices as thermostats, which switch equipment on or off in response to temperature changes. Thermostats are found in refrigerators and air-conditioning units.

As a metal expands or contracts it exerts a considerable force. The apparatus shown in Fig. 2.3 demonstrates how a cast iron pin may be broken when the bar is heated and then allowed to cool. When the bar is heated, it expands, and the nut is tightened to take up this expansion. As the bar cools, it contracts and pulls on the cast iron pin which then fractures. For this reason the tailstock of a lathe (Chapter 13) has to be adjusted when turning a long bar between centres. As cutting proceeds, the bar heats up and **expands. The centre would be damaged and the bar would bend if the tailstock were not adjusted from time to time.**

It is not very difficult to calculate the amount a metal expands or contracts using the following expression:
**Expansion = original length
× coefficient of expansion
× increase in temperature**.
Some typical values for the coefficient of linear expansion of some common metals are:
Mild steel   = 0·000 011 mm/°C
Copper   = 0·000 017 mm/°C
Aluminium   = 0·000 023 mm/°C
Brass   = 0·000 020 mm/°C

Example 2.1   Calculate the expansion (increase in length) of a copper bar 1·5 m long if its temperature rises from 20°C to 100°C and its coefficient of expansion is 0·000 017 mm/°C.
Solution
Original
length   = 1·5 m
              = 1500 mm
Rise in
temperature   = 100°C − 20°C
              = 80°C
Expansion   = 1500 × 0·000 017 × 80
              = <u>2·04 mm</u>

Example 2.2   Calculate the contraction (decrease in length) of an aluminium bar 90 mm long if its temperature falls by 60°C. Its coefficient of expansion (or contraction) is 0·000 023 mm/°C.
Solution
Original
length   = 900 mm
Fall in
temperature   = 60°C
Contraction   = 900 × 0·000 023 × 60
              = <u>1·242 mm</u>

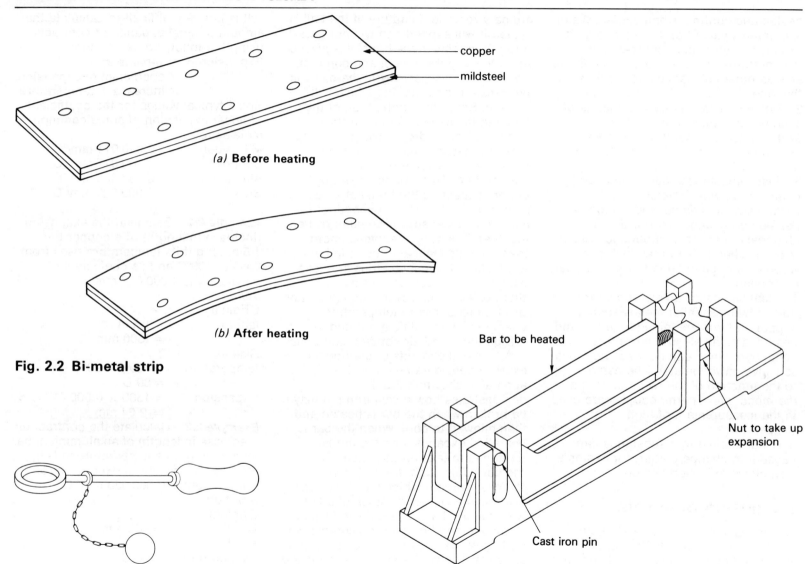

Fig. 2.2 Bi-metal strip

Fig. 2.1 Ball and ring

Fig. 2.3 Contraction apparatus

ENGINEERING SCIENCE

Transfer of heat energy

Heat energy can be transferred in three different ways:
Radiation
Conduction
Convection

Radiation

Heat energy is radiated from a hot body by means of *electro-magnetic* waves. These waves are the same as light waves and radio waves. They can be refracted by lenses and reflected by mirrors. This radiation is called *infra-red* since the radiation has a lower frequency (longer wave length) than red light in the visible spectrum. No medium (such as air or water) is needed to carry the radiation. For example the heat of the sun travels through space. This is shown in Fig. 2.4(a).

Conduction

Conduction is the name given to the transmission of heat energy by contact. In the example shown here, the heat source is in contact with the conductor (metal rod); which, in turn, is in contact with the thermometer. This is shown in Fig. 2.4(b).

In general, good electrical conductors are also good conductors of heat. Similarly good electrical insulators are also good insulators of heat. It should be noted that a good heat insulator does not necessarily withstand high temperatures.

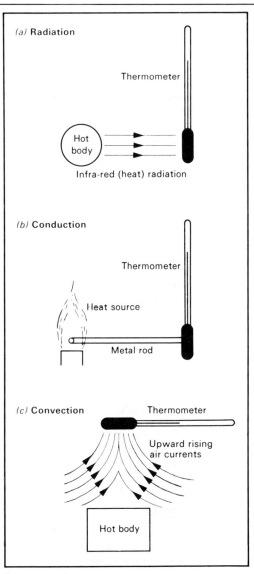

Fig. 2.4 Transmission of heat

Convection

Convection is the name given to the transmission of heat energy by the upward flow of a fluid (i.e. a gas or a liquid). This is shown in Fig. 2.4(c).

The fluid becomes less dense when it is heated and is displaced upwards by colder and more dense fluid. Examples of heat transmission by convection are:
1 the domestic hot water system found in many houses.
2 the cooling system in motor cars, though some pumping is generally necessary.

Quantity of heat

In the SI system, the unit of energy is the *joule*. Since heat is a form of energy, the unit of heat is also the joule (J). This is a very small unit and, in practice, it is more convenient to use the kilojoule (kJ) or the megajoule (MJ).

For example, the amount of heat required to raise the temperature of 1 kg of water by 1°C is approximately 4200 joules or 4·2 kilojoules. Figure 2.5 shows examples of the amounts of heat required to raise the temperature of various amounts of water.

Sensible heat and latent heat

So far we have only considered heat as the energy required to raise the temperature of a body. The heat taken in or given out when the temperature of a

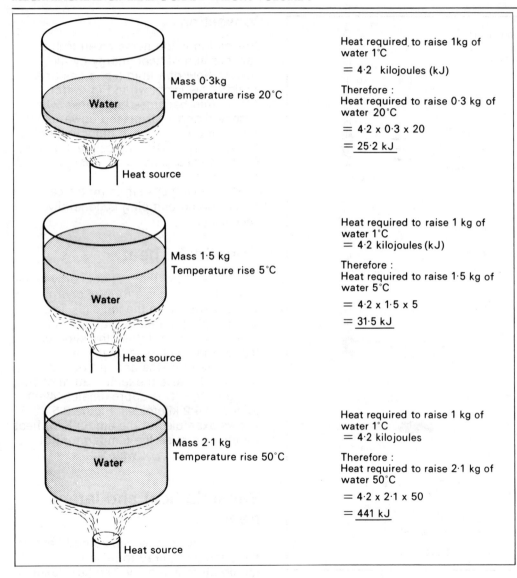

Fig. 2.5 Heat required to raise the temperature of water

body is raised or lowered is called *sensible heat*.

Heat can also change the state of a substance without changing its temperature. For example heat is required to melt a block of ice and change it into water. The heat required to change the state of a substance is called *latent heat*.

Examples of sensible heat and latent heat are given in Fig. 2.6 on page 32.

Specific heat capacity

Figure 2.7 shows various substances being heated up. In practice it will be found that these various substances require different amounts of heat to raise their temperatures by the same amount (see page 33).

The mass of the substances in Fig. 2.7 is limited to 1 kg and the temperature rise to 1°C. The amount of heat required to raise the temperature of each kilogramme of substance by 1°C is called the *specific heat capacity* of the substance.

The specific heat capacities for some common substances are given in Table 2.1.

Water-based cutting fluids are excellent coolants because water has a high specific heat capacity – higher than all the other substances in the table by a considerable amount. Each kilogramme of water will absorb a relatively large amount of heat before its temperature rises by 1°C.

Table 2.1 Specific heat capacity

MATERIAL	SPECIFIC HEAT CAPACITY (kJ/kg °C)
Alcohol	2·30
Aluminium	0·92
Brass	0·38
Copper	0·40
Glass (ordinary crown)	0·67
Glass (Pyrex)	0·84
Glycerin	2·44
Ice (−20 to 0°C)	2·10
Iron	0·46
Lead	0·13
Mercury	0·14
Paraffin oil	2·18
Solder (tinman's)	0·20
Steel (mild)	0·45
Water	4·19
Zinc	0·39

Example 2.3

A copper bar has a mass of 15 kg and a specific heat capacity of 400 J/kg °C. Calculate the heat energy required to raise its temperature from 200°C to 1000°C.

Solution

Heat transfer = Mass × specific heat capacity × change in temperature
= 15 kg × 400 J/kg °C × (1000 − 200)°C
= 15 × 400 × 800
= 4 800 000 joules (J)
= 4·8 megajoules (MJ).

Example 2.4

A quantity of water of mass 10 kg and a specific heat capacity of 4200 J/kg °C is cooled from 90°C to 10°C. Calculate the heat given up by the water.

Solution

Heat transfer = Mass × specific heat capacity × change in temperature
= 10 kg × 4200 J/kg °C × (90−10)°C
= 10 × 4200 × 80
= 3 360 000 J
= 3·36 MJ

Temperature

The temperature of a substance is its degree of hotness or coldness. It does not measure the heat in a substance. The hotness or coldness of a body can be determined roughly by touching it with the hand, but this is not practical and not always possible. To test the reliability of the hand to gauge temperature, try touching a wooden fence and then an iron railing on a hot day. They are both at the same temperature but the iron railing will certainly feel much hotter. A much more accurate and reliable way of measuring temperature is by using instruments such as thermometers or pyrometers. The thermometer, see Fig. 2.8, consists of a glass tube with a very fine bore. One end is formed into a bulb and a liquid, usually mercury, is inserted. This is done by forming a cup on the other end of the tube and putting mercury into the cup. The tube is then heated causing the air in the tube to bubble out through the mercury. As the tube cools, mercury takes the place of the displaced air. The tube is now heated to a little above the highest temperature it is to record and the end is sealed off. On cooling, the mercury falls to the bulb.

Mercury is generally used in a thermometer because:
1 it is easily seen;
2 it has a long range of usefulness, i.e. its boiling point is 357°C and its freezing point is −39°C;
3 it expands uniformly;

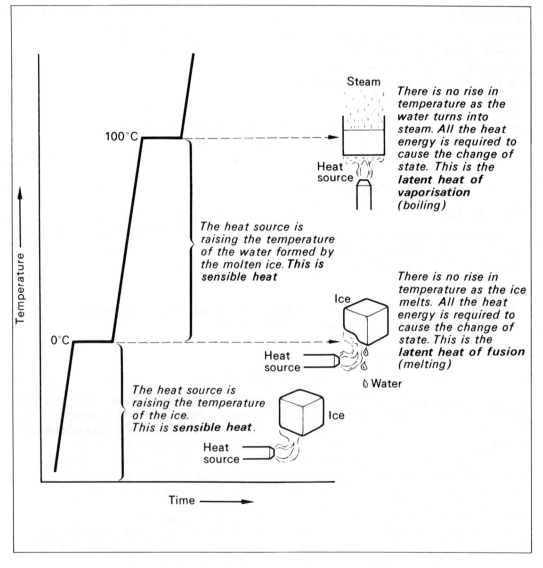

Fig. 2.6 Sensible heat and latent heat

4 it does not stick to the sides of the tube.

In very cold temperatures, that is below −39°C, mercury freezes and so another liquid must be used. Alcohol is the liquid usually preferred because its freezing point is very low, i.e. −112°C.

One other advantage of using alcohol is that it expands about six times as much as mercury for the same rise in temperature. However, it has the following disadvantages:
1 its boiling point is only 78°C;
2 it sticks to the side of the tube;
3 it is not easily seen and has to be coloured;
4 its expansion is not uniform.

The mercury in glass and the alcohol in glass thermometers can only be used at relatively low temperatures and they are generally inadequate for workshop applications.

However, mercury in steel thermometers and mercury vapour pressure thermometers can be used for most tempering processes and the chemical treatment processes associated with corrosion resistant coatings.

For the very much higher temperatures associated with heat treatment processes (see Chapter 4), instruments called *pyrometers* are used to measure the temperature of the furnaces and the work being heated. The more familiar of these are:
1 the thermocouple pyrometer;
2 the radiation pyrometer;
3 the optical pyrometer.

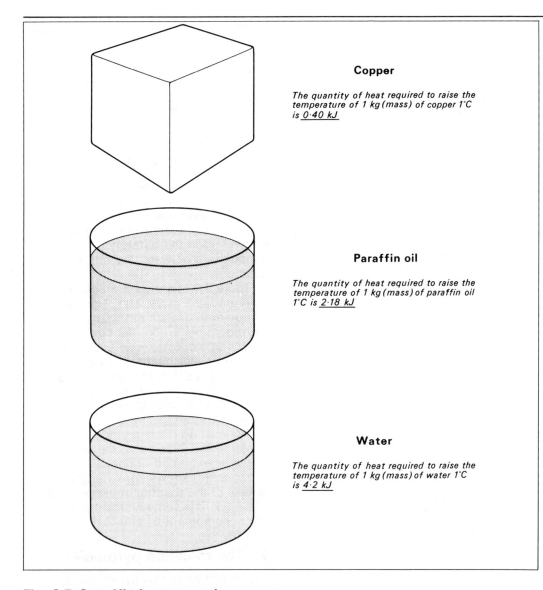

Fig. 2.7 Specific heat capacity

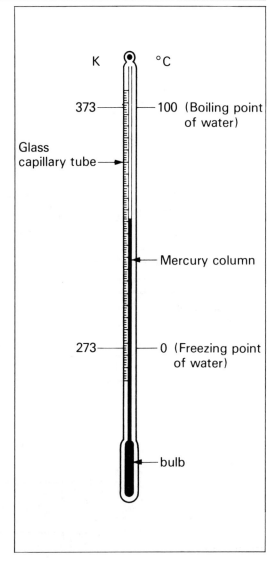

Fig. 2.8 Thermometer

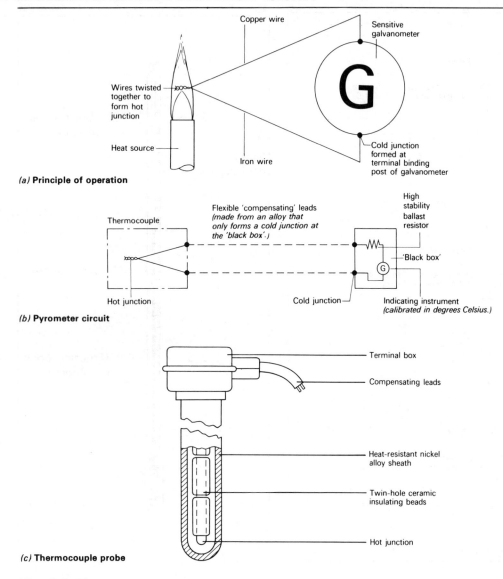

Fig. 2.9 Thermocouple pyrometer

1 The thermocouple pyrometer

This is the most widely used temperature-measuring device for heat-treatment processes. Figure 2.9(a) shows the principle of the *thermocouple*. If the junction of two different metals, such as iron and copper wires, is heated when it forms part of a closed electric circuit, an electric current will be generated in that circuit. The presence of the current will be indicated by a galvanometer. For a circuit of given resistance, the magnitude of the current flowing will depend upon the difference in temperature between the hot and cold junctions.

Figure 2.9(b) shows a practical thermocouple pyrometer. The complete instrument consists of three parts: the thermocouple probe, the compensating leads and the 'black-box' containing the indicating instrument. The component parts of this set of equipment make up a matched set that must always be kept together, otherwise the instrument will give false readings. In particular, the compensating leads connecting the probe to the 'black box' meter must *never* be extended or shortened.

Fig. 2.9(c) shows constructional details of the thermocouple probe and Table 2.2 lists some typical hot junction metal combinations and their sensitivities.

2 The radiation pyrometer

The principle of this pyrometer is identical to that described in 1 above

ENGINEERING SCIENCE

except that the thermocouple is not inserted into the furnace. Instead in the radiation pyrometer the radiant heat from the furnace or the component is concentrated and reflected on to the thermocouple by a parabolic mirror, as shown in Fig. 2.10.

3 The optical pyrometer

The principle of this instrument is shown in Fig. 2.11. The brightness of the filament of an electric bulb in the instrument is adjusted until it matches the brightness of the furnace as seen through the eyepiece. At this instance the filament is no longer visible. The brightness of the lamp filament depends upon the current flowing through it, and an ammeter that is calibrated in degrees of temperature is connected into the lamp circuit to indicate the temperature at which the lamp filament 'disappears'. (An ammeter is a device for measuring electric current.) This type of pyrometer requires a lot of skill on the part of the operator. It cannot be used below temperatures at which a hot body starts to glow: about 650°C in a darkened room.

Workshop estimation of temperatures

The temperature associated with various engineering processes can be estimated by recognising changes in the materials. With experience, these estimates can be surprisingly accurate. All solids glow and radiate visible light when heated

Table 2.2 Thermocouple combinations

THERMOCOUPLE	SENSITIVITY (millivolts/°C)	TEMPERATURE RANGE (°C)
Copper–constantan	0·054	−220 to +300
Iron–constantan	0·054	−220 to +750
Chromel–alumel	0·041	−200 to +1200
Platinum–platinum/rhodium	0·009 5	0 to +1450

Constantan = 60% copper, 40% nickel.
Chromel = 90% nickel, 10% chromium.
Alumel = 95% nickel, 2% aluminium, 3% manganese.
Platinum/rhodium = 90% platinum, 10% rhodium.

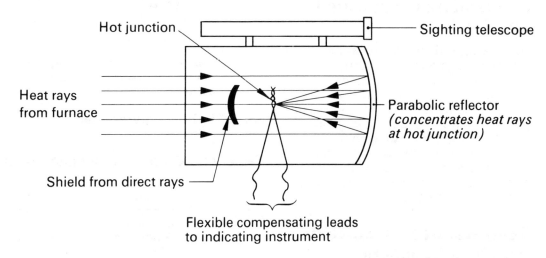

Fig. 2.10 Radiation pyrometer

above approximately 650°C. The radiated light changes in colour and brightness with changes in temperature. These changes in colour, and the temperatures at which they occur, are listed in Table 2.3.

At the lower temperatures associated with the tempering of ferrous metals, the colour of the oxide film that forms on the polished surface of the metal indicates the temperature of the metal. These colours and their associated temperatures are listed in Table 2.4. The higher the temperature, the thicker the oxide film and the darker it appears.

Temperatures associated with forging

Figure 2.12 gives the temperatures between which some common engineering materials should be forged. If the temperature is too low, cracks will occur in the metal, and if it is too high, grain growth will occur. Both grain growth and cracking weaken the forging and make the forged metal useless. This is why accurate temperature measurement and control in forging processes is important.

Temperatures associated with heat-treatment

The temperatures associated with the various heat-treatment processes – tempering, case-hardening, annealing and normalising – are referred to in Chapter 4.

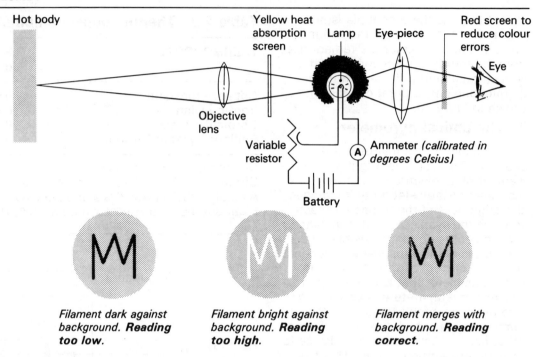

Fig. 2.11 Optical pyrometer

Table 2.3 Colours associated with temperature

COLOUR	TEMPERATURE °C
Dull red	500
Blood red	650
Cherry red	750
Bright red	850
Salmon	900
Orange	950
Yellow	1 050
White	1 200

Table 2.4 Tempering colours, temperatures and applications (carbon steels)

COLOUR	EQUIVALENT TEMPERATURE °C	APPLICATION
Very light straw	220	Scrapers; lathe tools for brass
Light straw	225	Turning tools; steel-engraving tools
Pale straw	230	Hammer faces; light lathe tools
Straw	235	Razors; paper cutters; steel plane blades
Dark straw	240	Milling cutters; drills; wood-engraving tools
Dark yellow	245	Boring cutters; reamers; steel-cutting chisels
Very dark yellow	250	Taps; screw-cutting dies; rock drills
Yellow–brown	255	Chasers; penknives; hardwood-cutting tools
Yellowish brown	260	Punches and dies; shear blades; snaps
Reddish brown	265	Wood-boring tools; stone-cutting tools
Brown-purple	270	Twist drills
Light purple	275	Axes; hot setts; surgical instruments
Full purple	280	Cold chisels and setts
Dark purple	285	Cold chisels for cast iron
Very dark purple	290	Cold chisels for iron; needles
Full blue	295	Circular and band saws for metals; screwdrivers
Dark blue	300	Spiral springs; wood saws

Table 2.5 Melting points of common metals

METAL	MELTING POINT (°C)
Aluminium	659
Bismuth	271
Brass	930–1010
Bronze	910
Cadmium	321
Chromium	1615
Copper	1083
Gold	1075
Iron (cast) 2·3% carbon +	1075–1275
Iron (pure)	1530
Lead	327
Manganese	1260
Molybdenum	2450
Nickel	1452
Platinum	1755
Silver	961
Steel 0·4 to 1·6% carbon	1400–1500
Tin	232
Tungsten	3400
Vanadium	1710
Zinc	419

Table 2.6 Melting points of soft solders

COMPOSITION		MELTING POINT	TYPE AND APPLICATION
Tin%	Lead%	°C	
0	100	325	Pure lead
10	90	305	High lead coarse solder
20	80	280	Coarse plumber's solders
30	70	260	Fine plumber's solder for angles, seams, etc.
40	60	237	
50	50	212	Coarse tinman's solder for use with copper bit
60	40	190	
66	34	180	Fine tinman's solder for blowlamp use
75	25	183	Fine and hard solders for blowpipe use
80	20	186	

A pewter solder with a very low melting point of 96°C has the following composition:
    Tin 20%   Lead 30%   Bismuth 50%
This solder will melt in boiling water.

Melting points of the more common metals

Table 2.5 gives the melting points of the more common metals and alloys. Where a range of temperatures is given, the actual melting point will depend upon the composition of the alloy.

Temperatures associated with soldering

Solders are mainly alloys of lead and tin. Sometimes bismuth or cadmium is added to the lead/tin alloy to lower its melting point. A very small percentage of antimony added to the alloy gives harder and stronger joints. A table showing the melting points and composition of the more common soft solders is shown in Table 2.6 (page 39).

Note: the melting point of the various solders decreases as the lead content decreases.

Force

We cannot see or draw *force* but we can see and feel the effects of it.

The *force of gravity* cannot be seen despite the fact that it is all around us, but when we drop something it falls to the ground because the force of gravity pulls all objects towards the centre of the earth. When we see an object fall to the ground, we see *the effect of the force*.

When you push a door open you exert a force on the door that causes movement, but when you push against the wall of a house no movement occurs despite the fact that you are exerting a force.

We can define force as that which moves or tries to move an object.

Why can we push a door open, yet not push over the wall of a house? Every time a force is applied to an object there is an *equal and opposite* force exerted by that object. This is called the reaction force. Figure 2.13 shows an example of an *applied force* and the *reaction force* that tries to act against it (see page 40).

The block of metal is being lowered on to the rubber block. Gravity acts on the mass of the metal causing it to exert a downward force. In Fig. 2.13(a) the metal is not yet in contact with the rubber. Therefore it is not yet applying an external force to the rubber and the rubber is not yet providing an *internal reaction force* in opposition to the *external applied force*.

In Fig. 2.13(b) it will be seen that the metal has started to press down on the rubber. As soon as the metal block touches the rubber, the rubber provides an internal reaction force in opposition to the downward force of the metal. At first this reaction force will be insufficient to balance the applied force and the metal block will continue to move downwards.

In Fig. 2.13(c) the rubber continues to distort (change shape) until the internal reaction force becomes large enough to balance the downward force of the metal and no further movement takes place.

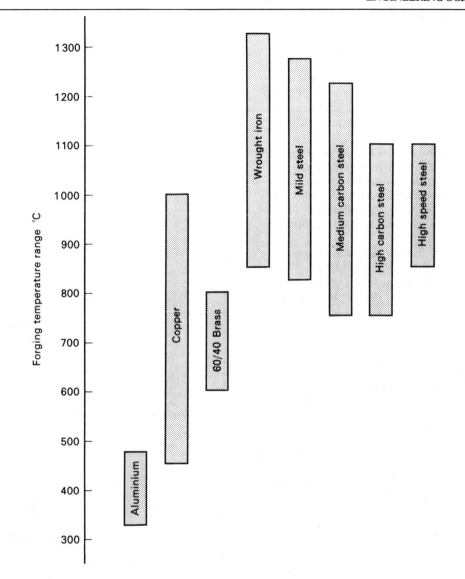

Fig. 2.12 Typical forging temperatures

MECHANICAL ENGINEERING CRAFT THEORY VOLUME 1

The rubber block is said to be in a *state of stress*.

The distortion of the rubber block when in a state of stress is called *strain*.

$$\text{stress } (\sigma) = \frac{\text{force } (F)}{\text{area of the rubber block}}$$

$$\text{strain } (\epsilon) = \frac{\text{change in thickness}}{\text{original thickness}}$$

Therefore, in addition to moving or trying to move solid objects, **a force is also that which changes or tries to change the shape of an object.**

Commonly used units of stress are: newtons per square millimetre, N/mm^2. mega-newtons per square metre, MN/m^2.

These are the same numerically:

$$5 \text{ N/mm}^2 = 5 \text{ MN/m}^2$$

Can you work out why this is? The answer is at the end of the chapter.

Effects of force

So far only the effect of a *compressive* force has been considered (see Fig. 2.13). Other ways in which a force may be applied to a body are shown in Fig. 2.14.

Example 2.5 A metal bar 10 mm square and 1500 mm long is subject to a *tensile force* of 25 kN. Calculate the tensile stress and the strain if the bar stretches 4·1 mm.

Solution

$$\text{tensile stress} = \frac{\text{force}}{\text{area}}$$

$$= \frac{25\,000}{10 \times 10}$$

$$= 250 \text{ N/mm}^2$$

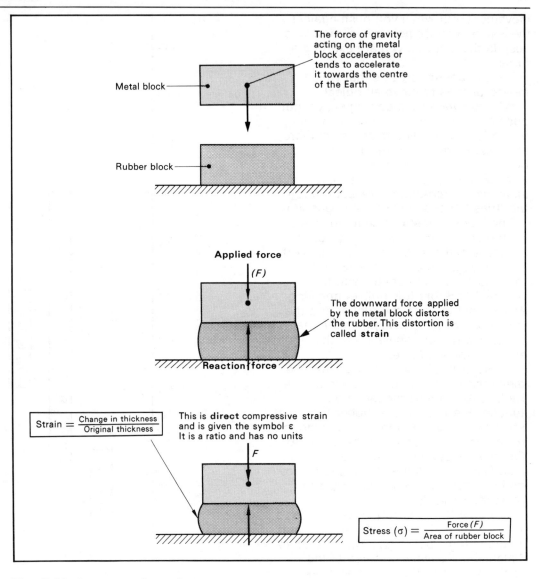

Fig. 2.13 Stress and strain

strain = increase in length / original length
= 4·1 mm / 1500 mm
= 0·000 82

Note: Strain is a *ratio* and therefore has no units.

Example 2.6 A brass block 250 mm square and 100 mm thick is subject to a compressive force of 3 MN. Calculate the compressive stress and the strain if the thickness is reduced by 0·5 mm.

Solution

compressive stress = force / area
= 3 000 000 / 250 × 250
= 48 N/mm²

strain = reduction in thickness / original thickness
= 0·5 / 100
= 0·005

Example 2.7 A steel plate of cross-sectional area 300 mm² is subject to a shear load of 45 kN. Calculate the shear stress and the shear strain if the original length is 125 mm and the distortion is 0·075 mm.

Solution

shear stress = force / area
= 45 000 / 300
= 150 N/mm²

shear strain = distortion / original length
= 0·075 / 100
= 0·000 75

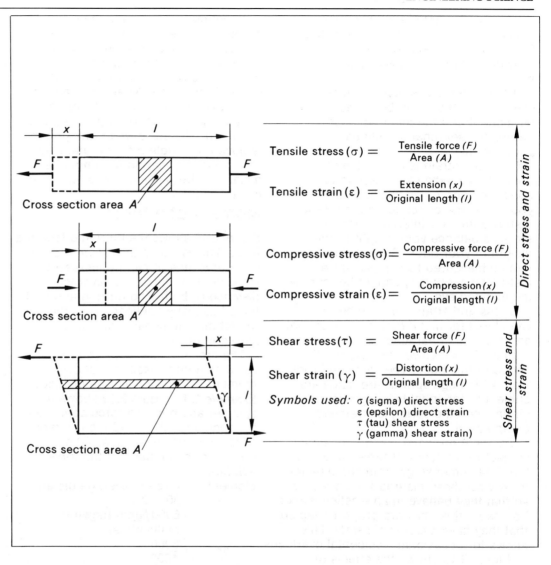

Fig. 2.14 Types of stress and strain

It should be noted that when the applied force is removed, the reaction force disappears and so does the strain, providing the material is *elastic*. (See page 93).

If the material is stressed beyond its *elastic limit*, the strain becomes permanent and the material takes a permanent set (changes shape permanently).

Often the strain is not visible to the unaided eye. When you step on to a concrete floor, or lay this book down on your desk, the concrete and the desk distort until their internal reaction stresses balance your weight or the weight of your book. Such distortions can be measured by very sensitive instruments, but they cannot be seen by the unaided eye.

Stress and strain can also be calculated for metal rods and tubes that are given *torsional* loads. However the mathematics involved are beyond the scope of this book. The wires and rods from which coil springs are made are subject to torsional twisting stress and strain when the spring is stretched or compressed.

Engineering materials are constantly subject to the types of force shown in Fig. 2.14, either singly or in combination. In service, these materials are stressed so that they behave in an elastic manner. To ensure this, they are proportioned so that they have a *factor of safety*. This allows for occasional, accidental overloads.

Figure 2.15 shows the effects of various types of load applied under practical working conditions.

Sometimes engineering materials are deliberately overstressed so that they behave in a plastic manner and take a permanent set. This enables the materials to be formed and cut as shown in Fig. 2.16. When the blank is bent, it is stressed beyond its elastic limit so that it flows to shape in a plastic condition. Therefore, when the punch is removed the angle bracket retains its shape. When shearing (cutting) sheet metal the stress is increased until the metal fails.

Moment of a force

Figure 2.17 shows the turning effect of a force. This is called the *moment of a force* or *torque*. It can be increased by increasing the force, the leverage distance or both. The turning effect of a force has many applications in the workshop, and some examples are shown in Fig. 2.18.

The moment of a force can be calculated quite easily as follows:
moment = force × leverage distance

Example 2.8 Figure 2.19 shows a spanner and nut. The force acting on the spanner is 30 N and the leverage distance (moment arm) is 200 m. Calculate the moment of the force.

Solution

$$\begin{aligned}\text{Moment} &= \text{force} \times \text{leverage distance} \\ &= 30 \times 200 \\ &= \underline{6000\ \text{Nmm}}\ (\text{newton millimetres}) \\ \text{or} &= \frac{6000}{1000} \\ &= \underline{6\ \text{Nm}}\ (\text{newton metres: the unit of torque})\end{aligned}$$

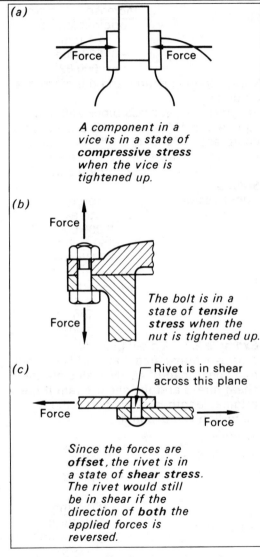

(a) A component in a vice is in a state of **compressive stress** when the vice is tightened up.

(b) The bolt is in a state of **tensile stress** when the nut is tightened up.

(c) Since the forces are **offset**, the rivet is in a state of **shear stress**. The rivet would still be in shear if the direction of **both** the applied forces is reversed.

Fig. 2.15 Practical examples of stress

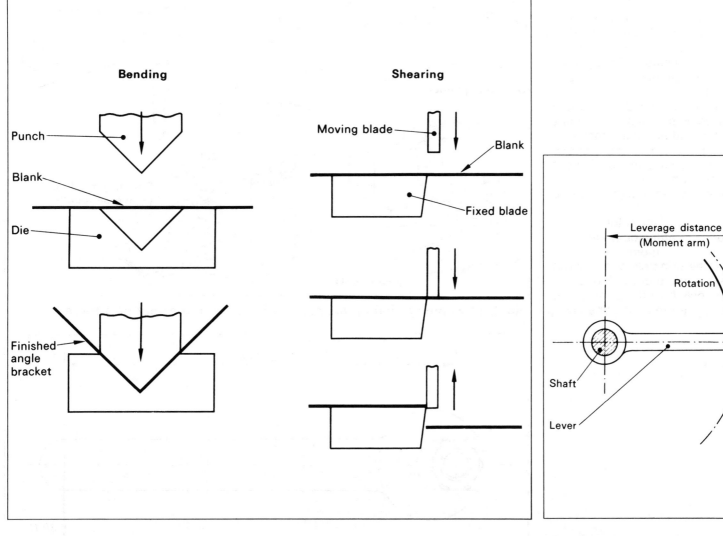

Fig. 2.16 Metal being formed and cut in the plastic state

Fig. 2.17 Moment (turning effect) of a force

Principle of moments

A lever is a device by which an effort can overcome a load. Whether the effort is greater or smaller than the load will depend upon the position of the pivot (fulcrum). Some examples of levers are shown in Fig. 2.20.

It will be seen from Fig. 2.20 that for the lever to remain stationary (in a state of balance) the load and the effort must be acting upon it in opposite directions. This observation is used in working out the forces acting on a lever.

For a state of equilibrium (balance) to exist:

$$\text{the total clockwise moments} = \text{the total anti-clockwise moments}$$

This is called **the principle of moments**. An example is worked out in Fig. 2.21. Figure 2.22 shows how the principle of moments is applied to a machine clamp (page 46).

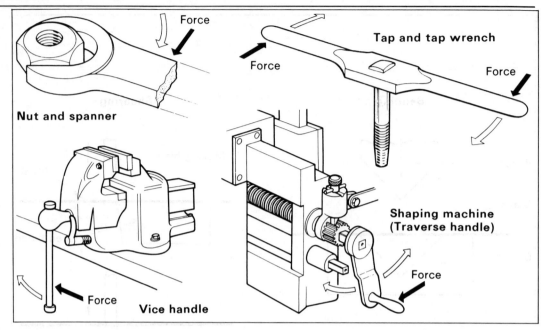

Fig. 2.18 Some workshop examples of the turning effect of a force

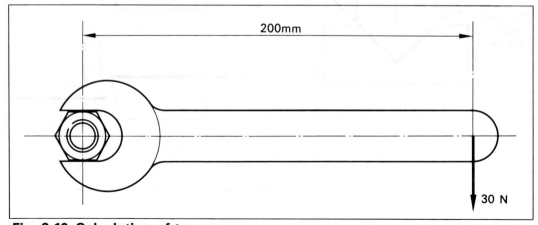

Fig. 2.19 Calculation of torque

ENGINEERING SCIENCE

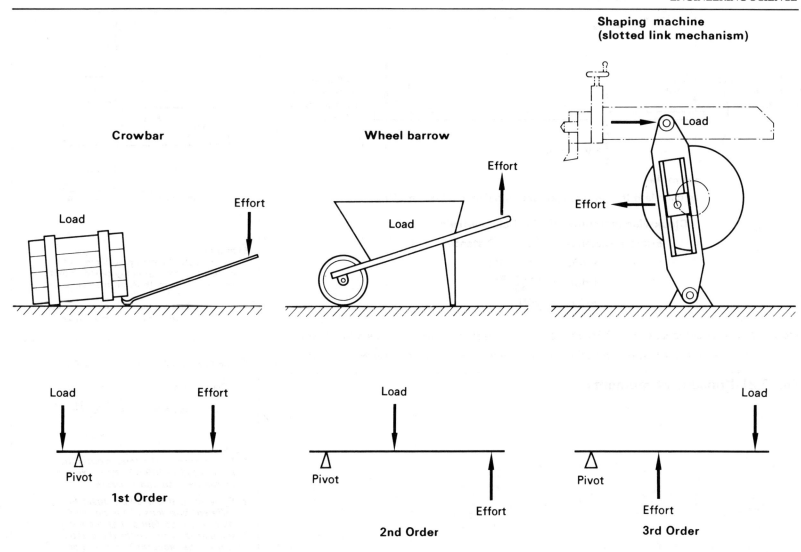

Fig. 2.20 Levers

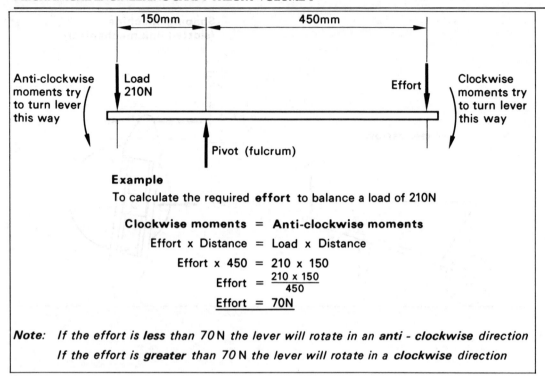

Fig. 2.21 Principle of moments

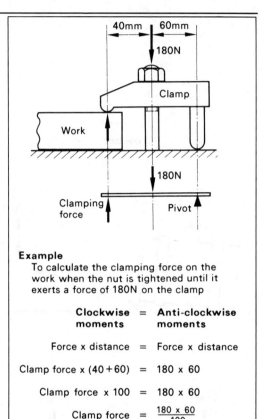

Fig. 2.22 Clamping force

Exercises

1. a) Describe briefly the difference between *heat* and *temperature*.
   b) Sketch in good proportion a mercury in glass thermometer and show on it the freezing point and the boiling point of water.
2. Describe, with the aid of sketches, a temperature measuring device suitable for use at the temperatures associated with the heat treatment of metals.
3. a) Describe a simple demonstration, using a ball and ring, to show the relationship between temperature and expansion.
   b) Describe a simple demonstration to show the force exerted on a cast iron pin by the contraction of a steel bar as it cools.
4. Describe, with the aid of sketches, how heat can be transmitted by:
   a) radiation
   b) convection
   c) conduction
   State an example of each of the above methods of heat transmission.
5. Calculate the expansion of a steel bar 2·5 m long if its temperature rises from 20°C to 250°C and its coefficient of expansion is 0·000 011 mm/°C.
6. Calculate the contraction of a copper bar 900 mm long if its temperature falls by 80°C. The coefficient of expansion (or contraction) for copper is 0·000 017 mm/°C.
7. A metal bar 5 mm square and 1 m long is subject to a tensile force of 8 kN. Calculate the *tensile stress* and the *strain* if the bar stretches 3·5 mm.
8. A metal plate of cross-sectional area 500 mm² is subject to a shear load of 45 kN. Calculate the shear stress and the shear strain if the original thickness is 25 mm and the distortion is 0·005 mm.
9. a) Sketch, in good proportion, *three* items of workshop equipment which use the principle of the lever to magnify the force applied by the user.
   b) Calculate the torque exerted by a spanner if a force of 25 N is applied through a leverage distance (moment arm) of 150 mm.
10. a) State the *principle of moments*.
    b) Calculate the force exerted on:
    (i) the component
    (ii) the packing
    by the machine clamp shown in Fig. 2.23.
    c) Why is it important that the bolt is nearer to the component than to the packing?

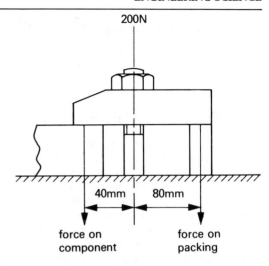

Fig. 2.23

Solution to problem on page 40:

Explanation of why
  5N/mm² = 5MN/m²
5MN/m² could be written as
5 000 000 N/1 000 000 mm²
or 5N/mm²
A stress of 5N on an area of 1 mm² is the same as a stress of 5 MN spread over an area of 1 m²

3. Engineering drawing

Introduction to projection

A well drawn picture or series of pictures can describe an object quickly and accurately. To describe the same object in writing often takes many hundreds of words and the reader might still misunderstand. This is why so many diagrams have been used in this book. Which is the easier, to draw an elephant, or describe it in words only to someone who has never seen such an animal?

Figure 3.1 shows a photograph of a typical engineering component. To draw this solid object on a flat sheet of paper, special techniques have to be used. These techniques are called *projections*. There are many different projections available to the draughtsman (the person who prepares engineering drawings) and some examples are shown in Fig. 3.2. The craftsman has to understand drawings, but he is rarely expected to prepare a drawing himself. However it is often useful to be able to prepare quick, accurate sketches of simple components, and sketching is considered on page 84.

Parallel perspective projection

This projection has only one vanishing point and is very simple to construct. It has the advantage that the circle on the

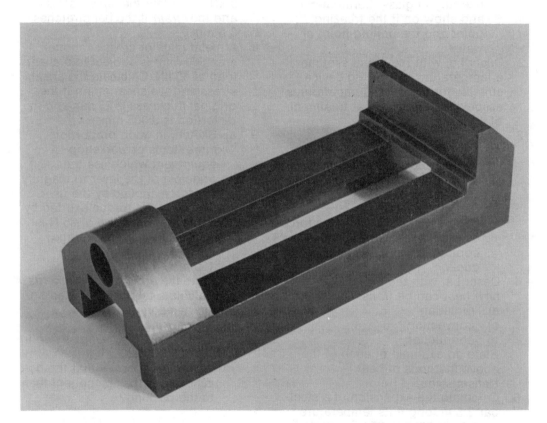

Fig. 3.1 Vice body

ENGINEERING DRAWING

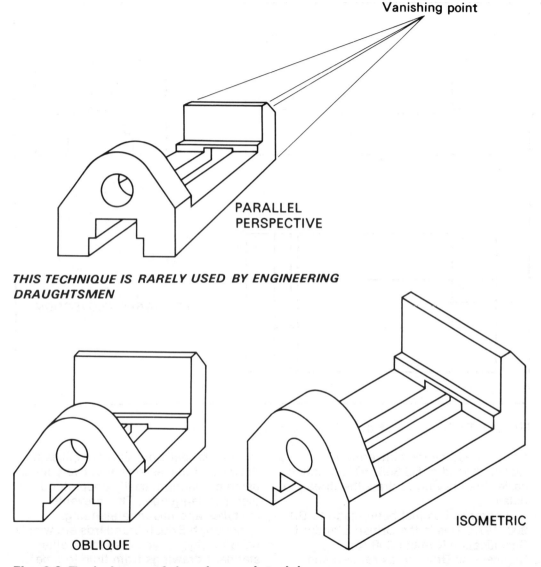

Fig. 3.2 Techniques of drawing – pictorial

front view can be drawn with compasses. Despite its simplicity this technique is rarely used by engineering draughtsmen.

Oblique projection

This projection is the simplest method of constructing a pictorial drawing as the curves do not require construction. Oblique projection is the least pleasing pictorially and much detail is lost in the foreshortening that occurs.

Isometric projection

This projection is the pictorial technique most widely used by engineering draughtsmen. Despite the fact that all the circles and curves have to be constructed, it is quick and relatively simple compared with perspective drawing. Isometric projection gives a reasonably proportioned, pictorial projection even when the receding lines are drawn the true length.

Orthographic projection

The pictorial drawings shown in Fig. 3.2 are easy to understand, and the solid object they represent is easy to visualise. However, they are all distorted to some degree to give the illusion of 'depth'.

The engineer is not concerned with the artistic merit of a drawing, only in whether it communicates information accurately and without the possibility of misunderstanding. The working drawings supplied to the craftsman are produced using a technique known as *orthographic projection.*

Figure 3.3 shows such a drawing, and it will be seen that no attempt has been made at pictorial representation. Usually, three separate drawings of the component are made from different viewpoints, on the same sheet of paper. Simple components sometimes have fewer views, and complex components more, but most have the three basic views shown.

Orthographic drawing allows each view to be drawn true to scale without distortion, and with practice the drawings can be interpreted accurately, quickly and easily.

The craftsman rarely has to produce an orthographic drawing, but he has to understand the basic principles so that he can interpret such a drawing.

Conventions

The engineering drawing is only a means by which the designer communicates easily with the craftsman. The drawing has no value in its own right and, if a better method of communication could be discovered, it would no longer be used.

The engineering drawing must be drawn as quickly and easily as possible to keep the cost down. To help speed the draughting (drawing) process, *standard conventions* are used to represent the more frequently used and awkward details. An example of the way a convention has been developed over the years is shown in Fig. 3.4. It will be seen that the method of representing a

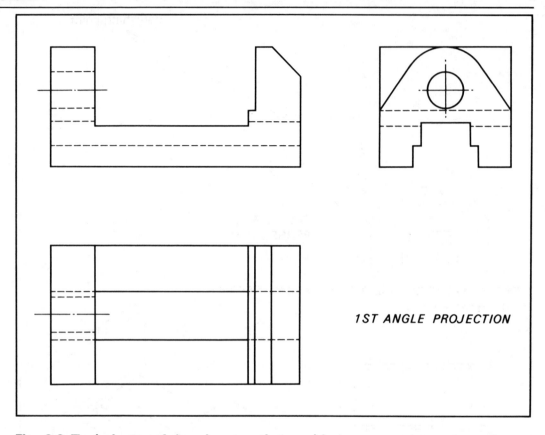

Fig. 3.3 Techniques of drawing – orthographic

screw thread by the convention recommended in BS 308: 1972 is much easier than having to draw the thread in detail.

Reference has just been made to BS 308: 1972. This is the British Standard Specification Number 308 for Engineering Drawing as revised and brought up to date in 1972. The use of such a standard not only simplifies the drawing; it makes sure that everyone is using a common, easily understood, pictorial 'language'. This prevents mistakes and misunderstanding.

Although British Standards are widely used in Nigeria, you may meet other standard drawings from time to time such as the German DIN system. Always

ENGINEERING DRAWING

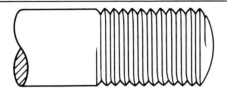

1. An early convention in which the helix required construction.

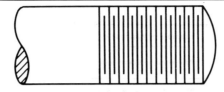

4. By standardising the line thickness the drawing of threaded components was further simplified.

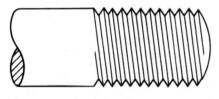

2. The first simplification was to simulate the helix using straight lines only.

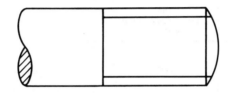

5. The alternative convention in B.S. 308:1964.

3. The next stage in simplification was the elimination of the Vee thread form.

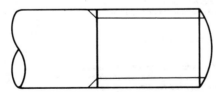

6. The preferred (most usual) convention in B.S. 308:1972.

Fig. 3.4 Evolution of the screw thread convention

check your drawing to make sure you understand which standard is being used.

British Standard Conventions in BS 308: 1972 can be divided into three main categories:
1 Types of line (Fig. 3.5, page 52).
2 Conventions of common features (Figs. 3.6, 3.7, 3.8, pages 53–5).
3 Abbreviations of written statements (Table 3.1, page 56).

Engineering drawing (1st angle projection)

Figure 3.9 on page 56 shows a photograph of a simple clamp. To produce an engineering drawing of this component, orthographic projection will be used.
1 Look at the side of the clamp and draw what you see on a sheet of paper (Fig. 3.10, page 57).
2 Look at the end of the clamp and draw opposite the clamp on your sheet of paper what you see. Fig. 3.10(a).
3 Look down on top of the clamp and draw underneath the side view what you see. Fig. 3.10(b).
You now have three, true to scale views drawn in *1st angle* orthographic projection. Third angle projection is used widely in America and will be considered in *Mechanical Engineering Craft Theory and Related Subjects: Volume 2*.

For simplicity, the drawing of the clamp is broken down into three operations. For more complex

Example	Type of line	Line width mm	Example of application
A ———————	Continuous (thick)	0·7	Visible outlines and edges
B ———————	Continuous (thin)	0·3	Fictitious outlines and edges Dimension and leader lines Hatching Outlines of adjacent parts Outlines of revolved sections
C ∼∼∼∼∼	Continuous irregular (thin)	0·3	Limits of partial views or sections when the line is not an axis
D -------	Short dashes (thin)	0·3	Hidden outlines and edges
E — · — · —	Chain (thin)	0·3	Centre lines Extreme positions of moveable parts
F — · — · —	Chain (thick at ends and at changes of direction, thin elsewhere)	0·7 0·3	Cutting planes
G — · — · —	Chain (thick)	0·7	Indication of surfaces which have to meet special requirements

(i) *Dashed lines.* Dashed lines should comprise dashes of consistent length and spacing, approximately to the proportion shown in the examples in the table.

(ii) *Thin chain lines.* Thin chain lines should comprise long dashes alternating with short dashes. The proportions should be generally as shown in the table but the lengths and spacing may be increased for very long lines.

(iii) *Thick chain lines.* The lengths and spacing of the elements of thick chain lines should be similar to those of thin chain lines.

(iv) *General.* All chain lines should start and finish with a long dash and when thin chain lines are used as centre lines they should cross one another at solid portions of the line. Centre lines should extend only a short distance beyond the feature unless required for dimensioning or other purposes. They should not extend through the spaces between views and should not terminate at another line of the drawing. Where angles are formed in chain lines, long dashes should meet at corners. Arcs should join at tangent points. Dashed lines should also meet at corners and tangent points with dashes.

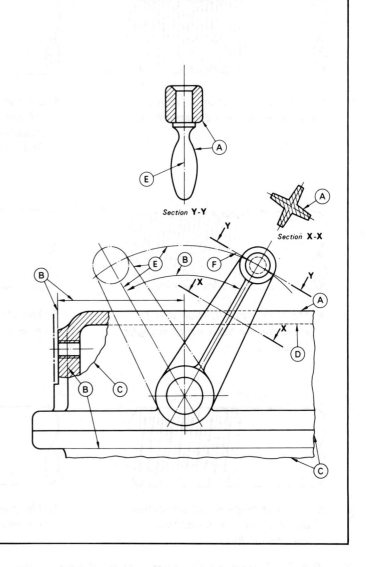

Fig. 3.5 Types of lines and their applications

ENGINEERING DRAWING

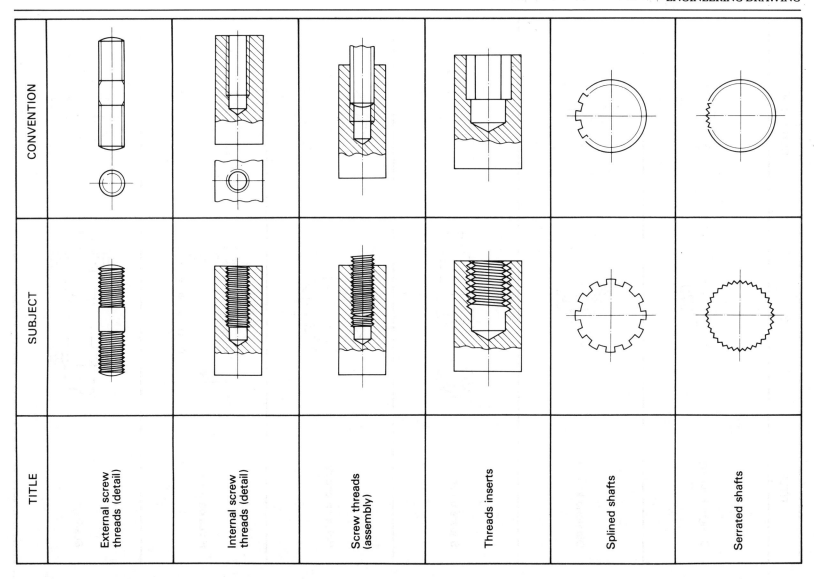

Fig. 3.6 Conventions for common features (1)

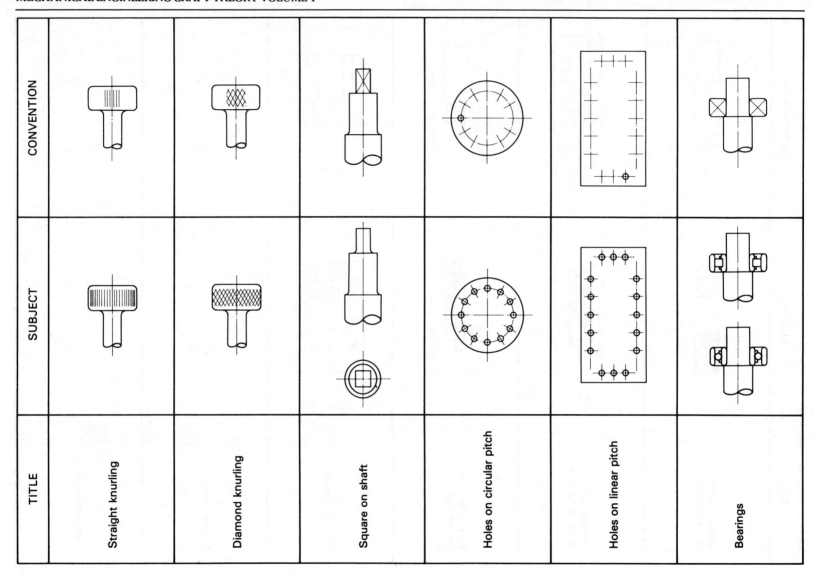

Fig. 3.7 Conventions for common features (2)

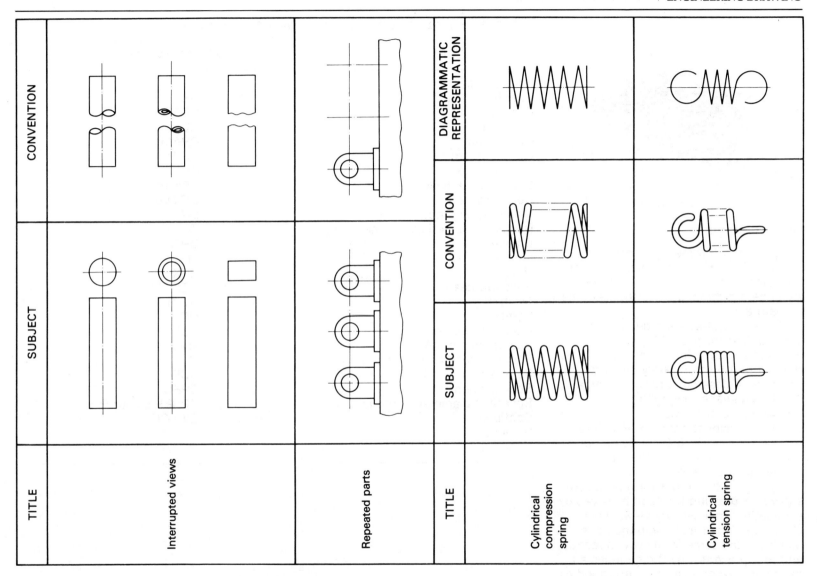

Fig. 3.8 Conventions for common features (3)

Fig. 3.9 Clamp

components all three views are often drawn at the same time; each piece of the component is drawn in all three views before moving on to the next line or feature.

Figure 3.11 shows the geometric construction for producing an orthographic drawing of the clamp. The skilled draughtsman rarely constructs every line unless he is constructing a developed shape (page 82).

Figure 3.12(a) shows a three-dimensional drawing of a simple bracket, whilst Fig. 3.12(b) shows an orthographic drawing of the same bracket (see page 59).

Figures 3.13(a) and 3.13(b) (page 60) show how drawing time can be saved by eliminating unnecessary views when drawing symmetrical components. A ball looks the same from every direction, and to represent it by three circles all the same size and carefully arranged as elevation, end elevation and plan view,

Table 3.1 Abbreviations for written statements

TERM	ABBREVIATION
Across flats	A/F
British Standard	BS
Centres	CRS
Centre line	CL or ℄
Chamfered	CHAM
Cheese head	CH HD
Countersunk	CSK
Countersunk head	CSK HD
Counterbore	C'BORE
Diameter (in a note)	DIA
Diameter (preceding a dimension)	⌀
Drawing	DRG
Figure	FIG.
Hexagon	HEX
Hexagon head	HEX HD
Material	MATL
Number	NO.
Pitch circle diameter	PCD
Radius (in a note)	RAD
Radius (preceding a dimension)	R
Screwed	SCR
Specification	SPEC
Spherical diameter or radius	SPHERE ⌀ or R
Spotface	S'FACE
Standard	STD
Undercut	U'CUT

ENGINEERING DRAWING

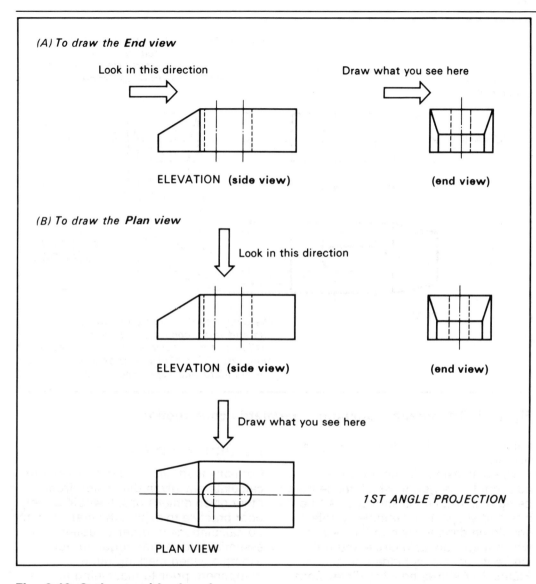

Fig. 3.10 Orthographic drawing

would be a waste of time. One circle and a note that the component is spherical is all that would be required.

Dimensioning

As well as showing the shape of the component, an engineering drawing must also show the size of the component. To avoid confusion and the chance of misinterpretation, the size (dimensions) of a component are added to the component drawing in a set manner laid down by B.S. 308: 1972. Figure 3.14 shows some of the basic rules governing dimensioning. Figure 3.14(a) shows how projection and dimension lines are used to relate the dimension to the drawing without confusion, whilst Fig. 3.14(b) shows the correct and incorrect methods of dimensioning a drawing (page 61).

Correct method of dimensioning a drawing Dimension lines should be thin, full lines. Wherever possible, they should be placed outside the outline of the drawing. The dimension line arrowhead must touch the projection line. Dimension lines should be well spaced so that they can be clearly read, and so that they do not obscure the outline of the drawing.

Incorrect method of dimensioning a drawing Centre lines and extension lines must not be used as dimension lines. Wherever possible, dimension line arrowheads must not touch the outline direct, but should touch the projection lines that extend from the outline. If the use of a dimension line within the outline is unavoidable, then try and use a leader line to take the dimension outside the outline.

Figure 3.15(a) shows how circles and shafts should be dimensioned. Note how the symbol ø is used to denote the word *diameter* as applied to a dimension.

Figure 3.15(b) shows how radii are dimensioned. Note that the radii of arcs of circles need not have their centres located (see page 62).

Figure 3.15(c) shows how notes may be used to avoid the need for the full dimensioning of certain features of a drawing.

Figure 3.16 shows how leader lines indicate where notes or dimensions are intended to apply. Such lines are terminated with arrowheads or dots. *Arrowheads* are used where the leader line touches the outline of the component or feature. *Dots* are used where the leader line finishes within the outline. Figure 3.16 shows an example of each termination (page 62).

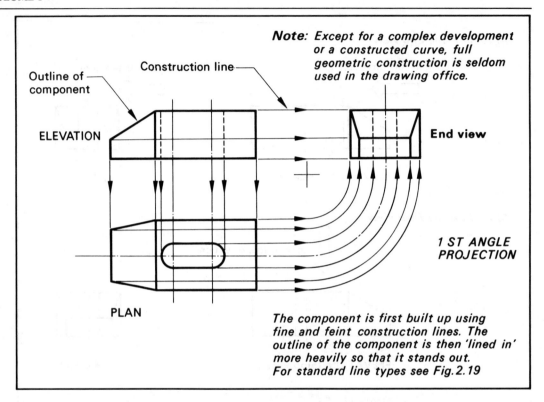

Fig. 3.11 Orthographic drawing – geometric construction

Duplication and selection of dimensions

In the same way as the number of views in a drawing are kept to a minimum, dimensions are selected so that the craftsman is not confused by unnecessary detail. Duplication of dimensions should also be avoided as it is unnecessary and can cause confusion. For example, a dimension may have to be revised, and extra appearances of the dimension may be missed.

The dimension should appear adjacent to the view in which the feature being dimensioned is shown as a true size and shape. For example, a hole should be dimensioned in the view in which it appears as a circle and not where it appears as hidden detail. Figure 3.17 shows how the dimensions should be positioned (page 63).

Auxiliary dimensions

Normally it should not be necessary to calculate any given dimension from other given dimensions. It would be very poor practice to expect the craftsman to do calculations in order to obtain essential information required: for example, when marking out a component prior to machining it.

The exception to this rule is when

ENGINEERING DRAWING

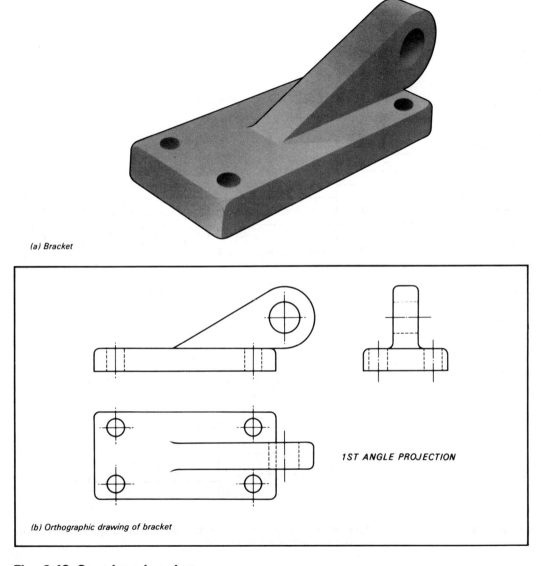

(a) Bracket

(b) Orthographic drawing of bracket

1ST ANGLE PROJECTION

Fig. 3.12 Cast iron bracket

unnecessary or auxiliary dimensions provide useful information such as an overall size. Auxiliary dimensions are not marked with a *tolerance* (see page 64) and are placed in a bracket as shown in Fig. 3.18. Auxiliary dimensions do not govern machining or inspection operations and are for information only.

Dimensioning from a datum

Cumulative errors occur whenever a feature is controlled by more than one tolerance. The example given in Fig. 3.19(a) shows how cumulative errors can occur. It will be seen that chain dimensioning gives a build up of tolerances that is greater than the designer intended. This cumulative effect can easily be eliminated by dimensioning each feature from the datum (see Fig. 3.19(b), page 64).

Cumulative errors can also occur when a number of components are assembled together as shown in Fig. 3.20. To avoid this, assembly dimensions are given. The individual components are then adjusted within their individual tolerances, or selective assembly is used so that the accumulated error is within the tolerance of the assembly dimensions.

It will be seen in Fig. 3.20 that the dimension A of the assembled components can vary as follows for the dimensions given:
Maximum
12·08 + 75·05 + 12·08 = 99·21 mm
Minimum
11·92 + 74·95 + 11·92 = 98·79 mm

59

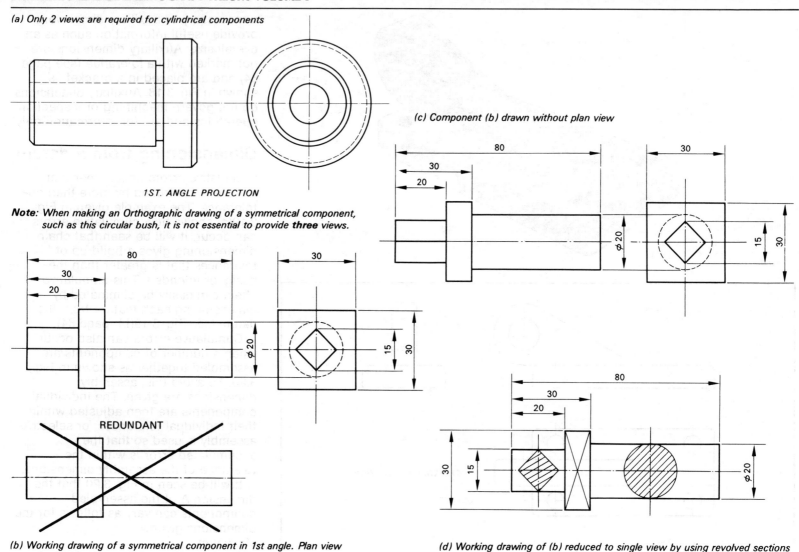

(a) Only 2 views are required for cylindrical components

1ST. ANGLE PROJECTION

Note: When making an Orthographic drawing of a symmetrical component, such as this circular bush, it is not essential to provide **three** views.

(c) Component (b) drawn without plan view

REDUNDANT

(b) Working drawing of a symmetrical component in 1st angle. Plan view redundant

(d) Working drawing of (b) reduced to single view by using revolved sections and B.S. convention for the square.

Fig. 3.13 Redundant views

ENGINEERING DRAWING

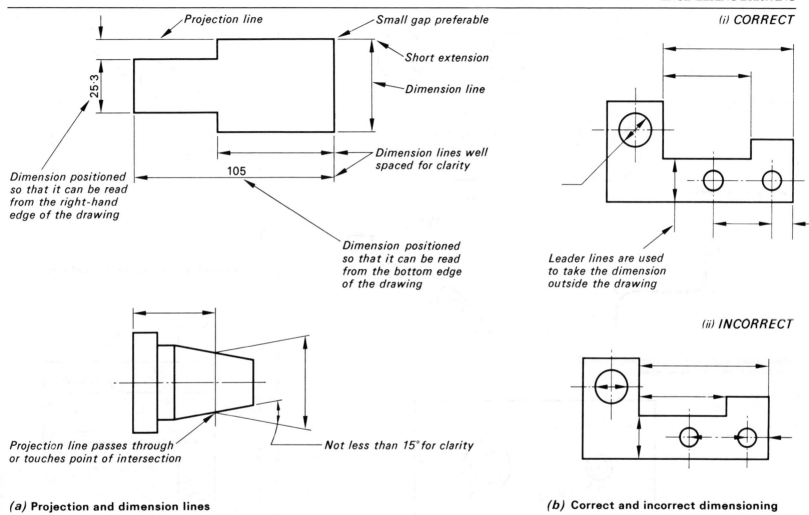

(a) Projection and dimension lines

(b) Correct and incorrect dimensioning

Fig. 3.14 Dimensioning – linear

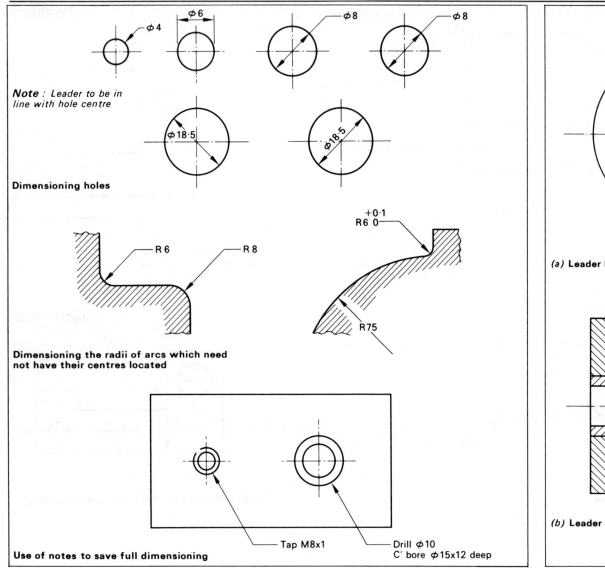

Fig. 3.15 Dimensioning – diameters and radii

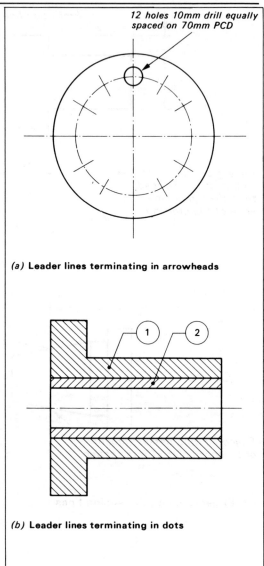

Fig. 3.16 Leader lines

ENGINEERING DRAWING

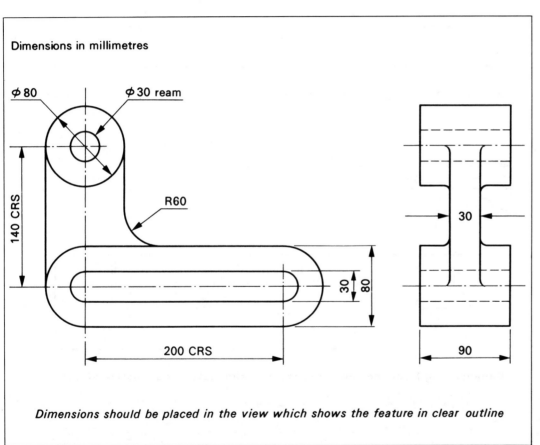

Fig. 3.17 Correct positioning of dimensions

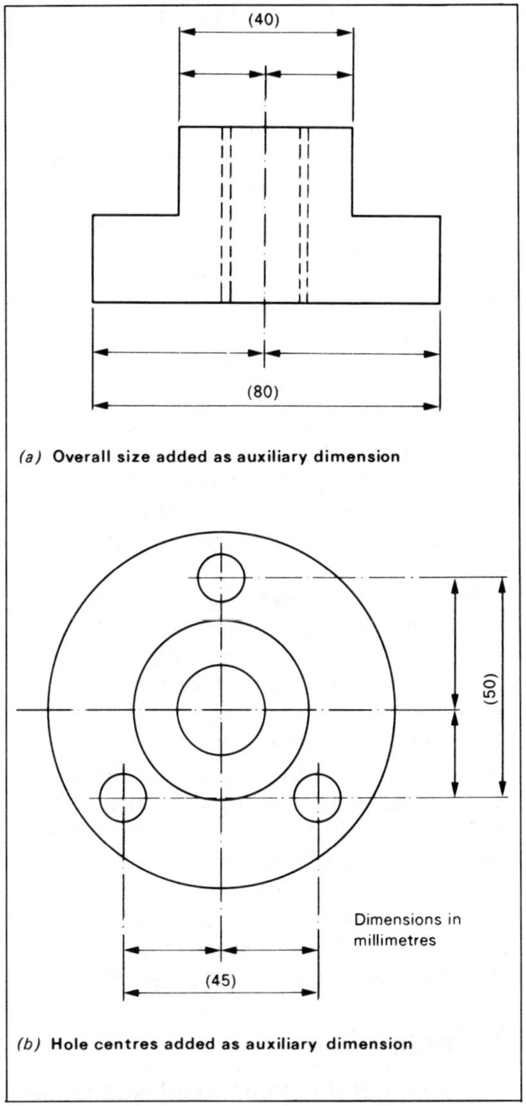

Fig. 3.18 Auxiliary dimensions

63

This variation may be too great for the assembled components to function properly. An assembly dimension could be given specifying A as, for example, 99 ± 0·1 mm. This dimension could be achieved by selective assembly, or by correction after assembly.

It has already been shown in Fig. 3.19 that it is better to dimension from a fixed datum. It is important that this datum is chosen for ease of marking out and manufacture.

Small components can be most conveniently marked out on the surface plate. Two mutually perpendicular datum edges should be used as a basis for dimensioning as shown in Figs. 3.21 and 3.22. The provision of datum edges on a small component is comparatively easy.

Figure 3.23 shows a component in which the bore is aligned to a datum surface (the base). In practice the base would be machined first, and the bore would be machined from it.

For large components, the preparation of mutually perpendicular datum edges can be a major and costly operation. In Fig. 3.24, the fixing holes for the two machines must align with each other, whilst their relationship to the edge of the bed plate is not important. In this instance a datum line (centre line) is used (see page 68).

Tolerancing

It is true that if a component was made exactly to size, no one would ever know as it could not be measured exactly.

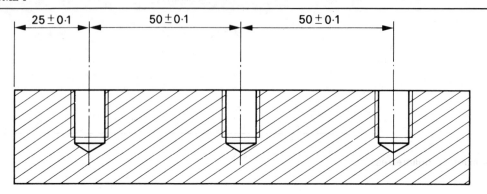

(a) **String dimensioning. Cumulative tolerance equals sum of individual tolerances**

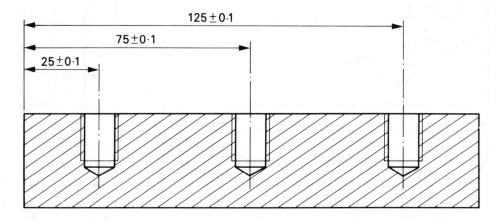

(b) **Dimensioning from one common datum to eliminate accumulative effect**

Fig. 3.19 Cumulative error

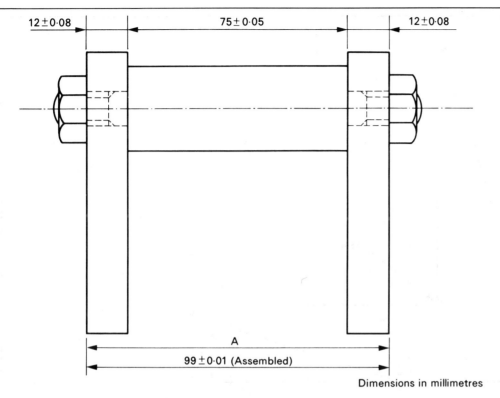

From the dimensions given, the dimension 'A' of the assembled components can vary as follows:

Maximum
   $12.08 + 75.05 + 12.08 = \underline{99.21\text{mm}}$
Minimum
   $11.92 + 74.95 + 11.92 = \underline{98.79\text{mm}}$

This variation may be too great to allow the assembly to function properly. An assembly dimension could be given specifying 'A' as, say, 99 ± 0.1 mm. This dimension could be achieved by selective assembly or by correction after assembly.

Fig. 3.20 Assembly dimensions

ENGINEERING DRAWING

Having calculated the ideal size for a dimension, the designer must then decide how much variation from that size he will tolerate. This variation between the smallest and largest acceptable size is called the *tolerance*. As well as specifying the magnitude of the tolerance, the designer must also indicate where the tolerance lies relative to the nominal size. Figure 3.25(a) shows various methods of tolerancing a dimension (page 69).

The effect of tolerancing on manufactured components and the types of fit obtained between mating components is shown in Fig. 3.25(b). Definitions relating to tolerance components are shown in Fig. 3.25(c).

Sectioning

Sectioning is used to show the internal details of machine parts that cannot be clearly shown by other means. The stages of making a sectioned drawing are shown in Fig. 3.26 on page 70. *Note*: steps (a), (b) and (c) are performed mentally in practice and only (d) is actually drawn.

The rules for producing and reading sectioned drawings can be summarised as follows:

1 Drawings are only sectioned when it is impossible to show the internal detail of a component in any other way.
2 Bolts, studs, nuts, screws, keys, cotters and shafts are not usually sectioned even when the cutting plane passes through them.
3 Ribs and webs are not sectioned

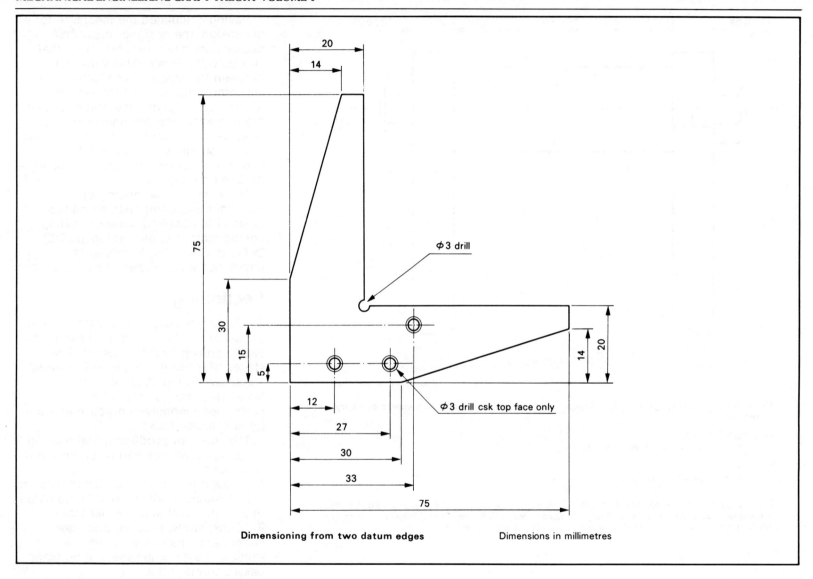

Fig. 3.21 Dimensioning from datum edges

ENGINEERING DRAWING

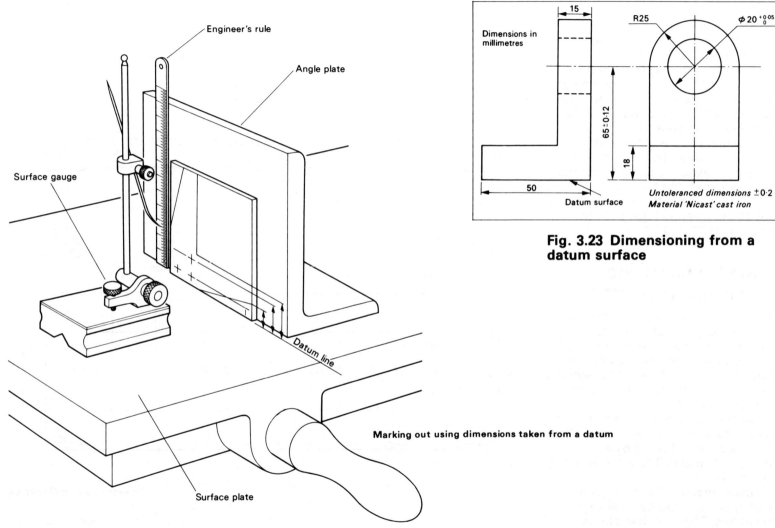

Fig. 3.22 Reason for dimensioning from datum edge

Fig. 3.23 Dimensioning from a datum surface

when parallel to the cutting plane.
4 The cutting plane must be indicated in the appropriate view.
5 Hidden detail is not shown in sectioned views when it has already been shown in another view.
6 The section shading (hatching) is normally drawn at 45° to the outline of the drawing. If the outline has an angle of 45° then the hatching angle can be changed to avoid confusion.
7 Adjacent parts are hatched in opposite directions. To show more than two adjacent parts the spacing between the hatched lines can be varied.

Some practical examples of sectioned drawings are given in Figs. 3.27 and 3.28 on pages 71 and 72.

Screwed connections (conventions and form)

The British Standard conventions for screw threads (B.S.308: 1972) were introduced on page 51. These should be interpreted carefully when sectioning components. Figure 3.29 shows how the screw thread conventions should be used (see page 73).

(a) *Male thread* The crest diameter is indicated by a heavy (outline) line. The root diameter is indicated by a continuous thin line. The male thread is never sectioned.

(b) *Female thread* The crest (core diameter) is indicated by a heavy (outline) line. The root diameter is indicated by a continuous thin line. When sectioned, the full depth and

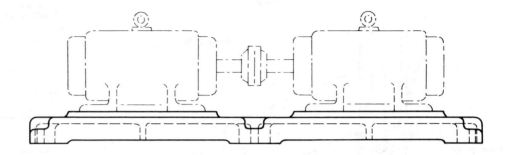

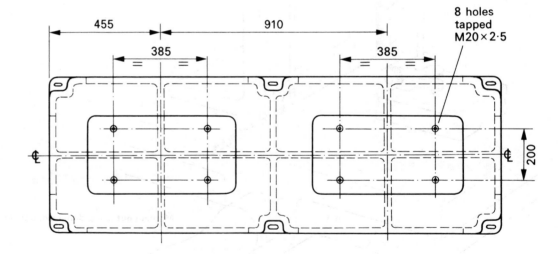

Dimensions in millimetres

Fig. 3.24 Dimensioning from a centre line datum

ENGINEERING DRAWING

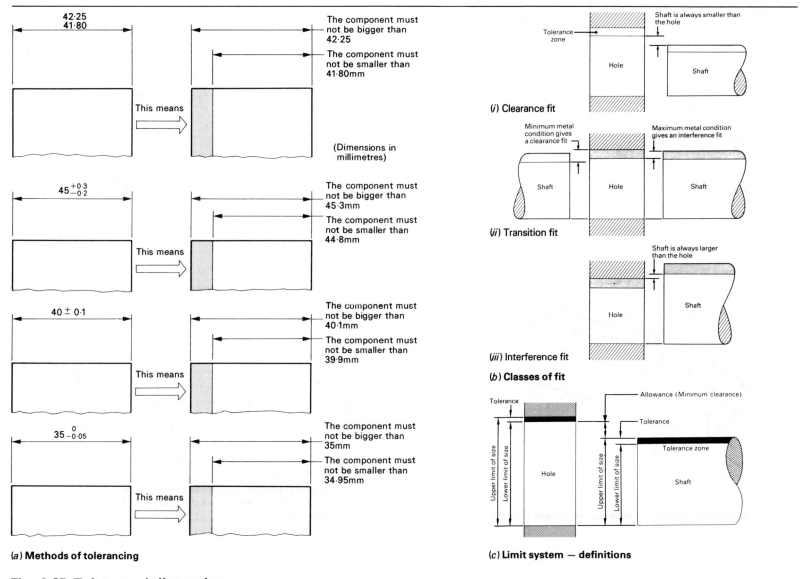

(a) Methods of tolerancing

(c) Limit system — definitions

Fig. 3.25 Toleranced dimensions

MECHANICAL ENGINEERING CRAFT THEORY VOLUME 1

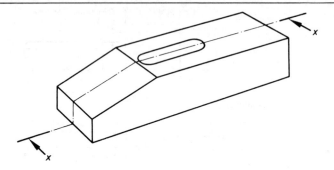

(a) The clamp is to be Sectioned along the line xx

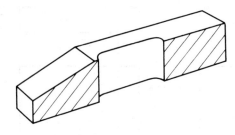

(c) That part of the clamp that lies in front of the cutting plane is removed leaving the sectioned component

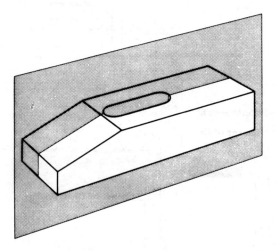

(b) The cutting plane is positioned on the line xx as shown

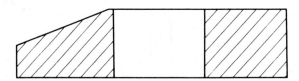

(d) Sectioned, orthographic elevation of the clamp shown in (a).

Note the section shading lines lie at 45° to the horizontal and are half the thickness of the outline.

Fig. 3.26 Section drawing

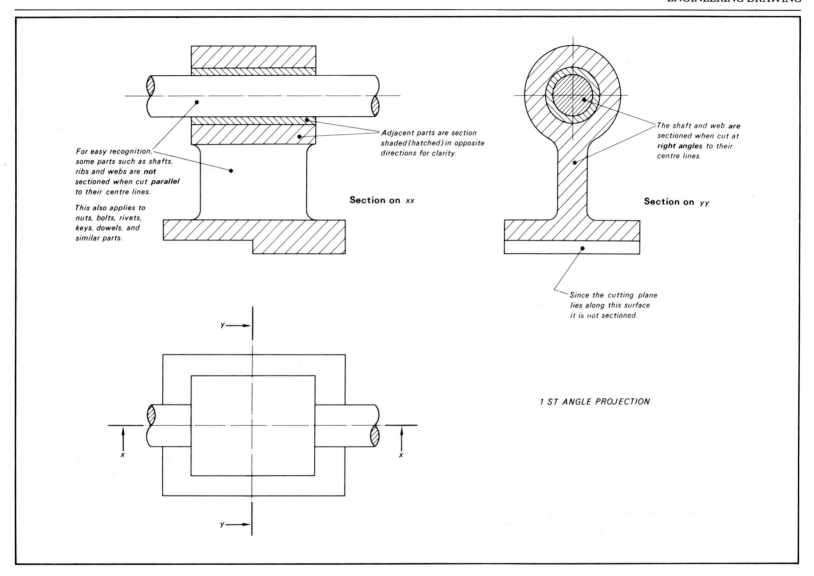

Fig. 3.27 Further sections

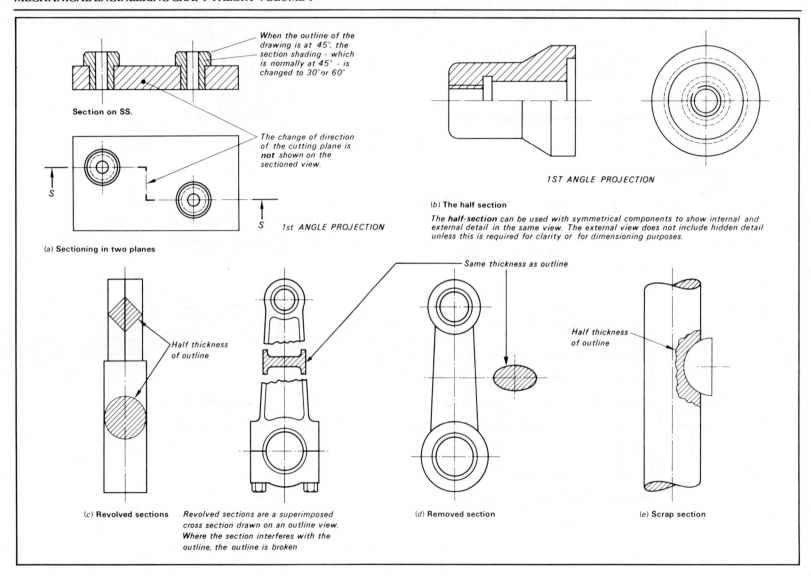

Fig. 3.28 Miscellaneous Sections

ENGINEERING DRAWING

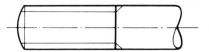

(a) **Male thread**
Crest diameter indicated heavy (outline) line. Root diameter by continuous thin line. The male thread is never sectioned.

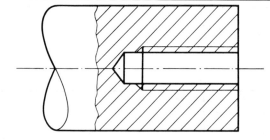

(b) **Female thread**
Crest (core dia.) is indicated by heavy (outline) line. Root diameter by continous thin line. When sectioned the full depth and length of the thread is section shaded (hatched)

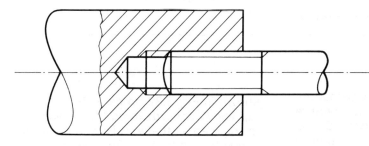

(c) **Male and female threads assembled**
When assembled, only the female thread is sectioned. Therefore the section shading is only carried across the female thread. Note change in thick and thin lines as thread moves from male to female. This is in accordance with (a) and (b) above

Fig. 3.29 Use of screw thread convention

length of the thread is section shaded (hatched).

(c) **Male and female threads assembled** When assembled, only the female thread is sectioned. Therefore the section shading is only carried across the female thread. Note the change in thick and thin lines as the thread moves from male to female. This is in accordance with 1 and 2 above.

One problem that always seems to face designers is how 'long' to make the internal thread in a component. The tendency is to show the full length of a hole through a component to be threaded. This wastes time and can lead to broken taps. (A tap is a tool for cutting threads (see page 211)). Unless a tap is started perfectly square to the hole, there will be a sideways force on it. The deeper it goes, the greater this force becomes and the more likely the tap is to break off in the hole. The craftsman can often save himself time and trouble by foreshortening the thread in the hole without reducing the effective strength of the joint, as shown in Fig. 3.30.

Obviously where a highly stressed component is concerned, as in an aircraft engine, the designer's requirements must be strictly adhered to.

(a) **Hole tapped right through**
Maximum strength is achieved by the time the hole is one diameter deep (in theory). To allow for variations in fit, this should be increased to 1½ times the diameter in practice.

(b) **Hole relieved** The back of the hole is opened up to the clearance size of the

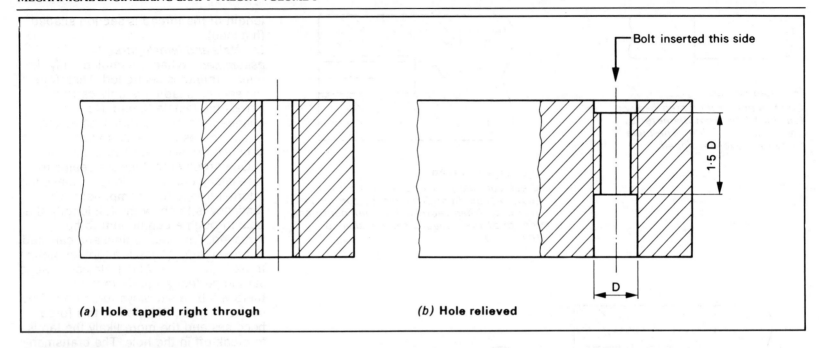

Fig. 3.30 Length of tapped hole

thread. If the hole is tapped from this side the clearance hole helps start the tap square in the hole. This reduces the risk of breakage. The front of the hole is cleared out about two threads deep to prevent the first thread 'picking up' as the bolt is tightened.

Figure 3.31 shows a section through a screw and nut and indicates what the various elements of the thread are called. These need to be memorised as the engineer has to make a wide variety of screwed connections. Such connections are used wherever it is necessary to assemble and dismantle components both during manufacture and for maintenance purposes. Some applications of screwed connections are given in Chapter 10 together with the techniques of cutting a thread.

Screw thread conventions (systems and proportions)

There are many screw thread systems currently in use throughout the world and some of the more common ones are shown in Fig. 3.32 on page 76.

(a) The *Whitworth* thread form was introduced as the world's first standard screw thread form by Sir Joseph Whitworth in the nineteenth century. It is the basis of all 55° thread systems. Many of these are obsolete now but will still be used for many years for maintenance purposes. Screw threads based on the Whitworth form are:
British Standard Whitworth: BSW
British Standard Fine: BSF
British Standard Pipe: BSP
(Parallel and tapered)

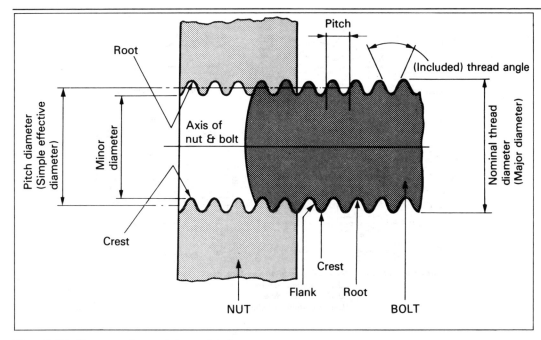

Fig. 3.31 Screw thread terminology

Coarse thread series: 1·6 mm to 68·0 mm diameter
Fine thread series: 1·8 mm to 68·0 mm diameter
Constant pitch series: 10 ranges from 1·6 mm diameter to 300 mm diameter

A typical metric screw thread would be specified as:

$$M8 \times 1$$

Where: M = Metric ISO system
8 = 8 mm diameter
1 = 1 mm pitch

(e) *Conduit* (*electrical*) thread systems are now based on the ISO-metric constant pitch system. This ensures a relatively shallow thread which will not weaken the thin wall of the conduit tube. The pitch is constant at 1·5 mm and the depth of the thread is 0·920 mm. Nominal diameters are: 16 mm, 20 mm, 25 mm and 35 mm.

The pitch/diameter relationship of a screw thread is important.

Coarse thread systems These are stronger and less inclined to 'strip' than fine thread systems, but they tend to vibrate loose. They are usually used on soft and/or low strength materials.

Fine thread systems These are not so strong but lock up tighter than coarse thread systems and are less inclined to work loose. They are usually used on harder, tough materials.

The studs used for fixing the cylinder head to a light alloy engine block would

(b) *The British Association* (*BA*) system provides a range of fine threads in small sizes for scientific instruments and electrical equipment. It is based on a 47½° form and has always been in metric dimensions. It is used internationally and provides a range not catered for in the ISO-metric system. There is no indication that it will become obsolete.

(c) The *Unified* system uses a 60° thread form, and is the basis of all modern threads. It has the maximum strength for a Vee form coupled with good self-locking (anti-vibration) properties. It is universally used in the United States of America and is widely used in the Automobile industry. There are three systems in current use.

Coarse thread series: UNC
Fine thread series: UNF
Special thread series: UNS

(d) The *ISO-metric* thread system is now used all over the world and will, eventually, supersede all other screw thread systems. Its form is based on the Unified system (60°) and there are three metric thread series:

have a coarse thread on one end for fixing into the light alloy block, and a fine thread on the other end to take the steel nut.

The general proportions for hexagon head bolts, nuts and lock nuts are shown in Fig. 3.33. Other types of screwed fixings together with locking and anti-vibration devices are considered on page 209.

Luckily the craftsman does not have to memorise all the screw thread proportions and systems as these are set out in the *screw-thread tables* of the various workshop handbooks. Table 10.2 gives an abstract from a typical table for metric screw threads.

Rivets

The proportions for some typical rivet heads are shown in Fig. 3.34(a) and some alternative rivet types are shown in Fig. 3.34(b). Further information on types of rivets, riveted joints, faults in riveted joints, etc. can be found on pages 224–227.

Hollow or 'pop' rivets are used for box sections in sheet metal work where it is only possible to get to one side of the surface of the metal, as shown in Fig. 3.35. The rivet is passed through the two pieces of metal being joined, and is then expanded by drawing the headed *mandrel* back through the rivet. A 'neck' in the mandrel ensures that the head breaks off and is left in the rivet to give it strength.

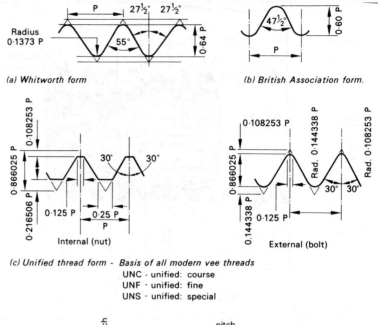

(a) Whitworth form

(b) British Association form.

(c) Unified thread form - Basis of all modern vee threads
UNC - unified: course
UNF - unified: fine
UNS - unified: special

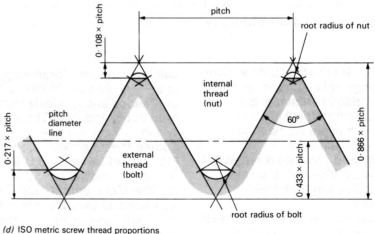

(d) ISO metric screw thread proportions

Fig. 3.32 Screw thread forms

ENGINEERING DRAWING

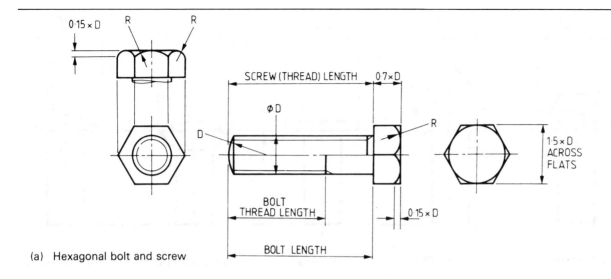

(a) Hexagonal bolt and screw

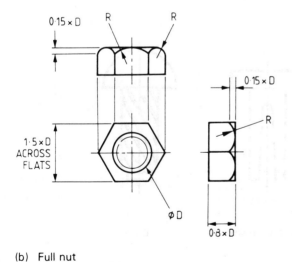

(b) Full nut

Fig. 3.33 Bolt and nut proportions

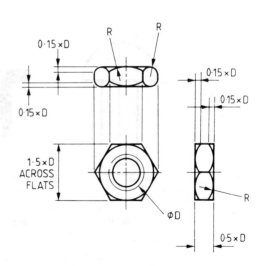

(c) Thin nut (lock nut or jam nut)

77

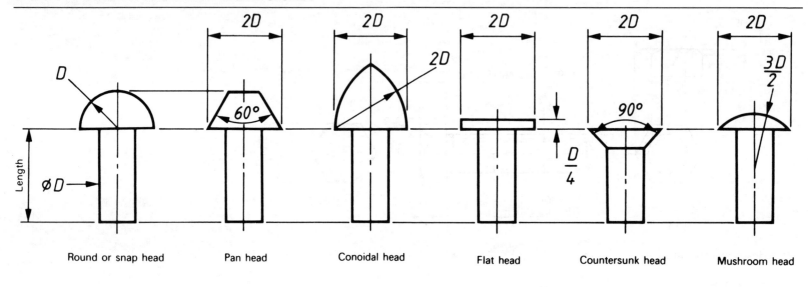
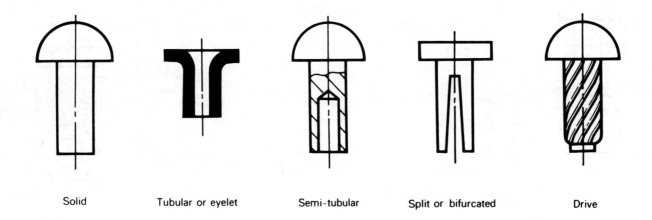

Fig. 3.34 Rivet types and proportions

ENGINEERING DRAWING

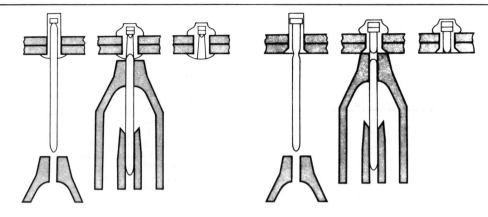

(a) Solid 'pop' rivets—sealed type, short and long break stem mandrels

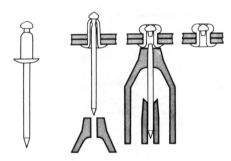

(b) Hollow 'pop' rivets—break stem at head, non seal type

Fig. 3.35 'Pop' riveting

Simple geometrical drawing

Many simple geometrical constructions are useful to the engineer in setting out work, particularly in sheet metalwork.

Division of lines

It is often more convenient and accurate to divide lines by geometrical construction rather than by direct measurement, especially when awkward sizes are involved. Figure 3.36(a) shows how a line may be halved (bisected) using compasses (page 80).

To bisect a line means to cut it into two equal parts.
1 Set your compasses to a radius that is greater than half the length of the line AC (i.e. greater than AB or BC).
2 With centre A draw an arc. With centre C draw another arc. The arcs should cross (intersect) at D and E.
3 Join D to E. The point at which DE cuts the line AC, B, is the centre of AC (i.e. AB = BC). DE will be at *right angles* to AC.

This construction can be used for drawing mutually perpendicular lines.

Figure 3.36(b) shows how a line may be divided into a number of parts using a tee-square and set square.

To divide a line into any number of equal parts (for example, five):
1 Draw a line AC at any convenient angle to AB.
2 Mark off with your compasses five equal divisions along AC.
3 Join point 5 on AC to the end of AB at B.
4 Using a set square and straight edge

as shown, draw lines through points 1, 2, 3, and 4, parallel to line 5B. AB is now divided into five equal parts.

Setting out angles — use of compasses

Angles that are multiples of 7½° can be set out very accurately using compasses alone. The basic angle from which all the others can be derived is the 60° angle shown in Fig. 3.37(a).

Let A be the apex of the angle.
1 With centre A draw an arc BC of large radius.
2 Step off BD equal in radius to AB.
3 Draw a line AE through D.
4 The angle EAB is 60°.

The construction of a 90° angle is shown in Fig. 3.37(b).

Let A be the apex of the angle.
1 With centre A draw an arc BC of large radius.
2 Step off BD and DE equal in radius to AB.
3 With centre D draw any arc F.
4 With centre E draw an arc equal in radius to DF.
5 Join AF with a straight line. Angle BAF is 90°.

The construction of a 45° angle is shown in Fig. 3.37(c).
1 Draw AB and AC at right angles (90°) to each other as described in Fig. 3.37(b).
2 With centre A, and with large radius, draw an arc to cut AB at D and AC at E.
3 With centres E and D draw arcs of equal radius to intersect at F.

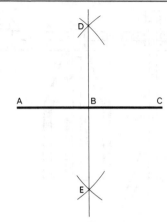

(a) Bisecting a line

(1) To bisect a line means to cut it into two equal parts
(2) Set your compasses to a radius that is greater than half the length of the line AC (i.e. greater than AB or BC)
(3) With centre 'A' draw an arc. With centre 'C' draw another arc. The arcs should cross (intersect) at 'D' and 'E'.
(4) Join 'D' to 'E' and where DE cuts the line AC at 'B' is the centre of AC (i.e. AB=BC)
(5) DE will be at RIGHT ANGLES to AC This construction can be used for drawing mutually perpendicular lines

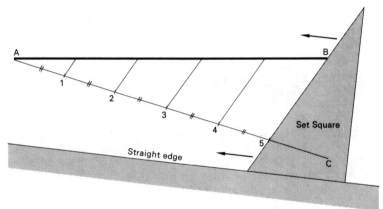

(b) Dividing a line into any number of equal parts

(1) To divide a line into any number of equal parts (say five)
(2) Draw a line AC at any convenient angle to AB
(3) Mark off with your compasses five equal divisions along AC
(4) Join point 5 on AC to the end of AB at 'B'
(5) Draw lines through points 1,2,3, and 4,, parallel to line 5B Using a set square and straight edge as shown AB is now divided into five equal parts.

Fig. 3.36 Division of lines

ENGINEERING DRAWING

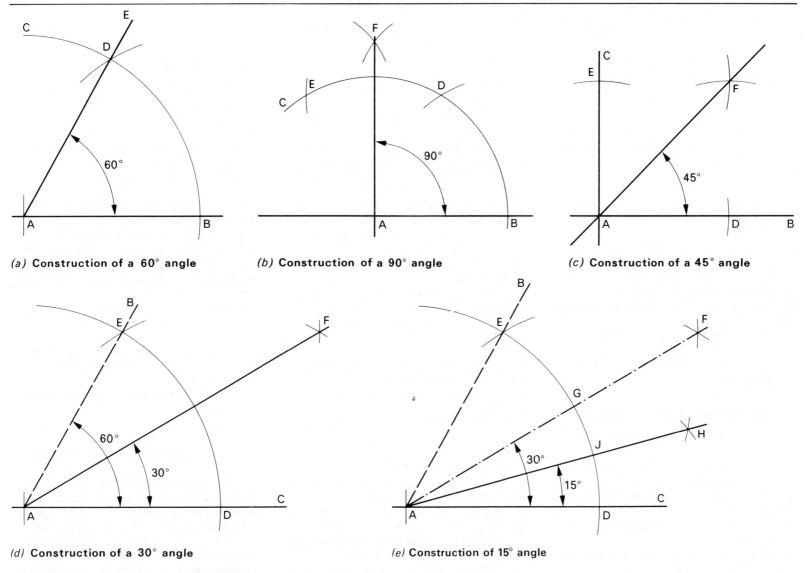

(a) Construction of a 60° angle

(b) Construction of a 90° angle

(c) Construction of a 45° angle

(d) Construction of a 30° angle

(e) Construction of 15° angle

Fig. 3.37 Construction of angles using compasses

4   Draw a straight line from A through F. Angle BAF is 45°. (AF bisects angle BAE.)

The bisection of the 60° angle to produce 30° is shown in Fig. 3.37(d).
1   Draw AB and AC at 60° to each other as described in Fig. 3.37(a).
2   With centre A, and a large radius, draw an arc to cut AB at E and AC at D.
3   With centres E and D draw arcs of equal radius to intersect at F.
4   Draw a line from A through F. Angle CAF is 30° (half 60°).

The successive bisection of the 30° angle to give 15° and 7½° is shown in Fig. 3.37(e).
1   Draw AC and AF at 30° to each other as described in Fig. 3.37(d).
2   With centres G and D draw arcs of equal radius to intersect at H.
3   Draw a line from A through H. Angle CAH is 15° (half 30°).
4   With centres J and D a further bisection can be made as described in 2, 3 and 4 above. This would give an angle of 7½°.

Construction of plane figures

Triangle   The construction of a triangle is shown in Fig. 3.38(a).
1   Draw AB, BC and CD equal in length to the sides of the required triangle.
2   With centre B and radius AB draw the arc AF.
3   With centre C and radius CD draw the arc DG.
4   Where the arcs intersect at E is an apex of the triangle.
5   Join BE and CE with straight lines to form the triangle BCE.

Square   The construction of a square is shown in Fig. 3.38(b).
1   Mark off one side of the square AB on the base line.
2   With centre A and radius AB draw the arc BC.
3   With centre B and radius AB draw the arc AD.
4   With centre E and radius AB step off F and G on arcs BC and AD respectively.
5   With centres E and F draw arcs of equal radius to intersect at H.
6   With centres E and G draw arcs of equal radius to intersect at J.
7   Erect perpendiculars AH and BJ.
8   The arcs BC and AD cut the perpendiculars AH and BJ at K and L respectively.
9   To complete the square join K and L.

Hexagon   The construction of a hexagon is shown in Fig. 3.38(c).
1   Mark off one side AB on the base line.
2   Erect perpendiculars AC and BD using one of the previously demonstrated constructions or a set square.
3   With centre A and radius AB draw an arc to cut the base line at E.
4   With centre E and radius AB draw an arc to cut the arc drawn in 3 at G.
5   With centre B and radius AB draw an arc to cut the base line at F.
6   With centre F and radius AB draw an arc to cut the arc drawn in 5 at H.
7   With centre G and radius AB draw an arc to cut the perpendicular AC at J.
8   With centre H and radius AB draw an arc to cut the perpendicular BD at K.
9   To complete the hexagon join AG, GJ, JK, KH and HB with straight lines.

Development

The developed shape for a component represents the flat piece of metal (blank) from which that component can be bent up.

The photograph (Fig. 3.39) shows a variety of shapes whose surfaces will now be developed geometrically. The examples in the photograph were made from card and it is quite easy to draw their developments on card or stiff paper, cut them out and test the accuracy of your drawing. Many sheet metal workers 'prove' their developments this way before cutting up expensive sheet metal.

Pyramid   The construction for the development of a pyramid is shown in Fig. 3.40(a).
1   Draw the elevation and plan of the pyramid with the slant side shown as true length.
2   With centre E and radius EB draw the arc BX.
3   Step off the base lengths AB, BC, etc. on the arc BX.
4   Join the points BADCB to the apex E.
5   The figure EBADCB (shaded) is the developed blank for the pyramid.

Frustum of a pyramid   It will be seen from the photograph (Fig. 3.39) that the frustum of a pyramid is a pyramid with the top cut off. The construction for the development of a frustum of a pyramid is shown in Fig. 3.40(b) on page 85.

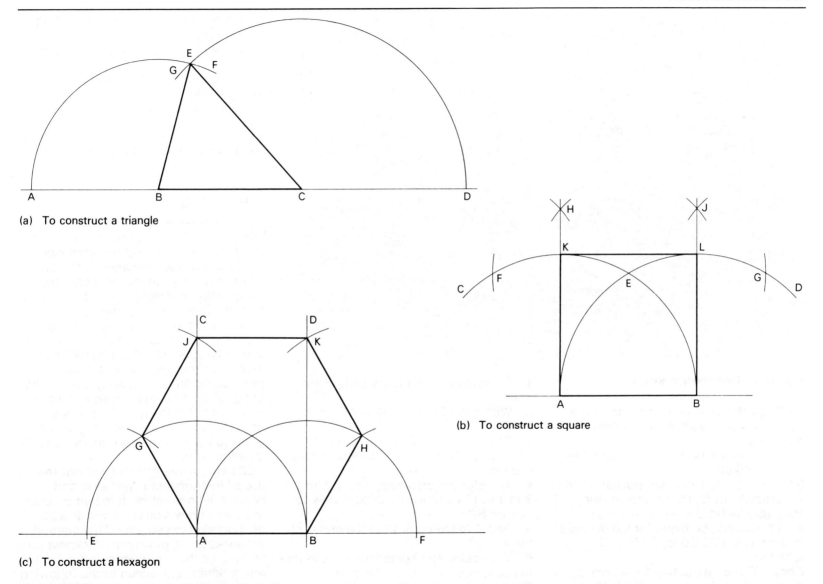

(a) To construct a triangle

(b) To construct a square

(c) To construct a hexagon

Fig. 3.38 Construction of plane figures

MECHANICAL ENGINEERING CRAFT THEORY VOLUME 1

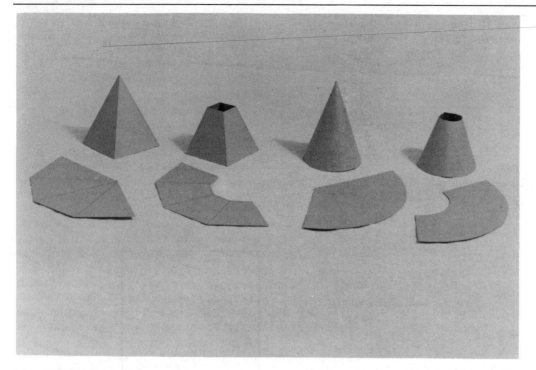

Fig. 3.39 Geometric solids

1 Draw the elevation and plan of the pyramid with the slant side shown as true length.
2 Develop the base of the pyramid as in Fig. 3.40(a).
3 Develop the truncated portion of the pyramid, A_1 B_1 C_1 D_1, as shown using the same technique as for the base.
4 The developed blank for the pyramid is the figure BADCB B_1 C_1 D_1 A_1 B_1 (shaded).

Cone The construction for a cone's development is shown in Fig. 3.40(c).

1 Draw the elevation and plan of the cone.
2 With centre A and radius AB draw the arc BC.
3 Divide the plan view into a number of equal parts. A 30°/60° set square was used in this example.
4 Transfer the distances 0 to 1, 1 to 2, 2 to 3 ... 11 to 12 from the plan view to the arc BC.
5 Join A to the point 12 at the end C of the arc.
6 The sector AB12 (shaded) represents the developed blank for the cone.

Frustum of a cone The construction for the frustum of a cone is shown in Fig. 3.40(d).
1 Draw the elevation and plan of the cone.
2 Construct the base development as in Fig. 3.40(c).
3 With centre A and radius AE draw a radius ED.
4 The developed blank is represented by the shaded figure OED 12.

Sketching

The craftsman is rarely, if ever, called upon to produce a formal drawing on the drawing board, but he often has to produce a quick freehand sketch of a component in good proportion. This sketch may be orthographic but is often pictorial (isometric or oblique).

In order to sketch well, a good pencil, properly sharpened, is essential. It is suggested that an 'H' pencil satisfies most requirements for sketching, particularly on good quality paper. The pencil should be sharpened to a point and kept sharpened. A chisel edge is used by draughtsmen working at the drawing board and is not really suitable for sketching.

Drawing a straight line without the use of instruments is not easy and needs a little practice. It is bad practice to try and draw a straight line as a series of short sketchy strokes. This method produces a line of varying thickness and looking as though it needs a shave. It is much better to proceed in the following manner: place the pencil at the start of

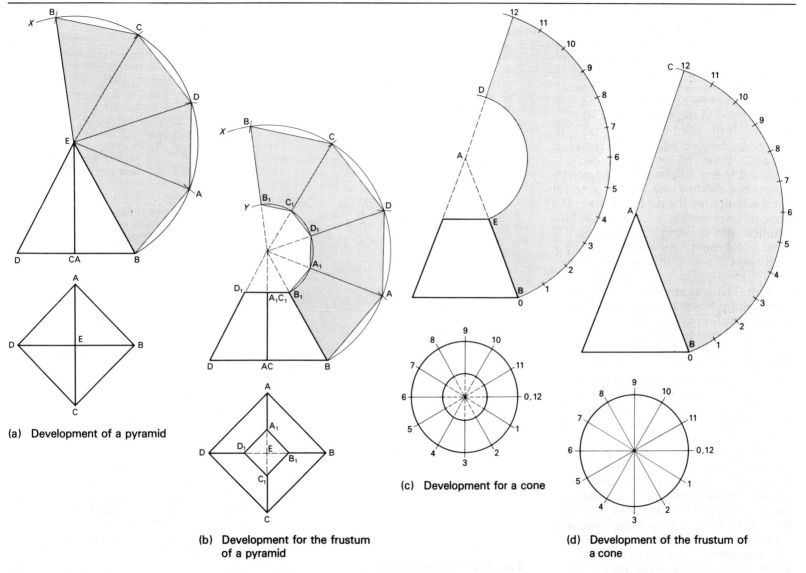

(a) Development of a pyramid

(b) Development for the frustum of a pyramid

(c) Development for a cone

(d) Development of the frustum of a cone

Fig. 3.40 Development of geometric solids

the line and draw, lightly and carefully, a very faint line. At first this line will be anything but straight but no matter, it will fulfil its function by acting as a guide. Now examine the line, noting where irregularities occur and draw in the finishing line correcting for the irregularities in the faint line as you proceed. If the faint line is very faint, it will not be noticed after the finished line has been drawn as the eye will be attracted to the finished line. Do not try to improve the line any further or to rub out the faint line. If a rubber is used, the clear distinct outline will be lost. A little practice with drawing straight lines will soon make them look as though they have been drawn with a straight edge.

To draw a circle is rather more difficult. The first step is to draw the axes (centre lines) to the circle. From the intersection of the axes, mark off distances equal to the radius of the circle as shown in Fig. 3.41(a). Now draw a faint line through the points marked remembering to go *through* the points and not *to* them. Examine the faint line for errors and then draw in the finished circle in one, continuous line.

Fig. 3.41(b) shows the steps in sketching a quadrant. In making freehand sketches, always draw the centre lines first, then the outline very faintly, and leave the heavier finishing lines until last. The faint lines will not show after the finishing lines have been drawn so there should be no need to use a rubber. A rubbing out always spoils a drawing by roughing up the paper and collecting dirt.

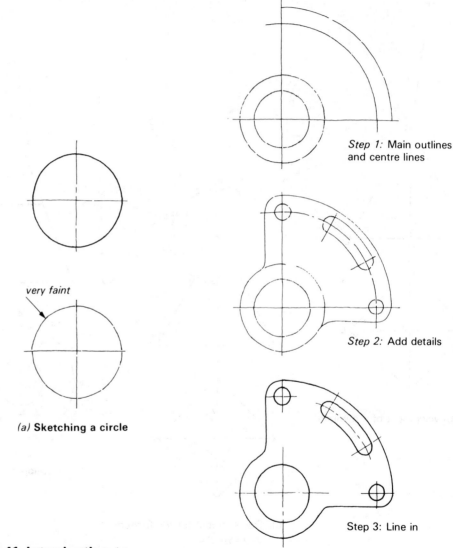

Fig. 3.41 Introduction to free-hand sketching

(a) **Sketching a circle**

Step 1: Main outlines and centre lines

Step 2: Add details

Step 3: Line in

(b) **Sketching a quadrant**

ENGINEERING DRAWING

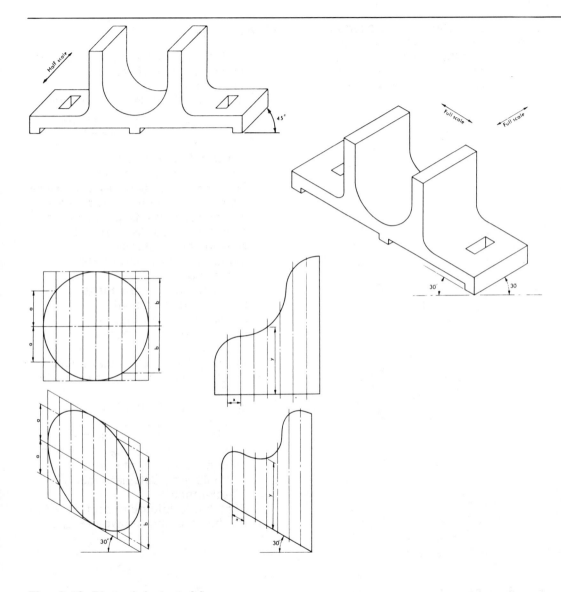

Fig. 3.42 Pictorial sketching

Some components are best sketched with the component set at an angle in order to show end view details or thickness not shown in the front view, to give a pictorial representation (see page 49). There are two different methods generally adopted for this purpose and these are illustrated in Fig. 3.42.

The bearing block shown in Fig. 3.42(a) is sketched showing an *oblique view*; the width of the bearing block is drawn at 45° but is usually drawn at half the scale used for the length and height. The biggest advantage of this method is its simplicity and it is very useful when sketching items of uniform width. Also circles and arcs of circles can be drawn with compasses.

The same bearing block is shown in Fig. 3.42(b) but this time it is sketched in isometric projection. In this method of sketching, all horizontal lines on the component are shown at 30° to the horizontal on the drawing, and are not drawn to a smaller scale as is done in the oblique view. In the isometric sketch, all the horizontal and vertical lines are drawn to the same scale. All vertical lines on the component are drawn vertically. Figure 3.42(c) shows how curves and circles have to be constructed as ellipses and parts of ellipses.

The method of sketching pictorial views is illustrated in Figs. 3.43 and 3.44. In both instances it will be seen that a 'box' is sketched very faintly, and then the outline of the component is sketched into the 'box'. Figure 3.44 shows a two-jaw chuck sketched in isometric projection. The procedure in both cases is the same: firstly the production of the very faint box-like construction lines and then the addition of details and the final drawing in.

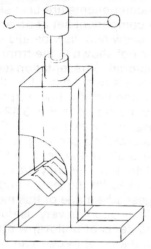

Step 1
General outlines (very faint)

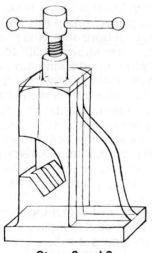

Steps 2 and 3
Add details and line in

Fig. 3.43 Sketching a pipe – vice

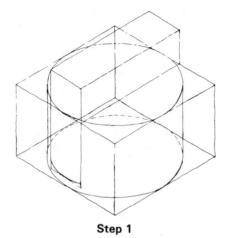

Step 1

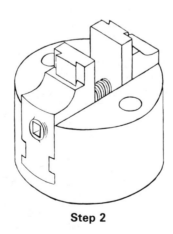

Step 2

Fig. 3.44 Sketching a chuck

Exercises

1. Sketch, approximately full size, the following items of workshop equipment:
   a) a double ended plug gauge for checking a bore $\frac{25 \cdot 02}{25 \cdot 00}$ mm diameter.
   b) a drill chuck key
   c) a double ended spanner
2. Fig. 3.45 shows two views of twelve simple components drawn in first angle projection. Copy the views shown and add the third, missing view in each instance.
3. Sketch the following BS308 conventions:
   a) an external screw thread,
   b) a square on a shaft,
   c) diamond knurling,
   d) a cylindrical compression spring,
   e) six holes on a circular pitch.
4. a) List the dimensioning errors in Fig. 3.46 (a).
   b) Show two methods of dimensioning the hole in Fig. 3.46 (b) if the maximum limit of size is 25·02 mm and the minimum limit of size is 25·00 mm. Calculate the tolerance.
5. Sketch a longitudinal section (AA) for the assembly shown in Fig. 3.47.

ENGINEERING DRAWING

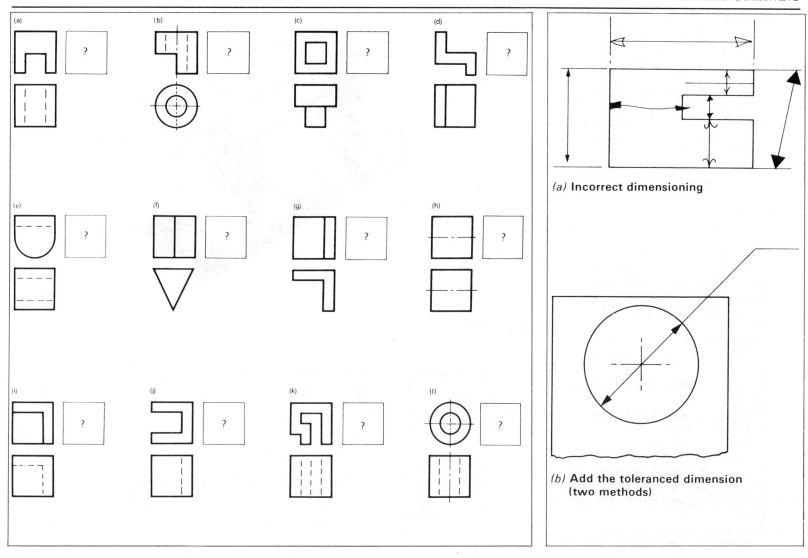

Fig. 3.45

Fig. 3.46

(a) Incorrect dimensioning

(b) Add the toleranced dimension (two methods)

6 a) Sketch, in good proportion, a section through two 75 mm square by 12 mm thick plates held together by an M12 hexagon bolt and nut. Include plain washers under the head of the bolt and the nut.
   b) Sketch the following locking devices used with screwed connections:
   (i) castle nut and split pin
   (ii) tab washer
   (iii) double coil spring washer
   (iv) lock nut
   (v) slit head nut (*either* aero-type *or* binx-type).

7 Use geometrical constructions to: a) divide a line 10 cm long into 7 parts, b) construct a 45° angle, c) construct a 30° angle (bisect a constructed 60° angle), d) bisect a line 6 cm long.

8 Use geometrical constructions to:
   a) draw a triangle of sides 6 cm, 4 cm, 5 cm
   b) draw a hexagon 50 mm across corners
   c) draw a hexagon with side length of 30 mm

9 Develop a blank for:
   a) a square based pyramid of side 50 mm and vertical height 80 mm,
   b) a cone with a base diameter of 50 mm and a vertical height of 75 mm.

10 Draw a pictorial view of the component shown in Fig. 3.48 in:
   a) isometric projection
   b) oblique projection

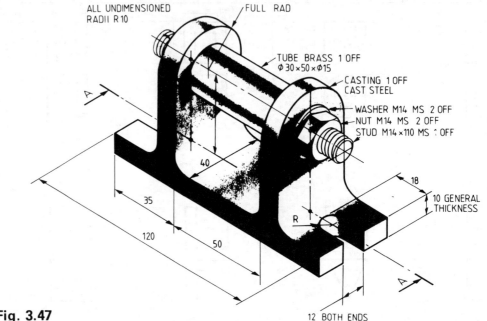

Fig. 3.47

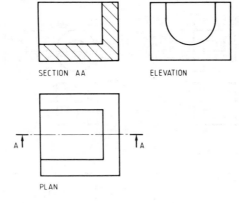

Fig. 3.48

4. Engineering materials and heat treatment

Properties of materials

Figure 4.1 shows three objects. The first is a connector joining electric cables. The plastic casing has been partly cut away to show the metal connector. Plastic is used for the outer casing because it is a good electrical insulator and prevents electric shock if a person touches the joint. It also prevents the connectors from touching and causing a short circuit. As well as being a good insulator, the plastic is cheap and tough, and easily moulded to shape. It was chosen for the casing because of these special *properties*. That is, the properties of cheapness, toughness, good electrical insulation, and ease of moulding to shape.

The metal connector and its clamping screws are made from brass. This is a yellow coloured metal that has been chosen because of its special properties. These properties are good electrical conductivity, ease of machining to shape, and corrosion resistance.

The second object to be shown in Fig. 4.1 is the connecting rod of a motor car engine. This is made from a special steel alloy that has properties of great strength and toughness and can be forged and machined to shape.

Fig. 4.1 Material selection

The third object shown in Fig. 4.1 is part of a machine tool called a lathe (see Chapter 13). The metal used is *cast iron*. This is a metal that is very strong, yet is quite easily melted, and can be poured into sand moulds so that it can be cast into very complicated shapes like the one shown. Strength, low melting point, and ease of casting are some of the properties of cast iron.

All the materials chosen in the above examples have special engineering properties that make them the best for the particular job they are doing. To understand about materials we must first understand what is meant by the more common engineering properties.

Tensile strength

Figure 4.2(a) shows a heavy load being held up by a rod fixed to a beam. The load is trying to *stretch* the rod. Therefore the rod is said to be in *tension*, and the material from which the rod is made needs to have *tensile strength* to resist the pull of the load.

Compression strength

Figure 4.2(b) shows a component being crushed by a heavy load. The load is said to be *compressing* the component. Therefore the component needs to be made from a material with a high *compression strength* to resist the load.

Shear strength

Figure 4.2(c) shows a rivet joining two pieces of metal together. The forces acting on the two pieces of metal are

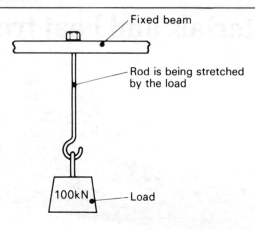

(a) **Tensile strength**

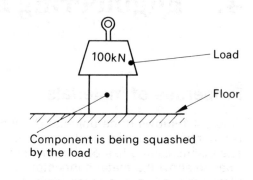

(b) **Compression strength**

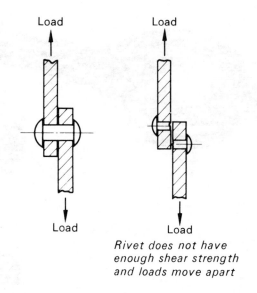

(c) **Shear strength**

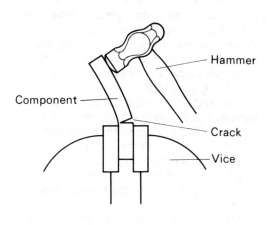

(d) **Impact strength**

Fig. 4.2 Material properties (strength)

trying to pull them apart. Because the loads are not exactly in line they are said to be *off-set* and the load on the rivet is called a *shearing* load. That is, the rivet is said to be *in shear*. If the rivet material does not have sufficient *shear strength* to resist the loads, the rivet will break and the loads will move apart as shown. The same effect can be caused by loads pushing on the ends of the two pieces of metal joined by the rivet.

Impact strength

To withstand *shock loads* such as a hammer hitting a piece of metal in a vice as shown in Fig. 4.2(d), a material requires *impact strength*. This is also called *toughness*. The axles of a motor vehicle require impact strength so that they do not break when the wheels hit bumps in the road. In Fig. 4.2(d) the piece of metal in the vice does not have sufficient impact strength (toughness) and is starting to crack.

Elasticity

Figure 4.3(a) shows a spring. This sort of spring is called a *tension spring* because it stretches and becomes longer when it is pulled, and returns to its original length when the pull is removed. Some springs become shorter under load, but return to their original length when the load is removed. These springs are called *compression springs*.

The materials from which both sorts are made must have the *property of elasticity* – the ability to deform under load and return to the original size and shape when the load is removed.

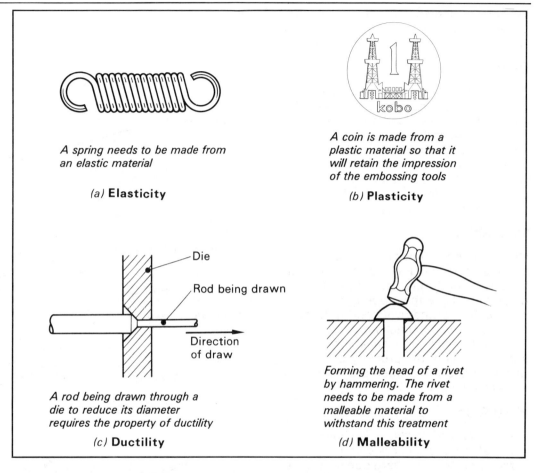

A spring needs to be made from an elastic material

(a) **Elasticity**

A coin is made from a plastic material so that it will retain the impression of the embossing tools

(b) **Plasticity**

A rod being drawn through a die to reduce its diameter requires the property of ductility

(c) **Ductility**

Forming the head of a rivet by hammering. The rivet needs to be made from a malleable material to withstand this treatment

(d) **Malleability**

Fig. 4.3 Material properties (flow)

Plasticity

This is the opposite property to that of elasticity. Instead of springing back into shape when the deforming load is removed, a plastic material remains deformed. The *property of plasticity* is used when a coin is made. A disc of soft metal is squeezed between two metal dies and takes the impression engraved into the dies. When the dies open the metal *remains deformed* in the shape of the coin, as shown in Fig. 4.3(b). When a piece of soft steel is bent to shape, it also shows the property of plasticity.

Ductility

When materials are deformed in a plastic manner, they may be squeezed into shape as described above, or they may be stretched into shape. Figure 4.3(c) shows a wire being pulled, or *drawn*, through a die to make the wire longer and thinner. Materials that can be *stretched* into shape are said to have the *property of ductility*.

Malleability

Metals are sometimes *hammered into shape* as shown in Fig. 4.3(d) in which a head is being formed on a rivet. The metal must have the *property of malleability* for the rivet head to form without the metal cracking.

Both ductility and malleability are special cases of the property of plasticity and these three properties are closely linked.

Hardness

The *property of hardness* is shown by materials that *resist scratching or indentation* by other hard bodies. Figure 4.4(a) shows a hardened steel ball being pressed first into a hard material and then into a soft material by the same load. The ball only makes a small mark, or indentation, in the hard metal, but it makes a deep indentation in the soft metal. Hardness is often tested in this manner.

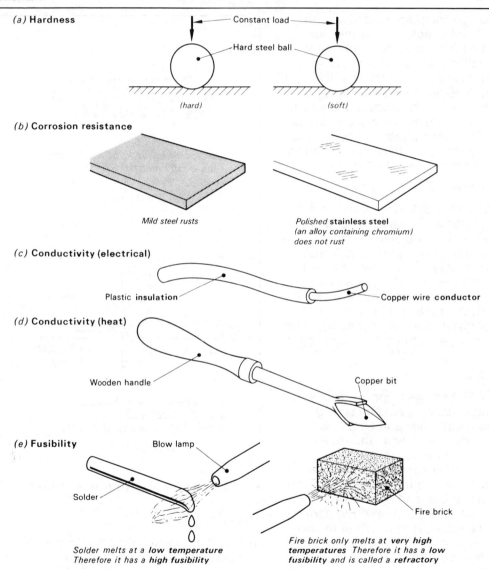

Fig. 4.4 Material properties (miscellaneous)

ENGINEERING MATERIALS AND HEAT TREATMENT

Corrosion resistance

Unprotected mild steel soon corrodes (goes rusty) in hot damp climates. Such conditions are found in southern Nigeria. Therefore mild steel does not have the property of *corrosion resistance*. Polished stainless steel, an alloy of steel and chromium, does not corrode in warm damp atmospheres, or any other naturally occurring atmospheres. Therefore it has the property of corrosion resistance.

Corrosion resistance is the ability of a material to *resist chemical or electro-chemical attack*. This is shown in Fig. 4.4(b).

Conductivity (electrical)

Figure 4.4(c) shows a piece of electrical cable. The copper wire conductor has the *property of electrical conductivity* as it *allows the passage of an electric current*. The plastic insulation has a low conductivity and resists the flow of an electric current so strongly that virtually no current can pass through it.

Conductivity (heat)

Figure 4.4(d) shows a soldering iron. The bit is made from copper as it is a good conductor of heat and so allows the heat to travel down to its tip and into the work being soldered. Therefore copper has the *property of thermal conductivity* as it *allows the passage of heat*. The wooden handle remains cool as it has a low thermal conductivity and resists the passage of heat through itself. This prevents the user from burning his hands.

Fusibility

This is the ease with which metals will melt. It will be seen from Fig. 4.4(e) that *solder melts easily* and so has the *property of high fusibility*. On the other hand, fire-brick only *melts at very high temperatures* and so it has the property of *low fusibility*. Materials that will only melt at very high temperatures are also called *refractories*.

Engineering materials

Almost every substance known to man has found its way into the engineering workshop at some time or other. Neither this chapter, nor indeed the whole book could hold all the facts about all these materials. The more important groups of materials are shown in Table 4.1 above. In this chapter we are mainly concerned with the *metals* and their properties.

Hot and cold working processes

The terms hot and cold working are used from time to time in this chapter and elsewhere in the book. Since the properties of a metal will change when subjected to hot and cold working processes, it is important to understand

Table 4.1 Engineering materials

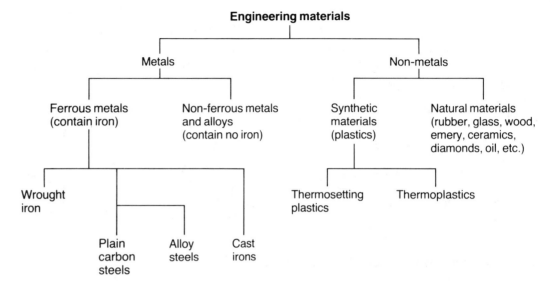

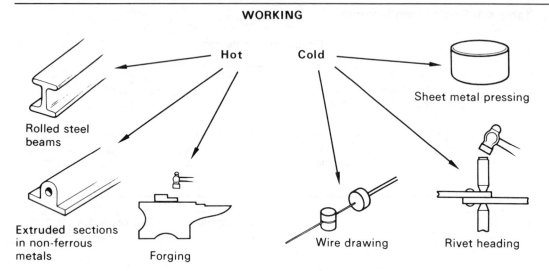

Fig. 4.5 Examples of hot and cold working

what is meant by these processes. There are many ways of shaping metal, but they may be grouped into *casting, cutting and working*.

Casting

Metal is heated until it becomes molten and is then poured into a mould made from a refractory material that will not be affected by the heat of the molten metal. The metal then cools and solidifies in the mould and takes the desired shape. The mould is then broken open and the metal is removed.

Cutting

Metal is cut to the desired shape using hand tools and machine tools. Metal cutting is considered in the later chapters of this book.

Working

Metal is said to be *worked* when it is squeezed or stretched into shape. After it has been shaped by squeezing or stretching, it is said to be in the *wrought condition*. Thus metal which is worked into shape must have the *property of plasticity* as described on page 93.

The metal is *hot-worked* or *cold-worked* depending upon the temperature at which the shaping takes place. These temperatures are not easy to define. For instance, lead hot-works at room temperature (which is why plumbers like working it), but steel does not hot-work until it is red-hot. The hot-working temperatures for a range of metals and alloys are given in Chapter 8.

When metals are examined under a microscope, it is seen that they consist of very small crystals or grains. A metal is rather like a lump of sugar, except that there are many more grains and they are much smaller. When most metals are bent and worked at room temperature, these crystals are distorted and the metal becomes hard and brittle. If this happens, *cold-working* has taken place and the metal has become *work-hardened*. For example, a thin strip of steel can be fastened in a vice and bent backwards and forwards. Eventually it becomes work-hardened and breaks off at the point at which it has been bent.

When cold-working metal at room temperature, the craftsman must stop before the metal breaks. The metal is then heated and allowed to cool down slowly so that the metal becomes soft again and further working can take place. This softening is called *annealing* and is described on page 115.

When metal is hot-worked, it does not work-harden because any distorted crystals reform instantly. If the metal could be prevented from cooling down there would be no limit to the amount of hot-working it could withstand. Further, metals can be shaped more easily and with less force when they are at the hot-working temperature. Figure 4.5 shows examples of hot and cold-working.

Common forms of supply

There is an almost unlimited range of forms in which metals can be supplied to a factory and Fig. 4.6 shows some of these forms. The processes by which the metal has been produced before reaching the factory will have a profound effect on its properties (see pages 91–95). Tables 4.2, 4.3, and 4.4 compare the advantages and limitations of hot-working, cold-working, and casting processes.

Ferrous metals

Figure 4.7 shows a bridge, a motor-lorry and a railway train. All these things have one common factor. They are largely made from steel because steel is very strong, is readily available in large quantities, and is the cheapest metal available.

Figure 4.8 shows a motor car engine cylinder block and the bed of a machine tool. These are made from cast iron because cast iron is cheap and can be easily cast into complicated shapes. It is also very strong, although not as strong as steel (see page 99).

Both steel and cast iron belong to a group of metals called *ferrous metals*. All *ferrous metals* are based on *iron*. The more important of these ferrous metals are listed in Table 4.5 on page 99.

Wrought iron

This material is widely used for making chains and hooks for lifting tackle. Although not as strong as mild steel, it

Table 4.2 Hot-working processes

ADVANTAGES	LIMITATIONS
1 Low cost.	1 Poor surface finish – rough and scaly.
2 Grain refinement from cast structure.	2 Due to shrinkage on cooling the dimensional accuracy of hot worked components is of a low order.
3 Materials are left in the fully annealed condition and are suitable for cold working. (Heading, bending, etc.)	3 Due to distortion on cooling and to the processes involved hot working generally leads to geometrical inaccuracy.
4 Scale gives some protection against corrosion during storage.	4 Fully annealed condition of the material coupled with a relatively coarse grain leads to a poor finish when machined.
5 Availability as sections (girders) and forgings as well as the more usual bars, rods, sheets and strip and butt welded tube.	5 Low strength and rigidity for metal considered.
	6 Damage to tooling from abrasive scale on metal surface.

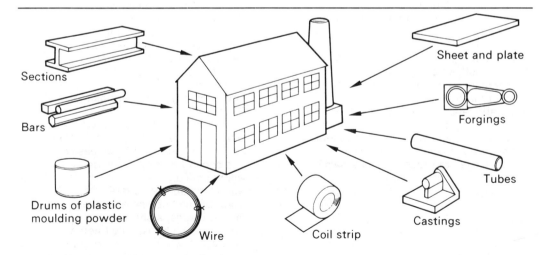

Fig. 4.6 Forms of supply

Table 4.3 Cold-working processes

ADVANTAGES	LIMITATIONS

1 Good surface finish.
2 Relatively high dimensional accuracy.
3 Relatively high geometrical accuracy.
4 Work hardening caused during the cold working processes:
  a) increases strength and rigidity;
  b) improves the machining characteristics of the metal so that a good finish is more easily achieved.
	1 Higher cost than for hot worked materials. It is only a finishing process for material previously hot worked. Therefore, the processing cost is added to the hot worked cost.
	2 Materials lack ductility due to work hardening and are less suitable for bending etc.
	3 Clean surface is easily corroded.
	4 Availability limited to rods, bars, sheets, strips and solid drawn tubes.

Table 4.4 Casting processes (gravity, sand only)

ADVANTAGES	LIMITATIONS
1 Virtually no limit to the shape and complication of the component to be cast. 2 Virtually no limit to the size of the casting. 3 Low cost as no expensive machines and tools are required as in forging. 4 Scrap metal can be reclaimed in the melting furnace. (Wrought and machined components have to be made from relatively expensive pre-processed materials.)	1 Strength and ductility low as structure is un-refined. 2 Quality is uncertain as local differences of structure and mechanical defects such as blow-holes cannot be controlled or corrected. 3 Low accuracy due to shrinkage. 4 Poor surface finish. 5 Component must be designed without sudden changes of section, so that molten metal flows easily and cooling cracks and warping will not occur. 6 Not all metals are suitable for casting. The best metals have a low shrinkage, a short freezing range and high fusibility (melt at relatively low temperatures), and have a high fluidity when molten.

Fig. 4.7 Use of steel

ENGINEERING MATERIALS AND HEAT TREATMENT

Table 4.5 Ferrous metals

NAME	GROUP	CARBON CONTENT %	SOME USES
Wrought iron	Wrought iron	Less than 0.05	Chain for lifting tackle, crane hooks, architectural ironwork.
Dead mild steel	Plain carbon steels	0.1 to 0.15	Sheet for pressing out such shapes as motor-car body panels. Thin wire, rod, and drawn tubes.
Mild steel	Plain carbon steels	0.15 to 0.3	General purpose workshop bars, boiler plate, girders.
Medium carbon steel	Plain carbon steels	0.3 to 0.5 0.5 to 0.8	Crankshaft forgings, axles. Leaf springs, cold chisels.
High carbon steel	Plain carbon steels	0.8 to 1.0 1.0 to 1.2 1.2 to 1.4	Coil springs, wood chisels. Files, drills, taps and dies. Fine-edge tools (knives, etc.).
Grey cast iron	Cast iron	3.2 to 3.5	Machine castings.

Fig. 4.8 Use of cast-iron

Table 4.6 Wrought iron.

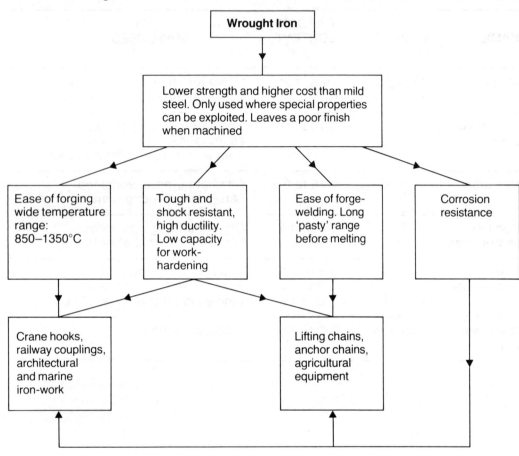

does not tend to work-harden in service and can be used for long periods without maintenance. Mild steel chains are stronger for a given size, but have to be annealed and inspected at frequent intervals. Wrought iron also forge-welds more easily than any other ferrous metal. This facilitates the manufacture of chain links. Its fibrous structure causes it to tear when overloaded instead of snapping suddenly and this gives time for emergency action to be taken. The slag filaments make it corrosion resistant. See Table 4.6.

Dead mild steel

The carbon content is deliberately left low so that the steel will have a high ductility. This enables it to be pressed into complicated shapes even while it is cold. It is slightly weaker than mild steel and is not usually machined as its softness would cause it to tear and leave a poor finish. It is used extensively for motor car body panels.

Mild steel

This is relatively soft and ductile and can be forged or drawn in the hot or cold condition. It is easily machined using high-speed cutting tools with a fairly large rake angle. Free-cutting qualities are available, containing traces of lead, tellurium, or sulphur. Although improving the machining properties, these additives tend to weaken the steel. A coolant is recommended to prevent chip welding.

Mild steel cannot be hardened by heating and quenching, but it can be case hardened after increasing the carbon content of the surface layers of the metal. It can also be work-hardened. See Table 4.7 on page 101.
The effects of varying the carbon content of plain carbon steels are shown in Fig. 4.9 on page 102.

Medium carbon steel

This is harder, tougher, and less ductile than mild steel, and cannot be bent or

formed in the cold condition to any great extent without cracking. It hot-forges well, but close temperature control is required to prevent:
1 'Burning' at high temperatures (over 1150°C), which leads to embrittlement.
2 Cracking below 700°C, due to work hardening.

It machines to a good surface finish, better than mild steel, with high-speed steel tools if the rake angle is reduced to increase the tool strength. A coolant should be used to prevent chip welding.

It can be hardened by heating and quenching. Quenching should be done in an oilbath if toughness is required and in water if maximum hardness is required. See Table 4.8 on page 103.

High carbon steels

These are harder, less ductile, and slightly less tough than medium carbon steel. Cold forming is not recommended, but they hot-forge well, providing the temperature is even more closely controlled. There should be an upper limit of 900°C and a lower limit of 700°C.

They can be machined with high-speed tools if a low cutting speed and a small rake angle are used. A cutting fluid with an extreme pressure additive is recommended to prevent chip welding. If a lot of high carbon steel components are to be machined, carbide tipped tools should be considered.

High carbon steels are hardened by heating and quenching. Only oil should be used for the quenching bath to prevent distortion and cracking. High carbon steel is used extensively for cutting tools. See Table 4.9 on page 103.

Table 4.7 Mild steel

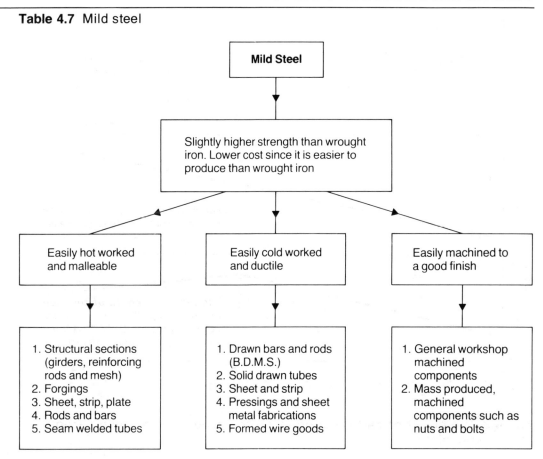

High-speed steel

This has largely superceded high carbon steel for power-operated cutting tools. It has the advantage of retaining its hardness at operating temperatures as high as 700°C, whereas high carbon steel starts to lose its hardness at 220°C and it is useless for cutting purposes at 300°C.

Its hardness after heat treatment should be in excess of 65 Rockwell 'C' scale.

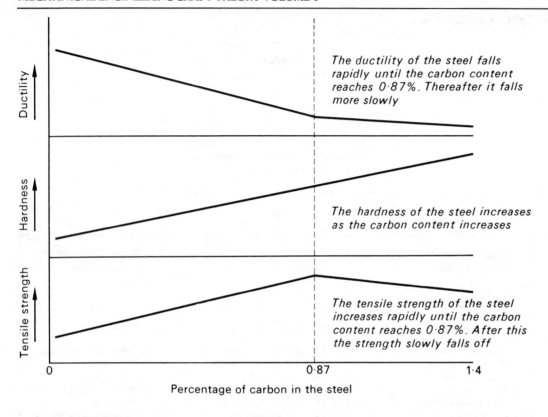

Fig. 4.9 The effect of carbon content on the properties of plain carbon steels (annealed)

A typical high-speed steel consists of:
Carbon 0·75%
Chromium 4·7%
Tungsten 22·0%
Vanadium 1·4%
Iron 71·15%

It will be seen that this steel contains other substances in addition to the iron and carbon of the plain carbon steels described so far. Therefore high speed steel is an *alloy steel*. Alloy steels are very much more expensive than plain carbon steels, but have superior properties. That is, they may be stronger, harder, more wear resistant or more corrosion resistant, etc. Cutting tools made from high speed steel last longer and can be operated at higher cutting speeds than high carbon steel tools and this makes them more economical despite their higher initial cost. Most of the machining operations described later in this book use high speed steel cutting tools. See Table 4.10 on page 104.

Grey cast iron

Grey cast iron is very similar in composition and properties to the crude pig iron produced by the blast furnace. It does not require the complex and expensive refinement processes of steels and so provides a useful, low-cost engineering material. See Table 4.11.

Malleable cast iron

This is a 'white' cast iron of low carbon content (2·5%–3·0%) that has been cast to shape in the ordinary way. The castings are then subjected to a heat treatment process that increases their strength and malleability very considerably.

There are two heat treatment processes:
1 Blackheart
2 Whiteheart

These names refer to the colour of a broken casting after heat treatment. See Table 4.12 on page 105.

Spheroidal graphite (S.G.) cast iron

This is also known as 'high duty' cast iron. When traces of the metals magnesium or cerium are added to

ENGINEERING MATERIALS AND HEAT TREATMENT

Table 4.8 Medium carbon steel

Table 4.9 High carbon steel

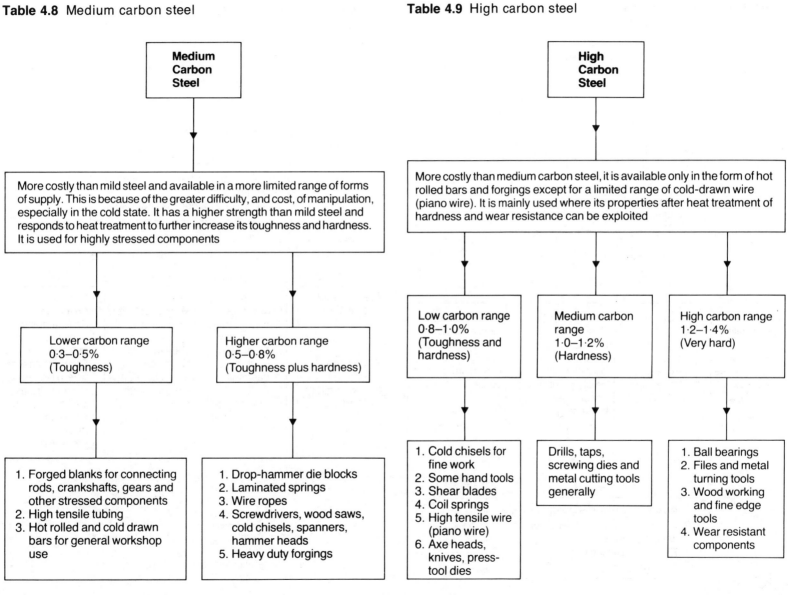

Table 4.10 High speed steel

High-speed Steel

High-speed steel is much more costly than high carbon steel because it is a heavily alloyed steel containing expensive metallic elements

Availability:
1. Hot rolled bar
2. Forged tool blanks
3. Ground tool bits

Hardness: At least 65 Rockwell C scale. Hardness is retained up to 700°C

Machineability: Easily machined to shape in the annealed condition. Easily ground to shape after hardening

Wear resistance: Resistant to abrasion due to the high chromium content

1. Widely used for metal-cutting tools
2. Used for components subject to wear and abrasion
3. Efficiency and life out-weighs high cost

Table 4.11 Grey cast iron

Grey Cast Iron

A low cost material that can be used for many purposes
Available to the foundry as virgin ingots

Mechanical properties:
1. High compressive strength
2. Low tensile strength
3. High rigidity
4. High stability after 'weathering'

Casting properties:
1. High fluidity and ability to make sound castings
2. Relatively low melting temperature 1130–1250°C

Machineability: Easily machined to a good finish once the 'skin' has been removed. Forms a discontinuous chip

Special properties: Self-damping does not vibrate or 'ring'. Prevents chatter when used for machine frames. Self-lubricating. Good anti-friction properties

A 'natural' for machine beds, frames and details
General castings

ENGINEERING MATERIALS AND HEAT TREATMENT

Table 4.12 Malleable cast iron

```
                    White
                    Cast
                    Iron
                  /       \
                 /         \
    Blackheart Process    Whiteheart Process
```

Blackheart Process
Castings are heated in boxes out of contact with air at 850–950°C for 50 to 170 hours. The effect of this prolonged heating is to break down the iron carbide to form small 'rosettes' of graphite. The final structure is of ferrite and fine carbon particles. It is soft and easily machineable. It is almost as malleable as cast mild steel

Whiteheart Process
Castings are packed in boxes with high quality iron ore. They are then heated to about 1000°C for between 70 and 100 hours. The ore draws the carbon out of the castings. The composition and properties of the casting will resemble a cast mild steel

Malleable Cast Iron
Used when a stronger, less brittle material than grey cast iron is required for: small machine details, conduit fittings, etc.

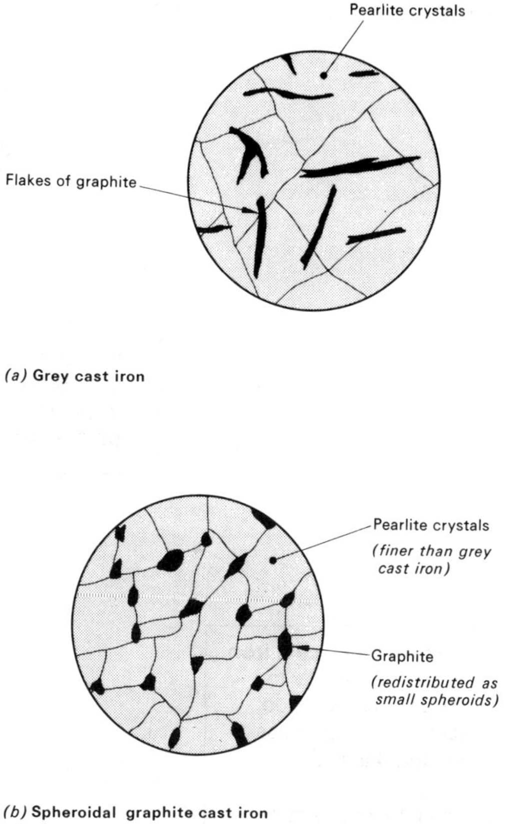

(a) Grey cast iron — Pearlite crystals, Flakes of graphite

(b) Spheroidal graphite cast iron — Pearlite crystals *(finer than grey cast iron)*, Graphite *(redistributed as small spheroids)*

Fig. 4.10 Cast iron micro structures

ordinary grey cast iron, the graphite flakes become redistributed throughout the mass of the metal as fine spheroids (see Fig. 4.10).

The ultimate tensile stress for a spheroidal graphite cast iron will be about 600 MN/m² compared with only 120 MN/m² for a grey cast iron. Spheroidal graphite castings are comparable with medium carbon steel forgings. In many motor car engines the traditional forged steel crank shaft is being replaced with an S.G. casting. Not only is the material itself cheaper than steel, but casting crankshafts to shape is cheaper than forging. The S.G. casting is also easier to machine.

If S.G. cast irons are soaked at 900°C for several hours, the tensile strength will fall to about 540 MN/m² but the elongation percentage (ductility) will

Table 4.13 Spheroidal graphite (S.G.) cast iron

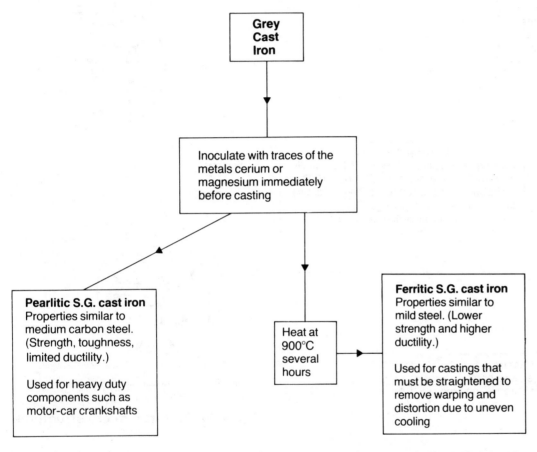

increase to between 10 and 27 per cent. This is approaching the properties of mild steel. See Table 4.13.

Alloy cast irons

These cast irons have special properties such as corrosion resistance, heat resistance, etc. They are summarised in Table 4.14 on page 107.

Non-ferrous metals

The term *non-ferrous metals* refers to the 38 metals other than iron that are known to man. The non-ferrous metals most used by engineers are listed in Table 4.15 on page 108.

In addition to the metals listed in Table 4.15, the following non-ferrous metals can be alloyed with plain carbon steels, either singly or in groups, to produce *alloy steels* that have special properties.

Nickel refines the grain size of the steel and increases *toughness*.

Chromium improves the response of the steel to heat treatment and permits slower cooling with a consequent reduction in cracking and distortion (see page 115). It also helps large steel sections to harden uniformly.

Manganese improves the *wear resistance* of steels.

Molybdenum reduces *temper brittleness* and ensures that a steel retains its strength when operating at high temperatures.

Cobalt and *tungsten* improve the ability of cutting tool steels to retain their *hardness* at high temperatures when used in metal cutting machines.

Vanadium enhances the properties of any other alloying elements present and also reduces the chance of *fatigue failure*. It is often found in spring steels for this reason.

Nickel and chromium are also used to improve the corrosion resistance of steels when present in fairly high quantities, as in stainless steels. They are also electro-plated on to steels and other metals to provide a decorative finish that is corrosion resistant.

ENGINEERING MATERIALS AND HEAT TREATMENT

Non-ferrous alloys

The pure non-ferrous metals are used mainly where their properties of corrosion resistance and electrical and thermal conductivity are needed. They are not widely used for mechanical engineering applications as their mechanical strength is too low. (Copper is an exception.) Their mechanical properties are greatly improved by alloying them together.

Brasses

These are alloys of copper and zinc. Table 4.16 on page 109 gives some typical examples.

Tin bronzes

These are alloys of copper, tin and a de-oxidizer.
Gunmetal
Copper, tin and zinc (de-oxidizer).
Phosphor bronze
Copper, tin and phosphorus (de-oxidizer).
 Table 4.17 gives some typical examples of both gunmetal and phosphor bronze (page 109).

Particular uses of copper and aluminium

Aluminium

Aluminium has two important properties:
1 low density (one third that of steel) which makes it useful for components that must be light in weight, for example, in aircraft.
2 high affinity for oxygen, which makes it difficult to extract it from its ore. This makes it relatively expensive despite the fact that it is the third most abundant element in the earth's crust. (Silicon and oxygen are the two most abundant.) See Table 4.18 for some uses of pure aluminium (page 110).

Copper

Copper is one of the most easily recognisable metals in the workshop because of its rich, red colour. Although considerably heavier and more expensive than steel, its special properties make it particularly suitable

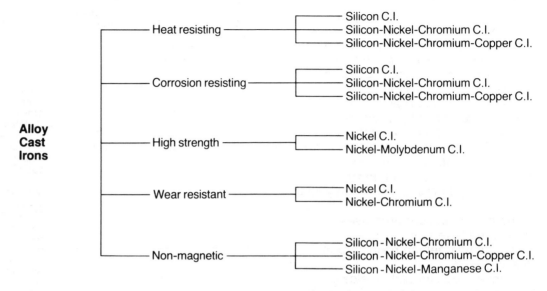

Table 4.14 Alloy cast irons

for a wide range of uses (see Table 4.19 on page 110).

The workshop identification of common metals and alloys

Many materials of different physical properties look very similiar and it is essential that some form of permanent identification is marked on them, for example, colour coding.
 However, bar 'ends' are often used up for small, occasional jobs and Table 4.20 gives some simple workshop tests of identification (see page 111).

Heat treatment

The properties of a metal may be modified by heating it to various temperatures and cooling it at various speeds. This is called *heat treatment*. The theories behind the processes involved are complex and beyond the scope of this book. However, by following certain set procedures, the desired effect can be obtained quite simply. Remember that each metal and alloy requires its own individual treatment, and any variation from the recommended procedure can only end in disappointment.

The heat treatment processes considered here are:
1 quench-hardening plain carbon steels;
2 tempering plain carbon steels;
3 case-hardening plain carbon steels;
4 annealing plain carbon steels;
5 normalising plain carbon steels;
6 annealing non-ferrous metals.

Quench-hardening plain carbon steels

Figure 4.11 summarises the methods by which the structure, and therefore the properties, of plain carbon steels can be changed by heat treatment processes.

The temperature to which the steel must be heated to change completely the initial structure and properties will depend upon the carbon content of the steel. Figure 4.12 (page 112) shows the temperatures from which plain carbon

Table 4.15 Common non-ferrous metals

METAL	DENSITY kg/m³	MELTING POINT °C	PROPERTIES	TYPICAL USES
Aluminium	2 700	660	Lightest of the commonly used metals. High electrical and thermal conductivity. Soft, ductile, and low tensile strength 93 MN/m².	The base of many engineering alloys. Lightweight electrical conductors.
Copper	8 900	1 083	Soft, ductile, and low tensile strength 232 MN/m². Second only to silver in conductivity, it is much easier to joint by soldering and brazing than aluminium. Corrosion resistant.	The base of brass and bronze alloys. It is used extensively for electrical conductors and heat exchangers, such as motor-car radiators.
Lead	11 300	328	Soft, ductile and very low tensile strength. High corrosion resistance.	Electric cable sheaths. The base of 'solder' alloys. The grids for 'accumulator' plates. Lining chemical plant. Added to other metals to make them 'free-cutting'.
Silver	10 500	960	Soft, ductile, and very low tensile strength. Highest conductivity of any metal.	Widely used in electrical and electronic engineering for switch and relay contacts.
Tin	7 300	232	Resists corrosion.	Coats sheet mild steel to give 'tin plate'. Used in soft solders. One of the bases of 'white metal' bearings. An alloying element in bronzes.
Zinc	7 100	420	Soft, ductile, and low tensile strength. Corrosion resistant.	Used extensively to coat sheet steel to give 'galvanized iron'. The base of die-casting alloys. An alloying element in brass.

Table 4.16 Typical brass alloys

NAME	COPPER %	ZINC %	LEAD %	TIN %	PROPERTIES AND USES
Cartridge brass	70	30			Very high ductility and moderate tensile strength which increases rapidly as the alloy is cold worked. Used in press work for severe deep drawing operations.
Standard brass	65	35			Cheaper than cartridge brass, but less ductile; suitable for most engineering purposes.
Basic brass	63	37			The cheapest cold working brass, lacking in ductility and can withstand simple forming operations only.
Muntz metal	60	40			Not suitable for cold working, but hot works well. Used for extruded sections and hot stamping.
Free-cutting brass	58	39	3		Not suitable for cold working but excellent for high speed machining.
Admiralty brass	69	30		1	Virtually cartridge brass plus a little tin to improve its corrosion resistance in salt-water conditions.
Naval brass	62	37		1	Virtually muntz metal plus a little tin to improve its corrosion resistance in salt-water conditions.

Table 4.17 Typical tin bronze alloys

NAME	COPPER %	TIN %	ZINC %	PHOSPHORUS %	PROPERTIES AND USES
Low-tin bronze	96	3.75		0.25	This alloy is severely cold worked to harden it so that it can be used for springs where good elastic properties must be coupled with corrosion and fatigue resistance.
Cast phosphor bronze	89.50	10		0.50	This alloy is suitable for sand casting. It has good anti-friction properties and is widely used in cast rods and tubes for making bearing bushes and worm wheels.
Admiralty gunmetal	88	10	2		This alloy is suitable for sand casting where fine grained pressure-tight components, such as pump and valve bodies, are required.

Notes:
1. **Brass.** Gives a poor quality porous casting and relies upon hot or cold working to consolidate the metal and give it adequate mechanical strength.
2. **Bronze.** Can only be cold worked if very little tin is present (low-tin bronze). It gives a good quality, sound, pressure-tight casting.
3. **Aluminium bronze and cupro-nickel alloys.** These are more expensive than 'tin bronzes', but are more corrosion resistant at high temperatures. They are used for boiler and condenser tubes.

Table 4.18 Aluminium

```
                        ┌─────────────┐
                        │  Aluminium  │
                        └──────┬──────┘
                               ▼
┌──────────────────────────────────────────────────┐
│ 1. Good conductor of heat and electricity        │
│ 2. Resistant to normal atmospheric corrosion     │
│ 3. Cheaper than copper                           │
│ 4. Produced in politically more stable countries │
└──────────────────────────────────────────────────┘
```

High purity aluminium

- **Properties:** Soft, ductile, of little use structurally. High conductivity
- **Uses:** Electrical conductors. Heat exchangers. (Difficult to solder).
- **Availability:** Drawn wire and rod, cold rolled sheet, extruded sections

Basis of a wide range of alloys

Commercially pure aluminium

- **Properties:** Contains up to 1% silicon and iron. This, together with cold working, gives adequate strength for many uses
- **Uses:** Non toxic oxides make it suitable for food processing plant and utensils. Die cast and wrought small machine parts
- **Availability:** Drawn wire and rod, cold rolled sheet, forgings, extruded sections

Table 4.19 Copper

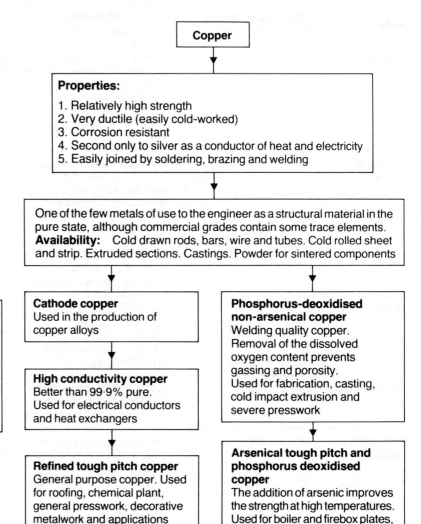

steels should be quench-hardened. The degree of hardness the steel achieves is solely dependent upon:
1 the carbon content;
2 the rate of cooling.

Effect of carbon content

There must be sufficient carbon present to form the hard iron carbides in the steel when it is heated and quenched. The effect of the carbon content when a steel is heated and quenched is shown in Table 4.21 on page 113.

Effect of rate of cooling

The rapid cooling necessary to harden a steel is known as *quenching*. The liquid into which the steel is dipped to cause this rapid cooling is called the *quenching bath*.

In the workshop, the quenching bath will contain either water or quenching oil (but on no account use lubricating oil).

The more rapidly a plain carbon steel is cooled, the harder it becomes. Unfortunately, rapid cooling can also lead to *cracking* and *distortion*. Therefore, the workpiece should not be cooled more rapidly than necessary to give the desired degree of hardness. For plain carbon steels, the cooling rates shown in Table 4.22 are recommended.

Overheating plain carbon steels

It is a common mistake to overheat a steel in the hope that it will become harder. As already stated, the hardness only depends upon the carbon content

Table 4.20 Workshop identification tests
(*These are not fool-proof and require some experience.*)

METAL	APPEARANCE	HAMMER COLD	TYPE OF CHIP	'SPARK TEST' ON GRINDING WHEEL
Mild steel ('black')	Smooth scale with blue/black sheen	Flattens easily	Smooth, curly, ribbon-like	Stream of yellow/white sparks, varying in length; slightly 'fiery'.
Mild steel ('bright')	Smooth, scale-free, silver grey surface			
Medium carbon steel	Smooth scale, black sheen	Fairly difficult to flatten	Chip curls more tightly and discolours light brown	Yellow sparks, shorter than m/s, and finer and more feathery
High carbon steel	Rougher scale, black	Difficult to flatten	Chip curls even more tightly and discolours dark blue	Sparks less bright, starting near grinding wheel, and more feathery with secondary branching (distinctive acrid smell)
High-speed steel	Rougher scale, black with reddish tint	Very difficult to flatten. Tends to crack easily	Long ribbon-like chip. Distinctive smell. Over-heats tool easily	Faint red streak ending in fork (distinctive acrid smell)
Cast iron	Grey and sandy	Crumbles	Granular, grey in colour	Faint red spark, ending in bushy yellow sparks (distinctive acrid smell)
Copper	Distinctive red colour	Flattens very easily	Ribbon-like, with razor edge	Should not be ground

of the steel and the rate of cooling. Once the correct hardening temperature has been reached, any further increase in temperature only slows the rate of cooling and tends to reduce the hardness. Further, overheating also causes *crystal growth* resulting in a weak and defective component.

On the other hand, if the hardening temperature is not reached, the component will not harden no matter how quickly it is cooled.

Tempering plain carbon steels

Hardened plain carbon steel is very brittle and unsuitable for immediate use. A further process known as tempering must be carried out to increase the toughness of steel at the expense of some hardness.

Tempering means reheating the steel to a suitable temperature and quenching it again. The temperature to which the steel is heated depends upon what the component is going to be used for. Table 4.23 (page 114) gives suitable temperatures for tempering components made from plain carbon steel.

Examples of hardening plain carbon steels

Example 4.1

To harden and temper a cold chisel made from octagonal chisel steel having a carbon content of 0·6%/0·7%.

From Fig. 4.14 it will be seen that the correct hardening temperature from a

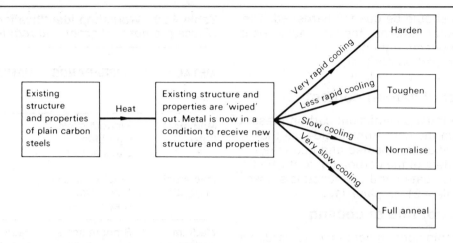

Fig. 4.11 Heat treatment of plain carbon steels

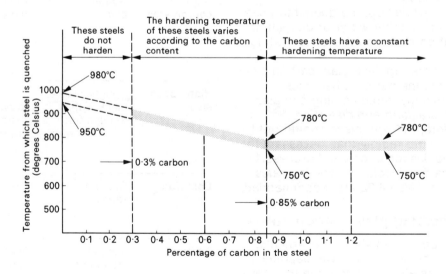

Fig. 4.12 Hardening and annealing of plain carbon steels

Table 4.21 Effect of carbon content

TYPE OF STEEL	CARBON CONTENT %	EFFECT OF HEATING AND QUENCHING (RAPID COOLING)
Mild	Below 0·25	Negligible
Medium carbon	0·3–0·5	Becomes tougher
	0·5–0·9	Becomes hard
High carbon	0·9–1·3	Becomes very hard

Table 4.22 Rate of cooling

CARBON CONTENT %	QUENCHING BATH	REQUIRED TREATMENT
0·30–0·50	Oil	Toughening[1]
0·50–0·90	Oil	Toughening
0·50–0·90	Water	Hardening
0·90–1·30	Oil	Hardening[2]

[1] Below 0.5 per cent carbon content, steels are not hardened as cutting tools, so water hardening has not been included.
[2] Above 0.9 per cent carbon content, any attempt to harden in water could lead to cracking.

0·6%–0·7% plain carbon steel lies between 820°C and 850°C (bright red heat). As the carbon content is fairly low, and a chisel is a simple shape, it can be safely quenched in water to achieve maximum hardness.

To temper the chisel, first polish the cutting end so that the temper colours caused by the oxide film can be observed. The shank is then heated as shown in Fig. 4.13, and the polished end is watched as the temper colours travel towards it.

If the chisel is to cut metal, the cutting edge should be a brownish-purple when it is quenched.

If the chisel is to cut brick or concrete, the cutting edge should be purple to give it greater impact resistance.

Letting the heat travel down from the shank ensures that the shank is left in a tough, rather than a hard condition so that it will not shatter when hit by a hammer.

Example 4.2 To harden and temper a press tool die made from a 1·2% plain carbon steel.

From Fig. 4.14 it will be seen that the correct hardening temperature for a 1·2% plain carbon steel lies between 750°C and 780°C (dull red heat). As the carbon content is high, and the die may be intricate in shape, it should be quenched in oil to prevent distortion and cracking.

Unlike Example 4.1, the press tool die must be of uniform hardness throughout. This can only be achieved by uniform heating. One simple method is to use a sand tray to spread the heat source as shown in Fig. 4.14. When the die is the correct tempering colour (dark brown for brass; brownish-purple for steel) it is again quenched in oil.

Case-hardening plain carbon steels

Shallow case

This process is used to surface-harden mild steel components (see Fig. 4.15).

Carburizing Heat the component to about 850°C in contact with a carbon rich compound, such as Kasenit, for a few minutes. This raises the carbon content of the metal surface to about 0·9 per cent and makes it suitable for hardening.

Hardening (*dipping off*) Since the high carbon case is already above the required hardening temperature (Fig. 4.12), it is only necessary to quench the component in water. If the compound has 'taken', there will be a loud crack and the component surface will have a characteristic mottled appearance.

Deep case

The process of superficial hardening only produces a shallow case a few hundredths of a millimetre thick. Obviously, any attempt to correct the size and geometry of the component by subsequent grinding will remove this shallow case. If grinding is called for, a much deeper case is required. This is produced as follows.

Carburizing Heat the component to about 850°C to 900°C in contact with a carbon rich compound, but this time hold it at this temperature for 3 to 4 hours. As well as producing a deep case, this prolonged heating coarsens the grain of the steel and weakens the component. To correct this, grain refinement is required.

Grain refinement Allow the component to cool down to room temperature, remove it from the carburizing compound, and reheat it to about 850°C to 900°C. Immediately quench in oil. This refines the grain of the core but not the case.

Hardening (*dipping off*) Reheat to only 750°C to 800°C and immediately quench in water. This hardens the case and refines its grain. It is not usual to temper case hardened components.

Table 4.23 Tempering temperatures

COMPONENT	TEMPER COLOUR	TEMPERATURE °C
Edge tools	Pale straw	220
Turning tools	Medium straw	230
Twist drills	Dark straw	240
Taps	Brown	250
Press tools	Brownish-purple	260
Cold chisels	Purple	280
Springs	Blue	300
Toughening (crankshafts)		450–600

In the workshop, the tempering temperature is usually judged by the colour of the oxide film that appears on a freshly polished surface of the steel when it is heated.

Some tools, such as chisels, want only the cutting edge hardened, the shank being left tough to withstand the hammer blows.

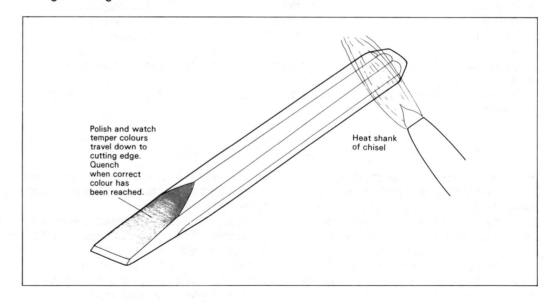

Fig. 4.13 Tempering a cold chisel

ENGINEERING MATERIALS AND HEAT TREATMENT

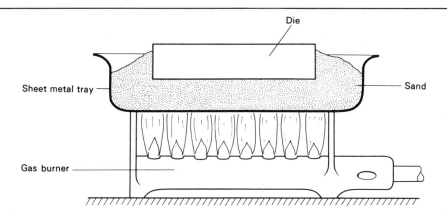

Fig. 4.14 Tempering a die uniformly

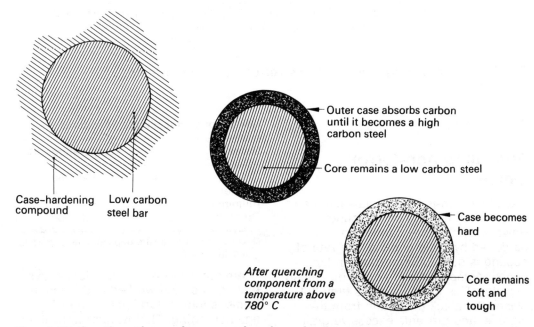

Fig. 4.15 Section through a case-hardened component

The component will now have a hard, fine-grained case, and a tough, fine-grained core.

Annealing plain carbon steels

The temperatures from which plain carbon steels are hardened and annealed are identical. The difference between the processes lies in the rate of cooling (Fig. 4.11). To anneal a plain carbon steel it is cooled very slowly by turning off the furnace, closing the flue dampers, and allowing both work and furnace to cool down together. Alternatively the component may be buried in lime or ashes.

Example 4.3 To anneal a component made from 0·6% carbon steel.

Since the steel is annealed and hardened from the same temperature, reference can be made to Fig. 4.11. It will be seen that the full annealing temperature for a 0·6% carbon steel is approximately 850°C.

The steel is raised to this temperature in the furnace and soaked until the temperature is uniform throughout. The furnace is turned off, the dampers are closed, and furnace and component cool down slowly together.

Example 4.4 To anneal a component made from 1·2% plain carbon steel.

The procedure is the same as in Example 4.3 except for the temperature from which the metal is cooled. Reference to Fig. 4.11 shows that the correct temperature for a 1·2% plain

115

carbon steel is between 750°C and 780°C. The metal is cooled slowly as before.

Normalising plain carbon steels

Normalising consists of heating to the temperatures shown in Fig. 4.16 and cooling more rapidly (in still air) than for annealing (in the furnace).

The ductility of the metal is lower, but the grain structure is more refined and the surface finish is better when the metal is machined. The strength of the metal is improved. This process also removes process stresses and prevents warping during or after finish machining.

Example 4.5 To normalise a 1·2% carbon steel forging after rough machining to relieve any residual stresses.

Reference to Fig. 4.16 shows that the normalising temperature for a 1·2% carbon steel is 850°C to 980°C. It will be noted that this is considerably higher than for annealing or hardening a 1·2% carbon steel. Despite the higher temperature, grain growth is avoided by the faster rate of cooling. After the steel has reached 950°C to 980°C it is removed from the furnace and allowed to cool down in still air. Care must be taken to avoid:
1 placing the component in a draught;
2 placing the component on a surface that will 'chill' it;
3 restricting the natural circulation of air around the component.

Annealing non-ferrous metals

Like steel, non-ferrous metals can be annealed by heating and cooling. However, since they cannot be hardened by rapid cooling, the rate of cooling is quite unimportant. In fact, copper components are often quenched in water. This not only saves time but cleans the black oxide film from the surface, and prevents excessive grain growth.

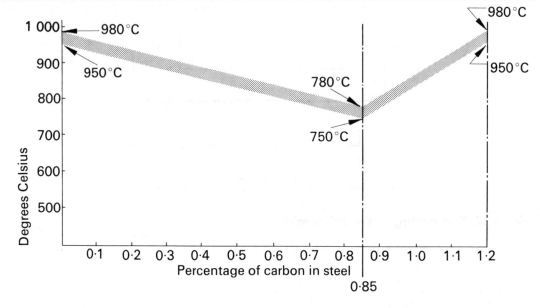

Fig. 4.16 Normalising temperatures for plain carbon steels

Non-ferrous annealing temperatures

Metal	Temperatures °C
Cold working brasses	600–650
Copper	650–750
Aluminium	500–550
Duralumin	480–500

(The duralumin range are popular general purpose aluminium alloys.)

There are very many aluminium alloys that can be cold worked and machined. Some, such as duralumin, suffer from age hardening. That is, after annealing, they commence to re-harden by

ENGINEERING MATERIALS AND HEAT TREATMENT

themselves. After standing for about five days they can no longer be cold worked and require re-annealing. Age hardening can be slowed up by refrigerating the component at −20°C after annealing.

Hardening faults

The effect of overheating causing cracking, grain growth and loss of hardness has already been considered on page 111. In addition, cracking and distortion can occur as the result of faulty design and incorrect quenching as shown in Figs 4.17 and 4.18.

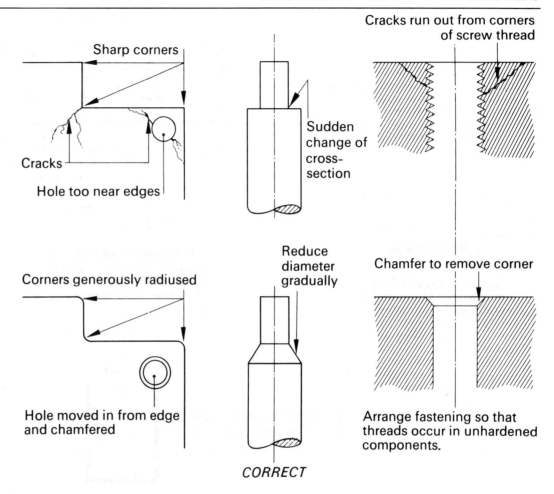

Fig. 4.17 Some causes of cracking

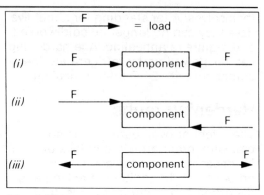

Fig. 4.19

Exercises

1. State which of the components shown in Fig. 4.19 is subjected to a:
   a) tensile load
   b) compressive load
   c) shear load
2. A soldering iron has a wooden handle, an iron shank (yoke), and a copper bit. With reference to their properties, explain why the maker of the soldering iron chose these materials.
3. Match the following properties to the components shown in the table: elasticity, plasticity, ductility, malleability.

Component	Property
rivet	
coin	
spring	
wire	

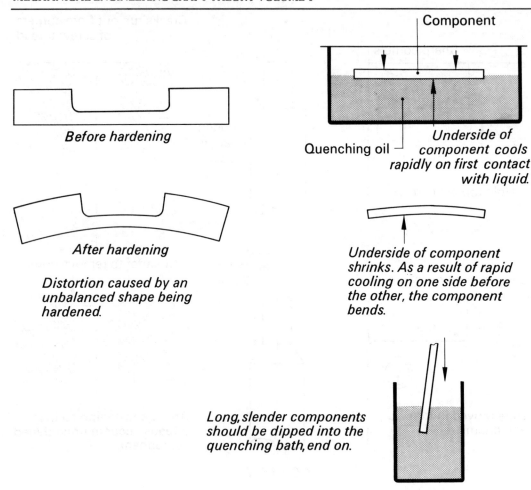

Fig. 4.18 Some causes of distortion

4 Give *one* of the properties and *one* of the engineering uses of *each* of the following:
   a) copper
   b) cast iron (grey)
   c) aluminium alloy
   (*WAEC* 1974)

5 Wrought steel bars may be purchased in (i) the *hot-worked*, and (ii) the *cold-worked* condition. Describe briefly the effect of each condition on (a) the properties, and (b) the appearance of the steel bars.

6 Describe briefly the *major* differences in properties and composition between mild steel and cast iron.

7 Describe briefly how a piece of high-carbon steel can be:
   a) hardened
   b) tempered
   c) annealed
   Explain how you would judge that the correct temperature was reached in *each* case.
   (*WAEC* 1974)

8 Decribe the *workshop tests* you would use to distinguish between:
   a) mild steel
   b) high carbon steel
   c) high speed steel

9 State which metals are used to make the following alloys:
   a) brass
   b) gunmetal bronze
   c) soft solder

10 a) Describe in detail how you would harden and temper a cold chisel made from 0·6% carbon steel. Pay particular attention to the temperatues used and how they would be judged.
   b) State the rate of cooling for each of the following processes.
   (i) quench hardening
   (ii) annealing
   (iii) normalising

5. Safety

The need for safety

The number of accidents reported in our industries has continued to increase over the years. Discussions with workers have revealed that more emphasis should be attached to safety education and training.

Some workers feel that industrialisation is the main cause of this increase in the accident rate. They now have to work with machines, which are increasing in number and are becoming more complicated and sophisticated than those used in industries a few years ago.

Some workers still believe that accidents are inevitable because, as they put it, 'Whatever happens to a man, God has written it as his destiny'. Some still believe that human beings many kilometres away can use hidden forces and 'magical actions' to cause their accidents.

A critical analysis of the causes of industrial accidents will show that these beliefs are unfounded, and that we alone are responsible for whatever happens to us in our workplaces. No accident happens because, 'it is God's wish'; no magician or enemy can sit in his home and 'send' or 'conjure' our misfortunes in the factories.

This chapter attempts to discuss some important points for the engineering craftsman and his place of work so that he will be able to work effectively without fearing accidents that may result in injuries to himself and his workmates and damage to expensive tools and equipment.

Causes of accidents

In general, there are two major causes of accidents:
1 unsafe practices on the part of the worker;
2 unsafe working conditions.

Unsafe practices on the part of the worker may result from ignorance of the correct operating and safety procedures, or a deliberate disregard for those procedures. For example he may 'forget' to wear his goggles when operating a grinding machine. He may decide to operate an unfamiliar machine without first seeking instruction in its use and making a careful study of the functions of its controls. He may use machines and equipment after drinking an excessive amount of alcohol so that his judgement is impaired, or he may choose to ignore all the safety procedures and endanger not only himself but his workmates as well.

Unsafe working conditions can be created by negligence on the part of:
1 the worker;
2 the employer (company).

The *worker* can contribute to unsafe working conditions by using worn or unsuitable tools. Often this is because he is too lazy to fetch the correct tool and tries to 'make do' with the nearest tool that comes to hand. Similarly, he can contribute to unsafe conditions by not maintaining his tools in good condition. A chisel with a mushroom head can cause blindness if a piece of metal flies off and enters the worker's eye when the chisel is struck with a hammer. The head of the chisel should be trimmed periodically on a grinding wheel. (See Fig. 5.1).

The *employer* can contribute to unsafe working conditions by installing dangerous machinery without adequate guarding; by allowing the floors of his factory to become slippery with oil so that it is dangerous to move about; by not allowing time and money for the proper maintenance of machines and equipment and by not providing a reasonable working environment. That is, adequate ventilation and lighting, a low noise level, and adequate toilet and washing facilities.

SAFETY

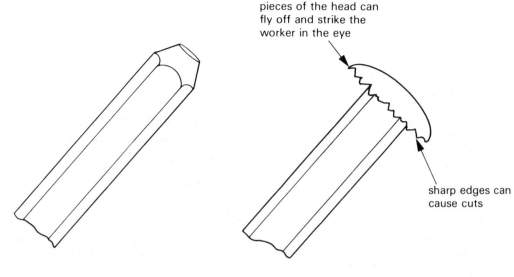

(a) Correctly trimmed chisel head

(b) Mushroom headed chisel

Fig. 5.1 Trimming a chisel head

Legislation

The Government realises that the negligence of both worker and employer can lead to serious accidents, and it is conscious of the unacceptably high accident rate in factories. As a result of this some rules and regulations for the safety of the working population have been made and are contained in the Factory Ordinance of June 1st 1958. Relevant portions of these regulations are extracted by each industry. These abstracts are then posted boldly in strategic areas and locations.

It is now the legal responsibility of employers of labour to help reduce the number of accidents by following the requirements of the Factories Ordinance regulations. They must also ensure that all safety recommendations and instructions are carried out by the employees. It is also the legal responsibility of the *worker* to use the safety equipment provided and to obey the requirements of the Factories Ordinance.

Employers must provide all the safety equipment necessary to ensure safe working conditions and prevent accidents. They can secure the services of special staff to:
1 train workers in the use and servicing of safety equipment;
2 ensure that the equipment provided by employers is actually used by employees;
3 ensure that working environments are kept safe;
4 ensure that the instructions of the Factories Ordinance are obeyed;
5 advise management on safety matters.

Workers, for their part, must be safety-conscious. They must develop safe practices to help reduce the accident rate and remain fit to work for as long as they wish. They must try to make full use of the training they receive and make full and safe use of the equipment and facilities provided by their employers.

The Government for its part makes sure that its recommendations are adhered to. Many publications on safety and various aspects of the Factories Ordinance can be obtained from the Government Printers in Lagos. Factory Inspectors are employed to visit industries and see that the recommendations are followed.

Government recommendations cover three major areas:
1 health;
2 safety;
3 welfare.

Health

The health section of the Ordinance makes recommendations for the maintenance of a healthy environment. Attention must be paid to cleanliness, temperature, ventilation, lighting and drainage. Floors should be cleaned, sanitary conveniences provided and work places should not become overcrowded.

Safety

The safety section of the Ordinance makes recommendations for fencing of machineries, cleaning, protection of the eyes, lifting, fire, etc. This chapter introduces this very important aspect of the Ordinance as it relates to the engineering craftsman.

Behaviour

It is very important to study all the safety instructions and regulations for the work in hand, but the craftsman should be aware of safe practice all the time. He must study the work to be done, the environment in which it is to be done, the tools to be used and the best method to be used. He must realise what the dangers will be if he adopts a wrong and thoughtless approach. He must always have a thoughtful and positive approach to safety for his own sake and the sake of his workmates.

Personal safety

To avoid injuries to yourself and your workmates on the shop floor, the following points must form part of the general code of behaviour:
1   Do not act foolishly on the shop floor.
2   Do not operate machines that you have not used before without learning about them.
3   Always be tidy in the workshop.
4   Always protect your eyes (see Fig. 5.2 on page 123).
5   Do not wear loose clothing (see Fig. 5.3 on page 123).
6   Do not lift heavy loads.
7   Always protect your feet (see Fig. 5.4 on page 124).
8   Do not use hand tools that are not in good condition (Fig. 5.5, page 124).
9   Make sure all moving machinery is fenced (see Fig. 5.6, page 125).
10   Do not run in workshops.
11   Do not throw tools or materials about the shop floor.
12   Remember to place warning notices on faulty machines.
13   Always keep away from suspended loads (see Fig. 5.7 on page 128).
14   Always co-operate with your colleagues.
15   Always protect your hands.
16   Always be tolerant and patient.
   To avoid damage to machines, the following points must be considered. We shall enumerate safety points for individual machine tools later.
1   Machines must always be cleaned.
2   Moving parts must be oiled regularly as set out in maintenance schedules.
3   Make sure you understand the functions of machine controls before operating them.
4   Always report all faults to your superiors.
5   Do not play with electrical connections.
6   Report all electrical faults.
   To your colleagues:
1   always be friendly;
2   always be co-operative;
3   try to understand their problems and be helpful;
4   do not be a bully to others;
5   always consider and respect the ideas of other people.

Safety rules for particular tools, machine tools and processes

Hand tools

(See Fig. 5.5).
Files   Files must not be used without handles. The tang can cause injury to the wrist. Files with chipped tips are also dangerous.
Spanners   Spanners of the correct sizes must be used for nuts to avoid injury to the user when the spanner slips. Oversize spanners also round off the edges of the nuts. Do not extend spanners with pieces of tube because this strains the spanner and the fastening.
Socket wrenches   Allen keys of the correct size must be used for socket screws (allen screws). Worn socket wrenches must never be used as they can slip and injure the user.
Hammers   Hammers must be securely fixed to the handles before use. A badly fixed head can fly off while in use and injure co-workers.
Chisels   Chisels with mushroomed heads must not be used as the sharp edges can cause injury to the user (see Fig. 5.1). For the protection of

SAFETY

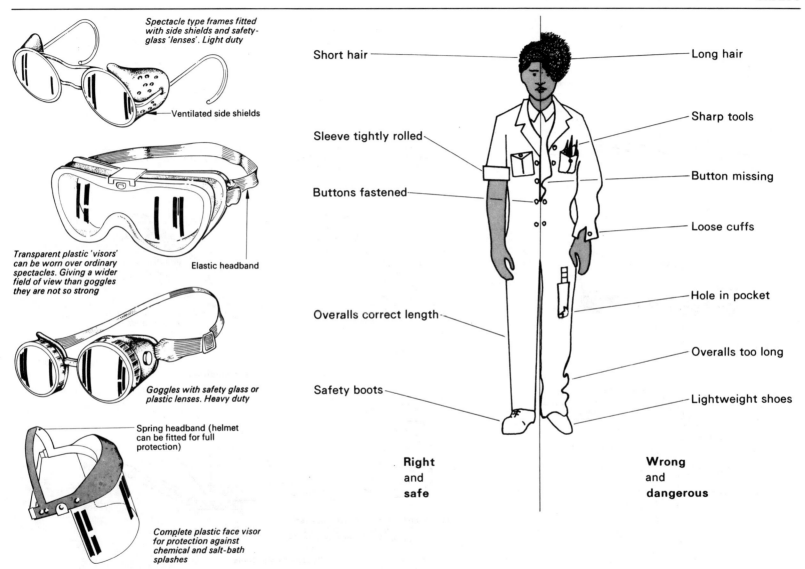

Fig. 5.2 Safety goggles and visors   Fig. 5.3 Correct dress

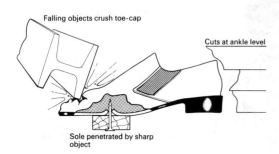

Fig. 5.4 Safety footwear

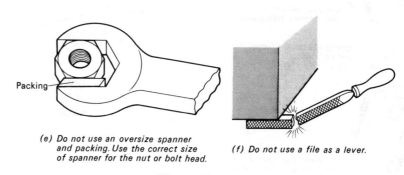

Fig. 5.5 Dangers in use of hand tools

co-workers during chipping, chiselling must be done against a screen.

Portable power tools

These can be either pneumatic or electrical, for example, hand drilling machines and grinding machines.

It is dangerous to use damaged electrical cables or airlines.

When using these tools, gloves, goggles and appropriate safety clothing must be worn.

Users of these tools must maintain a balanced posture to avoid slipping especially when the drill is breaking through whilst drilling.

Heavy objects must not be allowed to drop on to or obstruct cables and airlines. Electrical faults must be reported immediately.

Drilling

Work must be securely clamped on the drilling machine.

The drill itself must be properly held in the jaws of the chuck.

Use the machine guards provided (see Fig. 5.8 on page 127).

Do not wear loose clothing and flapping sleeves that could be caught by the rotating parts of the machine (see Fig. 5.3).

To drill thin objects, enough support must be provided, and careful and efficient clamping techniques must be used.

Do not use your hands to remove chips (swarf) when drilling.

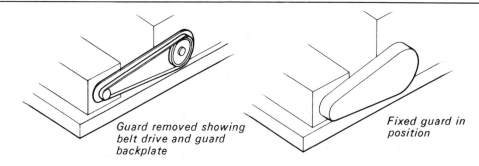

(a) **Fixed transmission guard**

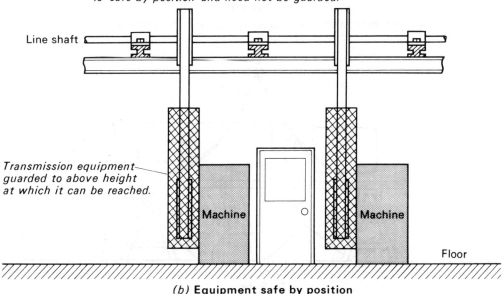

(b) **Equipment safe by position**

Fig. 5.6 Transmission guards

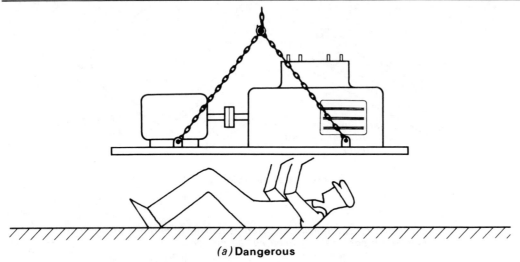

(a) **Dangerous**

It is highly dangerous to work under equipment slung from a hoist.

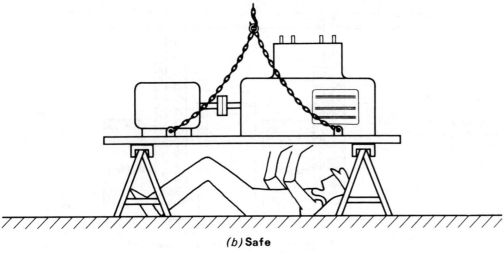

(b) **Safe**

Equipment should be lowered onto trestle stands before being worked on from underneath

Fig. 5.7 Working under equipment

Milling

Gloves must be worn when handling milling cutters, especially cylindrical cutters.

Do not handle the chips; they penetrate the hands easily and cause painful cuts. Work must be firmly clamped; clamps and bolts must be intelligently arranged to avoid obstructing the cutter and distorting the workpiece.

Obtain and correctly arrange packing to stop the work from slipping when the cutting load is applied.

Do not take measurements or gauge your work with the cutter rotating.

Always use cutter guards (see Fig. 5.9).

Always protect your eyes against flying chips.

Do not place heavy tools and attachments on the machine table directly. Use wooden packing to avoid damage to the machined surfaces.

Do not attempt to change the machine speed without first stopping the machine.

Always *isolate* the machine if any setting is to be done, or the cutter is to be changed.

Shaping

Stop the machine before changing speed.

Isolate the machine when any setting is being done.

Stand away from the chips which are always hot and can burn the flesh. It is

SAFETY

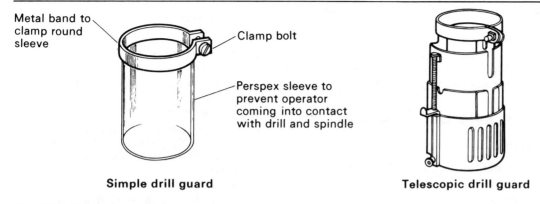

Fig. 5.8 Cutter guards

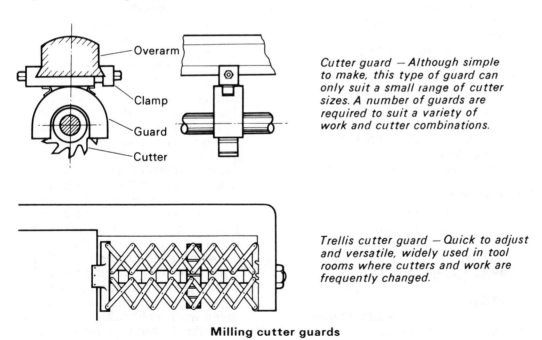

Cutter guard – Although simple to make, this type of guard can only suit a small range of cutter sizes. A number of guards are required to suit a variety of work and cutter combinations.

Trellis cutter guard – Quick to adjust and versatile, widely used in tool rooms where cutters and work are frequently changed.

Fig. 5.9 Milling cutter guards

advisable to shape against a shield for the safety of your workmates who may be standing close to your machine.

The tool must be withdrawn from the work completely before the machine is started up.

The machine must be stopped before gauging or measuring.

The work as well as the cutting tools must be firmly clamped.

Grinding

Safety glasses or goggles must be worn at all times when grinding.

Traverse the workpiece away from the wheel when setting or gauging.

Keep your hands away from the revolving wheel.

Always test grinding wheels to detect cracks before fitting them.

Always ensure that grinding wheels are dressed.

Set the dust extractor close enough to the wheel.

Keep the coolant shut off when the wheel is not rotating.

Make sure the work is held firmly on the magnetic chuck or other means of workholding.

Always magnetise the work when it is placed on the magnetic chuck.

Always de-magnetise when the work is to be removed, that is, always obey the rule 'work on, magnet on: magnet off, work off'.

Turning

Always isolate the machine when measuring or gauging the work or setting the work holding device.

Do not use your bare hands to remove the swarf.

Tool overhang must be kept to a minimum.

Keep clear of rotating chucks.

Do not leave the chuck key in the chuck.

Always ensure that the tool is set so that it does not foul the revolving chuck.

Clamps, clamping bolts, etc. must be carefully set when using a faceplate so that they do not foul the tool or the saddle when traversing.

The machine must first be stopped before the speed is changed.

Always protect the lathe slideway by placing a board across the bed when changing the chuck.

Welding

There must be good ventilation in order to remove fumes.

Appropriate protective clothing must be worn: gloves, goggles with suitable filters, aprons, head gear etc.

Do not roll up leggings and sleeves when welding because sparks and hot slag can cause serious burns.

Wear a boiler suit to protect the arms and legs.

Do not handle hot metals with your bare hands.

Make sure all connections are correctly made.

Do not repair faulty valves and regulators in the case of gas welding, but return them to a qualified fitter.

Get rid of all flammable materials at the welding site.

Arc welding equipment must be properly earthed.

Electric arc welding should not be done in damp areas.

Always keep connections, valves and cables free from oil or grease.

The safe way to work

Start

1 Obtain assignment (drawing or specimen).

Think

1 Think of job hazards.
2 Think of environmental hazards.
3 Think of precautions to be taken.
4 Think of the best way to do the work.

Prepare

1 Put on appropriate clothing.
2 Collect appropriate tools.
3 Inspect tools for damage.
4 Remove all possible job and environmental hazards.
5 Prepare an operation schedule.

Do the work

1 Use appropriate tools.
2 Work to a logical sequence.
3 Measure or gauge.
4 Finish.
5 Measure or gauge again.

Clean up

1 Collect, clean and return all tools and equipment to stores.
2 Clean the machine.
3 Tidy the working area.

Exercises

1 With the aid of examples describe what is meant by:
   a) unsafe practices on the part of the worker
   b) unsafe working conditions
2 What is the legal responsibility of (a) the employer, and (b) the worker under the Factory Ordinance of 1958?
3 a) Why should the engineering craftsman wear (i) overalls, (ii) goggles, (iii) safety shoes in the workshop?
   b) What precautions should be taken before operating an unfamiliar machine?
4 Sketch a drilling machine guard and describe the sort of accident that can occur if it is not used.
5 State *two* precautions that should be observed when machine drilling a piece of thin steel plate.
   (*WAEC* 1974)
6 Sketch a milling machine cutter guard, and state *five* precautions that should be taken when setting and operating a milling machine.
7 What special precautions should be taken when operating a double-ended off-hand grinding machine?
8 What precautions should one take when operating a centre lathe?
9 What special precautions should be taken when welding?
10 Describe the hazards associated with the use of the following hand tools: spanner, file, chisel, hammer.

6. Engineering measurement

Standard of length

Accurate measurement is the basis of good engineering practice. It is significant that craftsmen in many trades other than engineering use a wooden rule, whereas the engineer always uses a precision engraved steel rule. Further, the engineer only uses the rule for his least important measurements.

It is important that all rules and other measuring instruments are based on a common standard of length. This common standard ensures that parts made in one factory fit the corresponding parts made in another factory.

In 1960 the International Standard Metre was defined as being equal in length to 1 650 763·73 wave lengths of the orange radiation of Krypton isotope 86 gas as shown in Fig. 6.1.

Previously, various countries used bars of metal as their standards of length, but a natural light standard has several advantages over metal bars:
1   it does not change length or 'creep';
2   if destroyed it can easily be replaced;
3   identical 'copies' can be kept in all standards rooms and physical laboratories;

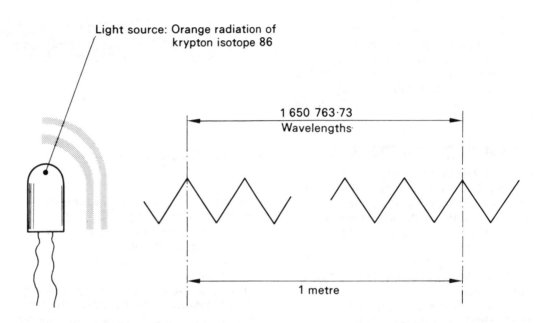

Fig. 6.1 The light standard of length

NAME	RANGE	READING ACCURACY
Steel rule	150 mm to 1 000 mm (1m)	0·5 mm
Vernier caliper	0/150 mm to 0/2 000 mm (2 m)	0·02 mm
Micrometer caliper	0/25 mm to 1 775–1 800 mm (1·8 m)	0·01 mm
Slip gauges	1·0025 mm to 375 mm (105-piece set)	0·0025 mm

Table 6.1 Workshop standards of length

4 it can be compared with other measuring instruments more easily and accurately than the old 'bar' standards of length.

Table 6.1 lists the more frequently used workshop measuring devices and indicates their range of sizes and reading accuracy. All of these measuring devices are related to the International Standard of Length. Note that the measuring accuracy may not be as good as the reading accuracy as it depends upon the skill and 'feel' of the user.

Measuring with the rule

Figure 6.2 shows a typical steel rule 300 mm long. This is a convenient size for most workshop applications, although some craftsmen prefer a 150 mm rule as it is convenient to carry in the pocket.

The steel rule should be:
1 made from hardened and tempered spring steel;
2 *engine divided*, that is, the graduations should be precision engraved into the metal;
3 Ground on the edges so that it can be used for scribing straight lines, and as a straight edge when testing a surface for flatness.
4 Satin chrome finished so as to reduce glare, make it easier to read, and prevent corrosion.

Figure 6.3 shows some typical applications of the rule. All measurements made with the rule are of limited accuracy because of the difficulty of aligning the graduations with the feature being measured. Despite the claims of many craftsmen, the rule should not be trusted for measurements that must be accurate to less than 0·5 mm.

The *engineer's rule*, used for making direct measurements, depends upon the visual alignment of a mark or surface on the work to be measured, with the nearest division on its scale. This may appear to be a relatively simple exercise, but in practice errors can very easily occur, as shown in Fig. 6.4. These errors can be minimised by using a *thin* steel rule.

It is important when making measurements with an engineer's rule, to have the eye directly opposite, and at 90° to the mark on the work. If the mark is looked at sideways, there will be an error known as *parallax*.

Reference to Fig. 6.4 will show that:
1 'M' represents the position of a mark that is to be measured by means of a rule laid alongside it. The graduations of measurement are on the upper face of the rule, as indicated.
2 If the eye is placed along the sighting line A-M, which is at 90° to the work surface, a *true reading* will be obtained at 'a', for it is then directly opposite 'M'.
3 If, however, the eye is not on this sighting line, but displaced to the right, as at 'R', the division 'r' on the graduated scale will appear to be opposite 'M' and an *incorrect reading* will be obtained. Similarly, if the eye is displaced to the left, as at 'L', an incorrect reading on the opposite side, as at 'l' will result.

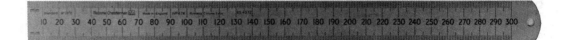

Fig. 6.2 The steel rule

ENGINEERING MEASUREMENT

The construction and use of calipers

Calipers are used to extend the application of the rule and increase the reading accuracy. They are used for transferring the distance between the faces of a component to the rule in such a way as to reduce sighting errors.

The constructional features and some uses of calipers are shown in Fig. 6.5.

By careful setting, and developing a sense of touch or 'feel', a surprisingly high degree of accuracy can be obtained when using calipers.

Firm joint calipers are usually used for larger measurements.

Spring joint calipers are usually used for fine work, as in instrument making and tool making.

As already stated, the accurate use of calipers depends upon a highly developed sense of feel that can only be acquired by practice. When using calipers, observe the following rules.
1 Hold the caliper gently near the joint.
2 Hold it square to the work.
3 No force should be used to 'spring' it over the work. Contact should only just be felt.
4 The caliper should be handled and laid down gently to avoid disturbing the setting.
5 Lathe work should be *stationary* when taking measurements. This is essential for safety and accuracy.

Transfer calipers

These are used to measure the sizes of

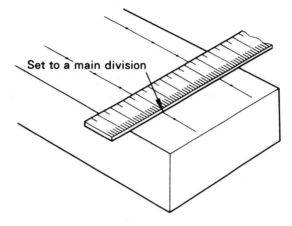

Measuring the distance between two scribed lines

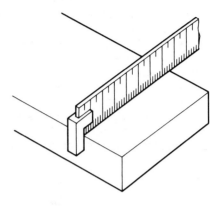

Measuring the distance between two faces using a hook rule

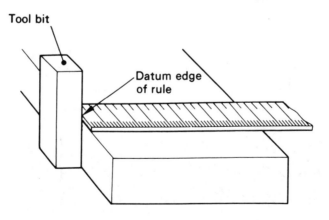

Measuring the distance between two faces using a steel rule and abutment

Fig. 6.3 Use of the rule

undercuts when it is impossible to insert or remove conventional calipers without disturbing their setting. Figure 6.6 shows inside and outside transfer calipers together with a typical application.

After setting the caliper, as shown in Fig. 6.6(a), the auxiliary leg is locked. The contact leg is released as shown in Fig. 6.6(b). After removal from the component, the contact leg is brought back into position against the auxiliary leg and the setting is measured.

Telescopic gauge

Although more expensive than inside calipers and of more limited range, the telescopic gauge is very popular for fine work due to its greater rigidity and improved 'feel'.

The construction and use of these gauges is shown in Fig. 6.7 (page 134).

These precision gauges are specially designed for use either as comparators, or for taking internal measurements which are otherwise hard to obtain. They are used in conjunction with external micrometers.

There is a series of five gauges of various ranges covering a total range from 13 mm–330 mm.

All working parts are made of a high-grade alloy steel. The measuring faces are hardened and radiused to suit the smallest diameter that can be measured by the gauge.

In use, the telescoping leg expands to the size of the bore or slot and is locked by a turn of the Knurled locking nut in the end of the handle; the gauge is then withdrawn from the work and measured with an external micrometer.

The micrometer caliper

The equipment so far described has only limited accuracy. As already stated, the unaided rule should only be trusted to 0·5 mm.

Most engineering work has to be measured much more accurately than this, especially where component parts must fit together as, for instance, a shaft with its bearing. To achieve this precision, measuring equipment of greater accuracy and sensitivity must be used.

One of the most familiar precision measuring devices found in the workshop is the *micrometer caliper*. Figure 6.8 shows the construction of a

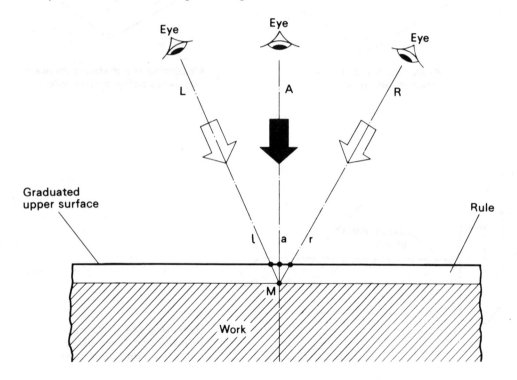

Fig. 6.4 Possible errors with direct eye measurement

ENGINEERING MEASUREMENT

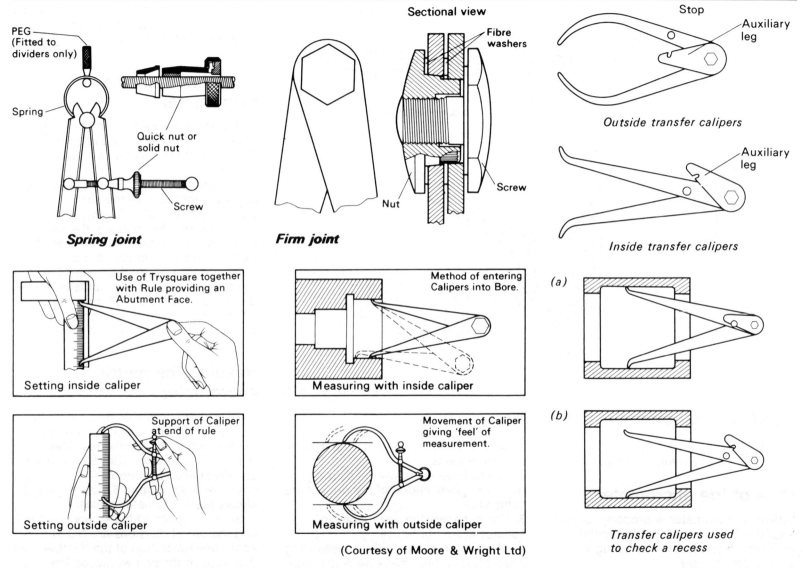

Fig. 6.5 Construction and use of calipers

Fig. 6.6 Transfer calipers

133

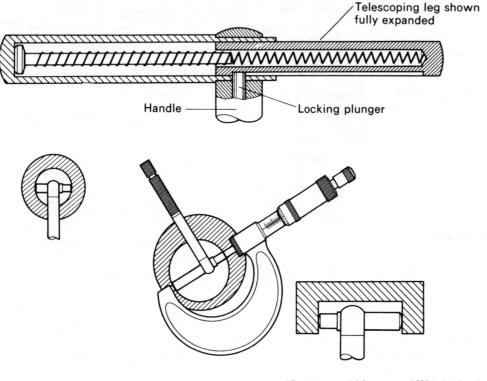

Fig. 6.7 Telescopic gauges

(Courtesy of Moore and Wright Ltd)

typical micrometer caliper and the names of the more important parts.

Care of the micrometer

Unless a micrometer is properly looked after it will soon lose its high initial accuracy. Therefore, when using a micrometer caliper:
1 Wipe the anvils and the work to be measured perfectly clean before making a measurement.
2 Do not use excessive measuring pressure. (Two 'clicks' of the ratchet are sufficient.)
3 Do not leave the anvil faces in contact when not in use.
4 Stop the machine before measuring. Attempting to take measurements with the machine working can lead to serious accidents and irreparable damage to the micrometer. This rule applies to all measuring instruments.

Adjustment of the micrometer

In the box with the micrometer will be found a small double-ended spanner. This is used for making two basic adjustments:
1 *Looseness in the screw*: This is taken up by a slight turn of the screw adjustment nut – Fig. 6.8 (6).
2 *Zero error*: Periodically the anvil faces should be cleaned and closed using the ratchet to give the correct measuring pressure. If the zero line of the thimble does not coincide with the datum line on the barrel, turn the barrel – Fig. 6.8(4) – with the 'C' spanner until the zero line coincides with the datum.

Reading the metric micrometer

The metric micrometer has a screw of 0·5 mm pitch. The barrel is graduated in 'whole' and 'half' millimetres. The thimble is graduated with 50 divisions equally spaced around its circumference. Figure 6.9 on page 136 shows the micrometer scales.

Since the pitch of the screw is 0·5 mm and the barrel divisions are 0·5 mm apart, one revolution of the thimble (and therefore of the screw) moves the thimble along a distance of one barrel

ENGINEERING MEASUREMENT

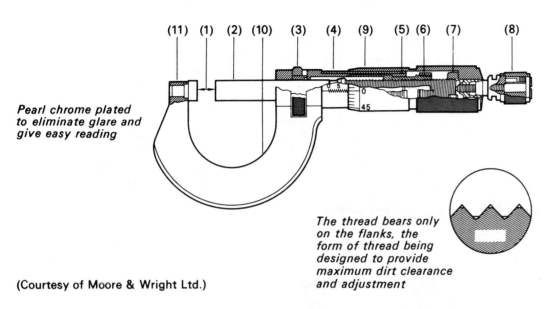

Pearl chrome plated to eliminate glare and give easy reading

The thread bears only on the flanks, the form of thread being designed to provide maximum dirt clearance and adjustment

(Courtesy of Moore & Wright Ltd.)

(1) **Spindle and anvil faces** — Glass hard and optically flat, also available with **Tungsten carbide** faces
(2) **Spindle** — Thread ground, and made from alloy steel, hardened throughout, and stabilised
(3) **Locknut** — effective at any position. Spindle retained in perfect alignment
(4) **Barrel** — Adjustable for zero setting. Accurately divided and clearly marked. Pearl chrome plated
(5) **Main nut** — Length of thread ensures long working life
(6) **Screw adjusting nut** — For effective adjustment of main nut effective
(7) **Thimble adjusting nut** — Controls position of thimble
(8) **Ratchet** — Ensures a constant measuring pressure
(9) **Thimble** — Accurately divided and every graduation clearly numbered
(10) **Steel frame** — Drop forged. Marked with useful decimal equivalents
(11) **Anvil end** — Cutaway frame facilitates usage in narrow slots

Fig. 6.8 Construction of the micrometer caliper

division. (The barrel divisions are placed on alternate sides of the datum line for clarity.) Therefore, since the thimble has 50 equal divisions, and one revolution of the thimble equals 0·5 mm, a movement of one thimble division equals:

$$\frac{0·5}{50} = 0·01 \text{ mm}$$

To find the reading, the following three things are added:
1 the largest visible 'whole' millimetre;
2 the largest visible 'half' millimetre;
3 the thimble division in line with the datum line.

The reading in Fig. 6.8 is as follows:
9 'whole' mm = 9·00 mm
1 'half' mm = 0·50 mm
48 hundredths of a mm = 0·48 mm
9·98 mm

The micrometer caliper can only measure over a range of 25 mm. Where distances greater than 25 mm are to be measured, larger micrometers increasing in steps of 25 mm are used. For example, Fig. 6.10 shows a range of micrometer calipers reading 0–25 mm, 25–50 mm, 50–75 mm. Micrometers continue to increase in steps of 25 mm up to a maximum of 1800 mm.

The vernier caliper

Figure 6.11 shows the vernier caliper, which can make inside and outside measurements on the one instrument. The micrometer caliper cannot do this. The vernier caliper reads from zero to the full length of its beam scale, whereas the micrometer only reads over a range of 25 mm. It is important to note

135

that for inside readings using the vernier caliper, the thickness of the jaws must be added to the scale reading.

Unfortunately the vernier caliper does not give such accurate readings as the micrometer caliper for the following reasons.
1 It is difficult to obtain a correct 'feel' due to its size and weight.
2 The scales are difficult to read even with the aid of a magnifying glass.
3 The reading accuracy is only 0·02 mm. (The reading accuracy of the micrometer is 0·01 mm.)

Metric vernier calipers are fitted with two types of scale: a 25 division scale on cheaper instruments, and on instruments with dual metric and 'inch' scales; and a 50 division scale on better quality instruments. The 50 division scale is easier to read as the graduations are spaced further apart for clarity.

Figure 6.12(b) shows the scales of a 25 division metric vernier caliper. The main scale is divided into centimetres, and sub-divided into millimetres and half millimetres. The vernier scale is divided into 25 equal divisions and it will be seen that these occupy 24 divisions (12 mm) of the main scale. Thus the length of each vernier division equals:

$\frac{1}{25}$ of 12 mm or 0·48 mm

But each main scale division equals ½ or 0·5 mm. Therefore, the difference between one fixed scale division and one vernier scale division is:

0·50 − 0·48 = 0·02 mm

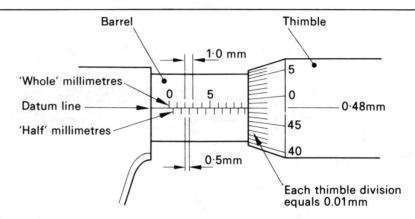

Fig. 6.9 Micrometer scales (metric)

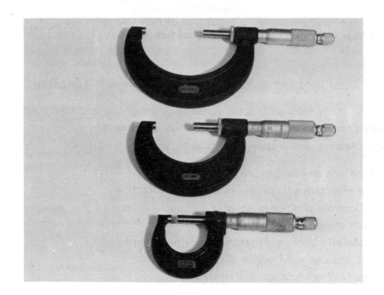

Fig. 6.10 A range of micrometer calipers

To find the reading, the following four things are added:
1 the largest whole centimetre before the vernier zero mark;
2 the largest whole millimetre before the vernier zero mark;
3 the largest half millimetre before the vernier zero mark;
4 *twice* the vernier division exactly opposite a main scale division.

The reading in Fig. 6.12(b) is as follows:

8 'whole' cm	= 80·00 mm
4 'whole' mm	= 4·00 mm
0 'half' mm	= 0·00 mm
Vernier scale 6 (× 2)	= 0·12 mm
	84·12 mm

The 50 division scale provides a clearer and more easily read instrument. Since 50 divisions on the vernier scale occupy 49 divisions on the main scale, each vernier division occupies:

$$\frac{1}{50} \text{ of } 49 \text{ mm} = 0.98 \text{ mm}$$

But *each* main scale division equals 1·0 mm. Therefore, the difference between one main scale division and one vernier division is:

1·0 mm − 0·98 mm = 0·02 mm

Therefore, although the 50 division scale is more clear and easier to read than the 25 division scale, it is no more accurate. Figure 6.12(a) shows a 50 division scale. Try and work the reading out for yourself before looking at the answer on page 146. Further applications of the micrometer and vernier principles are to be found in *Mechanical Engineering Craft Theory and Related Subjects: Volume 2.*

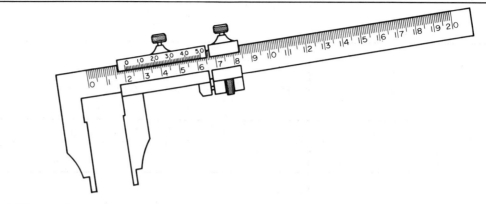

(a) The vernier caliper

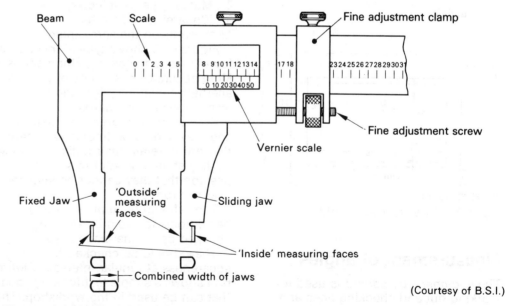

(Courtesy of B.S.I.)

(b) Names of the parts of the vernier caliper

Fig. 6.11 The vernier caliper

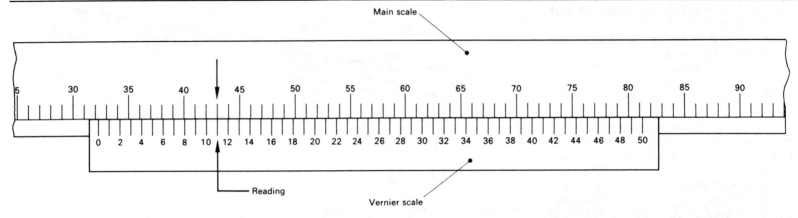

(a) 50 division

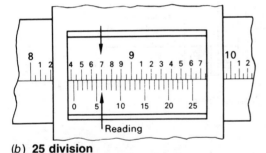

(b) 25 division

Fig. 6.12 The vernier scale

Measurement of angles

The *engineer's try square* is used for marking out and checking lines and surfaces that are at right angles to each other. Two surfaces or lines at right angles (90°) can be described as:
1 Perpendicular to each other;
2 Mutually perpendicular;
3 'Square' to each other.
All these mean the same thing.

Figure 6.13 shows typical try squares found in all engineering fitting shops. More accurate try squares of various alternative designs are found in inspection and standards rooms.

Try squares are precision instruments and they should be treated with care if they are to retain their initial accuracy.

They should be kept in such a position that they cannot be knocked over or dropped.

They should be kept separated from bench tools to avoid burrs being knocked up on the blade edges.

They should be checked for squareness at regular intervals. Figure 6.14 shows a simple test for a try square that can be used in the workshop. The square is placed on a clean piece of plate as shown, and a line is scribed against the edge of the blade. The square is reversed as shown and a second line is scribed, again using the blade as a guide. If the lines are not over the top of each other (coincident) then the square is faulty. This test is quite accurate, as the error is doubled and easily seen. Complicated equipment is required to make a precise check.

Two applications of the try square are shown in Fig. 6.15. In the first example the work is small and can be held up to the square. The stock is placed against the edge AB of the work and slid gently downwards. When the blade comes into contact with the edge BC, any lack of squareness between AB and BC will allow light to be seen between CB and the try square blade.

It is not always convenient to hold a large component and try square up to the light. In the second example in Fig. 6.15, a surface plate is used as a datum (see page 139) for both the work and the try square. The squareness of the component is checked using feeler gauges (page 141) as shown. If the

ENGINEERING MEASUREMENT

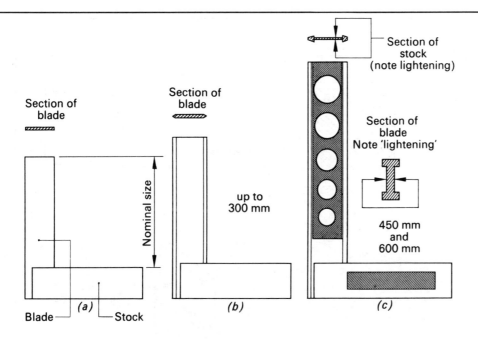

(a) Precision ground. Hardened and tempered blades. Conforming to B.S. No. 939 **Grade B**

(b) **Up to 300 mm**
Hardened stock and glass hard edges of blades. High precision blades having bevelled edges. Conforming to B.S. No. 939 **Grade A.A. (Ref)**

(c) **450 mm and 600 mm**
Hardened stock and glass hard edges of blades. High precision blades having bevelled edges. Conforming to B.S. No. 939 **Grade A.A. (Ref)**

Note special design developed in conjunction with N.P.L. to produce a square of the necessary accuracy to conform to B.S.I. specification, the conventional design being unsuitable for rigidity and overhang test for this specification

(d) Design and sizes as (c). The precision finished hardened stock and blade conforming to B.S. No. 939 **Grade A.**

Fig. 6.13 Engineers' try squares

component is square to the datum surface, the gap between it and the try square blade will be constant.

For marking out and checking angles other than 90°, a protractor is used. Figure 6.17 shows a simple protractor. This has a limited accuracy of ±0·5°, and for more accurate work the vernier protractor has to be used. This is shown in *Mechanical Engineering Craft Theory and Related Subjects: Volume 2.*
Figure 6.17(b) shows how the protractor is used.

The surface plate (datum surface)

In Fig. 6.15, a surface plate is being used as a datum for checking the squareness of a large workpiece. The word 'datum' means a fixed starting point. In engineering this meaning is extended to include lines and surfaces from which measurements are taken. In Fig. 6.15 the plate provides a fixed

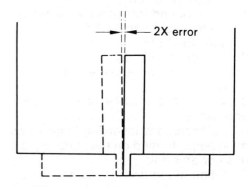

Fig. 6.14 Testing a try square

surface common to both the square and the workpiece and forms a basis for comparing the workpiece with the try square. Other forms of datum are shown in Fig. 6.18 on page 142. It will be seen that the datum chosen provides a common, fixed point, or line or surface from which measurements can be taken. Figure 6.18 (b) shows a datum surface being used as a basis for marking out a metal plate. All these applications will be considered further in Chapter 7.

The most commonly used datum for measurement and marking out is the *cast iron surface plate*, and an example is shown in Fig. 6.17. It is made from a close grained cast iron and is heavily ribbed so that it will not distort or twist even when it is carrying a heavy workpiece. The working surface is ground or scraped flat to a high degree of accuracy. For this reason, surface plates and tables must be used with the greatest care if they are to remain accurate. The following precautions should be observed:

1 all work and instruments placed on the plate must be free from sharp corners and burrs;
2 all work and instruments must be placed gently on the plate to prevent bruising it;
3 workpieces must be free from swarf and filings;
4 no operations involving hammering must be performed on the surface plate. It is *not* an anvil;
5 When not in use the surface plate should be lightly oiled and protected by a felt-lined wooden cover.

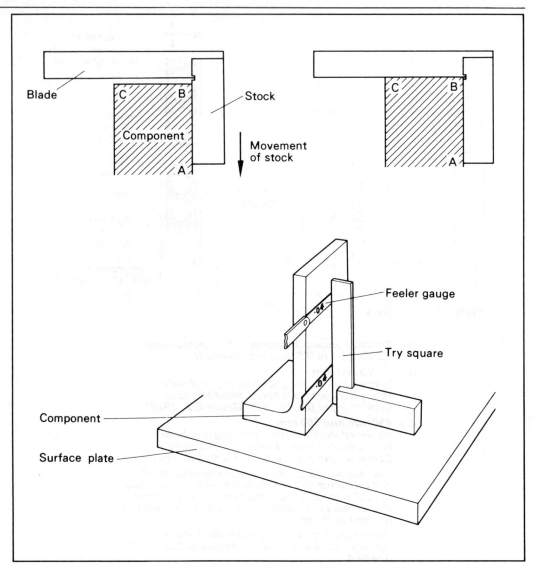

Fig. 6.15 Uses of the try square

Large surface plates are provided with legs or separate stands and are referred to as *surface tables*. For marking out purposes, the working surface is usually planed, but for fine measurement it is also scraped to a high degree of accuracy.

Surface plates are also made from glass and from a hard, dense stone called granite. Although not as common as cast iron, these materials have the advantage of being totally unaffected by tropical environments.

Feeler gauges

Figure 6.19(a) shows a typical set of feeler gauges. The blades are made from shim steel and the number marked on each blade is its thickness in hundredths of a millimetre. One use of feeler gauges was shown in Fig. 6.15 and further applications are shown in Fig. 6.19(b) (page 143).

Radius gauges

These are used for checking convex and concave radii, and are shown in Fig. 6.20. The blades are in sets with the radius increasing by 0·1 mm per blade. See page 144.

Gauging

The tolerancing of dimensions was introduced on page 64. Since it is not possible to measure an exact size, the designer specifies *limits* between which the dimensions will be acceptable. These limits are not chosen at random

Fig. 6.16 The surface plate

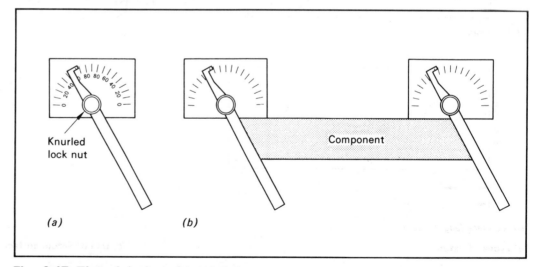

Fig. 6.17 The plain bevel protractor

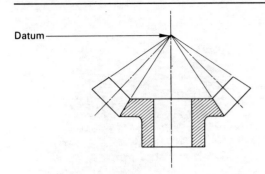

(i) A point datum (bevel gear)

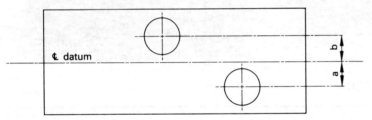

(ii) A line datum

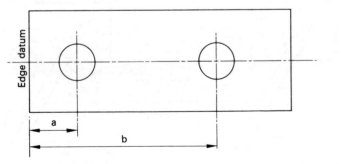

(iii) A surface (edge) datum

(a) Types of datum

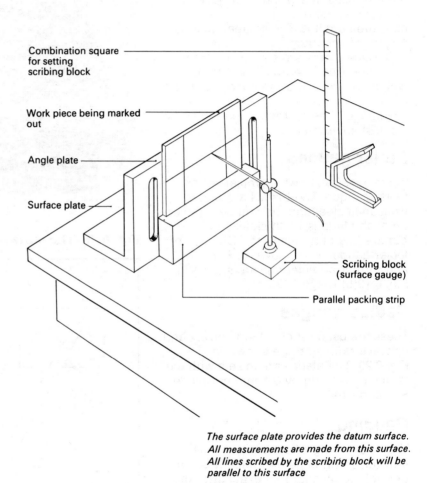

The surface plate provides the datum surface. All measurements are made from this surface. All lines scribed by the scribing block will be parallel to this surface

(b) Use of datum surface

Fig. 6.18 The datum

ENGINEERING MEASUREMENT

but are worked out from B.S. 4500 to suit:
1. the size of the dimension;
2. the accuracy required to make the component work satisfactorily;
3. the process by which the component will be made.

Some examples of dimensions showing limits are given in Fig. 6.21.

When only a small number of components have to be checked, they are usually measured using one of the instruments described earlier in this chapter. However, if a large number of similar components have to be checked then the cost of gauges is justified as they are quicker to use than measuring instruments and they require less skill. Gauges cannot determine the size of a component; they can only check if it lies within the design limits of size.

Caliper gauges

These are also called 'gap' and 'snap' gauges. They are used to check male components such as shafts. Typical caliper gauges are shown in Fig. 6.22 (page 144). Their principle of operation is similar to the plug gauge. That is, the component should pass between the 'go' jaws but should not pass between the 'not go' jaws. Unfortunately the caliper gauge does not check the geometry of the component.

Plug gauges

Plug gauges are used to check hole diameters. Figure 6.23 shows some typical plug gauges (page 145).

As long as the hole lies within the limits set by the designer, it is correct and its actual size does not matter. For example, the double ended plug gauge has a 'go' element and a 'not go' element. When checking a hole, the 'go' element should enter the hole but the 'not go' element should not.

If the 'go' element will not enter the hole, then the hole is undersize, or out of round, or both.

If the 'not go' element enters the hole, then the hole is too big.

The 'go' element is easily identified as it is always the longer.

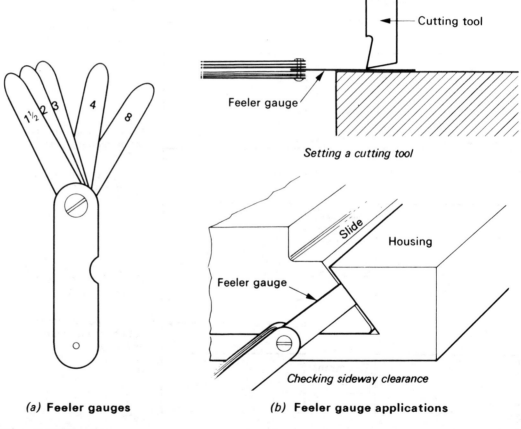

Setting a cutting tool

Checking sideway clearance

(a) **Feeler gauges**   *(b)* **Feeler gauge applications**

Fig. 6.19 Feeler gauges

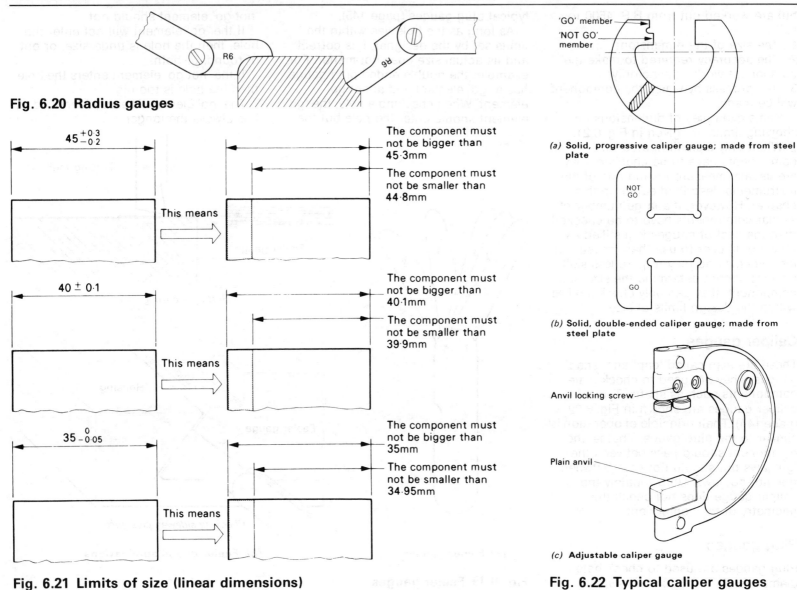

Fig. 6.20 Radius gauges

Fig. 6.21 Limits of size (linear dimensions)

Fig. 6.22 Typical caliper gauges

ENGINEERING MEASUREMENT

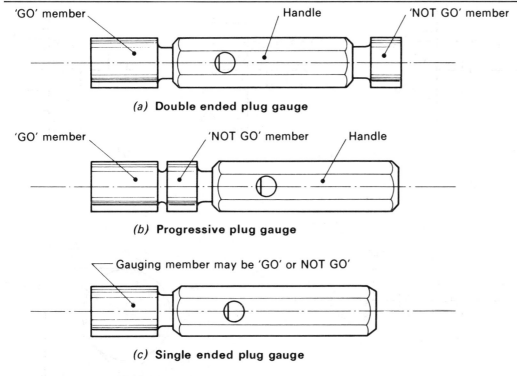

Fig. 6.23 Types of plug gauge

Ring gauges

For circular components, the ring gauge has the advantage that it can be used to check ovality. Often the machinist only uses a single 'go' gauge and his skill enables him to turn the shaft to give the correct 'feel' in the gauge. However, to be absolutely sure that the correct fit is obtained, separate 'go' and 'not go' gauges should be used. Figure 6.24 shows a typical ring gauge.

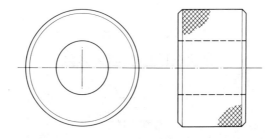

Fig. 6.24 Plain ring gauge

Exercises

1. a) State *four* essential features of an engineers rule.
   b) Show how a solid abutment is used to reduce errors when measuring from the edge of the component.
2. Sketch, in good proportion, a firm joint caliper and show:
   a) how it is set to a rule
   b) how it is used to measure the diameter of a steel rod
3. a) Sketch, in good proportion, a 0·25 mm micrometer caliper and name the parts of it.
   b) Explain how a micrometer caliper should be cared for so that it remains in good condition.
4. a) Describe how the micrometer caliper is adjusted (i) to remove zero error, (ii) to remove looseness in the screw.
   b) Write down the readings of the micrometer scales shown in Fig. 6.25.
5. a) Sketch, in good proportion, a vernier caliper and name the parts of it.
   b) Compare the advantages and limitations of the vernier caliper and the micrometer caliper.
6. a) Write down the vernier caliper reading shown in Fig. 6.26 (a)
   b) Calculate the hole diameter shown in Fig. 6.26 (b)
7. Sketch, in good proportion, an engineer's try square and name the blade and the stock.

MECHANICAL ENGINEERING CRAFT THEORY VOLUME 1

Show *two* ways in which it can be used to check that two edges or surfaces are square with each other.
8. Sketch a protractor (not vernier) suitable for checking surfaces that are at angles other than 90° to each other.
9. Figure 6.27 shows the scriber of a vernier height gauge touching the surface of a round bar held in a vee-block. The reading on the height gauge is 61·28 mm.
  a) What will be the reading on the height gauge when it is set for the scriber to pass through the centre of the bar?
  b) Describe briefly how the centre of a round bar can be established using a height gauge.
  c) Name an item of equipment that would provide a suitable datum surface for the above measurements and state *two* precautions that must be taken to avoid damaging the datum surface. (*WAEC* 1974)
10. Sketch, in good proportion, *three* of the following items of gauging equipment:
    a) double ended plug gauge
    b) caliper or 'snap' gauge
    c) ring gauge
    d) set of feeler gauges
    e) set of radius gauges

Reading on vernier scale in Fig. 6.12 = 32·22 mm

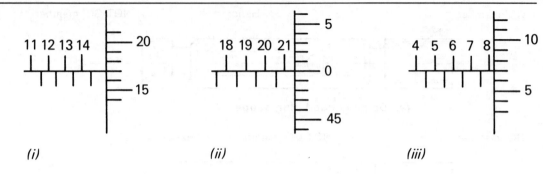

Fig. 6.25

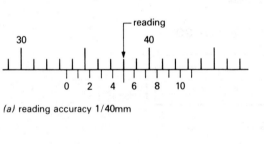

(a) reading accuracy 1/40mm

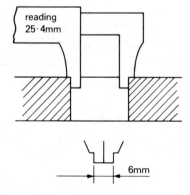

(b)

Fig. 6.26

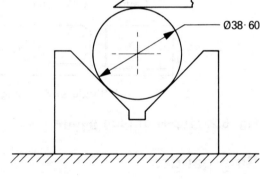

Fig. 6.27

7. Marking out

The need for marking out

The term *marking out* means the scribing of lines on a metal surface to show the profile or outline of the finished component, the profile or outline of any holes that are to be cut in the component, and the position of any hole centres. Except for very simple forming operations, such as 'squaring up' raw material ready for marking out, it is usually advisable to mark out a component before commencing to work on it by hand or machine.

Unlike a drawing made with a pen or pencil, scribed lines cut into the surface of the metal and remain there. The exception to the use of scribed lines is the marking out of tin plate. A scriber would cut through the plating of tin exposing the mild steel underneath. This would leave the mild steel base open to corrosion. For marking out tin plate a hard pencil should be used.

There are three reasons for marking out:
1 To provide guide lines that are worked to, and provide the only control for the size and shape of the finished component.
2 To indicate the outline of the component to the machinist as an aid to setting up and roughing down. The final dimensional control of the component in this instance comes from the use of precision measuring instruments in conjunction with the micrometer dials on the machine.
3 To determine that adequate machining allowance has been left on castings and forgings (see Fig. 7.1).

Preparation for marking out

To make the scribed lines show up clearly, the metal surface is usually coated with a contrasting colour.

Whitewash

This is usually applied to rough forgings

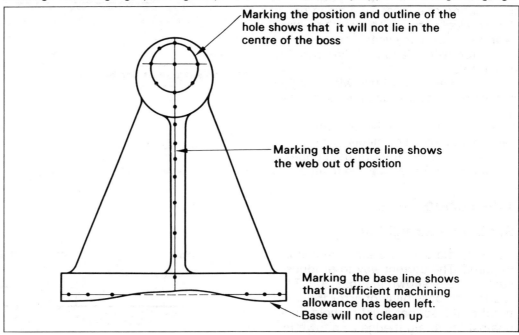

Fig. 7.1 Checking a casting

and castings that have a heavily oxidised surface (black scale).

Cellulose lacquer

This is made in a variety of colours and can be applied to any bright surface. When applied thinly it dries very quickly. It is best applied with a properly designed dispenser bottle to prevent evaporation.

Copper sulphate solution

A solution of copper sulphate in water and a few drops of nitric acid deposits a thin coating of copper on a clean plain carbon steel surface. This method has been used for many years, but compared with a lacquer it has certain disadvantages:
1 If it comes into contact with marking out instruments it stains and corrodes them.
2 It can only be applied to plain carbon and low alloy steels.
3 It is difficult to remove the copper coating once it has been deposited.

The scribed line

Scribing a straight line

For accurate work a clean, fine line is required. The correct way to produce such a line is shown in Fig. 7.2(a). To reduce the possibility of error the point of the scriber must be held up against the straight edge as shown in Fig. 7.2(b).

It is usual to mark the position of the

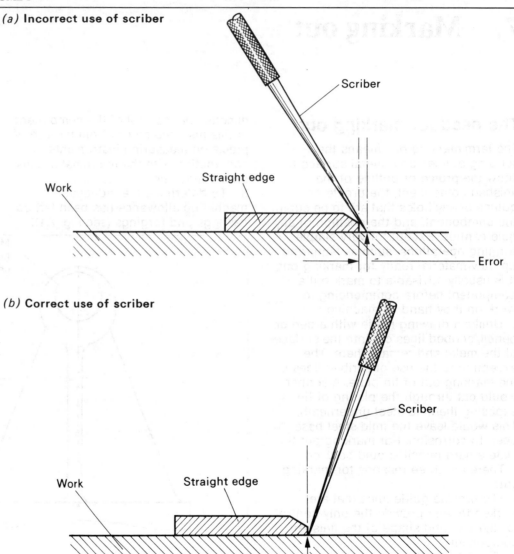

Fig. 7.2 Scribing a line

MARKING OUT

scribed line by making a series of dots along it with a *dot-punch*. This is similar to a centre punch, but lighter and sharpened to a finer point. Figure 7.3(a) shows such a punch and the method of marking a line.

The reasons for this operation are:
1 so that the line may be restored if it becomes obliterated;
2 so that there is a 'witness' to the accuracy of your work after removing surplus metal from a component. A little thought will show that if you file or machine down to a line so as to 'split the line', the line will no longer be visible. Further, because the line is no longer visible you have no proof that you have split it. If it has been dotted, then the half-dots remaining in the edge of the component are a witness to the accuracy of your work. This is shown in Fig. 7.3(b).

Scribing a line parallel to an edge

In addition to scribing straight lines using a scriber and rule, it is also necessary to scribe lines that are parallel to an edge. For this purpose *hermaphrodite* calipers are used. Because of their long name they are often called *jenny* or *odd-leg* calipers in the workshop. Fig. 7.4 shows how they are used.

Scribing a line parallel to a surface

To scribe lines parallel to a surface a *universal surface gauge* or *scribing*

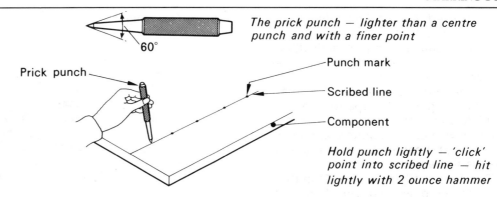

(a) Use of the prick punch

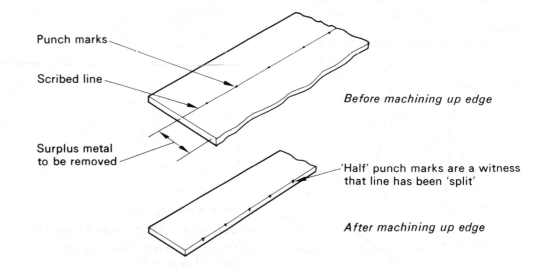

(b) Witness marks

Fig. 7.3 Preserving the scribed line

block is used. A typical example is shown in Fig. 7.5(a).

Surface gauges are provided with a firm but sensitive fine adjustment screw (5) for accurate work.

The hardened steel base (1) is of a suitable weight and shape to give stability and ease of handling. It has a vee groove along the bottom and at one end so that it can be used on round as well as flat work.

Two frictionally-held pins (2) in the base can be pressed down when working from a datum edge as shown in item (e) of the typical applications.

The *scriber* (6) can be clamped in any position on the *mast* (3) which can be adjusted quickly and set at any angle and locked in position by the *knurled screw* (4).

Fine adjustment is made by the

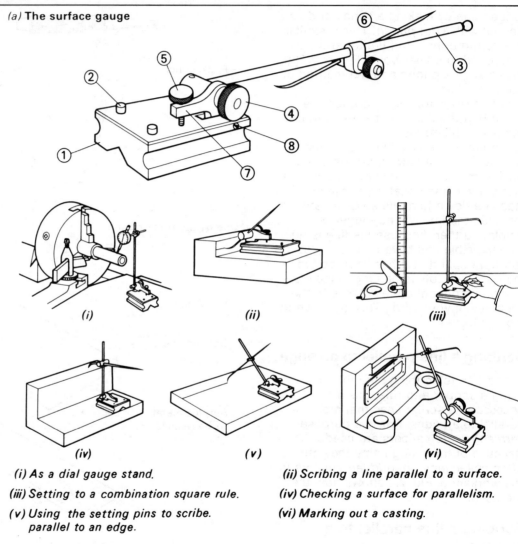

(a) The surface gauge

(i) As a dial gauge stand.
(iii) Setting to a combination square rule.
(v) Using the setting pins to scribe parallel to an edge.

(ii) Scribing a line parallel to a surface.
(iv) Checking a surface for parallelism.
(vi) Marking out a casting.

(b) Typical applications

Fig. 7.5 The universal surface gauge

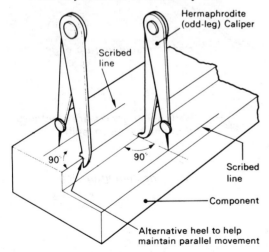

Fig. 7.4 Hermaphrodite calipers

MARKING OUT

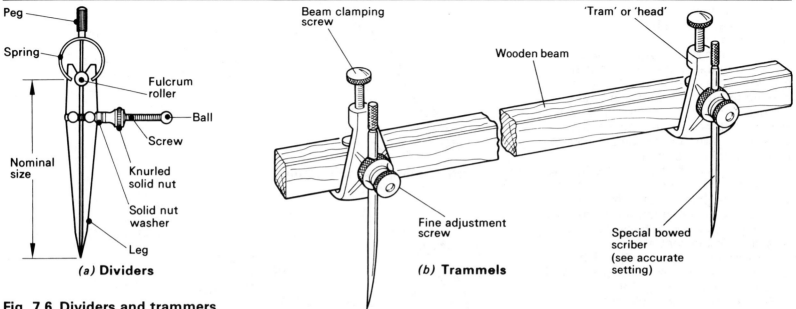

Fig. 7.6 Dividers and trammers

adjusting screw (5) through the *rocker arm* (7). The adjusting screw is positioned so that the gauge can be held and adjusted with one hand only.

Scribing a circular line

For scribing circular lines up to about 150 mm diameter, *dividers* are used as shown in Fig. 7.6(a). Above this diameter *trammels* or beam compasses are used as shown in Fig. 7.6(b)

Sharpening scribing instruments

The scribing points of scribers, dividers, trammels, and surface gauges must be kept needle sharp if fine lines are to be produced.
1 Sharpen regularly so that the minimum amount of metal is removed.
2 Never use a grinding wheel.
3 Always use a fine oilstone, as shown in Fig. 7.7.

Setting scribing instruments

Never rely on the eye alone for accurate setting. Use an engraved metal rule and set the instruments as shown in Fig. 7.8. The scribing point of the instrument is allowed to 'click' into the appropriate engraved mark on the rule.

The combination set

This useful set of attachments mounted on a special, very strong rule is shown in Fig. 7.9 on page 153.

The combination set consists of:
1 a *rule*, (1) hardened and ground and accurately engraved. It is usually 3 mm thick and has a centre slot to locate the various attachments. Because of its thickness, it is more rigid than an ordinary rule and can be used for many purposes.
2 the *square head*, (2) made from drop forged steel. It forms an adjustable try square with the rule and has a 45° bevel for marking out mitre joints. A spirit

level and a small scriber are also built into the head. The spirit level is only of very limited accuracy.

3 The *centre head*, (3) which is used for marking the centre of components (see Fig. 7.10). It enables a line to be scribed through the centre of any circular component which will lie within the arms of the vee. In practice, two lines are drawn at approximately 90° to each other. The centre of the component is at the point where the two lines cross. A third line should be drawn to check the point because two lines will always cross each other, but three lines will only pass through the same point if it really is in the centre.

4 The *bevel protractor*, (4) which is used in the same way as the plain bevel protractor shown in Fig. 7.9.

Figure 7.10 on page 154 shows some typical applications of the combination set.

Use of templates

To mark out a large number of components one at a time wastes time. It is quicker to mark out the required shape on a sheet of metal, or even thin wood; cut the shape out; check it for size, and use it as a guide for the scriber when marking out all the components. The template should be carefully marked with the job number and kept for future batches of work. Figure 7.11 on page 155 shows how a sheet metal component is marked out using a template.

Fig. 7.7 Sharpening a scribing point

Scribing points should be kept sharp by regularly dressing them with a fine oil slipstone as shown. That is by stroking the stone along the point never round it

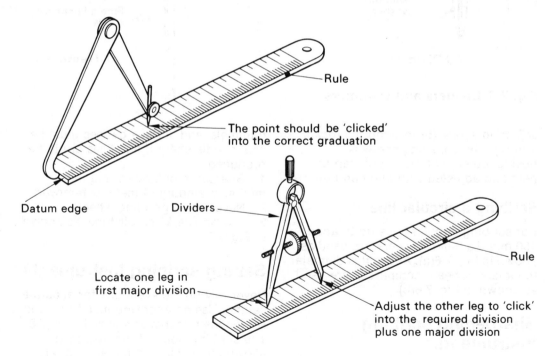

Fig. 7.8 Setting dividers and odd-leg calipers

Datum lines and datum edges

The datum as a fixed point, line or surface from which a measurement can be taken has already been introduced. (Figure 6.20).

Figure 7.12(a) shows the effect of chain dimensioning, in which each hole is dimensioned from the previous hole. If the dimension between each hole is on top limit (has the maximum tolerance) the build up of error between holes 1 and 5 is 4 × 0·1 mm, which is 0·4 mm. This is far greater than the designer intended.

Figure 7.12(b) shows the position of each hole dimensioned individually from the end of the component. The end of the component has become the *datum* and no hole can be more than ±0·1 mm out of position if it is within the limits set by the designer. Compare this with the error for chain dimensioning which can be as great as ±0·4 mm.

The centre line datum

Figure 7.13 shows a simple link that is to be made out of 6 mm thick mild steel plate. Such a simple component can be quite satisfactorily marked out using a centre line datum as shown in Fig. 7.14 (page 156). The procedure for marking out the link is as follows.

1 Scribe the centre line using a rule as a straight edge;
2 Step off the 75 mm hole centres using dividers;
3 Lightly dot punch the hole centres;
4 Scribe in the 18 mm diameter hole using dividers;
5 Scribe in the 18 mm radius with dividers, using the same centre as the previous hole;
6 Scribe in the 25 mm diameter hole using dividers;
7 Scribe in the 25 mm radius with dividers, using the same centre as the previous hole;
8 Join the 18 mm and 25 mm radii with

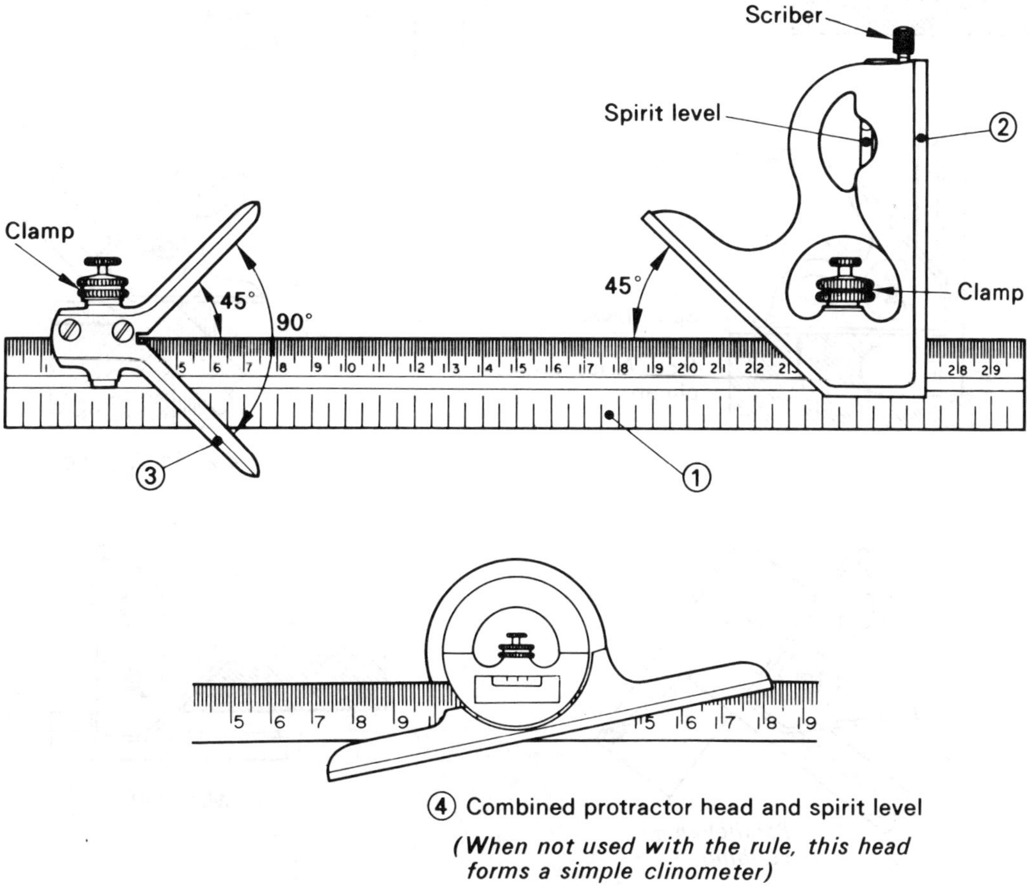
Scriber
Spirit level
②
Clamp
45°
90°
45°
Clamp
③
①
④ Combined protractor head and spirit level
(When not used with the rule, this head forms a simple clinometer)

Fig. 7.9 The combination set

tangential lines using a steel rule as a straight edge to guide the scriber.

The edge datum (service edge)

An alternative method of marking out the component shown in Fig. 7.13 is to use the edge of the plate as a datum for drawing the centre line and establishing the hole centres. The method of marking out using a datum edge, which is also sometimes called a service edge, is shown in Fig. 7.15 on page 157.

1 Scribe the centre line (ϕ) of the holes parallel to the datum edge using 'odd-leg' calipers;
2 Scribe the centre line of the first hole at right angles to the datum edge using a try square;
3 Mark off the position of the second hole centre using a steel rule;
4 Scribe the centre line of the second hole using a try square;
5 Dot punch the hole centres lightly;
6 Complete the marking out following the instructions given in numbers 4 to 8 on page 153 and in Fig. 7.14.

The datum surface

Use of a datum line is usually reserved for simple components, such as the example chosen, or for components made from large plates on which the production of a datum edge (or edges) is a major operation. For the component chosen, only one datum edge is required. However, most components required two datum edges, which must

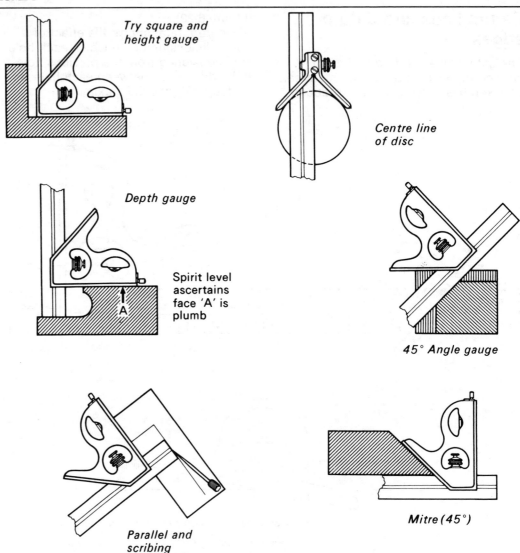

Fig. 7.10 Uses of the combination set

(Courtesy of Moore and Wright Ltd)

MARKING OUT

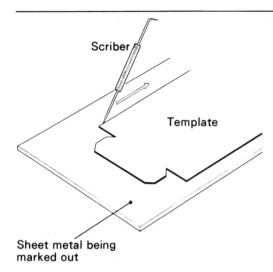

Fig. 7.11 Marking out from a template

be machined or filed accurately at right-angles to each other, as shown in Fig. 7.16 on page 158.

The hole is positioned from the datum edges by the dimensions x and y, which are at right-angles to each other. These dimensions are called the *co-ordinates* of the hole centre.

The most accurate method of marking out, and the easiest for large components, is to use a datum surface as shown in Fig. 7.17. This shows a surface table together with the equipment that would be required to mark out the link previously described. It will be seen that the surface plate provides the datum surface from which all the measurements are made. All lines scribed from this surface will be *parallel to the datum surface*.

The procedure for establishing the hole centres for the link using a datum surface are as follows.

1 File or machine two edges at right-angles (perpendicular) to each other, and at right-angles to the face being marked, as shown in Fig. 7.18(a);
2 The blank is placed on its end surface edge on the surface plate. In this example parallel packing is used to raise the blank to a convenient height. The scribing block is set to the combination square and rule.

This setting is transferred to the blank, and the line scribed will be parallel to the datum surface and therefore parallel to the datum edge of the blank as shown in Fig. 7.18(b). The second centre line is scribed at the same setting and will be parallel to the

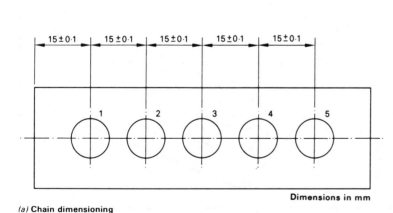

(a) Chain dimensioning

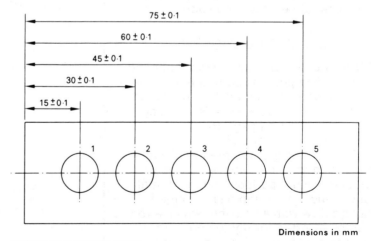

(b) Dimensioning from a datum

Fig. 7.12 Cumulative error

155

first centre line.

3 The blank is turned through 90° so that it rests on the other datum edge. This enables the remaining centre line to be scribed in at right-angles to the first two. The marking out of the link is completed as in numbers 4 to 8 on page 153 and in Fig. 7.14.

So far, only the marking out of flat-plate components has been considered. The greatest use of the marking-out table is when marking out three-dimensional solids, such as castings. An example is shown in Fig. 7.19 on page 160.

It will be seen that to support the casting in a horizontal position, *table jacks* are required. These are provided with swivel heads to compensate for sloping surfaces. *Wedges* are also used for this purpose when the height of the jack cannot be accommodated.

The use of vee-blocks

These are primarily intended for holding circular components so that the axis of the component is parallel to the datum surface that the vee-block is standing on. Figure 7.20 on page 160 shows a typical vee-block and clamp.

The 90° vee grooves are parallel and central to the sides, and square to the ends to ensure perfect alignment in all directions. The clamp has a knurled head screw with a hole into which a rod can be inserted for tightening it up. Sufficient clamping force is exerted to prevent rotation or slipping of the workpiece.

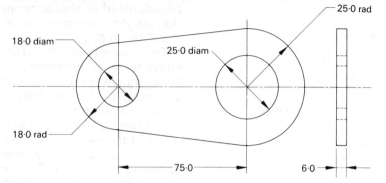

Fig. 7.13 Link

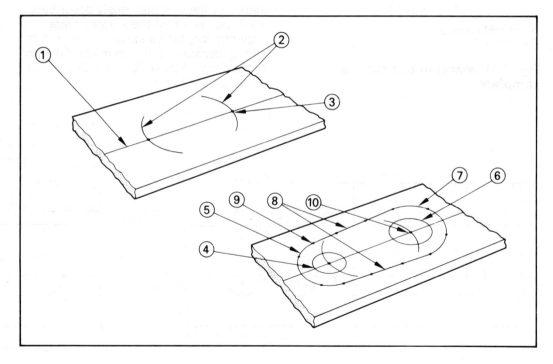

Fig. 7.14 Marking out from a centre line datum

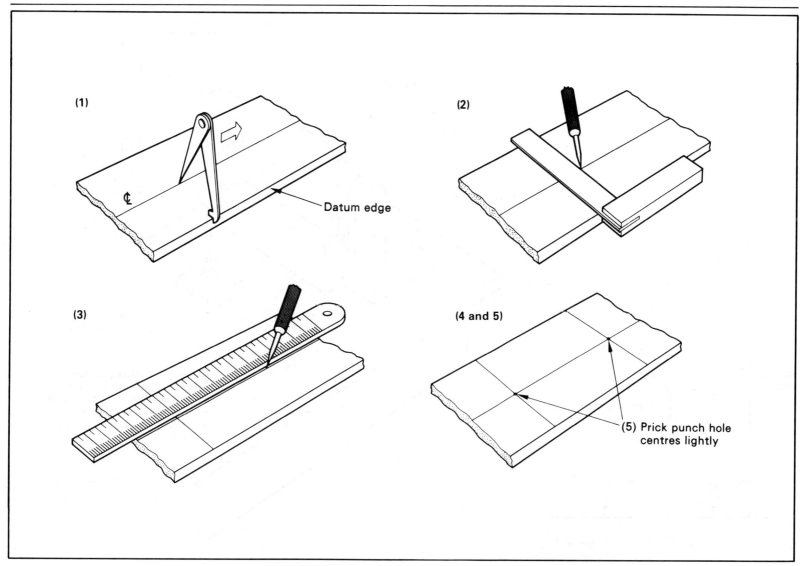

Fig. 7.15 Marking out from a datum edge

MECHANICAL ENGINEERING CRAFT THEORY VOLUME 1

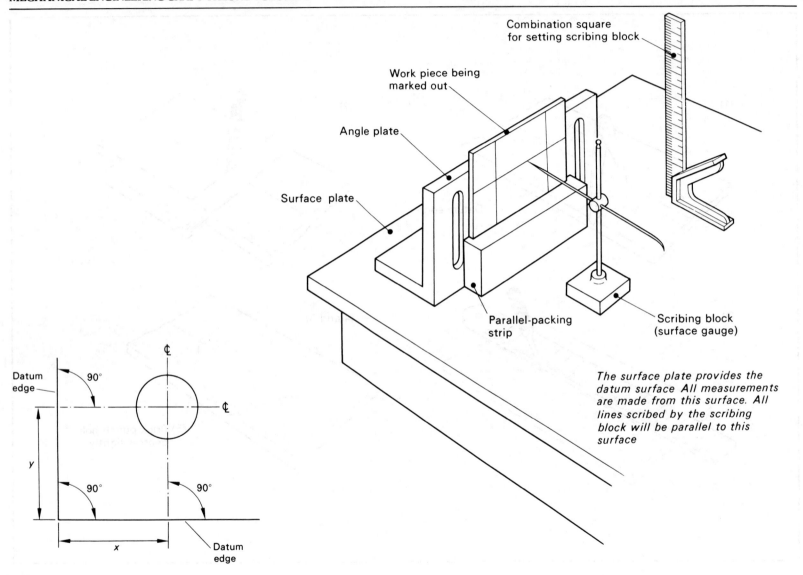

Fig. 7.16 Use of co-ordinates

Fig. 7.17 Marking out from a datum surface

MARKING OUT

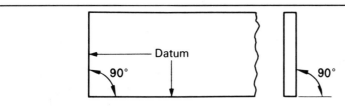

(a) Prepare datum surfaces

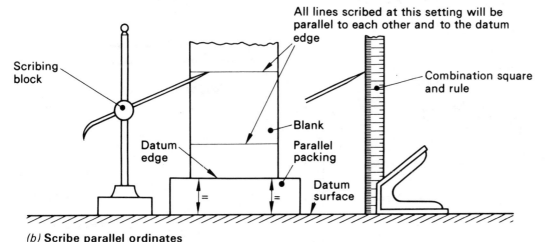

(b) Scribe parallel ordinates

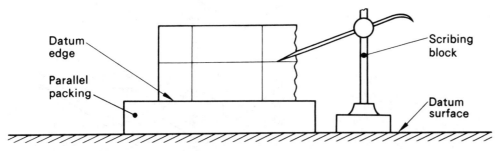

(c) Scribe co-ordinates perpendicular to (b)

Fig. 7.18 Marking out procedure when using a datum surface

Note: The *stirrup clamp* is only strong enough to hold the component while marking out. It would be highly dangerous to rely on it while machining.

Figure 7.21 shows a typical application of the vee-block while marking out. The vee-block is also used as a work-holding device during machining, and examples are given in the appropriate chapters.

Where long bars are to be supported, two vee-blocks are used. To ensure that the workpiece axis is parallel to the datum surface, these vee-blocks must be a *matched pair*. They are sold as a pair so always make sure they are kept as a pair.

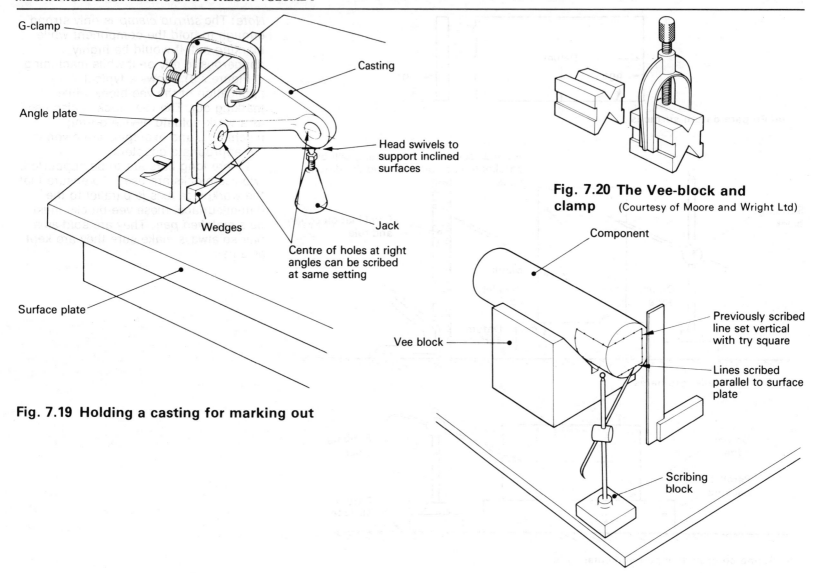

Fig. 7.19 Holding a casting for marking out

Fig. 7.20 The Vee-block and clamp (Courtesy of Moore and Wright Ltd)

Fig. 7.21 Use of the Vee-block

MARKING OUT

Exercises

1. Describe *three* ways of coating the surface of a component ready for marking out, and describe any precautions that should be taken.
2. Describe with the aid of sketches how a scribed line may be preserved and how a 'witness' can be left when machining a 'split the line'.
3. a) With the aid of sketches, show how lines can be scribed parallel to an edge using hermaphrodite (odd-leg) calipers.
   b) Describe, with the aid of sketches, how the points of scribing instruments should be sharpened.
4. Describe with the aid of a sketch how the points of a pair of dividers are set to an engineer's rule.
5. With the aid of a sketch, show how the centre of a circular component can be found using the centre finder and rule of a combination set.
6. Sketch, in good proportion, the set up for marking out a thin steel plate using the following equipment: scribing block; angle plate; surface plate; rule and combination square.
7. State *three* reasons for marking out a component prior to machining it.
8. Using the headings shown below, prepare an operation layout for preparing the blank and marking out the profile shown in Fig. 7.22 from a piece of bright mild steel plate 115 mm long, 62 mm wide and 12 mm thick. (*WAEC* 1974)

| No | Operation | Equipment used |

9. Describe, with the aid of sketches, the procedure for marking out the key-way shown in Fig. 7.23. Pay particular attention to the method of holding the shaft while marking it out.
Keyway
6 mm wide
3 mm deep
35 mm long
10. Sketch, in good proportion, the set up for marking out this φ 25 hole in the casting shown in Fig. 7.24. The base of the casting has been machined and can be used as a datum.
11. Using the headings shown in question 8, prepare an operation layout for marking out the centre lines of the φ 25 mm hole (Fig. 7.24) and scribing the profile of the hole using dividers. Marking out should be confined to surface AA of the casting, which has been previously white-washed.

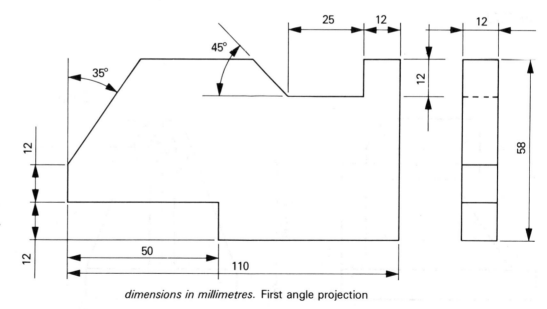

dimensions in millimetres. First angle projection

Fig. 7.22

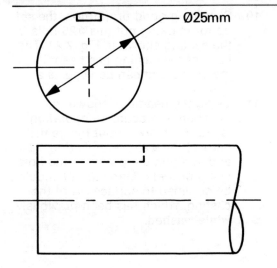

Fig. 7.23

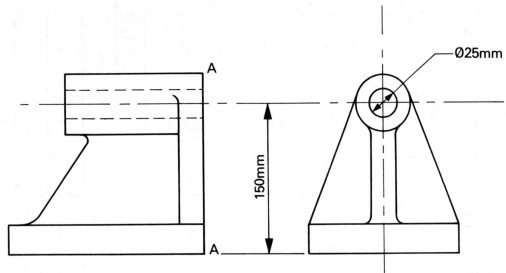

Fig. 7.24

8. Forging

Principles of hot forging

The process of *forging* is the hammering of metal to shape after it has been heated to the temperature at which it becomes plastic. That is, above the temperature of recrystallisation (page 96). Therefore forging is a hot working process.

The component shown in Fig. 8.1 may be machined from bar-stock such as bright drawn mild steel, or it may be forged to shape. It will be seen from Fig. 8.1(b) that when it is machined from bright drawn bar, the grain lies parallel to the axis of the component. However, when the component is forged to shape, as shown in Fig. 8.1(c), the grain flow is changed so that it is at right angles to the axis of the component where the flange has been formed. This makes the forged component much stronger than when it is machined from the bar, if the same material is used in both cases.

If the component shown in Fig. 8.1 is to be used for a gear blank, this difference in grain direction is very important. Figure 8.2(a) shows that the grain of the machined blank is parallel to the teeth of the gear, causing planes of weakness. The teeth break off relatively easily. Figure 8.2(b) shows that the grain of the forged blank is at right

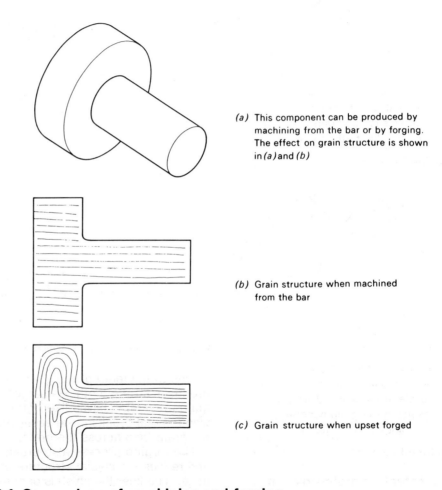

(a) This component can be produced by machining from the bar or by forging. The effect on grain structure is shown in (a) and (b)

(b) Grain structure when machined from the bar

(c) Grain structure when upset forged

Fig. 8.1 Comparison of machining and forging

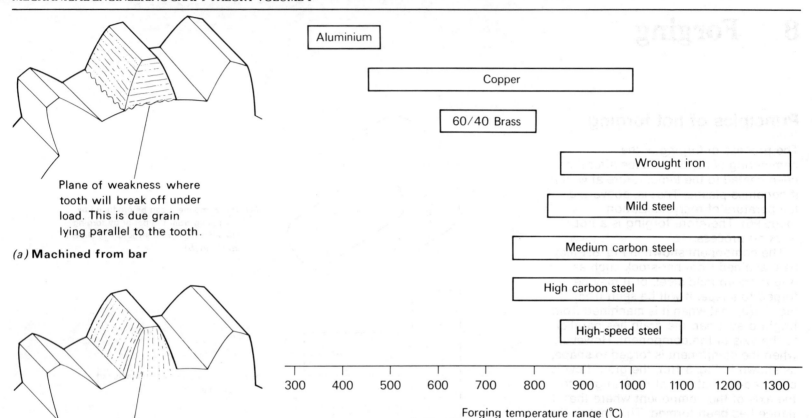

Plane of weakness where tooth will break off under load. This is due grain lying parallel to the tooth.
(a) Machined from bar
The tooth is very much stronger when the grain flows radially from the centre of the blank. This results in the grain lying at right angles to the tooth.
(b) Machined from bar

Fig. 8.2 Effect of grain flow on component strength

Aluminium
Copper
60/40 Brass
Wrought iron
Mild steel
Medium carbon steel
High carbon steel
High-speed steel
300
400
500
600
700
800
900
1000
1100
1200
1300
Forging temperature range (℃)

Fig. 8.3 Forging temperatures

angles to the teeth of the gear. This produces strong teeth. Remember that grain in metal behaves like grain in wood, metal breaks more easily along the grain than across the grain.

The forging process also breaks up and refines the crystal structure of the metal. The finer the crystals become, the tougher and stronger the metal becomes. The temperature at which the metal is forged is important. Figure 8.3 gives the upper and lower temperatures for forging various metals. If the upper temperature is exceeded, burning and grain growth will occur. Below the lower temperature work hardening will occur and the component may crack and become weakened.

It is important to relate the cooling time of the component to the time taken to complete the forging process. Figure 8.4 shows some examples of what can happen.

In Fig. 8.4(a) the forging process and the cooling cycle take the same time. This is ideal as no grain growth occurs after forging has finished, neither is there any work hardening and cracking.

In Fig. 8.4(b) the forging time is very much shorter than the cooling time. Grain growth occurs after forging has finished and this reduces the strength of the component. To prevent this, either the component is not heated to the maximum forging temperature, or the forged component is given a grain refinement heat-treatment process after it has cooled down.

In Fig. 8.4(c) the forging time is longer than the cooling time and reheating is necessary. As in 8.4(b), the maximum forging temperature of the reheat must be carefully judged, or grain refinement after cooling must be carried out.

The skill of the blacksmith lies in matching the forging temperature to the process. However, in production forging, or where large components are being forged, grain refinement is carried out after cooling. Although this is expensive, it is cheaper than scrapping a large and costly component, or a large quantity of mass-produced components.

The advantages of the forging process may be summarised as follows.
1 Forging uses less raw material; less time is needed and less swarf is produced when machining from a forging than when machining from the solid.
2 The forged component is stronger than the same type of component made from a casting, or machined from the solid.

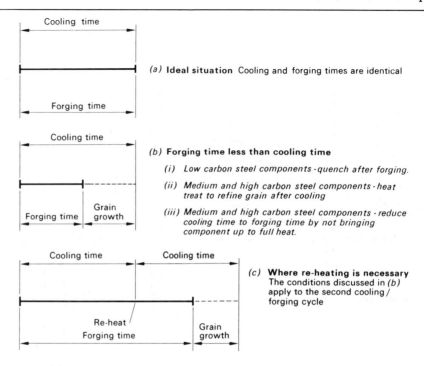

Fig. 8.4 The forging cycle

The hearth

'Hot bending' is usually the only forging operation carried out in the average workshop. The hearths are usually gas or oil-fired and have the advantage of being clean in use: they do not throw off abrasive dust that could settle on the slideways of nearby machines, causing excessive wear.

However, if *all* the forging operations are needed, the traditional open-fire hearth is essential. Figure 8.5 shows a typical hearth which burns coke breeze or anthracite peas. The blowing equipment is also shown (page 166).

This type of hearth can be fired to produce a wide range of temperatures, from a dull red heat for bending to white

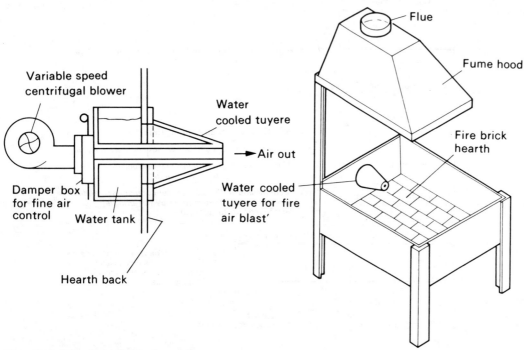

Fig. 8.5 Blacksmith's hearth

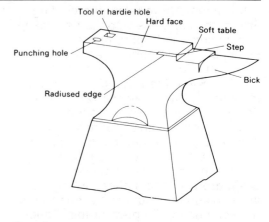

Fig. 8.6 The anvil

heat for forge welding. The area of the fire can also be controlled. Unfortunately, this type of hearth produces a lot of abrasive dust. Therefore, it is best kept in a separate shop, away from machine tools.

The anvil

The anvil is used to support the work while it is hammered. Figure 8.6 shows a typical *single bick London pattern anvil*.

The anvil itself is made from a number of forgings that are forge-welded together. The workface is usually made of a medium carbon steel and is hardened.

The anvil is supported on an angle iron or malleable cast iron stand to bring it up to a convenient working height. The *radiused* edges are used for simple bending operations, and the *soft table* is used for cutting metal off; the cutting edge of the chisel or set is not damaged as it breaks through the metal being cut. The *bick* is used for forming curved components, and the *hardie hole* is for holding various tools such as fullers, swages, hardies, etc.

Work holding

Because of the high temperatures at which metals are forged, it is not possible to hold them in the hand. Tongs are used to hold the work and their mouths vary in shape to suit the work being held. A range of tongs is shown in Fig. 8.7.

Hammers

These are used to form the workpiece, either by striking the metal directly or by striking forming tools (see below). Two of the various hammers used by the blacksmith are shown in Fig. 8.8.

The smaller hand hammer is used by

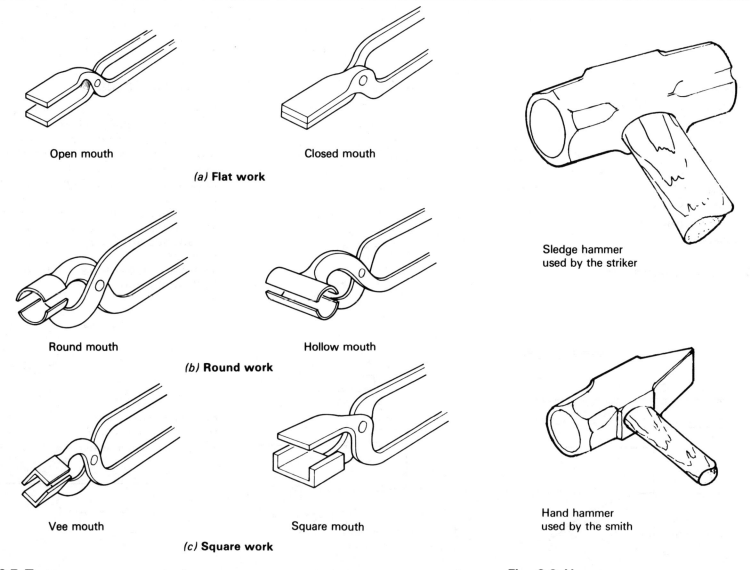

Fig. 8.7 Tongs

Fig. 8.8 Hammers

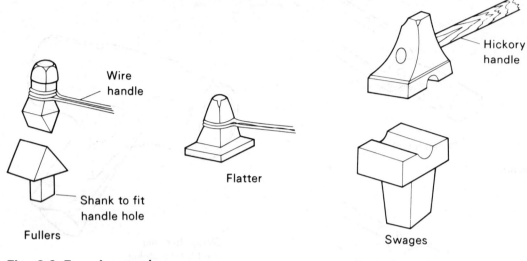

Fig. 8.9 Forming tools

Forming tools

Figure 8.9 shows a variety of forming tools used by the blacksmith.

1 *Fullers* are used to make vee grooves in the edge of the metal bar being forged. This helps to increase the length of the bar and thin it down at the same time.

2 *Flatters* or *flat-hammers* are used to smooth out the bar after fullering.

3 *Swages* are used to form round sections.

The use of these tools will be described in the following section.

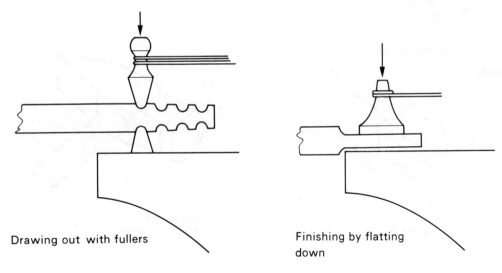

Fig. 8.10 Drawing down

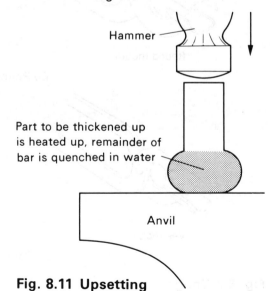

Fig. 8.11 Upsetting

FORGING

For all these operations the metal must be at yellow heat

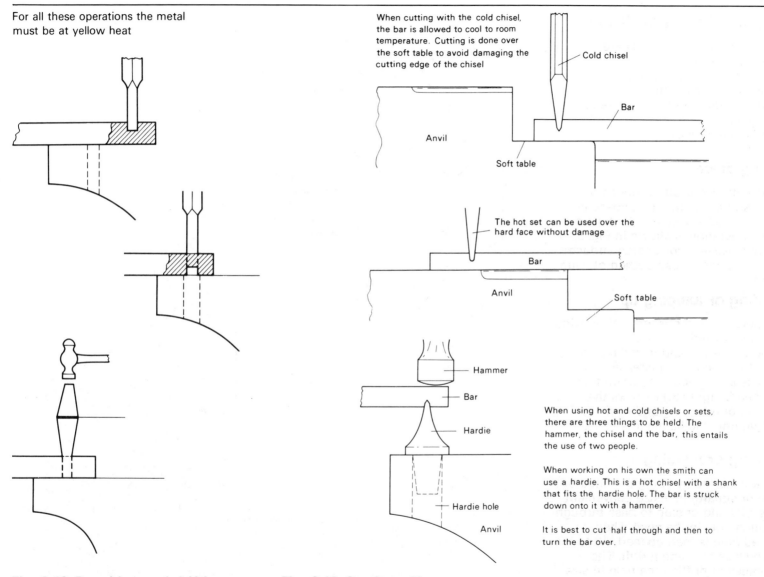

Fig. 8.12 Punching and drifting

Fig. 8.13 Cutting off

When cutting with the cold chisel, the bar is allowed to cool to room temperature. Cutting is done over the soft table to avoid damaging the cutting edge of the chisel

The hot set can be used over the hard face without damage

When using hot and cold chisels or sets, there are three things to be held. The hammer, the chisel and the bar, this entails the use of two people.

When working on his own the smith can use a hardie. This is a hot chisel with a shank that fits the hardie hole. The bar is struck down onto it with a hammer.

It is best to cut half through and then to turn the bar over.

Basic forging operations

The basic forging operations are:
1. drawing down;
2. upsetting or jumping up;
3. punching or piercing;
4. cutting with hot or cold chisels;
5. swaging;
6. bending and twisting;
7. welding.

Drawing down

This operation is used to reduce the thickness of a bar and to increase its length. The tools used are the *fullers*, and this operation is shown in Fig. 8.10. The fullers leave a corrugated surface so the component is smoothed off with a *flatter*.

Upsetting or jumping up

This operation is the reverse of drawing down and is used to increase the thickness of a bar and to reduce its length. Generally, the increase in thickness is only local, as when forming a bolt head. Figure 8.11 shows the operation of upsetting and it will be seen that only the hammer is used.

Punching or piercing

Holes are started by being punched out (round or square) in a size convenient for the piercing or slug to pass through the punch hole in the anvil. The punched hole is then opened out to the required size by using a drift. The advantages of drifting the hole to size are:

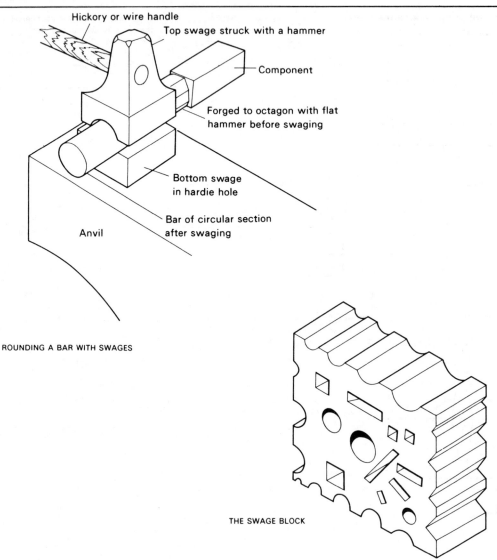

Fig. 8.14 Swaging

1 The surface finish in the hole is improved;
2 The metal round the hole is swelled out to form an 'eye' and so any weakening of the component is avoided.

Figure 8.12 shows the operations of punching and drifting to produce a hole.
1 Punch a pilot hole partway through.
2 Turn the bar over and punch the slug out through the punch hole in the anvil.
3 Gradually open up the hole by drifting from both sides with increasing size of drift. A drift is a tapered punch which increases the size of the hole by spreading the metal round it to form an 'eye'. This maintains the volume of metal round the hole and, therefore, the strength of the component.

Cutting with hot or cold chisels

Metal can be cut hot or cold, depending upon the equipment used. The *cold chisel* will be considered on pages 179 and 196. The *hot chisel* is more slender so that it can 'knife' its way through the hot, plastic metal. When cutting cold, the work is supported on the soft table of the anvil to avoid damaging the cutting edge of the chisel as it breaks through.

Sets

These are heavy duty chisels fitted with wire or hickory handles and struck with the sledge hammer.

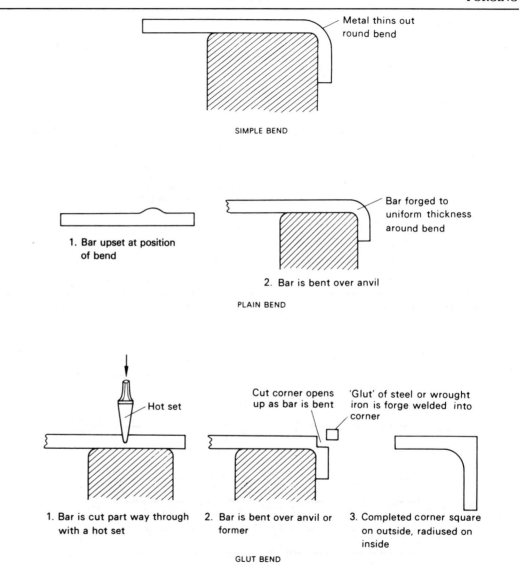

Fig. 8.15 Bending

(a) Straight scarf joint

Stages in making a scarf joint using Laffite welding plate

1. 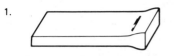 Upset each bar end

2. 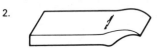 Scarf is formed on each bar end.

3. Bars are heated to a dull red heat. A piece of Laffite welding plate is placed in the joint. The joint is lightly hammered until the bars are stuck together.

4.

Joined bars are reheated to a light welding heat.

5.

Bars are forged out flat at welding heat to complete joint.

Stages in making a scarf joint using silver sand as a flux

1. 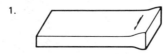 Upset each bar end.

2.  Scarf is formed on each bar end.

3. Bars are quickly withdrawn from the hearth-tapped on anvil to remove dirt, sprinkled with silver sand where weld is required.

4.

The bars are quickly positioned and hammered together to form the weld.
(a) First blows-top, middle to drive out scale
(b) Second blows-top, thick end that weld is complete with lower thin end before it is chilled by anvil.
(c) Third blows-top, thin end.

5. Take another heat and forge until joint is no longer visible.

(b) Cleft joint

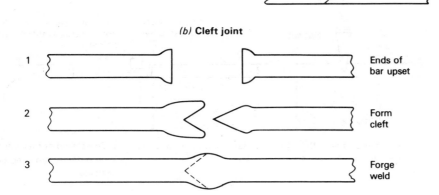

1 — Ends of bar upset
2 — Form cleft
3 — Forge weld

Fig. 8.16 Forge welding

Hardies

The use of chisels and sets requires an extra pair of hands. If the blacksmith is working on his own he can insert a chisel with a special shank into the hardie hole in the anvil and strike the work down onto it. These chisels are called *hardies*.

Operations involving the use of chisels, sets, and hardies are shown in Fig. 8.13.

In all the examples shown it is best to cut half through and then to turn the bar over.

Swaging

This is the operation of rounding a component. The component is broken down into an octagon with the flatter, and then rounded off between a pair of swages or between a single swage and the swage block, as shown in Fig. 8.14.

Bending and twisting

This operation is shown in Fig. 8.15. The point to note when bending is that there is a tendency for the metal to thin out round the bend causing weakness. This can be overcome by either upsetting the bar prior to bending, or forge welding an additional piece of metal, or glut, into the bend. The latter method forms a very strong corner.

Welding

This is difficult and requires great skill. When done correctly, the resulting joint is stronger than either arc or oxy-acetylene welding. Forge welding is restricted to wrought iron and mild steel. A flux is necessary, and this may be a proprietary brand such as *Laffite*, or a natural material such as silver sand. The former is the easier to use. There are various types of weld, and two examples are given in Fig. 8.16.

The most suitable materials for forging are wrought iron and mild steel. Wrought iron is the best metal to use for forge welding operations. Medium and high carbon steels can also be forged but the temperatures involved are critical, and much care and skill are required. Some non-ferrous metals can be forged but the skills required are outside the scope of this chapter. Generally non-ferrous metals are machine forged on a quantity production basis using special and expensive dies.

Exercises

1. State *two* major advantages in forging a component to shape rather than machining it from the solid.
2. State the effect of:
   (i) overheating a blank during forging
   (ii) continuing to forge after the blank has cooled below forging heat
3. Sketch a typical anvil, name its more important features and describe what the following are used for.
   a) hardie hole
   b) bick
   c) soft table
4. With the aid of sketches describe the following forging processes:
   a) drawing down
   b) upsetting
5. Sketch, and describe the use of, *two* of the following forging tools:
   a) fullers
   b) flatters
   c) swages
6. With the aid of sketches, describe *two* methods of hot cutting on the anvil using sets and hardies.
7. Describe, with the aid of sketches, how an eye can be formed in the end of a flat bar using a punch and drifts.
8. Describe, with the aid of sketches, the process of producing a scarf weld in wrought iron by forging.
9. Explain how an angle bracket can be forged from a steel bar 40 mm × 10 mm × 500 mm long, taking care to avoid thinning the metal as it is bent to a right angle.
10. Describe, with the aid of sketches, the method of forming the end of a 6 mm diameter rod into an 'eye' using the bick of the anvil. The inside diameter of the 'eye' is to be approximately 40 mm. Explain the importance of partial quenching to avoid heat spread during this operation.

9. Metal cutting

We are not completely certain what happens when metal is cut despite all the research that has been, and is being, carried out. However, certain fundamental principles have emerged which, if adhered to, will ensure reasonable success.

Clearance angle

One of the first controlled cutting operations we perform must be the sharpening of a pencil with a penknife. It is unlikely that any formal instruction is received before our first attempt. By trial and error we soon find out that the knife blade must be brought to the wood at a definite angle if success is to be achieved, as shown in Fig. 9.1.

Figure 9.1 shows the need for the angle γ (gamma) which is called the *clearance angle*. The clearance angle allows the tool to bite into the workpiece and reduces friction, so the tool lasts longer.

Tool angle

If, instead of a wooden pencil, a piece of soft metal such as brass is cut, the cutting edge of the blade soon becomes blunt. If this edge is examined under a magnifying glass it will be seen that the

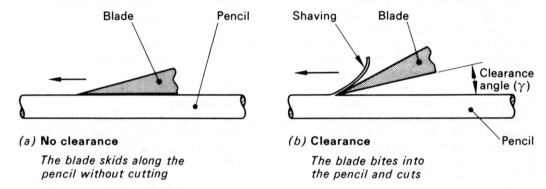

(a) **No clearance**
The blade skids along the pencil without cutting

(b) **Clearance**
The blade bites into the pencil and cuts

Fig. 9.1 The clearance angle

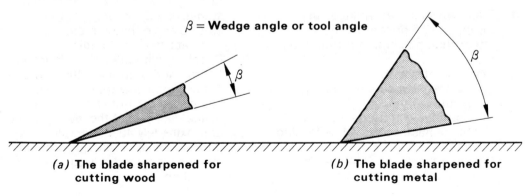

β = Wedge angle or tool angle

(a) **The blade sharpened for cutting wood**

(b) **The blade sharpened for cutting metal**

Fig. 9.2 Tool angle

METAL CUTTING

cutting edge has crumbled away. For the blade to cut brass successfully, the cutting edge must be ground to a less acute angle to give greater strength, as in Fig. 9.2.

β (beta) is the angle to which the blade is ground and it is called the *tool angle* or *wedge angle*.

The greater the tool angle, the stronger is the tool. Unfortunately, as angle β is made larger, the effort required to force the tool through the material becomes larger as well.

Rake angle

Angle α (alpha) in Fig. 9.3 is called the *rake angle*. This is a very important angle as it controls the geometry of the chip formation of any given material. It therefore controls the mechanics of the cutting action of the tool.

It is shown with the angles previously considered in Fig. 9.3.

Summary

Clearance angle (δ) This angle is kept to the minimum required for the tool to cut (5° to 7°). If the angle is too small the tool will rub and wear out quickly, or even refuse to cut. If the angle is too large, the tool is weakened and tends to 'dig in' and 'chatter', producing a poor finish.

Rake angle (α) Increasing this angle makes cutting easier when ductile and low-strength materials are being cut, but the strength of the cutting edge is reduced.

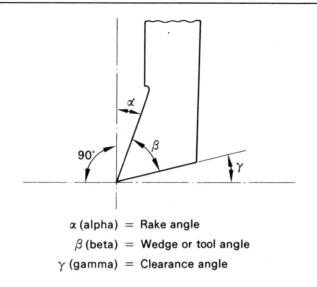

α (alpha) = Rake angle
β (beta) = Wedge or tool angle
γ (gamma) = Clearance angle

Fig. 9.3 Cutting tool angles

Some typical rake angles for high speed steel tools	
Material being cut	Rake
Cast iron	0°
Free-cutting brass	0°
Ductile brass	14°
Tin bronze	8°
Aluminium alloy	30°
Mild steel	25°
Medium carbon steel	20°
High carbon steel	12°
'Tufnol' plastic	0°

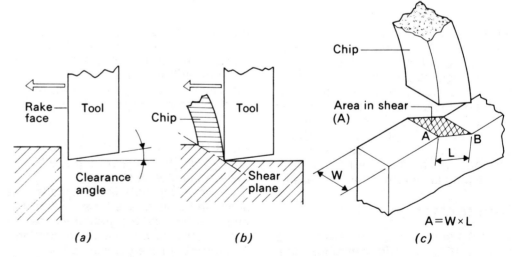

Fig. 9.4 The shear plane

175

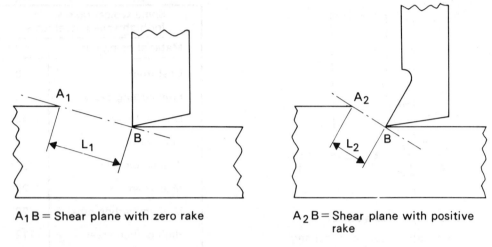

A_1B = Shear plane with zero rake

A_2B = Shear plane with positive rake

Comparing L_1 with L_2, it is apparent that the shear plane is shortened by increasing the rake angle from zero to a positive value

Fig. 9.5 The effect of rake on the shear plane

Tool angle (β)   Increasing this angle makes the tool stronger, but increases the required cutting force. Increasing the tool angle also backs up the cutting edge with a greater mass of metal, which conducts away the heat of cutting more quickly and prolongs tool life.

The clearance angle is kept constant when tools are designed but the rake angle and tool angle are adjusted to make a long lasting tool that cuts easily.

Chip formation

Figure 9.4 shows what happens when a simple cutting tool with clearance but a zero rake angle is used to cut a ductile material such as mild steel. The material being cut builds up ahead of the cutting tool until the cutting forces cause it to shear away from the parent metal along the shear plane (AB). The length of the shear plane multiplied by the width of the cut gives the area in shear for the metal being cut. This is shown in Fig. 9.4(c) where the chip has been 'lifted away' from the work piece to expose the area in shear.

For any given material, the smaller this area can be made, the lower will be the cutting force, and the greater will be the cutting efficiency. Since any reduction in the width of the cut will cause a reduction in the rate of metal removal, the most effective way of reducing the shear area is to reduce its length AB.

It has been shown by experiment that if the rake face of the tool is inclined away from the perpendicular, the shear plane tends to become normal to the rake face. That is, giving a tool a rake angle decreases the length of the shear path. Figure 9.5 shows how the shear path (and therefore the shear area) decreases as the rake angle increases for a ductile material.

Further, an inclined rake face enables the chip to peel away from the parent metal without having to turn through such an acute angle. Thus a high rake angle reduces the cutting force by reducing the shear area, and it also reduces the pressure of the chip on the rake face of the tool. Both these factors lead to increased cutting efficiency.

Unfortunately there is a limit to how far the rake angle can be increased. It has already been mentioned that any increase in rake angle results in a decrease in tool strength, so tool design becomes a compromise between cutting efficiency and tool strength and life.

There are three basic types of chip produced when cutting metals. These are:
1   the *discontinuous* chip;
2   the *continuous* chip;
3   the *continuous* chip with *built-up edge*.

Discontinuous chip

The shearing of the chip from the parent metal of the workpiece has already been discussed. This shearing action and the

METAL CUTTING

chip formation are shown in Fig. 9.6(a). The metal is very severely strained in forming the chip. If it is a brittle material, it may fracture in the primary deformation zone: that is, in the vicinity of the shear plane. This will give rise to the discontinuous type of chip illustrated in Fig. 9.6(b). Discontinuous chips are formed when brittle materials such as cast iron and free cutting brass are cut. Low cutting speeds and lack of rake can produce discontinuous chips when cutting ductile materials such as mild steel.

As brittle materials form a discontinuous chip with a constant shear plane angle, little advantage is gained from giving the tool a rake angle. Therefore brittle materials are usually cut with a zero rake angle. This permits the maximum possible wedge angle, which results in an increase in tool life.

Continuous chip

This is the long, ribbon-like chip that is produced when machining ductile materials such as mild steel, copper and aluminium that behave as a rigid plastic when cut. Although the chip shears from the parent metal along the shear plane, it does not separate up into 'plates', as shown in Fig. 9.6(a).

The formation of a continuous chip is shown in Fig. 9.7(a). Some very soft and ductile materials, with a low strength, tend to 'tear' away from the parent metal of the workpiece rather than shear cleanly. This results in a rough surface that has to be cleaned up by a very keen cutting edge, as shown in Fig. 9.7(b).

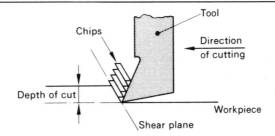

(a) Chip formation

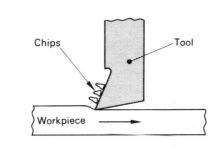

(b) Discontinuous chip

Fig. 9.6 Discontinuous chip

Note:
1 A blunt tool will cause a chip to shear away from the parent metal but will leave a rough torn surface.
2 A soft material tends to tear instead of shearing cleanly. Often the tear will be below the plane of cutting so that the component is undersize and will not clean up even with a sharp tool. This is why it is difficult to produce a good surface when cutting soft, ductile materials such as copper and fully annealed mild steel.
3 Soft materials such as copper and aluminium can be machined to a high finish by cutting at very high speeds using diamond-tipped tools. Under these conditions the metal behaves as if it is very much harder and stiffer at the point of cutting.

Continuous chip with built-up edge

Under some conditions, the friction between the secondary deformation zone of the chip and the rake face of the tool is very great. Metal from the chip becomes pressure-welded to the rake face, making it rough. The increased roughness increases the friction, and this leads to a building up of layer upon layer of chip material as shown in Fig. 9.8(a) on page 179. This is referred to as a built-up edge.

Eventually the amount of material grows to such an extent that it tends to become unstable and breaks down. The particles of built-up material that flake away weld themselves to the chip and to the workpiece as shown in Fig. 9.8(b). This produces a dangerously jagged chip and a rough surface on the workpiece. The formation of a built-up edge is called *chip welding*.

Chip welding should be prevented because it shortens tool life, increases power consumption and spoils the surface finish. Some methods of prevention are listed below.

1 Reducing friction This can be achieved by increasing the rake angle; using a lubricant between the rake face and the chip; polishing the rake face.

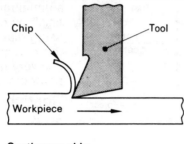

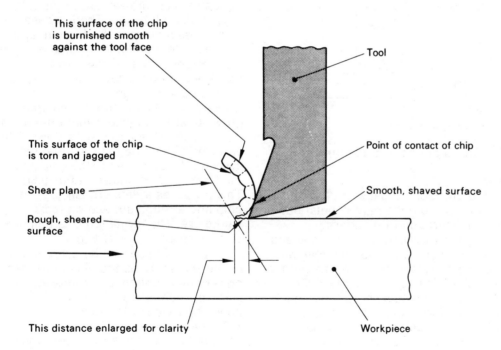

Fig. 9.7 Continuous chip

2 Reducing temperature This can be achieved by reducing friction and by reducing the cutting speed.

3 Reducing pressure between the chip and the tool This can be achieved by increasing the rake angle; reducing the feed rate; using oblique instead of orthogonal cutting (See page 278.)

4 Preventing metal-to-metal contact This can be achieved by using a high-pressure lubricant between the chip and the tool. Such lubricants contain chlorine and sulphur additives, which build up a non-metallic film on the tool face. Active sulphur compounds attack copper and its alloys and should not be used on such materials. The use of non-metallic cutting tool materials will also prevent chip welding if carefully selected. These will be considered in a later book.

The chip breaker

The long and ribbon-like continuous chip has razor-sharp edges and can inflict deep, painful and dangerous cuts. It should never be moved with the bare hands. A swarf rake should be used to drag it away from the working zone of the machine. Better still, it should be prevented from forming in the first place: a *chip breaker* can be built into the tool as shown in Fig. 9.9. The same effect can be achieved in a high-speed tool by grinding a step in the rake face just behind the cutting edge.

The chip breaker forces the chip into a tighter spiral than it would normally form. This work-hardens the chip and

METAL CUTTING

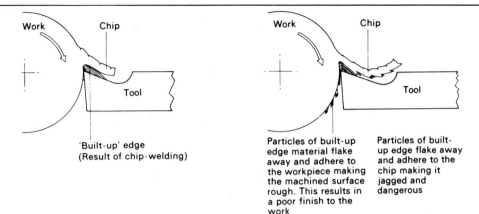

(a) Layering of chip material on rake face of tool during chip-welding

(b) Instability of built up edge if chip-welding becomes excessive

Fig. 9.8 Chip welding (built up edge)

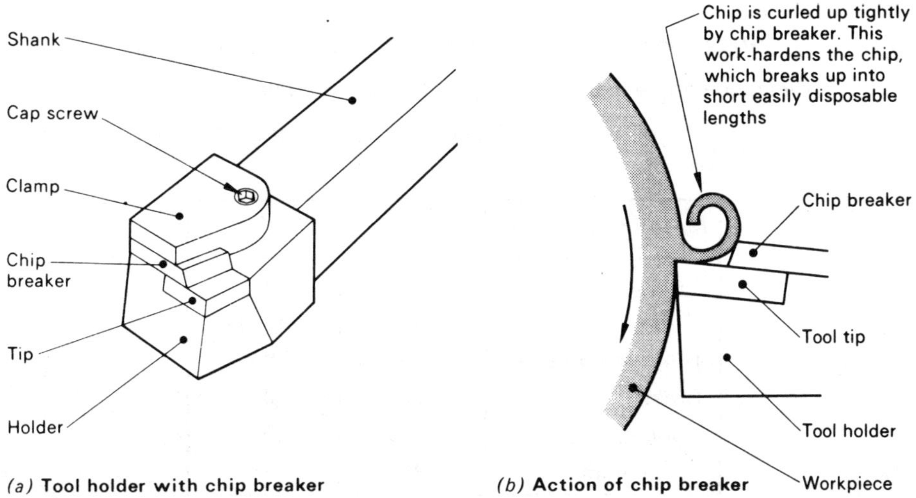

(a) Tool holder with chip breaker

(b) Action of chip breaker

Fig. 9.9 Chip breaker

makes it sufficiently brittle to break up into short lengths which are easily disposed of.

Application of cutting angles

Chisel

The basic wedge angle (page 174) applies to all metal-cutting tools. On pages 179 and 184 of this chapter, a variety of metal cutting tools will be considered, and the manner in which the basic wedge is applied will be examined.

Figure 9.10(a) shows how the point of a cold chisel forms a metal cutting wedge with rake and clearance angles. This allows a controlled cutting action. In Fig. 9.10(b) the chisel is inclined to the work at too small an angle. This destroys the clearance angle and prevents the cutting edge from biting into the workpiece. This causes the cut to become progressively shallower.

In Fig. 9.10(c) the chisel is inclined at too steep an angle. This destroys the rake angle and also makes the clearance angle too large. The result is that the chisel digs into the workpiece with loss of control of the cutting processes. Figure 9.11 shows the correct point angles and inclination angles for various materials. These can provide appropriate rake and clearance angles for the given materials.

File

Like any other cutting tool, the file tooth must have correctly applied tool angles

179

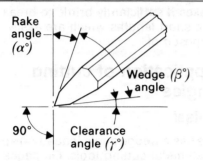

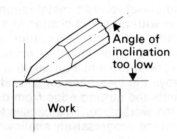

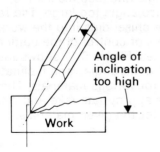

Fig. 9.10 The chisel – correct use

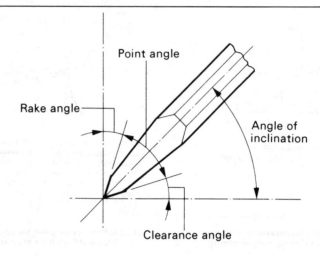

The point angle of a chisel is equivalent to the wedge angle of a lathe or shaping machine tool. The point angle together with the angle of inclination forms the rake and clearance angles

Rake angle = 90° − { angle of inclination + ½ point angle }

Clearance angle = 90° − { rake angle + point angle }

or = angle of inclination − ½ point angle

Material to be cut	Point angle	Angle of inclination
Cast iron	60°	37°
Mild steel	55°	34½°
High carbon steel	65°	39½°
Brass	50°	32°
Copper	45°	29½°
Aluminium	30°	22°

Fig. 9.11 Chisel angles

METAL CUTTING

in accordance with the principles laid down earlier in this chapter. The file tooth is formed by a chisel-type cutter hitting the file blank at an angle as shown in Fig. 9.12(a). This provides a single or 'over-cut'. Single cut files or 'floats' are used to work on hard material that would chip an ordinary file tooth. They are particularly effective on brittle materials such as cast brass, free-cutting brass and cast iron.

In order to give easier and smoother filing with greater control, a second or 'up-cut' is required. This produces a definite tooth, as distinct from simple ridges. However, its formation gives the tooth a burr, as shown in Fig. 9.12(b). If a brand new file is used on tough material such as medium or high carbon steel, or die steel, the burr chips off, leaving the file blunt and inefficient. A brand new file should always be 'broken in' on softer and weaker materials such as brass and mild steel.

It will be seen from Fig. 9.12(c) that, unlike the chisel, the file tooth has negative rake.

Hacksaw

The teeth of a heavy duty hacksaw blade that is used on power sawing machines are shown in Fig. 9.13(a). It will be seen that the teeth form a series of metal cutting wedges. Like all multi-tooth cutters designed to work in a slot, the hacksaw blade has to be provided with swarf (secondary) clearance as well as cutting (primary) clearance. This provides room for the chips to be carried out of the slot, without clogging

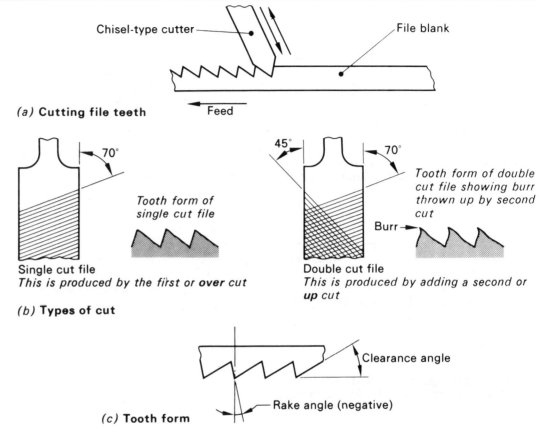

Fig. 9.12 File teeth

the teeth, whilst maintaining a strong cutting edge.

The finer teeth of a hand saw blade have only a simple wedge shape as shown in Fig. 9.13(b). Here, swarf clearance is provided by exaggerating the primary clearance. Tooth strength is maintained by the use of zero rake angle to increase the available wedge angle to a maximum.

Scraper

The scraper is used to remove metal locally from a surface with a high degree of accuracy. The end of the scraper is ground square to the blade so

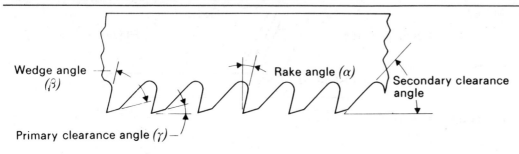

(a) **Heavy duty power saw blade**
(Tooth form gives high strength coupled with adequate chip clearance)

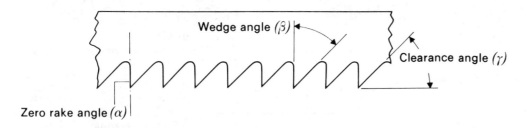

(b) **Light duty hand saw blade**
(Simplified tooth form for fine tooth blades)

Fig. 9.13 Hacksaw blade teeth

that a negative rake angle is formed as shown in Fig. 9.14(a). Clearance is provided by the angle of inclination at which the scraper is held. Figure 9.14(b) shows how the vertical component of the cutting reaction force holds the scraper off the work and prevents it digging in. If positive rake is applied, the direction of action of the vertical component force is reversed. This tends to pull the scraper into the work and reduces the fitter's control.

Thread-cutting tap and die

Figure 9.15(a) shows a section through a thread-cutting tap. The 'teeth' are form-relieved and the clearance face is curved, so the clearance angle is formed by the tangent to the thread form at the cutting wedge. The rake angle is formed by the flute, thus the metal cutting wedge is still in evidence. Because the tap is a form cutter with a form-relieved clearance, re-sharpening is more specialised than for the simple single point tools referred to so far.

Figure 9.15(b) shows how the metal cutting wedge is applied to the thread-cutting die.

Twist drill

This is dealt with in greater detail in Chapter 12. However, Fig. 9.16(a) shows how the basic metal cutting wedge is used in this cutting tool. Because the rake angle is formed by a helical groove, the rake angle varies from point to point along the lip of the drill, as shown in Fig. 9.16(b). The variation is from positive at the outer corner to negative near the centre of rotation. The fact that cutting conditions are poor at the point of the drill does not affect the quality of the hole produced by the outer corner, where the cutting conditions are relatively good.

Lathe and shaping machine tools

These are dealt with in greater detail in Chapters 13 and 14. However, Fig. 9.17(a) shows how the metal cutting wedge is used in a simple parting-off tool. Since this tool has to work in a slot, it is given side clearance and body clearance as well as a front clearance

METAL CUTTING

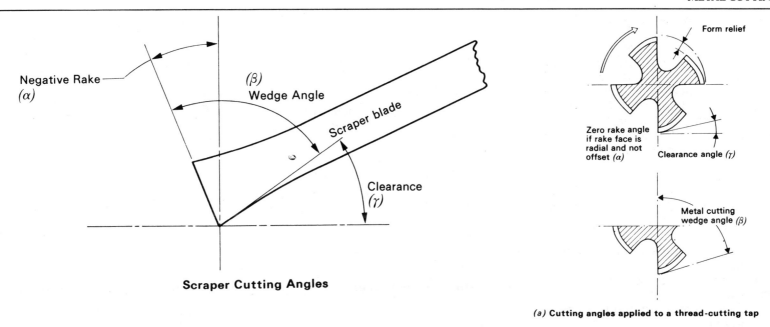

Scraper Cutting Angles

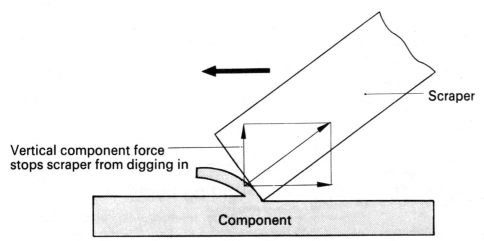

Fig. 9.14 The scraper

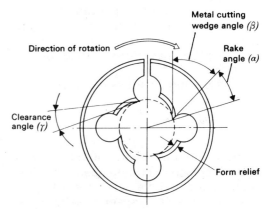

(a) Cutting angles applied to a thread-cutting tap

(b) Cutting angles applied to a thread-cutting die

Fig. 9.15 The thread cutting tap and die

angle formed by the basic wedge. Figure 9.17(b) shows how rake and clearance angles are applied to the more complex oblique cutting tool, and how they form compound angles. (Orthogonal and oblique cutting will be considered in Chapter 13). The same principles apply to shaping machine tools except that the angles are rotated through 90° as shown in Fig. 9.17(c).

Tool life

Tool life is controlled by many factors and the more important ones are listed below.
1 The rigidity of the work, tool and machine;
2 The cutting fluid used and its application;
3 The angles to which the tool has been ground;
4 The rate of feed and depth of cut;
5 The properties of the material being cut;
6 The properties of the cutting tool material;
7 The cutting speed (see below).

Cutting speed

Cutting speed is one of the most important factors determining tool life; a small increase in cutting speed rapidly reduces the tool life, while a small decrease in cutting speed greatly increases tool life.

This is because any change in cutting speed results in a change in the heat energy generated at the cutting edge.

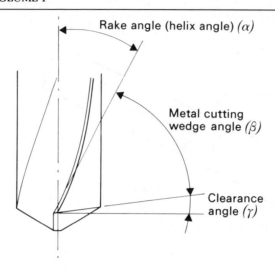

(a) Cutting angles applied to a twist drill

Fig. 9.16 The twist drill

An increase in cutting speed results in an increase in the heat energy generated. If this heat cannot be dissipated (got rid of) quickly enough, then the temperature of the tool increases and it starts to soften and becomes blunt faster. Heat is generated during cutting due to:
1 the internal breakdown of the metal structure of the workpiece during cutting;
2 the friction between the chip and the tool.

The effect of increasing cutting speed

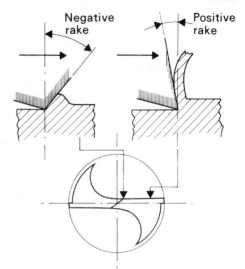

(b) Variation in rake angle along lip of drill

(*NOTE*: Rake angle at periphery is equal to helix angle of flute)

can be reduced by using a suitable cutting fluid to cool and lubricate the cutting tool. Actual cutting speeds and feeds for drilling, turning (lathe), shaping and milling will be considered in the chapters dealing with these processes.

Cutting fluids

Cutting fluids are designed to fulfil one or more of the following functions:
1 to cool the tool and the workpiece;
2 to lubricate the chip/tool interface

METAL CUTTING

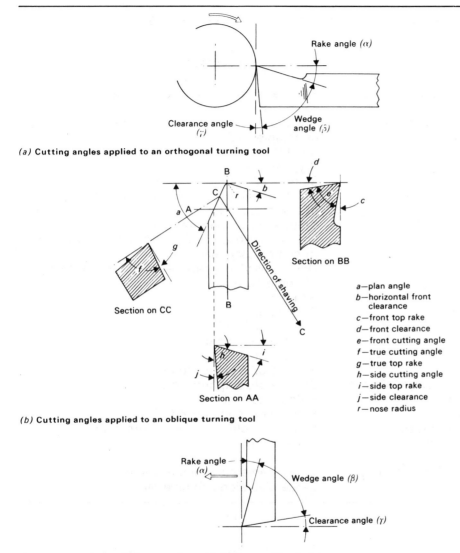

(a) Cutting angles applied to an orthogonal turning tool

a—plan angle
b—horizontal front clearance
c—front top rake
d—front clearance
e—front cutting angle
f—true cutting angle
g—true top rake
h—side cutting angle
i—side top rake
j—side clearance
r—nose radius

(b) Cutting angles applied to an oblique turning tool

(c) Cutting angles applied to an orthogonal shaping machine tool

Fig. 9.17 Single point cutting tools

and reduce tool wear due to friction;
3 to prevent chip welding (formation of a built-up edge);
4 to improve the surface finish of the workpiece;
5 to flush away the chips (swarf);
6 to prevent corrosion of the work and machine.

There are many types of cutting fluid and it is always best to consult the expert advisory service offered by the coolant manufacturers. The correct selection and use of cutting fluids can increase the productivity of a machine shop far more cheaply than any other method. Although money has to be spent on the fluid, expensive tools do not have to be replaced so often. Table 9.1 is a guide to the selection of cutting fluids for general machining of various materials using high speed steel tools.

Sheet metal cutting principles

Sheet metal is not rigid enough to be cut well by the single point and multi-tooth cutters normally used when machining. A hacksaw with a very fine pitch blade will cut sheet metal, but it is an exception. Anyone who has tried to drill a large hole in thin sheet metal, and has seen the torn and ragged hole that results, will appreciate the difficulty.

The quickest and easiest way to cut sheet metal is by *shearing* it. Cutting tools for sheet metal are called *shears* because, long before it was realised that all mechanical metal-cutting tools cut with a shearing action, it was obvious that this was the principle by which 'shears' cut.

There is a wide range of machines for shearing sheet metal, from snips to static and portable power machines. In each case the basic principle of metal cutting is the shearing action of a moving blade in relation to a fixed blade. This is true of hand operated machines and power operated machines.

The standard type of bench shear, and all guillotines, are used for straightline cutting. The basic principles of these machines is that the moving blade (inclined to the fixed blade) is brought down to meet the fixed blade (bottom blade), as shown in Fig. 9.18(a).

The moving cutting member of a shearing machine may be operated by:
1 *Hand-lever* – bench shearing machines;
2 *Foot treadle* – treadle guillotines;
3 *Electric motor* or *hydraulics* – power guillotines.

If the cutting members of a guillotine or shearing machine are arranged parallel to each other, the area under shear is the cross-section of the material to be cut, that is 'length × thickness', as shown in Fig. 9.18(b).

The top cutting member of a shearing machine is always inclined to the bottom member to give a *shearing angle* of approximately 5°. Figure 9.18(c) shows this arrangement of the blades. The area under shear is reduced and so the force required to shear the material is reduced as well.

Table 9.1 Recommended cutting lubricants for use with high speed steel tools

MATERIAL	CUTTING LUBRICANT
Aluminium and aluminium alloys	Soluble oil, paraffin (do not use alkali solutions)
Magnesium and magnesium alloys	Dry. If possible, keep the drill cooled with a jet of compressed air
Copper	Soluble oil, lard oil
Brass	Dry, soluble oil
Phosphor bronze	Soluble oil, lard oil
Slate	Dry. If possible, keep the drill cooled with a jet of compressed air
Monel metal	Soluble oil, sulphurized oil
Bakelite	Dry. If possible, keep the drill cooled with a jet of compressed air
Cast iron	Dry. If possible, keep the drill cooled with a jet of compressed air
Chilled cast iron	Soluble oil
Malleable iron	Soluble oil
Nimonic	Neat oil, lard oil
Wrought iron	Soluble oil, sulphurized oil
Zinc	Soluble oil
Mild steel	Soluble oil, sulphurized oil
Alloy steel – all tensile strengths	Soluble oil, sulphurized oil
High manganese steel	Sulphurized oil
Steel forgings	Soluble oil, sulphurized oil
Stainless steels (austenitic, martensitic and ferritic – standard grades)	Small diameters: tallow or turpentine. Large diameters: soluble oil
Stainless steels (free-cutting grades)	Small diameters: sulphurized oil Large diameters: soluble oil

METAL CUTTING

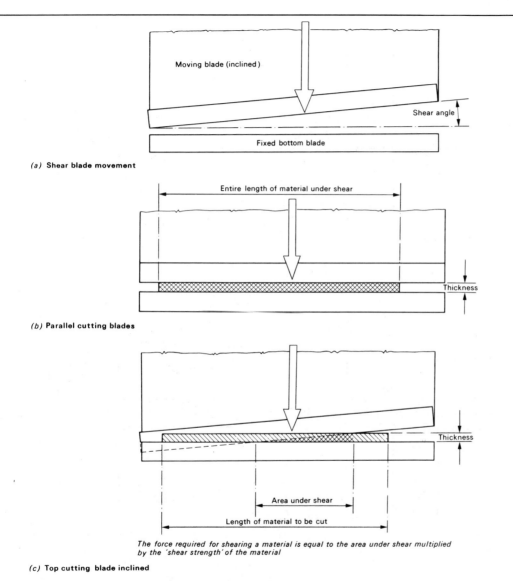

(a) Shear blade movement

(b) Parallel cutting blades

The force required for shearing a material is equal to the area under shear multiplied by the 'shear strength' of the material

(c) Top cutting blade inclined

Fig. 9.18 The effect of shear angle (shearing machine)

Figure 9.19 shows how the shearing action is used to cut metal. The shear blades are provided with a *rake angle* of approximately 87° and there must be *clearance* between the cutting edges of the blades to assist in the cutting action. The importance of clearance will be discussed later in this section.

Stage 1 The top cutting member moves downwards and exerts continuing pressure on the metal. The top and bottom surfaces of the metal are deformed.

Stage 2 As the pressure increases, the internal grains of the metal are deformed. This is *plastic deformation* before *shearing*.

Stage 3 After a certain amount of plastic deformation the cutting members begin to penetrate. The uncut metal *work-hardens* at the edges.

Stage 4 Fractures begin to run into the work-hardened metal from the points of contact of the cutting members. When these fractures meet, the cutting members penetrate the whole of the metal thickness.

Figure 9.20 shows details of the cutting blades of hand shears. It will be noticed that the design principles are the same as those used for guillotine shear blades (page 189).

Blade clearances are very important and should be set to suit the material being cut. An approximate rule is that the clearance should not exceed 10 per cent of the thickness to be cut, and must be varied to suit the particular material. For example, mild steel 10 per cent of the thickness being cut; brass 4 per cent and aluminium 3 per cent.

The off-hand grinding machine

The grinding process will be described fully in *Mechanical Engineering Craft Theory and Related Subjects: Volume 2* but it is essential to understand the basic principles of sharpening simple tools right from the start. The double-ended, off-hand grinding machine is widely used in toolrooms and jobbing workshops to sharpen the chisel, drill, lathe tool and shaping machine. The basic precautions that should be observed by the users of grinding machines are:
1 wear goggles;
2 check that the guard is in place;
3 check that the work rest is properly adjusted so that the tool being ground cannot be dragged down between the wheel and the work rest;
4 examine the wheel to see that it is neither chipped, glazed nor loaded. A glazed wheel is shiny in appearance and will not cut correctly. This overheats the tool being ground and may cause wheel failure. A loaded wheel has its pores clogged with soft metal and it will not cut correctly. Glazed and loaded wheels have to be 'dressed' to correct the cutting surface.

Figure 9.21(a) shows a typical double-ended, off-hand grinding machine used for sharpening small tools (page 190). This machine differs from all the others described in this book as the

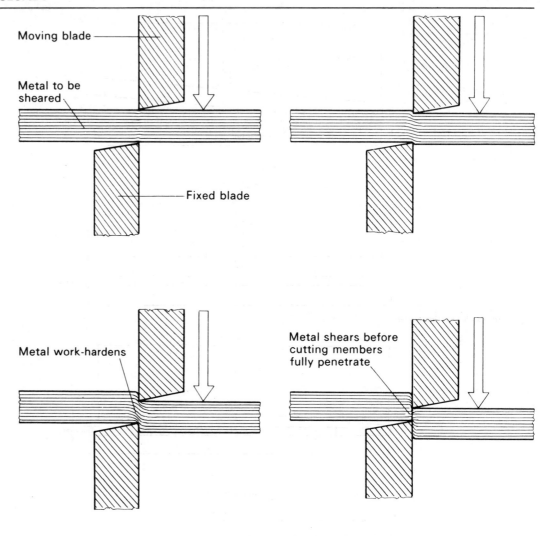

Fig. 9.19 The action of shearing metal

METAL CUTTING

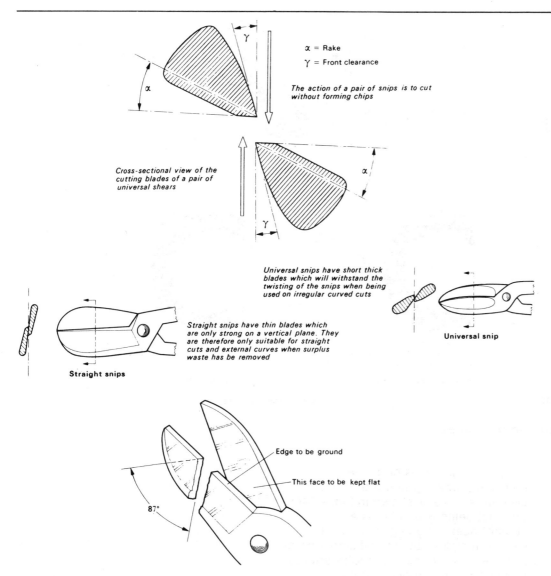

Fig. 9.20 Details of the cutting blades of hand shears

workpiece is held by hand. This can be set up quickly and allows flexible movement, but precise control is difficult. Templates and tool protractors should be used to check the cutting and profile angles until skill is acquired in grinding cutting tools. Particular attention should be paid to the special safety precautions listed at the end of this chapter as the simplicity of this machine encourages the use of careless and dangerous practices. The tool rest and guard should be adjusted as shown in Fig. 9.21(b).

Re-sharpening cutting tools

Chisel

This is ground as shown in Fig. 9.22. The cutting edge should be slightly radiused by rocking the chisel from side to side (page 191). This also helps to even up the wear on the wheel face.

Twist drill

This is most easily ground on the side of the wheel as shown in Fig. 9.23(a). The flat surface that this provides makes it much easier to produce a true point. The straight cutting lip should lie vertically against the side of the wheel, and the drill should be rocked against the wheel about the axis XX. When the drill has been ground, it should be checked on a point gauge as shown in Fig. 9.23(b). This ensures that the angles are equal, and the scale checks that the lip lengths are equal. It will be explained

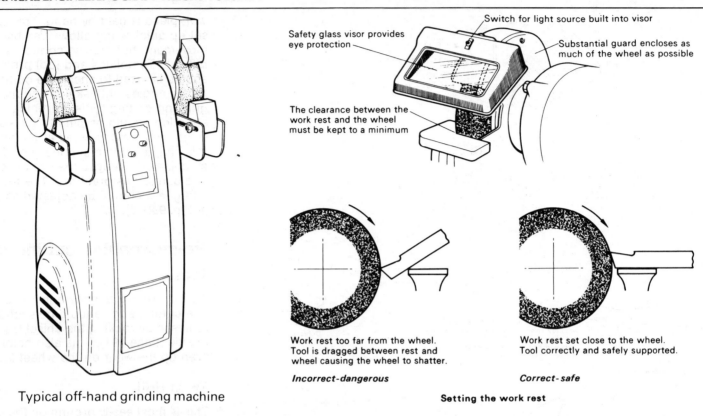

Fig. 9.21 Double ended, off-hand grinding machines

on page 240 that equal angles and lip length are necessary for accurately sized holes.

Single point tools

Lathe and shaping machine tools can also be ground on the off-hand grinding machine. Unfortunately, flat surfaces cannot be produced because of the wheel radius. This is particularly noticeable when grinding the front clearance angle as shown in Fig. 9.24(a). The tool being ground in is a straight-nose roughing tool, but the same principles apply to all single point tools. After grinding, the angles should be checked on a tool protractor as shown in Fig. 9.25 on page 192.

METAL CUTTING

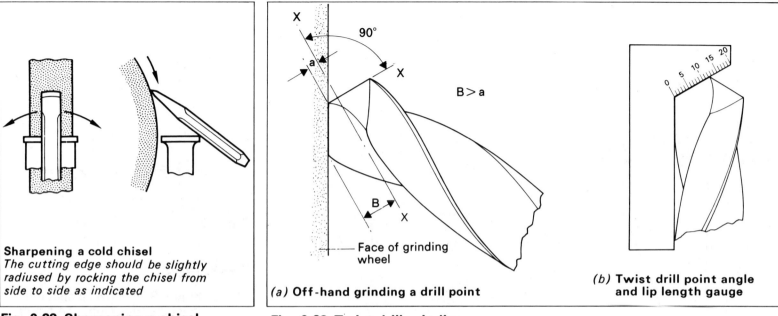

Fig. 9.22 Sharpening a chisel

Sharpening a cold chisel
The cutting edge should be slightly radiused by rocking the chisel from side to side as indicated

(a) Off-hand grinding a drill point

(b) **Twist drill point angle and lip length gauge**

Fig. 9.23 Twist drill grinding

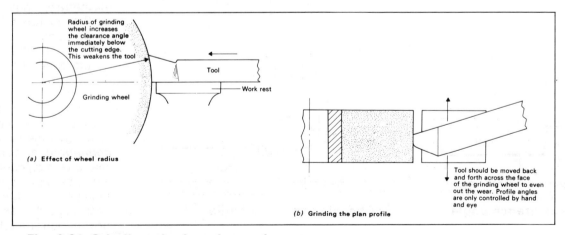

(a) Effect of wheel radius

(b) Grinding the plan profile

Fig. 9.24 Grinding single point tools

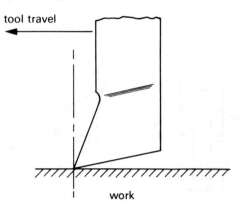

Fig. 9.26

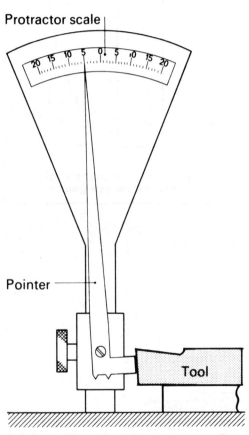

(a) **Checking the clearance angle**

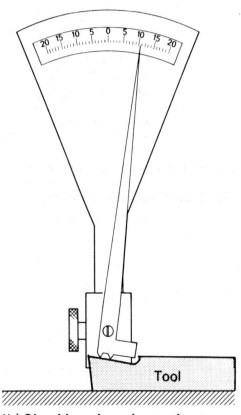

(b) **Checking the rake angle**

Fig. 9.25 Tool protractor

Exercises

1. a) Figure 9.26 shows a shaping machine tool. Copy the figure and indicate on it:
   (i) the rake angle
   (ii) the clearance angle
   (iii) the tool angle
   b) State suitable rake angles for the general machining of:
   (i) cast iron
   (ii) mild steel
   (iii) medium carbon steel
   (iv) phosphor bronze
2. Name *two* metals that give a *continuous* chip, and *two* metals that give a *discontinuous* chip when being machined with a postive rake cutting tool.
3. With the aid of sketches, explain how a 'built-up edge' occurs on a cutting tool and the effect it has on

the cutting operation. Suggest some means of preventing it from forming.
4. Sketch, in good proportion, the side view of a cold chisel and indicate the following angles:
   a) clearance angle
   b) point angle
   c) rake angle
   d) angle of inclination

State a suitable point angle for cutting mild steel.

5. With the aid of sketches, show how rake and clearance angles are applied to the following cutting tools:
   a) a lathe parting-off tool
   b) a twist drill
   c) a hacksaw blade tooth
   d) a screw-cutting tap
   e) a scraper
6. Sketch, in good proportion, the plan profiles of the following turning tools:
   a) a straight nose roughing tool
   b) a knife (bar) turning tool
   c) a left-hand facing tool
   d) a parting-off tool

Indicate the direction of the top rake angle in each case by means of an arrow.

7. List *five* important factors that influence the life of a cutting tool, and explain why it is better to operate a machine slightly slower rather than slightly faster than the optimum cutting speed.
8. List *five* important functions of a cutting fluid and give *two* reasons why ordinary mineral lubricating oils are unsuitable as cutting lubricants.
9. Explain, with the aid of sketches, how sheet metal is cut by the shearing action of guillotine blades.
10. With the aid of sketches, show how a cold chisel should be sharpened on an off-hand grinding machine and discuss the precautions that should be taken.

10. Fitting

The term *fitting* is used for those operations that the engineer performs by hand at the bench. The production of accurate components by hand demands great skill from the engineering craftsman. Every apprentice is disappointed with his slow progress at first, but constant practice will help him acquire the skill. Although this is hard work, great satisfaction is felt when the skill is finally acquired.

Fitter's bench

There is no single design for the ideal bench. However, for accurate work the following factors are very important.
1   The bench must be made from heavy timbers on a metal frame so that it is as solid and rigid as possible.
2   It must be positioned so that there is enough natural light and artificial, shadowless light.
3   The height of the bench should allow the top of the vice jaws to be in line with the underside of the fitter's forearm when he holds it parallel to the ground.
4   There should be adequate racking and storage facilities for small tools and instruments.

Figure 10.1 shows a typical fitter's bench embracing these factors.

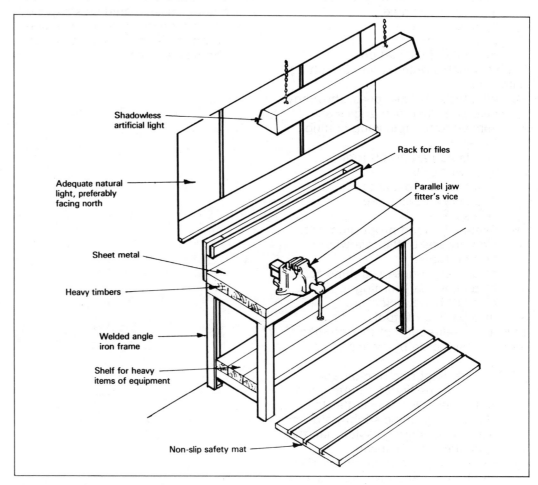

Fig. 10.1 Fitter's bench

FITTING

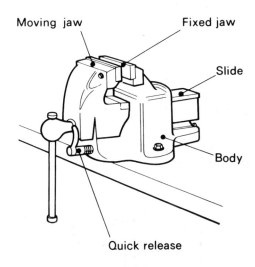

Fig. 10.2 Fitter's vice

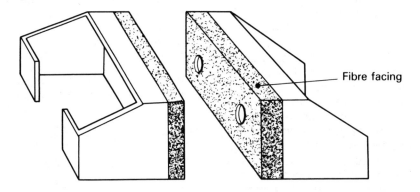

Fig. 10.3 Vice shoes

Vice

The fitter uses a *parallel jaw* vice of the type shown in Fig. 10.2. This is often fitted with a quick-release device which saves time when the vice is being adjusted for wide or narrow work.

For accurate work the vice must be kept in good condition.
1   Oil the screw regularly.
2   Ensure that the vice is heavy enough for the job in hand.
3   Heavy hammering and bending should be done on the anvil.
4   When chipping, the thrust of the chisel should be against the fixed jaw.
5   Never hammer on the top surface of the slide.

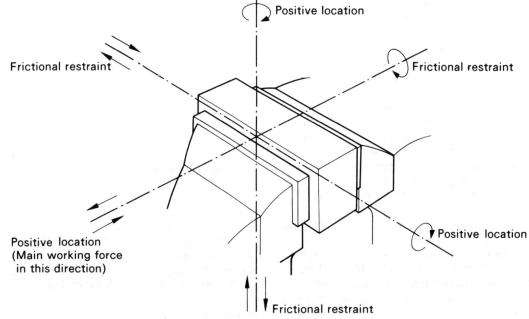

Fig. 10.4 Location in the vice

195

The jaws of the vice are serrated to prevent the work slipping when roughing down. However, these serrations can mark and ruin a finished component. When holding on a finished surface, fibre or soft metal clamps or vice-shoes are fitted over the jaws. These are shown in Fig. 10.3.

The work held in a vice must be given adequate support against the cutting force, and also against the clamping force of the vice itself. It must also be held securely so that it does not move as it is worked on. Figure 10.4 shows the restraints on the workpiece and it will be seen that some of these are positive whilst others are frictional. For heavy cutting, the work should be positioned so that the cutting forces are resisted by positive restraints.

As well as holding the work securely, the work must be positioned in the vice so that it is not distorted by the cutting force. Figure 10.5 shows how the work should be positioned. In Fig. 10.5(a) the cutting force is applied too far from the vice jaws and it will have sufficient leverage to bend the workpiece. The work is said to have excessive over-hang. Even when the force is too small to bend the workpiece permanently, it will make it vibrate and give off an irritating squealing noise. When the workpiece is held with the least possible over-hang, the cutting force does not bend the workpiece or make it vibrate. Correct positioning of the workpiece in the vice is shown in Fig. 10.5(b).

Cylindrical work is often difficult to

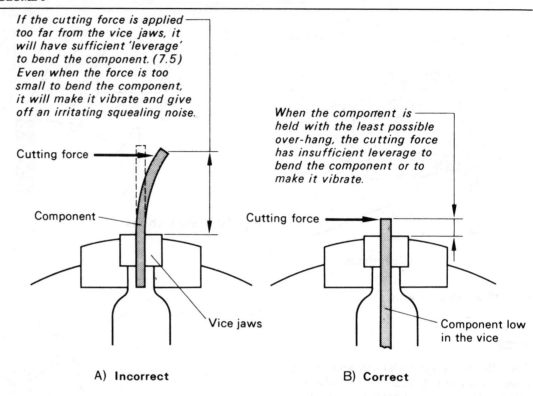

Fig. 10.5 Positioning work in the vice

hold securely in a parallel jaw vice as there is line contact at only two points. Introducing a vee block between the workpiece and the fixed jaw provides three-point support and greater security as shown in Fig. 10.6 on page 197.

Cold chisel

Cold chisels are used for rapidly breaking down a surface. It is the quickest way to remove metal by hand, but the accuracy is low and the finish is poor. Despite the fact that the chisel is only a simple roughing tool, it is still important that the principles regarding tool angles are correctly applied. The theory of the metal cutting wedge was applied to the cutting edge of the cold chisel on page 179.

Figure 10.8 on page 198 shows a selection of cold chisels and their applications. Another application of the flat chisel is the cutting of sheet metal and thin plate as shown in Fig. 10.7. Here the metal is being sheared between the chisel and the top of the fixed jaw of the vice. The line along which the cut is to be made should be as near the top of the vice jaws as possible, otherwise the metal will bend and the cut edge will be badly burred over.

The chips produced by the cold chisel tend to fly off at great speed and are potentially dangerous, so the following precautions should be taken:
1   wear safety glasses or goggles;
2   do not chip towards anyone else;
3   place a chipping screen in front of your vice.

File

Filing operations range from roughing down and deburring blanks, to complex and very accurate finishing operations on flat and curved surfaces. Like any other cutting tool, the file should be used with the correct cutting angles. These were discussed on page 181.

To make a plane surface, the file must be moved parallel to the plane of the required surface. Unfortunately, there are no slideways available to guide the file, only the muscular co-ordination of the user that comes with practice.

There are many different types of file, and to specify a particular type the following information must be given

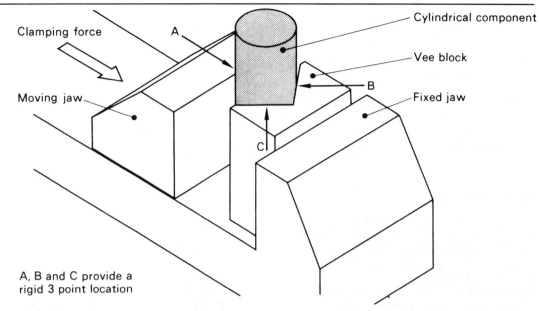

Fig. 10.6 Holding cylindrical work

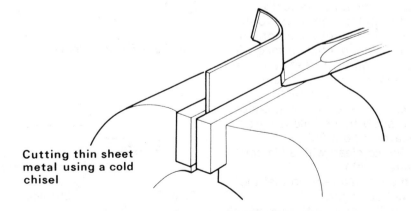

Fig. 10.7 Cutting thin sheet metal using a cold chisel

(see BS 498: 1960): 1 Length; 2 Grade of cut; and 3 Shape.

The length and other features of the file are shown in Fig. 10.9. The grade or cut of the file depends upon its length. The shorter the file, the smaller is the pitch of the teeth for any given grade. Table 10.1 gives the pitch range and applications of the grades that are normally available. The shape of the file depends on its use and Fig. 10.10 shows a range of files for typical uses.

Using the file

Correct height   For correct control of the file, the top of the vice jaws should be level with the forearm when it is held parallel to the ground, as shown in Fig. 10.11(a) on page 200.

Correct stance   The file can only be controlled if the body is correctly balanced. Fig. 10.11(b) shows how the feet should be placed relative to the vice.

Correct grip   During each stroke of the file, the weight must be gradually transferred from the front hand to the back hand. If this is not done correctly the file will rock and a flat surface will not be made. Figure 10.12 shows how the file should be held for various operations (page 200 and 201).

Care of files   Files are rarely treated well, and a badly treated file is hard to use and leaves a poor finish.
1   Keep the file clean with a *file card* (special wire brush).
2   Keep the file in a rack so that the teeth are not damaged.
3   Use new files on non-ferrous metals until the teeth are broken in. If a new file

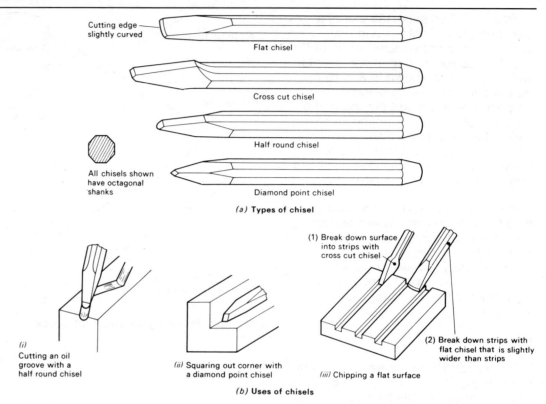

Fig. 10.8 Cold chisels

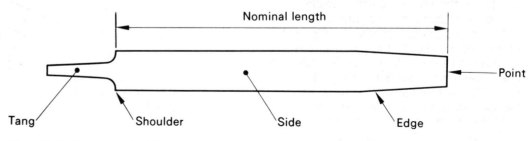

Fig. 10.9 Engineer's file

Table 10.1 File grades

GRADE	PITCH (mm)	USE
Rough	1·8–1·3	Soft metals and plastics
Bastard	1·6–0·65	General roughing out
Second cut	1·4–0·60	Roughing out tough material Finishing soft materials
Smooth	0·8–0·45	General finishing and draw filing
Dead smooth	0·5–0·25	Not often used except on tough die steels where high steels where high accuracy and finish is required

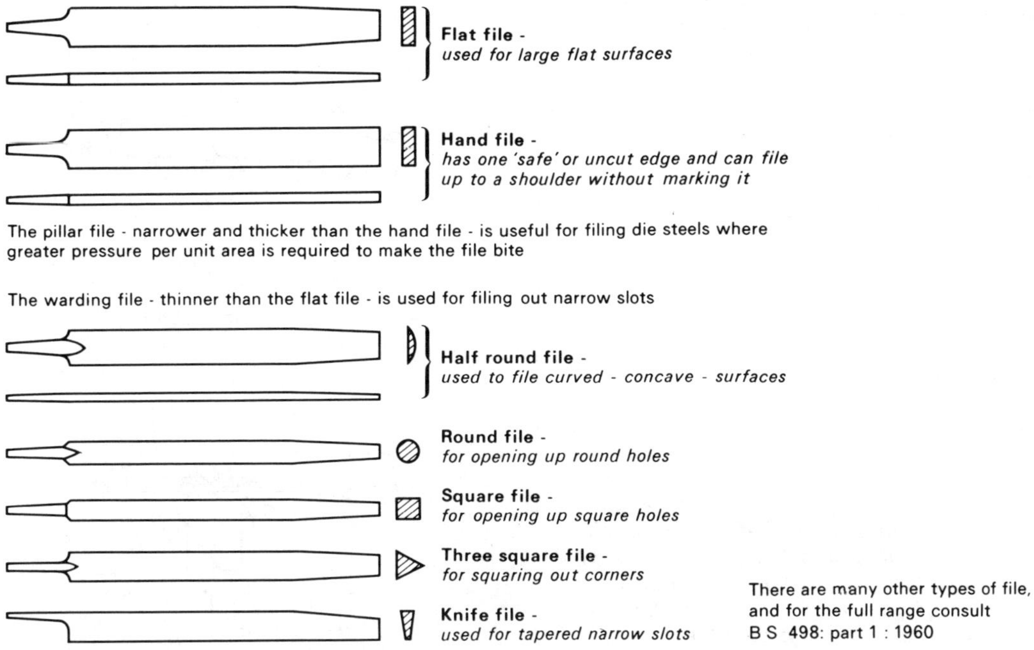

Flat file - used for large flat surfaces

Hand file - has one 'safe' or uncut edge and can file up to a shoulder without marking it

The pillar file - narrower and thicker than the hand file - is useful for filing die steels where greater pressure per unit area is required to make the file bite

The warding file - thinner than the flat file - is used for filing out narrow slots

Half round file - used to file curved - concave - surfaces

Round file - for opening up round holes

Square file - for opening up square holes

Three square file - for squaring out corners

Knife file - used for tapered narrow slots

There are many other types of file, and for the full range consult B S 498: part 1 : 1960

Fig. 10.10 Sections and uses of files

is used on steel, the burr on the teeth may chip and the file will be ruined as a cutting tool.
4 Never file quickly; this only wears out the file and the user. Slow even strokes using the full length of the file are best.
5 The file only cuts on the forward stroke; ease the downward pressure on the return stroke.

Hacksaw

Figure 10.13(a) shows a typical engineer's hacksaw with an adjustable frame that will accept a range of blade sizes. For the best results the blade should be carefully selected for the work in hand. It must be correctly fitted and correctly used. Figure 10.13(b) shows the basic elements of the hacksaw blade. Metal cutting wedge theory was applied to the tooth geometry on page 181. In the case of the hacksaw blade, however, additional side clearance has to be provided to prevent the blade wedging in the slot. This is done by giving the teeth 'set' so that the slot they cut is wider than the thickness of the blade, as shown in Fig. 10.14(a). Set is provided in two ways as shown in Fig. 10.14(b) (page 202)

Staggered tooth set With this type of set, the teeth are bent to the left and right of the centre line of the blade. Every third or fifth tooth is left straight as a 'clearing tooth'. This type of set can only be applied to coarse pitch blades where the teeth are large enough to be bent.

Wave set Where the pitch is fine (as for tube and sheet cutting blades) the teeth are too small to be given an individual set. Here, the cutting edge of the blade is waved so that set is applied to groups of teeth.

Most of the hints given for the care of

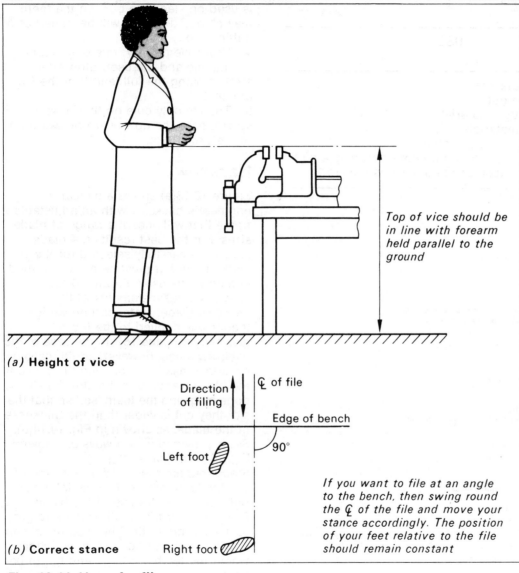

Fig. 10.11 Use of a file

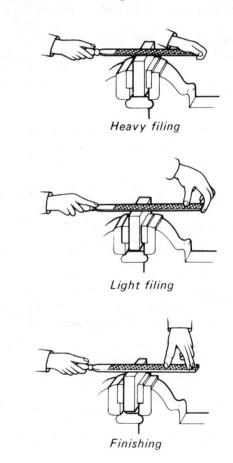

Fig. 10.12 Correct grip

a file apply equally to a hacksaw blade. In addition, never change a blade part way through a cut. The greater set of the new blade will cause it to jam in the slot already cut, and break. If a change of blade is unavoidable, start a new cut to the side of the old one.

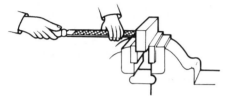

Filing a blind hole

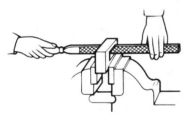

Filing a vertical surface Slotted components

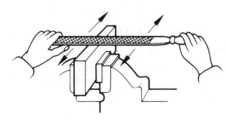

Draw filing

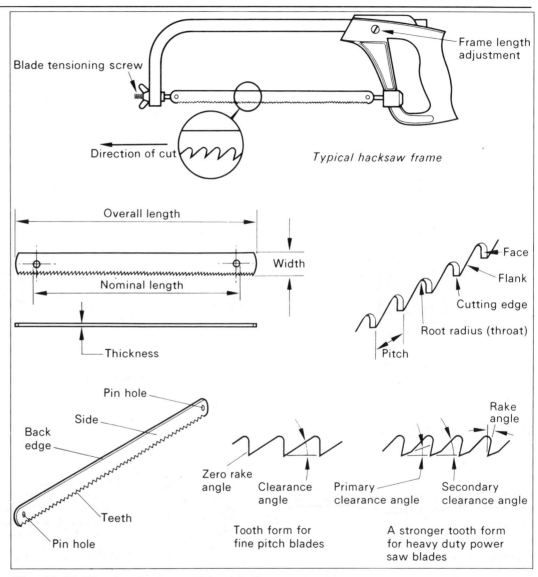

Fig. 10.13 The hacksaw and its blade

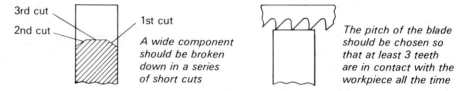

Material	Pitch (mm) Solid metal	Pitch (mm) Tube and sheet
Ferrous metal	1·4 – 1·6	0·8
Non-ferrous metal	1·8 – 2·1	1·0 – 1·2

A wide component should be broken down in a series of short cuts

The pitch of the blade should be chosen so that at least 3 teeth are in contact with the workpiece all the time

Fig. 10.15 The hacksaw blade – selection and use

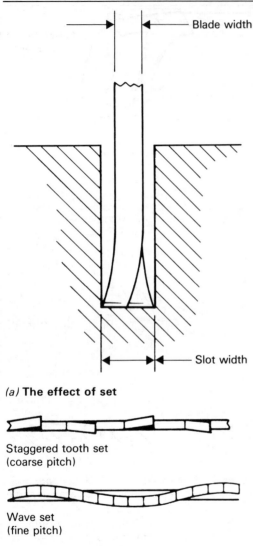

(a) The effect of set

Staggered tooth set (coarse pitch)

Wave set (fine pitch)

(b) Types of set

Fig. 10.14 Tooth set

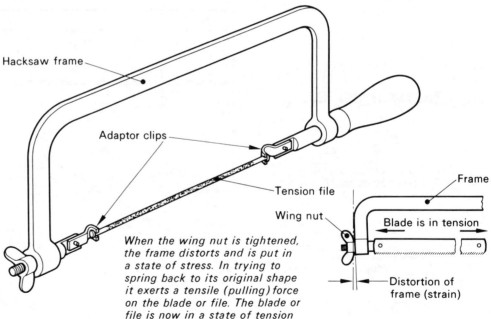

When the wing nut is tightened, the frame distorts and is put in a state of stress. In trying to spring back to its original shape it exerts a tensile (pulling) force on the blade or file. The blade or file is now in a state of tension

Fig. 10.16 The tension file

When using a hacksaw, the stance is the same as for filing. Saw at about 60 strokes per minute for high speed steel blades, or at about 40 to 50 strokes per minute for low tungsten blades. Figure 10.15 gives some useful hints for using a hacksaw.

1 When cutting a wide piece of metal, break it down into a series of short cuts.
2 The pitch (distance from point to point) of the teeth depends upon the type of metal being cut, and its thickness.
3 The pitch of the blade should be chosen so that *at least three teeth* are in contact with the workpiece all the time.

The ordinary blade is useless for profiling round a curved component. For this sort of work a tension file is used. This is a long thin circular file held in tension in the hacksaw frame to keep it stiff. The file and its adaptor clips are shown in Fig. 10.16. When the wing nut is tightened, the frame distorts and is put in a state of stress. In trying to spring back to its original shape, the frame exerts a tensile (pulling) force on the blade or file. The blade or file is now in a state of tension.

Use of hand tools

The example in this section requires the use of a drilling machine. By this stage most young engineers will have already used a simple drilling machine during practical skill training. If not, then Chapter 12 should be read in conjunction with this section.

Figure 10.17 shows a link to be made

Table 10.2 *Making the link*

(The marking out of the link has already been described in Chapter 7. This table is concerned with the manufacture of the link.)

METHOD 1	METHOD 2
1. Set up for drilling whilst sides of blank are still parallel.	1. Set up for drilling whilst sides of blank are still parallel.
2. Drill pilot holes.	2. Drill pilot holes.
3. Drill for reaming.	3. Drill for reaming.
4. Ream to size.	4. Ream to size.
5. Remove surplus metal with hacksaw or band saw leaving minimum metal to clean up.	5. Remove surplus metal by chain drilling and chiselling.
6. File smooth.	6. File smooth.
7. Deburr.	7. Deburr.
8. Check.	8. Check.
9. Grease up.	9. Grease up.

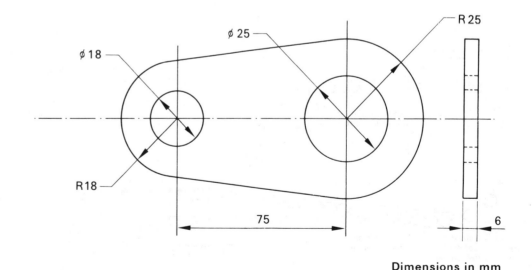

Dimensions in mm

Fig. 10.17 Link

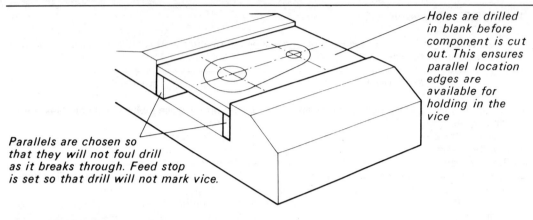

Parallels are chosen so that they will not foul drill as it breaks through. Feed stop is set so that drill will not mark vice.

Holes are drilled in blank before component is cut out. This ensures parallel location edges are available for holding in the vice

Fig. 10.18 Drilling the link

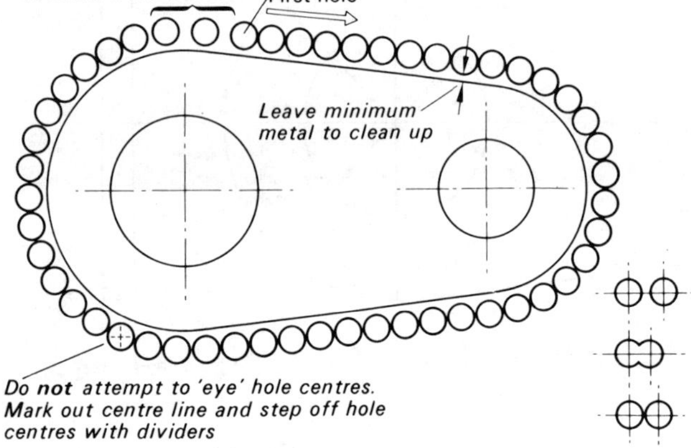

Table 10.3 *Cutting-speed calculations for drilling*

1. Cutting-speed calculation for 17·5 mm diameter drill.

Reference to Chapter 12 shows that a suitable speed for drilling mild steel with an H.S.S. twist-drill is 30 m/min

$$N = \frac{1\,000 S}{\pi D} \quad \text{where: } S = 30 \text{ m/min}$$
$$\pi = 3 \cdot 14$$
$$D = 17 \cdot 5 \text{ mm}$$

$$= \frac{1\,000 \times 30}{3 \cdot 14 \times 17 \cdot 5}$$

$$= \underline{546 \cdot 1} \text{ rev/min}$$

A suitable spindle speed would be between 500 and 550 rev/min

Share out last few holes to avoid a thick web — First hole

Leave minimum metal to clean up

Incorrect — web too thick

Incorrect — holes too close: drill will break

Correct — holes just touch

Do not attempt to 'eye' hole centres. Mark out centre line and step off hole centres with dividers

Fig. 10.19 Chain drilling

from bright drawn mild steel. The marking out of this link has already been described in Chapter 8. This chapter is concerned with the manufacture of the link using bench tools and a drilling machine. Table 10.2 gives two methods of making the link.

The mistake many young craftsmen make is to rush into cutting out the component from the stock material as the first operation. A little thought will show that once this component is cut out, it will be very difficult to hold in a

FITTING

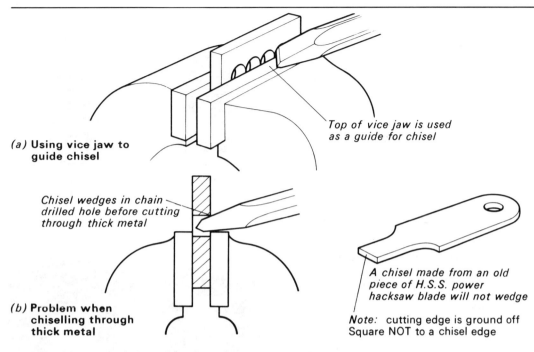

(a) Using vice jaw to guide chisel

Top of vice jaw is used as a guide for chisel

Chisel wedges in chain drilled hole before cutting through thick metal

A chisel made from an old piece of H.S.S. power hacksaw blade will not wedge

Note: cutting edge is ground off Square NOT to a chisel edge

(b) Problem when chiselling through thick metal

Fig. 10.20 Use of the chisel to remove surplus metal

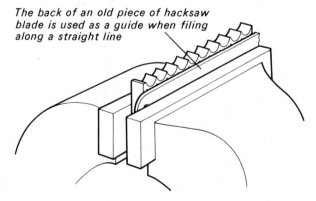

The back of an old piece of hacksaw blade is used as a guide when filing along a straight line

Fig. 10.21 Filing to a straight line

vice for the drilling operations. That is why the operation sequence given in Table 10.2 recommends that all drilling operations are done first. Figure 10.18 shows a suitable set-up.

As the link is relatively thin compared with the diameter of the holes, it is advisable to drill a 6 mm diameter pilot hole and then open it up: in two steps for the 18 mm diameter hole, and three steps for the 25 mm diameter hole. Because of the relatively thin material being drilled there will be a strong tendency for these large drills to chatter and leave a hole that is rough and not round. It is advisable to leave about 0·5 mm in the holes after the last drilling operation and finish with a reamer (see page 243) using a suitable cutting fluid (not mineral oil). Table 10.3 gives the cutting-speed calculations for the drilling operations.

Table 10.2 gave the options of sawing away the surplus material around the link, or chain drilling and chiselling. For a component of this size and shape there is little to choose between the two methods. If the stock material was thicker, chain drilling would be the better way. Figure 10.19 shows the additional holes that would have to be drilled whilst the blank was still set-up for drilling the two large holes.

Figure 10.20(a) shows how the surplus metal is removed using a cold chisel with the top of the vice jaw acting as a guide. Note that as in any chipping operation the following precautions must be observed:

1 wear safety glasses or goggles;

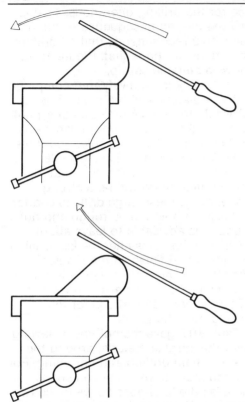

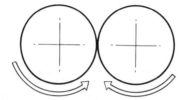

1. **Incorrect** — Filing up and over a radius requires an unnatural arm action. This results in an untrue curve

2. The action of generating a curve with a file is similar to two gears rotating when meshed together

3. **Correct** — Filing in this direction gives a natural arm action leading to a true curve.
   Note: The direction of the movement compared with the gears in (2)

Fig. 10.22 Filing – generation of a curve

(a) Socket head set or grub screw

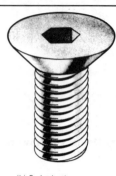

(b) Socket head countersunk screw

(c) Socket head cap screw

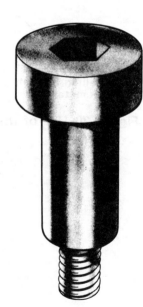

(d) Socket head shoulder screw

Fig. 10.23 Socket head screws

2 do not chip towards anyone else;
3 place a chipping screen in front of your vice.

Figure 10.20(b) shows the problems that can occur when the material is thick and how these problems can be overcome by using a special chisel made from a piece of H.S.S. (High Speed Steel) hacksaw blade.

For an illustration of how thin sheet metal can be cut at the vice using a shearing action between the vice jaw and the chisel see Fig. 10.8 on page 197.

The roughed out link is now completed by filing away the serrations left by the chain-drilling operation and finishing the component by draw filing. Filing the flat sides to blend with the rounded ends can be difficult and the use of a piece of old hard back hacksaw blade can be used as a guide as shown in Fig. 10.21.

The techniques of filing have already been introduced on page 198. Some difficulty is often encountered in filing the radii at the ends of a component of this shape and the correct technique is explained in Fig. 10.22. Finally the component should be de-burred and the sharp edges should be removed. It should then be checked for dimensional accuracy.

Screwed fastenings

Various types of screwed fastening are used where components must be assembled and dismantled regularly. The various screw thread systems, thread forms and the general proportions for hexagon bolts, nuts and plain washers have already been described in Chapter 3.

Some other types of screwed fastening will now be considered. Figure 10.23 shows a range of *socket head screws*. These are made from forged blanks and the threads are rolled, not cut. For a given size they are much stronger than machine cut, hexagon head bolts. The head can be sunk into counterbored holes to give a flush surface, and this improves the safety as well as the appearance of the assembly, although it increases the cost. These fixings are used extensively in jigs and fixtures, as well as in machine tools. Socket head screws are also known as

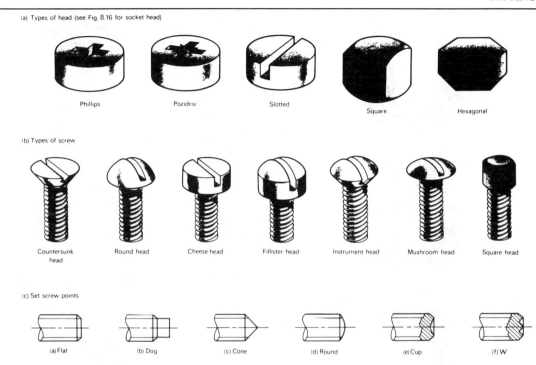

Fig. 10.24 Set screws

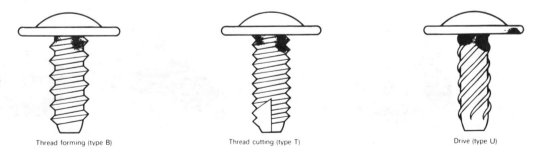

Fig. 10.25 Self-tapping screws

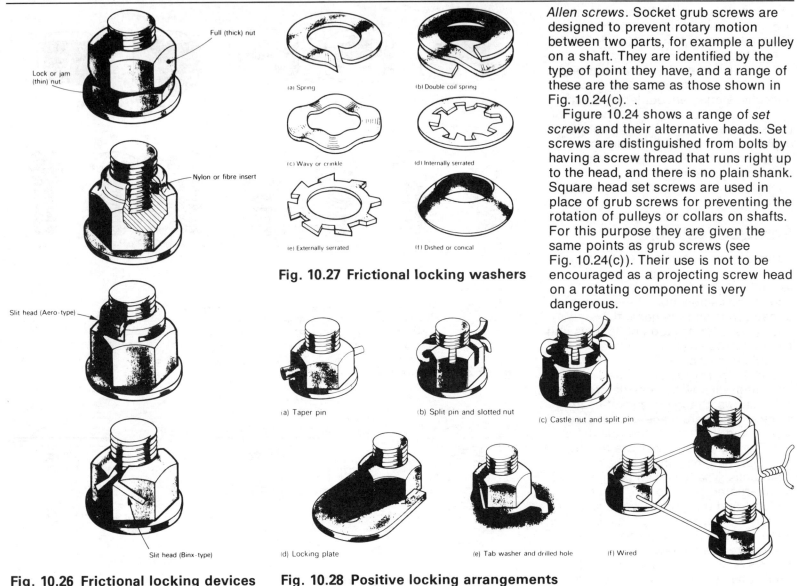

Fig. 10.27 Frictional locking washers

Fig. 10.26 Frictional locking devices

Fig. 10.28 Positive locking arrangements

Allen screws. Socket grub screws are designed to prevent rotary motion between two parts, for example a pulley on a shaft. They are identified by the type of point they have, and a range of these are the same as those shown in Fig. 10.24(c).

Figure 10.24 shows a range of *set screws* and their alternative heads. Set screws are distinguished from bolts by having a screw thread that runs right up to the head, and there is no plain shank. Square head set screws are used in place of grub screws for preventing the rotation of pulleys or collars on shafts. For this purpose they are given the same points as grub screws (see Fig. 10.24(c)). Their use is not to be encouraged as a projecting screw head on a rotating component is very dangerous.

Self tapping screws are shown in Fig. 10.25. They form their own thread in a previously drilled pilot hole. There are three basic types, which are shown in Fig. 10.25 and described below.

Type B The thread is formed as the material around the pilot hole is displaced. Type B screws are used for joining sheet metal, plastics and malleable non-ferrous metals.

Type T The thread is cut into the wall of the pilot hole. Type T screws can be used for joining a wide range of materials such as plastics, aluminium, brass, cast iron and sheet steel. Since the thread is formed by cutting and not by flow, the material into which they are inserted does not have to be ductile or malleable.

Type J These are *drive screws*. That is, they are hammered or forced into the pilot hole. They are suitable for plastics, aluminium, brass, cast iron and steel sheet.

Although all three types are shown with flanged heads to prevent them pulling through thin sheet metal or plastic, they are also available with the same types of head shown in Fig. 10.24.

Locking devices

To prevent screwed fastenings becoming loose because of vibration, various locking devices are employed. These can be classified as:
1 *frictional* locking devices;
2 *positive* locking devices.

Most threaded fasteners rely on friction. In service, these fasteners can be made more reliable if more friction is designed into the arrangement. This is achieved by using special frictional locking nuts, or by using a frictional locking washer instead of a plain washer.

Lock nut This is shown in Fig. 10.26(a). The lock nut, also known as a *thin nut* or a *jam nut*, is designed to jam or lock against a full nut. The stronger, full nut, takes all the tensile load; hence it is placed on top of the thin nut.

Insert nut This is shown in Fig. 10.26(b). A nylon or fibre insert squeezes into the threads as the nut is tightened and increases the stiffness of the nut.

Slit nut Two examples are shown in Figs. 10.26(c) and 10.26(d). The thread in the slit portion of the nut is slightly out of pitch with the main body of the nut. Considerable friction and stiffness is provided as the slit portion of the nut is sprung into pitch with the main body of the nut.

Spring washers These are used with conventional nuts, or under the heads of set pins and bolts where these are fitted into tapped holes. The washers collapse as the fastening is tightened and then attempt to spring back to shape. This forces the flanks of the mating threads together causing considerable friction. A range of spring lock washers is shown in Fig. 10.27.

Where there is excessive vibration, or personal danger from a fastener coming loose, as in the controls of a vehicle or aircraft, positive or mechanical locking arrangements are used (Fig. 10.28).

Use of screwed fastenings

Figure 10.29 shows some typical applications of screwed fastenings, which are described below.

Bolt and nut A section through a bolted joint is shown in Fig. 10.29(a). It will be seen that the joint line between the two components lies across the shank of the bolt to give maximum shear strength. *The joint must never lie across the thread of the bolt.*

Stud and nut This type of fixing is used where a joint is dismantled regularly. Most of the wear comes on the nut and stud, which can eventually be replaced cheaply. This prevents regular wear of the tapped holes in the casting or forging, which would be expensive to replace. See Fig. 10.29(b).

Cap head socket screws These are much more expensive than ordinary hexagon head bolts. This is because socket screws are made from high tensile steel, and they are heat treated to make them very strong, tough and wear resistant. They are widely used in the manufacture of machine tools. The example shown in Fig. 10.29(c) shows how the head is sunk into a counterbore to provide a flush surface.

Figure 10.30 shows a range of keys and spanners used for assembling and dismantling screwed fastenings. Spanners are carefully proportioned so that their length enables a man of normal strength to tighten the fastening correctly. A spanner that is too long will provide too much leaverage, and the fastening will be weakened or

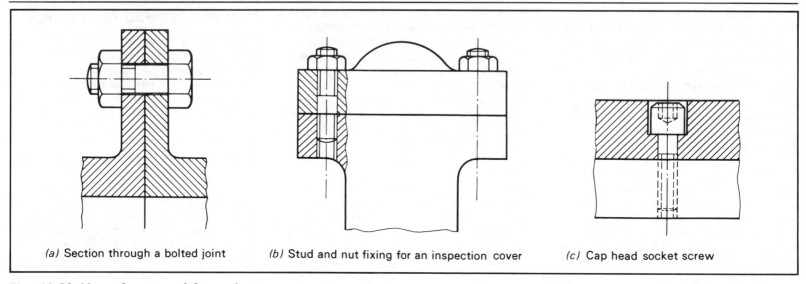

Fig. 10.29 Use of screwed fastenings

may even break off. This is why a spanner should never be lengthened with a piece of tube. The exception to this is the larger size of socket screw key in which the length of the key is deliberately shortened so that it can be used in restricted spaces. Here a short length of conduit may be slipped over the key to provide a more comfortable grip as well as increased leaverage.

In order to ensure that critical screwed fastenings are tightened correctly, a *torque spanner* should be used. Figure 10.31 shows such a spanner. Torque spanners fall into two categories. One type uses a slipping clutch. This can be set to slip when the nut is correctly tightened, and prevents

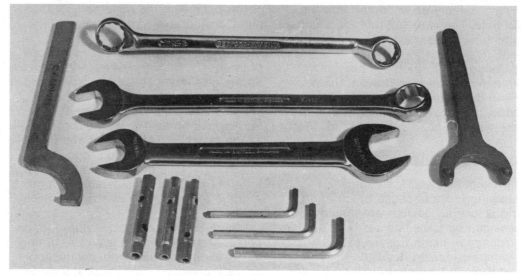

Fig. 10.30 Keys and spanners

over-tightening. The other type has a spring-loaded handle as shown in Fig. 10.31. The pointer indicates the torque being exerted on the nut on a scale. This relies heavily on the skill of the fitter for its correct functioning. However, it is much cheaper and simpler in construction.

Screw thread taps and dies

Screw thread taps are used to cut internal threads in engineering components. Figure 10.32 shows the essential features of a tap and also the three taps that make up a set of taps. In a cheap set, the difference between the taper, second and plug tap is only the length of the taper lead. In a good set of ground thread taps, the thread form is also reduced in diameter on the taper tap. This allows the second and plug taps to clean up the thread initially cut and produce a thread with a good surface finish. The cutting action of the tap has already been discussed on page 182.

The tap is rotated by means of a tap wrench. This should be selected to suit the size of the tap. Too small a wrench results in excessive force being used to turn the tap. Too large a wrench results in lack of 'feel'. In either case there is lack of proper control that will result in a broken tap. Figure 10.33 shows a selection of typical tap wrenches.

It is essential that the tap is aligned with the tapping size hole both axially and radially. Radial alignment is controlled by the taper and, if present,

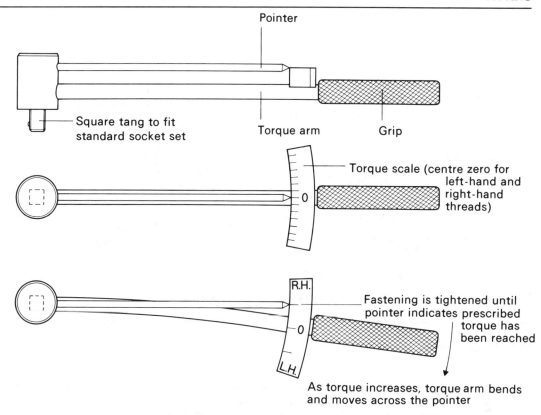

Fig. 10.31 Typical torque spanner

the pilot. Axial alignment is under the control of the fitter. If the tap is started with lack of alignment a defective thread will be cut. In a thick component, the forces on the tap will become unbalanced and the tap will break in the hole.

Screw thread dies are used to cut external threads on engineering components. The split button die is most widely used by the fitter, and a typical example together with the die stock is shown in Fig. 10.34. This type of die can also be used in the tailstock die holder of the centre lathe (page 269). It will be seen that the die has three adjusting screws. The centre screw spreads the die and reduces the depth of cut, while the outer screws close the die and increase the depth of cut.

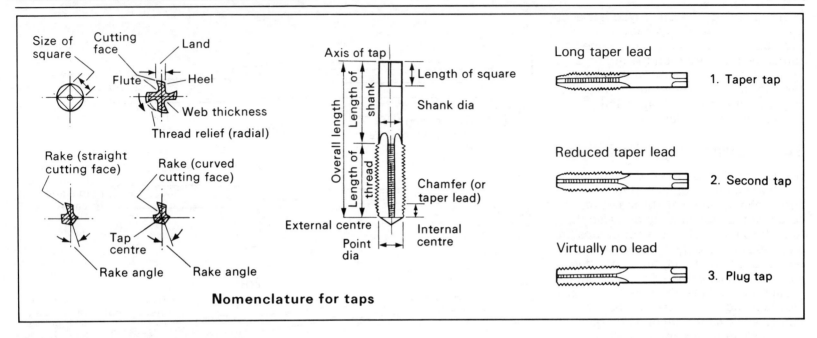

Fig. 10.32 Screw thread taps

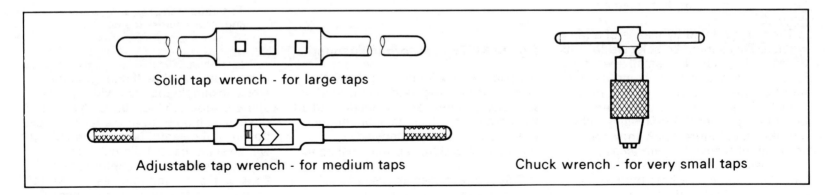

Fig. 10.33 Tap wrenches

Table 10.4 Screw Thread Tables

ISO PRECISION FINE THREADS — ALL DIMENSIONS IN MILLIMETRES

Nominal size and thread diameter- first choice	Pitch of thread	Major Diameter	Effective Diameter	Minor Diameter (external)	Minor Diameter (internal)	HEXAGON* Across flats (Max)	HEXAGON* Across corners (Max)
M 8	1·00	8·00	7·35	6·77	6·92	13·00	15·00
M 10	1·25	10·00	9·19	8·47	8·65	17·00	19·6
M 12	1·25	12·00	11·19	10·47	10·65	19·00	21·9
M 16	1·50	16·00	15·03	14·16	14·38	24·00	27·7
M 20	1·50	20·00	19·03	18·16	18·38	30·00	34·6
M 24	2·00	24·00	22·70	21·55	21·84	36·00	41·6
M 30	2·00	30·00	28·70	27·55	27·84	46·00	53·1
M 36	3·00	36·00	34·05	32·32	32·75	55·00	63·5
M 42	3·00	42·00	40·05	38·32	38·75	65·00	75·1
M 48	3·00	48·00	46·05	44·32	44·75	75·00	86·6
M 56	4·00	56·00	53·40	51·09	51·67	Not listed	Not listed
M 64	4·00	64·00	61·40	59·09	59·67	Not listed	Not listed

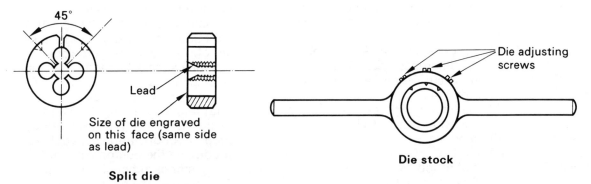
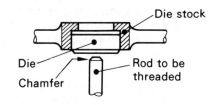

Fig. 10.34 Dies and die-stock

It is difficult to control a screw threading die, and any attempt to cut a full thread in one pass of the die usually results in a 'drunken' thread with a poor finish. A first, shallow cut should be taken with the die spread open by the centre screw. This is followed by one or more finishing cuts with the outer screws gradually closed down until the thread is a correct fit in the nut.

The forces acting on the teeth of a tap or a die are very great, and ordinary lubricating oils are of little use when cutting screw threads. An extreme pressure lubricant such as tallow is the most suitable lubricant for cutting threads by hand.

Screw thread tables

Table 10.4 gives an abstract from the ISO (International Standards Organisation) Precision Metric Fine Threads. All the dimensions given are in millimetres. Such information is invaluable to the engineer and is available in various tables and pocket-books that the fitter and machinist should always have. The difference between the minor diameter (external) and the minor diameter (internal) is the clearance between the crest of the thread in the nut and the root of the thread on the bolt.

Example Select a suitable tapping size drill for an M8 fine thread.

Solution From Table 10.4 it will be seen that the minor diameter (internal) for an M8 thread is 6·92 mm. Reference to metric drill tables shows that the nearest preferred sizes are 6·70 mm to 7·50 mm in steps of 0·1 mm for parallel shank jobber twist drills. Therefore the nearest size would be 6·9 mm or 7·0 mm. It is always better to go up a size than be under size, to prevent a torn thread. Therefore the 7·0 mm drill would be used with a negligible loss of strength.

Exercises

1. State *two* differences between a fitters bench vice and a machine vice.
   (*WAEC* 1974)
2. Sketch, in good proportion, the following types of cold chisel and describe their uses.
   a) flat chisel
   b) half-round chisel
   c) diamond point chisel
   d) cross-cut chisel
   State the safety precautions that should be taken when using a cold chisel.
3. a) With the aid of a sketch, show the difference between a cross-cut file and a single-cut (float) file.
   b) Sketch, in good proportion, the following types of file:
   (i) hand file
   (ii) flat file
   (iii) half-round file
   (iv) three-square file
4. a) State the *three* features by which a file is specified.
   b) State *three* precautions that must be taken to keep a file in good condition and cutting properly.
5. a) State the *two* features by which a hacksaw blade is specified.
   b) Show, with the aid of sketches, the *two* methods by which 'set' is applied to the teeth of hacksaw blades.
   c) What factors influence the choice of a particular type of hacksaw blade?
6. a) List the *three* types of screw-cutting tap that make a set and describe the difference between them.
   b) What is the purpose of the split in a circular (button) die?
   (*WAEC* 1974)
7. Explain the difference between 'self tapping' and 'drive' screws and describe where each type is used.
8. Sketch, in good proportion, *two* frictional locking devices and *three* positive locking devices.
9. Explain what is meant by an M10 × 1·5 thread, and describe with the aid of sketches how you would produce such a thread in a 20 mm thick plate using a drilling machine and hand tools.
10. With reference to Fig. 7.22 and using the headings shown below, prepare an operation schedule for producing the component shown, using standard bench tools only. Assume that the blank has already been marked out.

No	Operation	Equipment used

11. Sheet metal working

The skilled sheet metal worker is a specialist craftsman of the highest order. He can take a flat sheet of metal and beat it and roll it into the compound curves of, for example, a motor car mudguard. Any attempt to describe all the techniques available to him would fill this book many times over. Usually, however, the mechanical engineer is only called upon to understand and use the most basic of these techniques.

Cutting tools

Sheet metal is cut with shears. These range from hand shears, or tin snips, to power guillotines capable of slicing through 6 mm thick plate. Their principle of operation was discussed on page 185.

Hand shears

These are used for tin plate and thin sheet metal up to about 1 mm in thickness. Hand shears are made in various shapes so that both flat and curved surfaces can be cut out easily. A selection of shears is shown in Fig. 11.1(a).

Bench shears

Although hand operated, the force acting on the shear blades is magnified

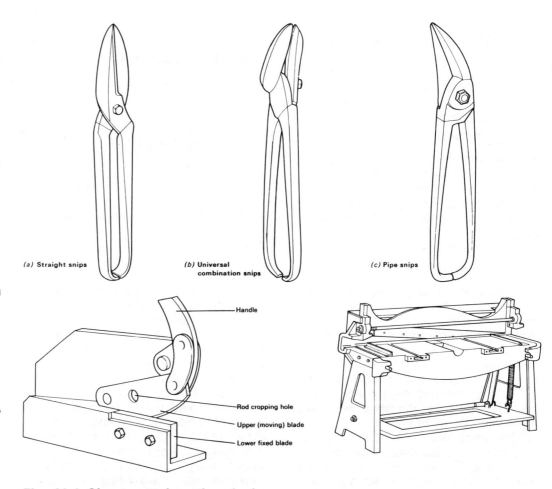

Fig. 11.1 Sheet metal cutting devices

by a system of levers. This enables thicker sheets up to 3 mm thick to be cut. Figure 11.1(b) shows typical bench shears.

Guillotine shears

These are used for rapidly breaking down large sheets into strips and rectangular blanks. They cannot be used for cutting curved profiles. Treadle-operated shears can cut sheets up to 1·5 mm thick by 1 m in length at each stroke. Figure 11.1(c) shows a typical treadle-operated guillotine shear.

Hole punching

It will be shown on page 254 that drilling holes in thin sheet metal is not only difficult but it can be dangerous as well. The alternative and superior techniques available for producing holes in sheet metal are:
1 trepanning (see page 244);
2 hole sawing (see page 246);
3 hole punching.

For thin sheet metal, the punched hole is superior for roundness, accuracy and finish. The blank or stock metal has a shearing force exerted on it by the punch and die. The principle of hole punching is shown in Fig. 11.2. The hole diameter is equal to the punch diameter.

There are various ways in which holes may be punched in thin sheet metal and these are described below.

Simple press tool A simple press tool may have to be used as shown in Fig. 11.3(a). The force required to close the tool and pierce the sheet is provided by the fly press shown in Fig. 11.3(b).

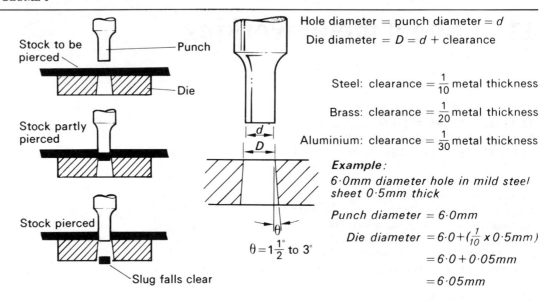

Fig. 11.2 Theory of hole punching

Hole diameter = punch diameter = d

Die diameter = $D = d$ + clearance

Steel: clearance = $\frac{1}{10}$ metal thickness

Brass: clearance = $\frac{1}{20}$ metal thickness

Aluminium: clearance = $\frac{1}{30}$ metal thickness

Example:

6·0mm diameter hole in mild steel sheet 0·5mm thick

Punch diameter = 6·0mm

Die diameter = $6·0 + (\frac{1}{10} \times 0·5mm)$

= $6·0 + 0·05mm$

= $6·05mm$

The kinetic energy of the rotating 'fly' (with or without the addition of heavy iron balls on the 'horns' of the fly) causes the ram of the press to descend by means of a multi-start screw and nut. A medium size hand press (No. 3) can exert a closing pressure of 20 kN with an average effort on the fly handle. Details of the simple press tool are shown in Chapter 2.

Chassis or erector's punch For punching holes in previously fabricated panels, the piercing tool and press shown in Fig. 11.3 is not convenient, and the chassis or erector's punch shown in Fig. 11.4 should be used. A pilot hole that is larger than the draw bolt is drilled first and this can be relatively rough. The punch and die are sited on each side of the panel to be pierced; the draw bolt is passed through the die and screwed into the punch. As the draw bolt is tightened up, it closes the punch and die and provides the shearing force to pierce the hole.

Safety

Bench and guillotine shears are designed to slice through sheet steel with ease. They will also slice through flesh and bone with ease. Never use shearing machines or hole punching tools unless:
1 you have been fully instructed in their use;

SHEET METAL WORKING

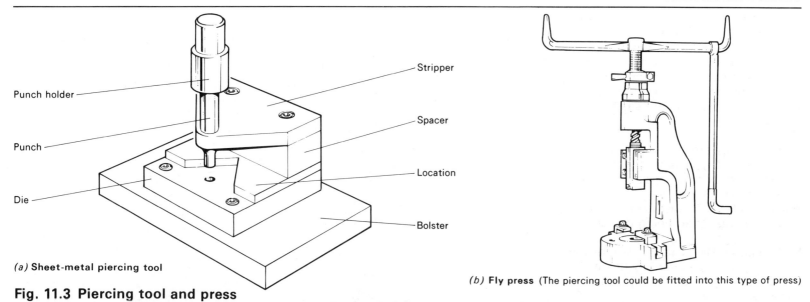

(a) Sheet-metal piercing tool

(b) **Fly press** (The piercing tool could be fitted into this type of press)

Fig. 11.3 Piercing tool and press

2　you have permission to use them;
3　appropriate guards are in place.

Hand forming tools

The full range of tools will not be described: only those necessary for the operations described in the next section of this chapter will be considered.

Hammers and mallets

A selection of these is shown in Fig. 11.5(a) on page 218.

Tinman's mandrel

This is shown in Fig. 11.5(b). It is made of steel and has one square end and one half-round end. The square end is used for forming and riveting rectangular

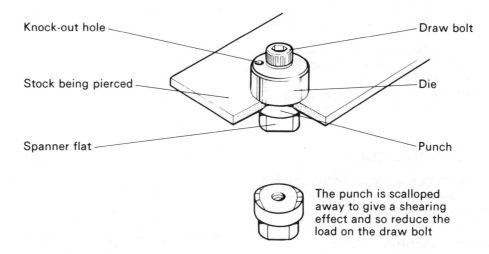

The punch is scalloped away to give a shearing effect and so reduce the load on the draw bolt

Fig. 11.4 Chassis or erector's punch

217

work, and the half-round end is used for circular and curved work.

The square end also contains a tapered hole for holding stakes and bick irons (see below). The mandrel is firmly attached to the bench by strap clamps so that it can be reversed easily.

Stakes

Some of these are shown in Fig. 11.5(c). As only folded work is being considered at this stage, bossing or panel beating heads have been omitted.

Hatchet stake   This is used for tucking in wired joints, sharpening bends and dressing edges.

Half-moon stake   This is used for the same operations as the hatchet stake when they are needed on curved surfaces.

Bick iron   This is used to support the hammer or mallet blow while shaping hollow and tapered work, knocking up, wiring and dressing edges.

Funnel and side stake   This is used for supporting conical and cylindrically shaped components.

Creasing iron   This is used for swaging small work, and hand wiring flat sheets. It is also used for forming hinges.

Forming machines

In this section, a range of hand operated forming machines are considered. For larger work and thicker materials, power operated machines are available.

Folding machine

Folding bars for use in a vice are only

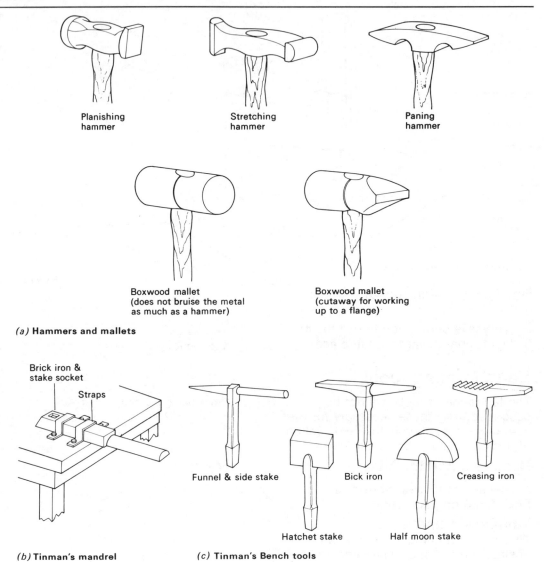

Fig. 11.5 Sheet metal equipment bench

SHEET METAL WORKING

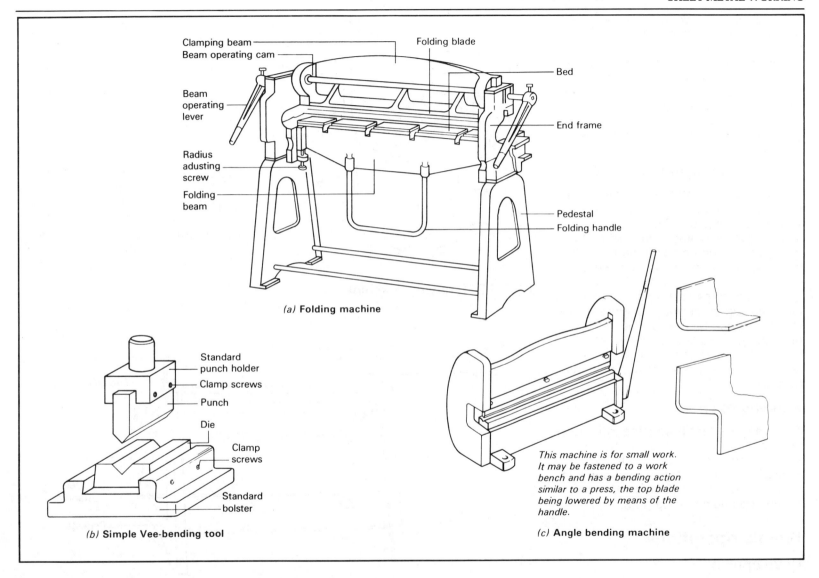

Fig. 11.6 Bending machines

suitable for short work. For larger work the folding machine shown in Fig. 11.6(a) is used.

Alternatively, pressure bending tools may be used. These consist of a 'vee' punch and die as shown in Fig. 11.6(b) which can be mounted in a fly press for short work. For longer work the angle bending machine shown in Fig. 11.6(c) may be used.

Universal Jennying machine

This is a very versatile bench-mounted machine that can be used for swaging, wiring, and jennying. The rollers on the spindle can be changed according to the operation being performed. The machine and its rollers are shown in Fig. 11.7.

The operations performed on this machine can be performed successfully with the bench tools described previously. However, once it is set up, the machine is quicker, and it is used when a number of similar components have to be made.

Bending rollers

These are used for producing cylindrical components. The grooves at the end of the top and bottom rollers enable previously wired or folded components to be rolled without damage. Bending rollers are shown in Fig. 11.8.

Simple operations

Development

Consider the template box shown in

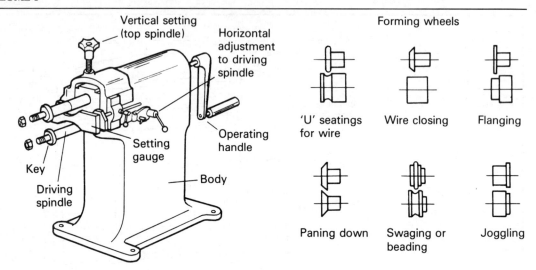

Fig. 11.7 Jennying machine

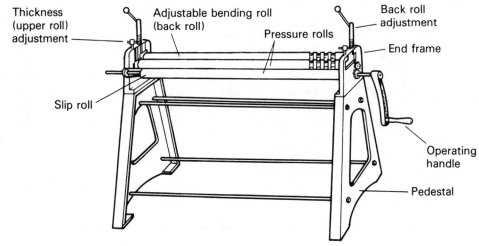

Fig. 11.8 Bending rolls

SHEET METAL WORKING

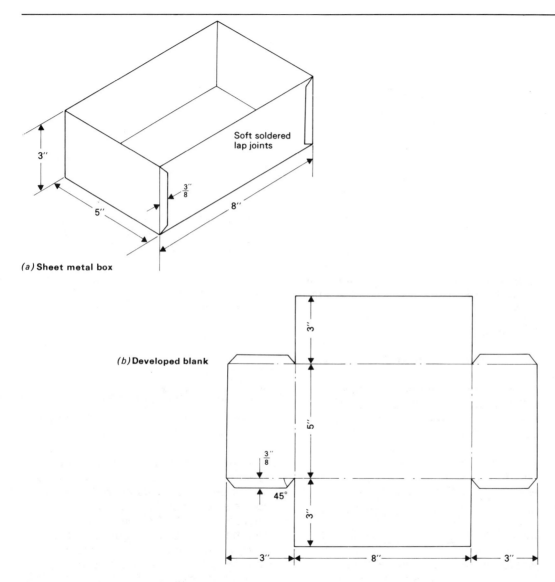

Fig. 11.9 Layout for forming a box

Fig. 11.9(a). Before this box can be made, its shape must be cut from a flat sheet of metal as shown in Fig. 11.9(b). This flat shape is called the *developed blank*. If a number of boxes are to be made, it is wasteful to draw out the blank from first principles each time. In this case a pattern or template is first produced (see Chapter 7). This may be in stiff sheet metal, hardboard or thin plywood. It is laid on the sheet from which the blank is to be cut and a scriber is run round the edge of the pattern.

Folded edge (bending)

The tin box shown in Fig. 11.9(a) would not be very pleasant to use. It would lack rigidity, and the edges would be sharp and dangerous. One way of stiffening up the edges and making them safe is shown in Fig. 11.10(a).

Wired edge

This is a superior method of finishing an edge, but requires more skill to produce than the folded edge previously described. The stages in wiring an edge are shown in Fig. 11.10(b).

Folded joints (self-secured)

The different types of self-secured joints and their advantages, limitations and applications will be discussed on page 222. The technique of forming a grooved seam, as shown in Fig. 11.11 (page 223), will now be considered.
1 The edges are folded to form 'locks'. There are two methods of doing this. The joint edges may be folded over and

slightly closed (the gap being a little wider than the thickness of metal that it has to accommodate). Edges prepared in this manner present no interlocking problems when making seams on 'flat' surfaces, as shown in Fig. 11.11(d).

Alternatively, the joint edges are folded over to an approximate angle of 60°. Edges prepared in this manner are better for interlocking seams on cylindrical articles of small diameter, as shown in Fig. 11.11(e).

2 The two 'locks' (one up and one down) are hooked together, as shown in Fig. 11.11(b).

3 The joint is finally secured (locked together) using a grooving tool as shown in Fig. 11.11(c). A different width of grooving tool is required for each width of joint being secured.

The *paned down* joint, used for joining two cylindrical components, is shown in Fig. 11.12(a). The *knocked up* joint, used for sealing the ends of cylindrical components, is shown in Fig. 11.12(b).

The cylindrical joints shown in Figs. 11.12(a) and (b) require a knowledge of flanging as a preliminary operation. A method of flanging a component is shown in Fig. 11.12(c).

Simple bend allowance

When metal is formed by bending, allowance has to be made for the corner. This allowance will depend upon the radius of the corner and the thickness of the material.

Figure 11.13 shows the development

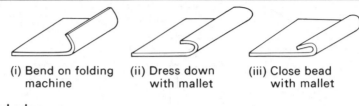

(a) **Beaded edge**

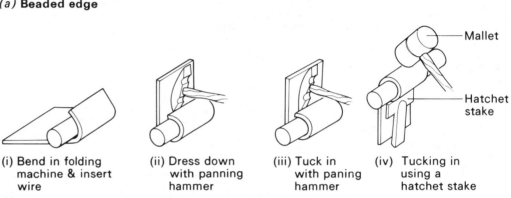

(b) **Wired edge**

Fig. 11.10 Beading and wiring edges

of blanks for components with acute, reflex, and right angle bends. It will be seen that the developed length is made up of the developed corner (DC) plus the unaffected metal (A and B) each side of the corner (see page 224).

Length of blank = A + B + DC
where: DC = $\theta/360 \times 2\pi R$
but: $\dfrac{2\pi}{360}$ = 0·0175 (constant)
therefore: DC = $\theta \times R \times 0\cdot 0175$

where: θ = 180° – angle of bend
R = values given in Fig. 11.13.

Self-secured joints

These joints are formed by folding and interlocking thin sheet metal edges together so that they are **made secure** without an additional jointing process. Their use is confined to fabrications or components constructed with light gauge sheet metal less than 1·6 mm thick. Figure 11.14 shows some commonly used self-secured joints.

Very often self-secured joints are employed in the manufacture of containers that have to hold foodstuffs and liquids. In this case it is necessary

SHEET METAL WORKING

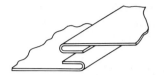 

(a) Edges of joint folded to form 'Locks'

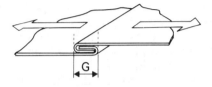 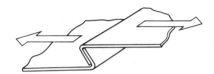

(b) Folded edges interlocked (G represents the width of Groove)

Top and bottom sections flanged

Flange dressed up   Flange paned down

(a) Paned down joint

(b) Knocked up joint

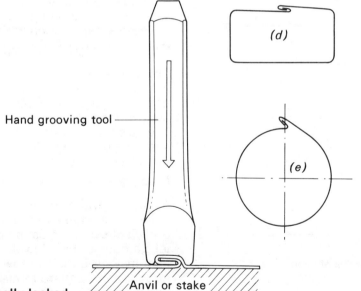

(c) Joint finally locked

Fig. 11.11 The grooved seam

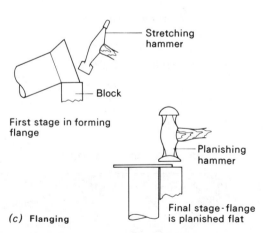

(c) Flanging

Fig. 11.12 Paned down and knocked up joints

Development of blanks for components with acute, reflex or right angular bends

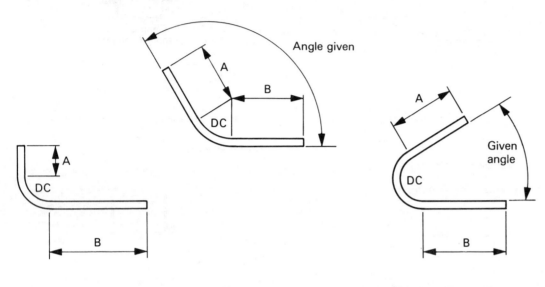

Material thickness			Approx. 'R' value
S.W.G.	Inches	mm.	
1 / 10	.300 / .128	7.620 / 3.251	½ stock thickness + inside radius of bend
11 / 18	.116 / .048	2.346 / 1.219	stock thickness + inside radius of bend
19 / 30	.040 / .0124	1.016 / 0.315	⅓ stock thickness + inside radius of bend

Fig. 11.13 Bend allowance

to seal the joints and seams. Latex rubber inserts, and soft solder with a high tin content are used.

Riveted joints

Riveting is a method of making permanent joints. The process consists of drilling or punching the plates to be riveted, inserting the rivet, then closing it by an applied compression force so that it completely fills the hole and forms a rigid joint.

A variety of riveted joints is used in construction and fabrication work:
1   single riveted lap joint;
2   double riveted lap joint;
3   single-strap butt joint;
4   double-strap butt joint.

These are illustrated in Fig. 11.15.

Single riveted lap joint

This is the simplest of all riveted joints and is widely used for joining both thick and thin plates. The plates to be joined are overlapped by a short distance. Then a single row of rivets, conveniently spaced along the middle of the lap, completes the joint.

Double riveted lap joint

A lap joint with two rows of rivets is known as a *double riveted lap joint*. Sufficient overlap must be provided to take a double row of rivets. This type of joint may have the two rows of rivets arranged in a square formation. This is known as *chain riveting*. If the rivets are arranged diagonally to form triangles, this is called *zig-zag riveting*.

SHEET METAL WORKING

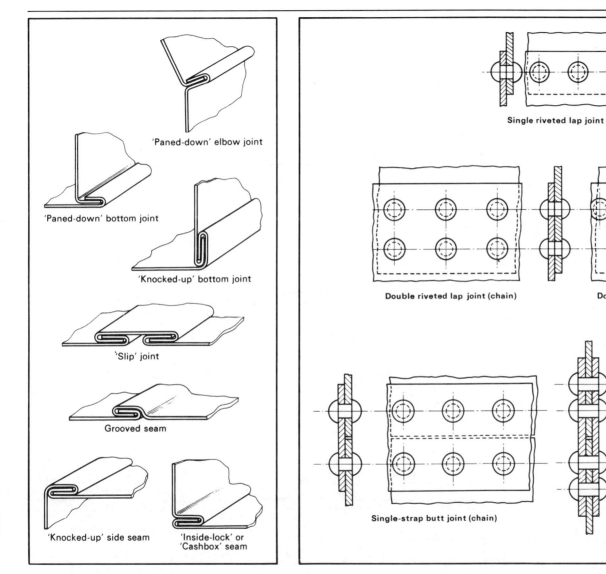

Fig. 11.14 Self secured joints

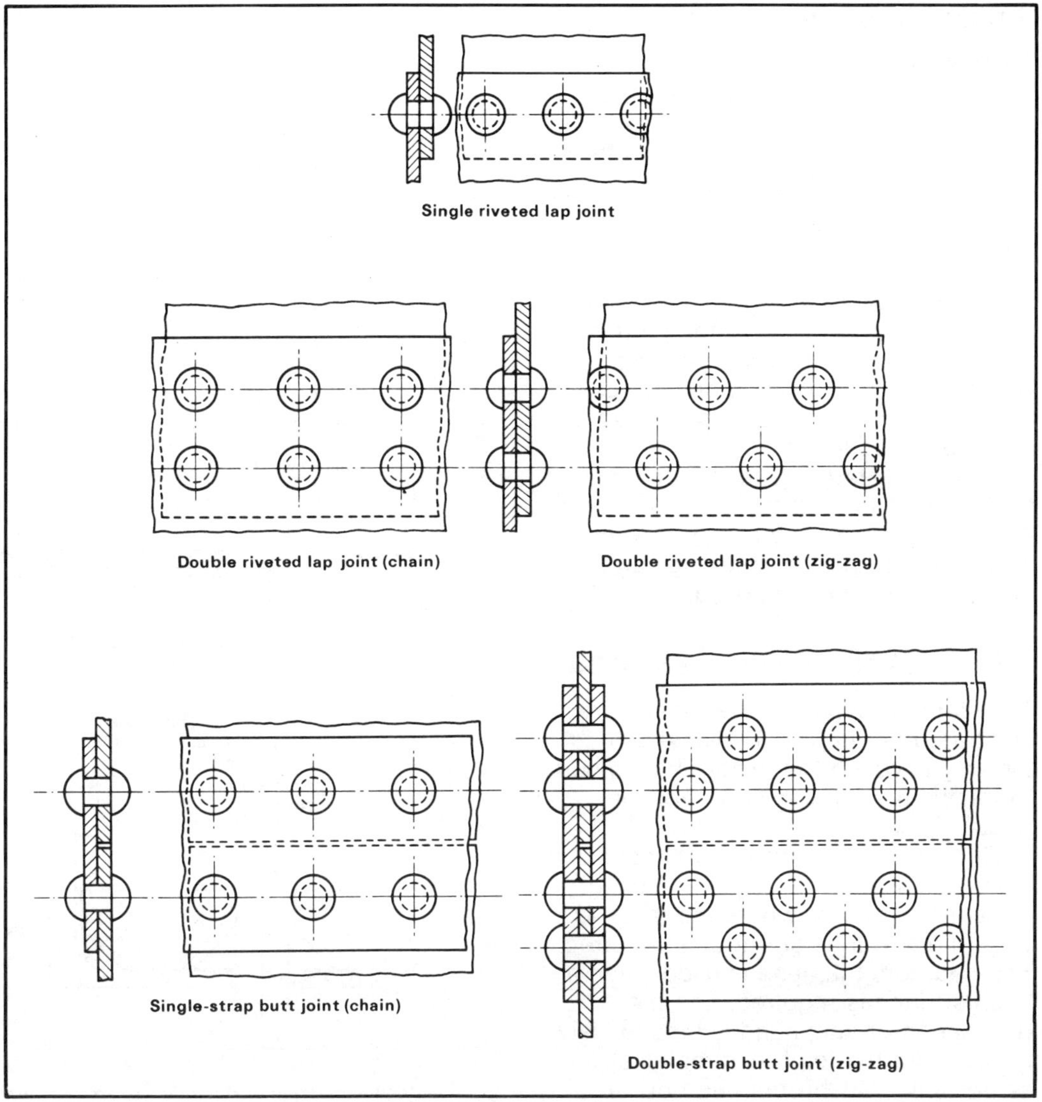

Fig. 11.15 Types of riveted joint

Single-strap butt joint

To make a riveted butt joint it is necessary to use a separate piece of metal called a *strap* to join the two component edges. The arrangement of this strap is shown in Fig. 11.15 on page 225.

Double-strap butt joint

When two cover plates are riveted on either side of a butt joint, the joint is known as a *double-strap butt joint*. When single or double straps are used for riveted butt joints the rivets may be arranged as follows:
1 *Single riveted*: One row of rivets on each side of the butt;
2 *Double, triple or quadruple riveted*: in which case the chain or zig-zag formation may be employed.

Types of rivet and rivet-head

The standard types of rivet heads are illustrated in Fig. 11.16. Also shown is the way in which thin material is joined to thick material with countersunk rivets.

Tinners (see below) and flat-head rivets are used in most general sheet metal fabrications, where the metal is very thin and little strength is required. The countersunk head is used when a flush surface is required, and the roundhead or snaphead is most widely used where the joint must be as strong as possible. Mushroom head or 'knobbled' rivets, as they are called in the steel construction industry, are used

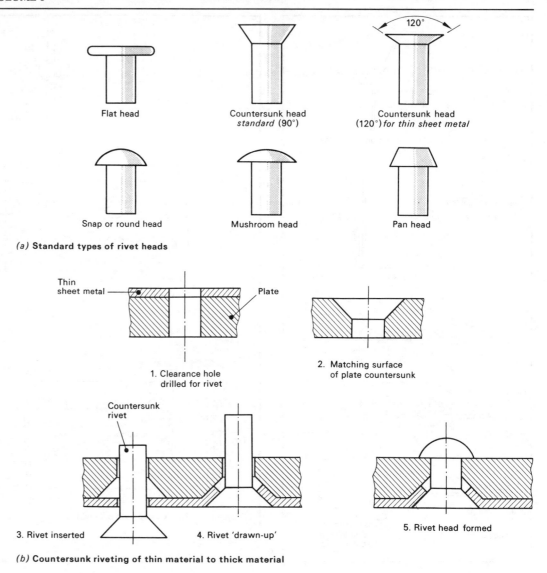

(a) Standard types of rivet heads

(b) Countersunk riveting of thin material to thick material

Fig. 11.16 Rivet heads and applications

SHEET METAL WORKING

where it is important that the rivet head does not stick up above the surface too much. They are used on outer fuselage 'skins' of aircraft in order to decrease 'drag'. In the case of steel chutes and bunkers they are used to reduce obstruction on the inside surfaces. Pan head rivets are very strong and are widely used for girders and heavy constructional engineering.

'Tinners' are similar to flat-head rivets. They are made of soft iron and are usually coated with tin to prevent corrosion and to make them easier to soft solder.

Always use the correct rivet for a particular metal to be riveted. When riveting aluminium, for example, use aluminium rivets; and when riveting copper use copper rivets.

Defects in riveted joints

When making joints with rivets, the following points should be followed to prevent many common defects:
1 use the correct allowance for edge clearance and pitch when marking out;
2 all drilled or punched holes should be made to the correct clearance size to suit the rivet diameter, or as specified on the drawing;
3 remove any 'burrs' from around the edges of all holes before finally assembling the parts to be joined;
4 ensure that holes are correctly aligned and matched before inserting the rivet;
5 use the proper type of rivet as specified on the drawing;
6 use rivets of the correct length;
7 when inserting rivets, do not attempt to force or drive them into the hole;
8 always use the correct tools for the job.

Some of the common forms of defects associated with riveted connections are illustrated in Fig. 11.17.

Soft soldering

Soft soldering is a low temperature thermal process in which the metal of the components being joined is not melted. The process involves the use of a suitable low-melting-temperature alloy of tin and lead. This is bonded by heat and a suitable flux to an unmelted parent metal. Therefore, soft solders must have a lower melting point than the metals they join.

In a soft soldered joint each of the joint surfaces is *tinned* by a film of solder. Tinning means applying an even coat of *solder* to a surface. The two films of solder are made to *fuse* with the solder filling the space between them.

When a soft solder is applied to a prepared metal joint that has been heated to a required temperature, it:
1 flows between the surfaces of the joint, which remain unmelted;
2 completely fills the space between the surfaces;
3 adheres thoroughly to the surfaces;
4 solidifies.

A definite chemical reaction takes place when metals such as brass, steel and copper are tinned correctly. The metal surface, and the tin in the solder, react together to form an 'intermetallic compound' which can be examined under a microscope. This acts as a 'key' for most of the solder in the joint.

The intermetallic compound layer gets thicker if the joint is kept at the soldering temperature. Solder cannot be completely wiped, drained or mechanically prised off the parent metal when in the molten state. The parent metal surface remains permanently wetted or 'tinned' by a film of a solder.

In general there are two stages in making a soft-soldered joint:
1 tinning the metal surfaces;
2 filling the spaces between the tinned surfaces with solder.

These stages are shown in Fig. 11.18. The metal to be soldered is supported on a wood or asbestos block (heat insulator). This prevents unecessary heat loss from the joint by conduction.

Table 11.1 on page 229 gives a selection of typical soft solders in general use, together with their properties and uses. The complete list is to be found in BS 219: 1959.

The 'tinning action' of solder cannot take place unless the two surfaces to be joined are *chemically* clean. This means that the surfaces must be free of oxide film, as well as dirt and grease.

Bare metal should be exposed at the mating or joining surfaces before starting any thermal joining process. This includes soft soldering, brazing or welding. Dirt, grease, oils and oxides cannot be soldered and act as barriers between the molten solder and the metal surfaces to be joined.

CAUSE OF RIVETING DEFECT	RESULTANT EFFECT	CAUSE OF RIVETING DEFECT	RESULTANT EFFECT
Sheets not closed together — rivet not drawn up sufficiently	Weak joint. Rivet shank swells between the plates Not enough shank protruding to form correctly shaped head	Rivet too short	Not enough shank protruding to produce a correctly shaped head Plate surface damaged Countersinking not completely filled
Rivet holes not matched	Weak mis-shapen head Rivet deformed and does not completely fill the hole	Rivet too long	Too much shank protruding to form required head 'Flash' formed around head (Jockey cap) Countersinking over-filled
Insufficient hole clearance	Rivet not completely 'drawn through'. Not enough shank protruding to form head  Original head of rivet 'stands proud', the formed head is weak and mis-shapened	Rivet set or dolly not struck square	Badly shaped head - off centre Sheet damaged by riveting tool
Hole too large for rivet	Hole not filled  Rivet tends to bend and deform. Head weak and poorly shaped	Drilling burrs not removed	Not enough shank protruding to form the correct size head 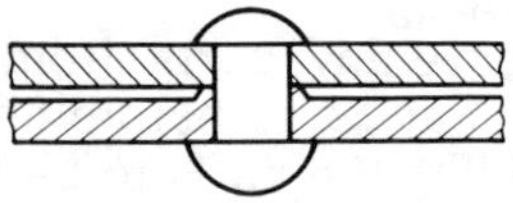 Plates or sheets not closed together. Unequal heads

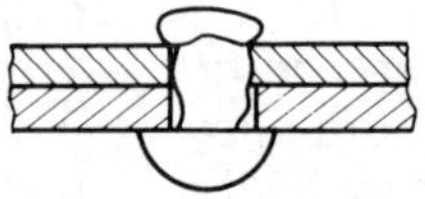

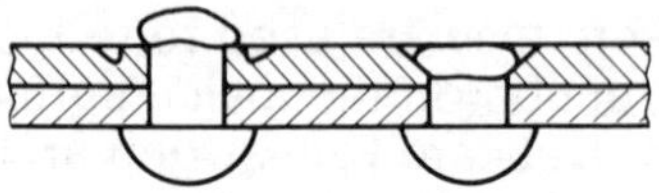

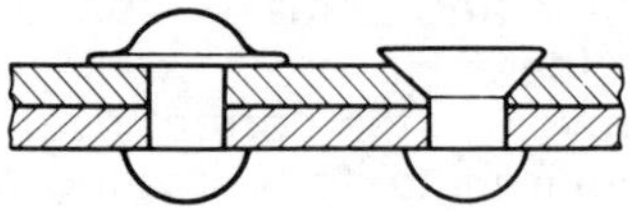

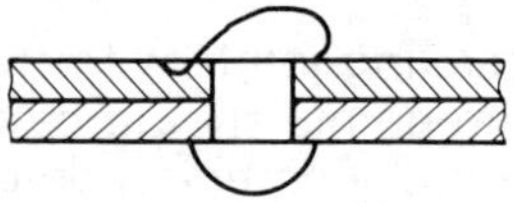

Fig. 11.17 Common defects in riveting

SHEET METAL WORKING

*The metal to be soldered is supported on a wooden block (**heat insulator**) to prevent unnecessary heat loss by **conduction***

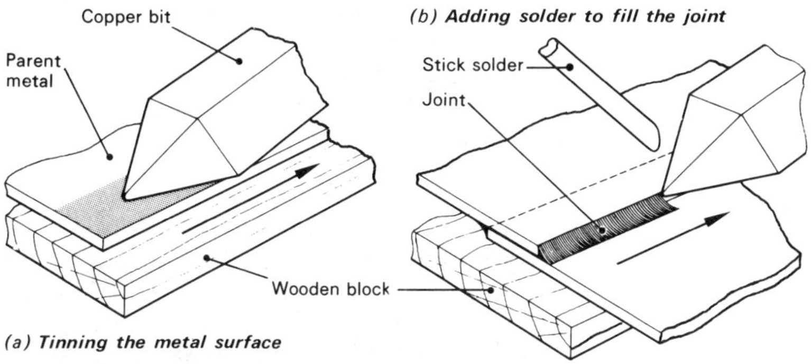

Fig. 11.18 Basic stages in soft soldering

(a) Tinning the metal surface
(b) Adding solder to fill the joint

Soldering fluxes

When a metal is cleaned and exposed to the air at room temperature, it acquires a thin oxide coating within a few minutes. Oxygen combines with metals to form oxides even more rapidly at high temperatures. These oxides must be prevented from **forming** as the metal is reheated to the soldering temperature. A soldering flux is used for this purpose.

The requirements of a good flux are:
1. it must remain liquid at the soldering temperature;
2. it must act as a cover over the joint in its liquid state and exclude the air;
3. it must dissolve any oxide film that is on the surfaces being joined;
4. it should be readily displaced from the joint surfaces by the molten solder.

Figure 11.19 shows the essential functions of a soldering flux: how it removes the oxide, prevents more oxide from forming and allows the molten solder to 'wet' the surface of the joint. A molten solder is said to 'wet' a surface when it leaves a continuous, permanent film. It must not **form** globules and roll off (see page 230).

Fluxes used for soft soldering operations may be classified as:
1 active; 2 inactive (passive).

1 Active fluxes

The active fluxes dissolve the oxide film on a metal quickly. At the same time, they prevent further oxidation. Unfortunately all active fluxes leave a corrosive residue along the edges of the joint after soldering. These flux residues are *hygroscopic*. This means that they absorb water from the atmosphere. As soon as the residue becomes damp, it corrodes the metal. If an active flux has to be used, the workpiece must be washed clean after soldering.

2 Passive fluxes

Electrical and some other work cannot

Table 11.1 Types of solder

B.S. Solder	Composition %			Melting range (°C)	Remarks
	Tin	Lead	Antimony		
A	65	34.4	0.6	183–185	Free running solder ideal for soldering electronic and instrument assemblies. Commonly referred to as **electrician's solder**.
K	60	39.5	0.5	183–188	Used for high-class tinsmith's work, and is known as **tinman's solder**.
F	50	49.5	0.5	183–212	Used for general soldering work in coppersmithing and sheet metal work.
G	40	59.6	0.4	183–234	**Blow-pipe solder.** This is supplied in strip form with a D cross-section 0.3 mm wide.
J	30	69.7	0.3	183–255	**Plumber's solder.** Because of its wide melting range this solder becomes 'pasty' and can be moulded and wiped.

A molten solder is said to 'wet' when it leaves a continuous permanent film on the surface of the parent metal instead of rolling over it.

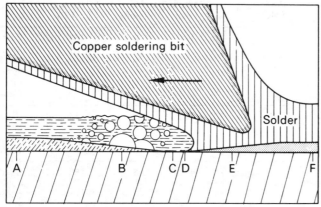

(Courtesy: Tin Research Institute)

Diagrammatic representation of the displacement of flux by molten solder.

A Flux solution lying above oxidised metal surface.
B Boiling flux solution removing the film of oxide (e.g. as chloride).
C Bare metal in contact with fused flux.
D Liquid solder displacing fused flux.
E Tin reacting with the basis metal to form compound.
F Solder solidifying.

Fig. 11.19 The essential functions of a soldering flux

be washed effectively after soldering. In these situations, passive fluxes are used. These prevent oxidation during soldering, but will not remove oxide already present on the joint faces. The faces have to be prepared by mechanical cleaning.

Types of soldered joints

Soft soldering, as a joining method, relies almost entirely on adhesion for its strength. Soft-soldered joints are at their strongest at room temperature. Their mechanical strength decreases rapidly as the temperature increases. The strength of a soft soldered joint is determined by three basic factors.
1 The strength of the solder itself. This depends on its composition (i.e. the ratio of tin to lead). Surplus solder does not add strength to the joint.
2 The strength of the bond between the bulk of the solder and the surfaces that it 'tins', i.e. the joint interfaces.
3 The design of the joint. Where strong joints are required, the joint edges may be interlocked before soldering. (See the self-secured joints section on page 222).

The three most common soldering operations are: *tacking, sweating* and *floating*.

Tacking

The process of tacking is shown in Fig. 11.20. Tacking means spot soldering at regular intervals instead of making a continuous run. The tip of a hot copper bit is loaded with soft solder. The heat causes the solder to penetrate the joint where the bit touches it. During tacking, the mating surfaces of the joint are pressed tightly together with a wooden stick, or the 'tang' of an old file. Tacking is used for joining long seams. Tack first at the middle, and then at each end of the seam. Finally tack at equal intervals on either side of the middle. This ensures a uniform spread of temperature and prevents the metal warping or buckling because of uneven expansion and contraction.

Sweating

This produces a continuous joint as shown in Fig. 11.21. A thin coating of a suitable flux is applied to the clean mating surfaces. An even coating of solder is applied to the surfaces to be joined. Solder flows more readily between surfaces that have been pre-tinned. The joint edges are then placed together with their tinned surfaces in contact. They are held by pressing down on them with a stick or

SHEET METAL WORKING

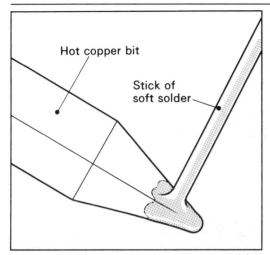

(a) Loading the copper bit with soft solder

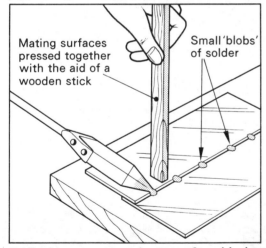

(b) Tacking a seam prior to soft soldering
Any excess solder may be removed by simply shaking or flicking the bit.

Fig. 11.20 Soft soldering processes – tacking

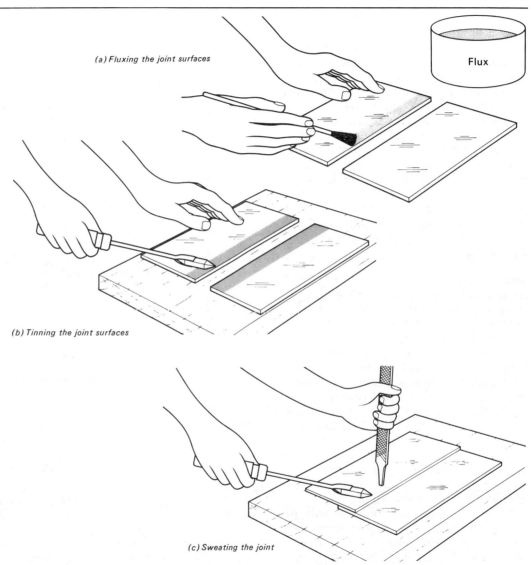

Fig. 11.21 Soft soldering processes – sweating

an old file. A heated soldering iron is placed on one end of the seam, ensuring that maximum surface contact is made between a facet of the bit and the joint metal. As the solder between the two surfaces begins to melt and flow out from under the edges, the bit is slowly drawn along the seam. The stick or old file must be moved with the bit and pressed on the joint to keep the thickness to a minimum. Sweating is only successful if there is an adequate and constant supply of heat energy. The soldering bit must be large enough for the job, which must be supported on wood or asbestos to prevent heat loss.

Floating

This is used to seal self-secured joints as shown in Fig. 11.22. One method uses a specially shaped bottoming soldering iron as shown in Fig. 11.22(a). The joint is fluxed inside and outside and held at 45° on a wooden block. A small quantity of soft solder in the form of 'buttons' or 'blobs' is dropped into the container and melted with the heated and tinned bottoming iron. This molten solder is then carefully flooded along the inside of the joint as the container is slowly rotated. The quantity of solder is controlled by steady handling of the soldering iron, adding blobs of solder when required.

If a bottoming iron is not available, an alternative method is to use a flame as a heat source, as shown in Fig. 11.22(b). An asbestos glove should be worn as protection against the flame and the heat radiated from it. The flame is

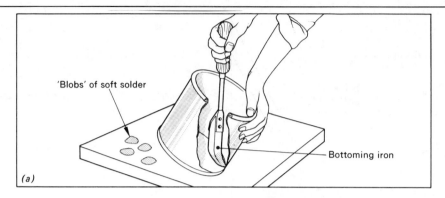

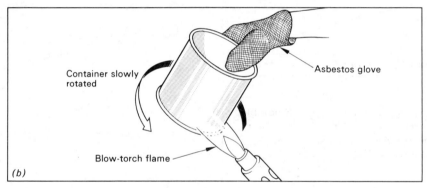

(c) Section through a knocked-up bottom

Fig. 11.22 Soft soldering processes – floating

carefully applied to the outside of the joint, and the same procedure is adopted as in Fig. 11.22(a). A section through the sealed joint is shown in Fig. 11.22(c).

Exercises

1. Sketch *three* sheet metal working tools and briefly describe a use for each of them.
   (*WAEC* 1974)
2. Name suitable applications for each of the following sheet metal cutting tools:
   hand shears
   bench shears
   guillotine shears
3. With the aid of sketches, show two methods of cutting large diameter holes in sheet metal or thin plate.
4. With the aid of sketches describe how the following protected edges are produced.
   a) folded edge (beading)
   b) wired edge.
5. Describe, with the aid of sketches, how *two* of the following self-secured joints may be made:
   a) grooved joint
   b) paned down joint
   c) knocked up joint
6. Sketch *two* of the following types of riveted joint:
   a) single riveted lap joint
   b) double riveted lap joint
   c) single-strap butt joint
   d) double-strap butt joint
7. a) By means of a sketch, show the difference between 'chain' riveting and 'zig-zag' riveting.
   b) Sketch the following rivet types:
   (i) mushroom head
   (ii) flat head
   (iii) countersunk head
8. Describe, with the aid of sketches, the effect of the following faults when making a riveted joint:
   a) rivet shank too long
   b) excessive clearance between the rivet and its hole.
9. a) State the difference between an *active* soldering flux and a *passive* soldering flux and give an example of each type.
   b) Describe, with the aid of sketches, how the bit of a soldering iron is 'tinned' prior to use.
10. Describe in detail the procedure for soft soldering the lap joint shown in Fig. 11.23 between two pieces of tin plate.

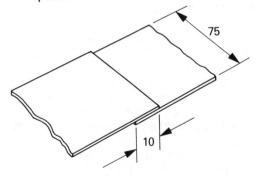

Dimensions in millimetres

Fig. 11.23

12. Drills, drilling machines and drilling

Types of drill

The drill does not produce a precision hole. It only removes the maximum volume of metal from the hole in a minimum period of time. If a hole of accurate size, roundness, and finish is required, the drilling operation must be followed by reaming or single-point boring.

Figure 12.1 shows three types of drill found in the workshop.

The 'D' bit

This can be ground from silver steel, or from cylindrical high-speed steel or stellite tool bits. It will not drill from the solid and should be treated more as a reamer than a drill: it leaves an accurate hole of good finish but only removes a small amount of metal. It is particularly effective when drilling free-cutting brass as it does not tend to 'draw' and run out.

The flat drill

This can be forged easily from silver steel rod. It is not very efficient, but it will drill from the solid and can be used in emergencies when a twist drill of the correct size is not available.

The twist drill

This is the most common type of drill. It

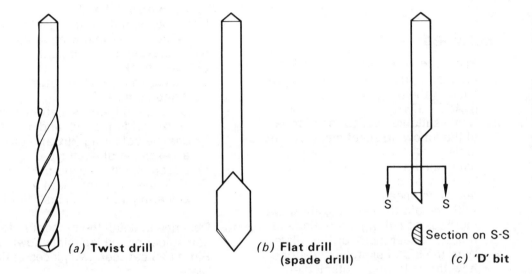

Fig. 12.1 Types of drill

cuts from the solid. and under satisfactory conditions it will open up existing holes.

The modern twist drill is made from a cylindrical blank by machining two helical grooves into it to form the flutes. The flutes run the full length of the body and have several functions:
1. they provide the rake angle;
2. they form the cutting edges;
3. they provide a passage for the coolant;
4. they facilitate swarf removal.

The flutes are not parallel to the axis of the drill but are slightly tapered. They become shallower towards the shank of the drill as shown in Fig. 12.2(a). This allows the web to be thicker at the shank than at the point of the drill, and provides a compromise between strength and cutting efficiency. A thick web would give maximum strength, but a thin web is required at the point to give an efficient 'chisel edge' for drilling from the solid. Thus a drill that has become shorter from repeated

DRILLS, DRILLING MACHINES AND DRILLING

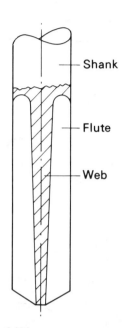

(a) **Web thickens**
To give strength to the drill the web thickens towards the shank and the flutes became shallower. Point thinning becomes necessary as the drill is ground back.

(b) **Body clearance**
The body of the drill is tapered towards the shank to give clearance in the drilled hole.

Fig. 12.2 Taper in the twist drill body

re-grinding needs 'point thinning'.

The lands are also ground with a slight taper so that the overall diameter of the drill is less at the shank than at the point, as shown in Fig. 12.2(b). This prevents the drill from binding in the hole, and so increases drill life and efficiency. The effects shown in Fig. 12.2 have been exaggerated to make them easier to see.

Figure 12.3 shows a typical twist drill and names its more important features. Although a taper shank drill is shown, the same nomenclature applies to parallel shank drills (page 236).

Twist drill cutting angles

Like any other cutting tool, the twist drill must be provided with the correct tool angles. Figure 12.4(a) shows how these compare with the corresponding angles for a single point lathe tool (page 237).

Clearance angle

The *clearance angle* of a twist drill can be adjusted during grinding of the point. Insufficient clearance leads to rubbing and over-heating of the cutting edges. This leads to softening and early drill failure. Excessive clearance reduces the strength of the cutting edge and leads to chipping and early drill failure. It will also cause the drill to dig in and chatter.

Rake angle

The *rake angle* of a twist drill cannot be altered easily because it is formed by the helix of the flutes. This is fixed at the time of manufacture and can only be changed slightly during re-grinding.

Some control of the rake angle is possible by choosing drills with the correct helix angle for the material being cut. Figure 12.4(b) shows the various types available.

As well as varying the clearance and rake angles of the drill, its performance can also be improved by modifying the point angle from the standard 118° for certain materials. When a large number of drills of the same size are being purchased, the web and land can also be varied. Figure 12.5 shows how the

235

point angle, web and land can be varied in different materials (page 238).

Twist drill cutting speeds and feeds

A drill must operate at the correct cutting speed and feed. The cutting speeds and feed rates given in this chapter are based on the following conditions.
1 The work is rigidly clamped;
2 The machine is in good condition;
3 A coolant is used if required;
4 The drill is correctly selected and ground for the material being cut.

The rates of feed and the cutting speeds for twist drills are lower than for most other machining operations for the following reasons.
1 The twist drill is weak compared with other cutting tools as the cutting forces are only resisted by the slender web. Further, the point of cutting is away from the point of support (the shank). This results in a tendency to flex and chatter.
2 It is relatively difficult for the drill to eject the chips from deep holes.
3 It is difficult to keep the cutting edges cool when they are enclosed in the hole. Even when a coolant is used it is difficult to apply it to the cutting edge. The flutes tend to 'pump' the coolant out of the hole and they become obstructed by the chips that are ejected.

Table 12.1 gives a range of cutting speeds suitable for jobbing work using standard high-speed steel twist drills

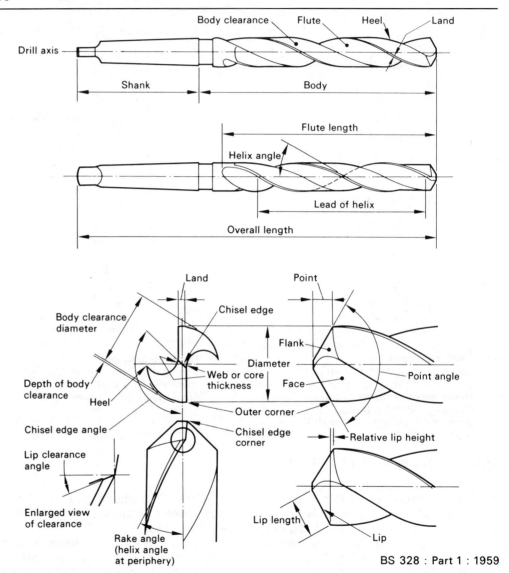

Fig. 12.3 Twist drill nomenclature

BS 328 : Part 1 : 1959

DRILLS, DRILLING MACHINES AND DRILLING

Table 12.1 Cutting speeds for HSS twist drills

MATERIAL BEING DRILLED	CUTTING SPEED (m/min)
Aluminium	70–100
Brass	35–50
Bronze (phosphor)	20–35
Cast iron (grey)	25–40
Copper	35–45
Steel (mild)	30–40
Steel (medium carbon)	20–30
Steel (alloy-high tensile)	5–8
Thermo-setting plastic (Low speed due to abrasive properties)	20–30

Table 12.2 Feeds for HSS twist drills

DRILL DIAMETER (mm)	RATE OF FEED (mm/rev)
1·0–2·5	0·040–0·060
2·6–4·5	0·050–0·100
4·6–6·0	0·075–0·150
6·1–9·0	0·100–0·200
9·1–12·0	0·150–0·250
12·1–15·0	0·200–0·300
15·1–18·0	0·230–0·330
18·1–21·0	0·260–0·360
21·1–25·0	0·280–0·380

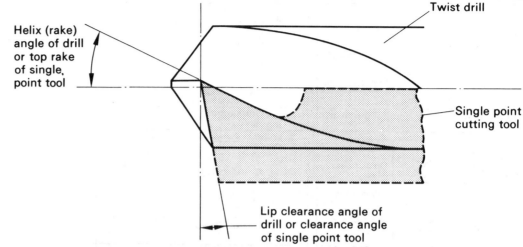

(a) Twist drill rake and clearance angles

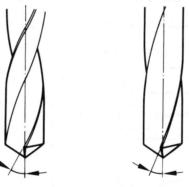

Normal helix angle for drilling low and medium tensile materials

Reduced or 'slow' helix angle for high tensile materials

Straight flute for drilling free cutting brass, drill does not try to draw in

Increased helix angle or 'quick' helix for drilling light alloy materials

(b) Helix angles

Fig. 12.4 Twist drill cutting angles

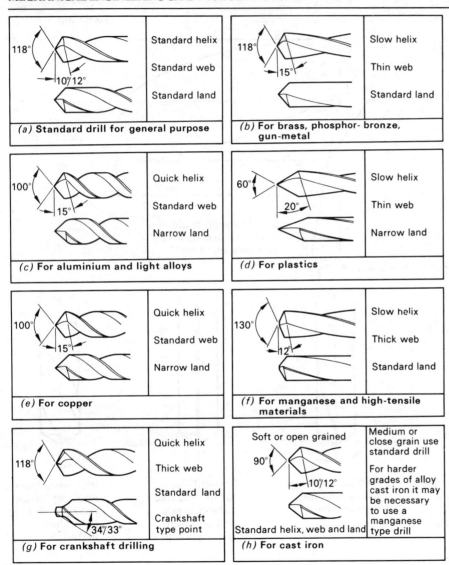

Fig. 12.5 Point angles

under reasonably controlled conditions. Table 12.2 gives the corresponding rates of feed. If the recommended speed or feed is not on the drilling machine gear box, always select an alternative speed or feed that is *less* than the desired rate.

Example 12.1 Calculate the spindle speed (S) for mild steel is 30 m/min, drill 12 mm in diameter, cutting mild steel.

Solution

$$N = \frac{1000S}{\pi d}$$

where: N = spindle speed in rev/min
S = cutting speed in m/min
d = drill diameter (mm)
π = 3·14

From Table 12.1, a suitable cutting speed (S) for mild steel is 30 m/min, thus:

$$N = \frac{1000 \times 30}{3 \cdot 14 \times 12}$$
$$= 796 \cdot 2 \text{ rev/min}$$

A spindle speed between 750 and 800 rev/min would be satisfactory.

Example 12.2 Calculate the time taken in seconds for the drill in Example 12.1 to penetrate a 15 mm thick steel plate.

Solution

1 From Example 12.1 the spindle speed has already been calculated as 796 rev/min (nearest whole number);
2 From Table 11.2 it will be seen that a suitable feed for a 12 mm drill is 0·2 mm/rev.

$$t = \frac{60P}{NF}$$

where: t = time in seconds
P = depth of penetration (mm)
N = spindle speed (rev/min)
F = feed (mm/rev)

$$= \frac{60 \times 15}{769 \times 0\cdot 2}$$

= 5·7 seconds
(to one decimal place)

Types of twist drill

Figure 12.6 shows the five standard types of twist drill normally available.

Jobber series

These are the *parallel shank* drills normally found in the workshop.

Stub drill

These have the same parallel shank proportions as the drill above but shorter *flutes*. They are used where greater rigidity is required.

Long series

These again have the same parallel shank proportions as the jobber series but longer flutes. They are used for drilling deep holes.

Morse taper shank drills

These have the same *flute length* as the jobber series, but have *taper shanks* made to the *Morse* system of *tapers*.

Core drills

These are available with both parallel and taper shanks. Their flute length is the same as for the jobber series.

They have three flutes, which give

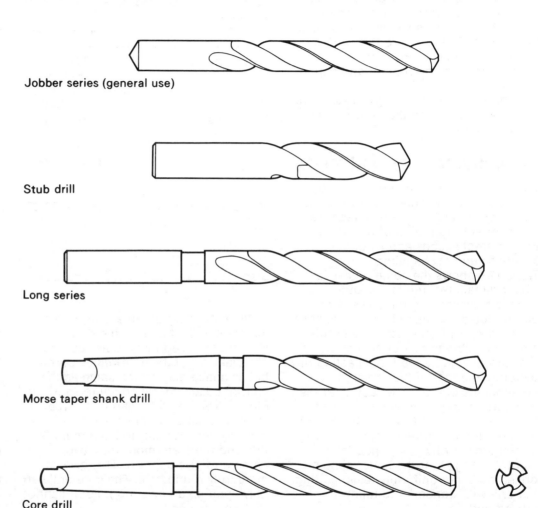

(Courtesy B.S.I.)

Fig. 12.6 Types of twist drill

increased strength and rigidity. Hence core drills are widely used for opening up existing holes, especially cored holes in castings. This is where the name 'core drill' comes from.

They have no chisel point and cannot cut from the solid.

Table 12.3 gives the range of standard metric sizes in which the above types of drill are available.

Twist drill failures and faults

Twist drills can fail early or produce holes that are inaccurate, out of round and of poor finish for several reasons:
1 incorrect regrinding of the point;
2 incorrect speeds and feeds;
3 abuse and mishandling.

Table 12.4 shows the common causes of twist drill failures and faults and suggests causes and remedies. Most cutting tools are guided by their shanks or spindles. Unfortunately, twist drills are too flexible to rely on this alone: they are guided by the forces acting on the cutting edges. If the radial components of the forces acting at the two cutting edges are equal, they will push the drill point towards the axis of rotation. If the cutting edges are not symmetrical, (if they are unequal in length or angle), or the material being drilled does not uniformly resist cutting, the drill will 'wander' and follow a curved path.

When drilling from the solid, the drill is controlled by the chisel point (see Fig. 12.7(a) on page 242). The hole will be round but may be oversize.

Table 12.3 Metric size drills (mm)

TYPE	DIAMETER	STEPS	
Jobber series	0·20–1·00	0·02/0·03	
	1·05–3·00	0·05	
	3·10–14·00	0·10	
	14·25–15·00	0·25	
Stub drills	0·50–25·00	0·20/1·00	Steps increase rapidly with diameter
Long series	2·00–25·00	0·05/0·25	Steps increase similarly to the jobber series
Morse taper shank	3·00–100·00	0·02/1·00	Steps increase the same as for the jobber series up to 15 mm, then more rapidly.

When opening up an existing hole, the point is floating and the drill is largely controlled by its outer corners. The diameter of the hole will be correct, but its shape may be the same as the constant diameter lobed figure shown in Fig. 12.7(b). The fault can be overcome by using a core drill for opening up an existing hole. A core drill is a multi-flute drill and there are more than two corners to give support. This gives a more truly round hole. The core drill can only open up an existing hole: it cannot drill from the solid.

Blind hole drilling

A blind hole is one that stops part way through a component. There is an essential difference between drilling a *through* hole and drilling a *blind* hole. When drilling a blind hole, there must be a way of knowing when the drill has reached the right depth. Most drilling machines have an adjustable depth stop attached to the quill as shown in Fig. 12.8. The depth stop is engraved with a rule type scale on its front face. This scale is used to set the knurled stop nut and lock nut, as shown in Fig. 12.9(a). The hole is then drilled to depth, as shown in Fig. 12.9(b) (page 243).

Generally, blind holes are only toleranced to rule accuracy: the scale on the depth stop is a satisfactory measure of the hole depth. However,

Table 12.4 Twist drill fault-finding chart

FAILURE	PROBABLE CAUSE	REMEDY
Damaged point	1. Do not use a hard-faced hammer when inserting the drill in the spindle 2. When removing the drill from the spindle, do not let it drop on to the hard surface of the machine table	Do not abuse the drill point
Rough hole	1. Drill point is incorrectly ground or blunt 2. Feed is too rapid 3. Coolant incorrect or insufficient	Regrind point correctly Reduce rate of feed Check coolant
Oversize hole	1. Lips of drill are of unequal length (Fig. 12.7) 2. Point angle is unequally disposed about drill axis 3. Point thinning is not central 4. Machine spindle is worn and running out of true.	Regrind point correctly Recondition the machine
Unequal chips	1. Lips of drill are of unequal length 2. Point angle is unequally disposed about drill axis	Regrind point correctly
Split web (core)	1. Lip clearance angle too small 2. Point thinned too much 3. Feed too great	 Regrind point correctly Reduce rate of feed

FAILURE	PROBABLE CAUSE	REMEDY
Chipped lips	1. Lip clearance angle too large 2. Feed too great	Regrind point Reduce rate of feed
Damaged corners	1. Cutting speed too high, drill 'blues' at outer corners 2. Coolant insufficient or incorrect 3. Hard spot, scale, or inclusions in material being drilled	Reduce spindle speed Check coolant Inspect material
Broken tang	1. Drill not correctly fitted into spindle so that it slips 2. Drill jams in hole and slips	Ensure shank and spindle are clean and undamaged before inserting Reduce rate of feed
Broken drill	1. Drill is blunt 2. Lip clearance angle too small 3. Drill point incorrectly ground 4. Rate of feed too great 5. Work insecurely clamped 6. Drill jams in hole due to worn corners 7. Flutes choked with chips when drilling deep holes	Regrind point Reduce rate of feed Re-clamp more securely Regrind point Withdraw drill periodically and clean

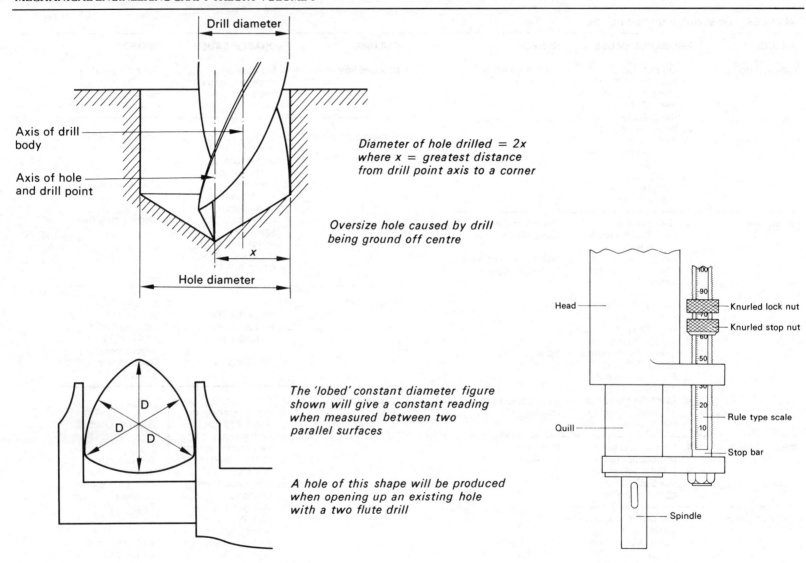

Fig. 12.7 Hole faults

Fig. 12.8 Depth stop attachment

flat-bottomed holes are often toleranced to greater accuracy and the stop nut is set differently. The sequence of operations shown in Fig. 12.10 should be used to produce a flat-bottomed blind hole to a precise depth.

Reamers and reaming

It has already been stated that a hole produced by a twist drill is likely to be out of round, oversize and with a rough finish. To some extent this can be overcome by drilling the hole undersize and opening it up with a multi-flute core drill.

The *reamer* has many more flutes than the core drill and is designed as a finishing tool. It will only remove a small amount of metal, but it leaves a round hole of good finish and accurate size.

Figure 12.11 shows three types of machine reamer. They differ from the hand reamer in having Morse taper shanks to fit the machine spindle and having no taper lead, only a bevel lead.

Fluted reamers are end-cutting devices only; the radial land prevents cutting taking place along the flutes. Rose-action reamers cut both on the end and on the periphery, and the flutes are backed off to give a clearance angle. Long fluted machine reamers are always end-cutting, but chucking reamers may have a fluted or a rose-cutting action. Fluted reamers give the best results with steels and similar ductile materials, whereas rose-action reamers are better for cast iron and bronze materials. These materials tend to close on the reamer, and peripheral cutting prevents seizure and broken tooling. Similarly rose-action reamers are preferable when reaming plastic materials.

Although standard reamers are made for right-hand cutting, they have flutes with a left-hand helix. This serves two purposes:
1 to prevent the reamer being drawn into the hole by the screw action of the helix;
2 to eject the chips ahead of the reamer and prevent them being drawn back up the hole, where they would mark the finished surface.

The reamer always follows the axis of the existing hole: it cannot correct positional errors. If the original hole is out of position or out of alignment with its datum, then these errors must be corrected by single point boring before reaming.

Miscellaneous operations

In addition to drilling holes, the following operations are also performed on the drilling machine;

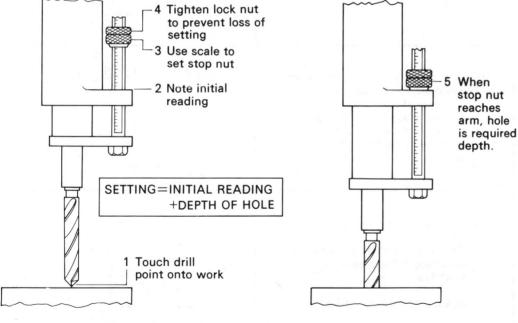

(a) **Setting depth stop**   (b) **Drill hole to depth**

Fig. 12.9 Use of depth stop to drill blind hole

1 trepanning;
2 countersinking;
3 counterboring;
4 spot facing.

Trepanning

It is dangerous to try to cut large diameter holes in sheet metal with a twist drill, and the resulting hole will not be satisfactory. The metal will not be thick enough to guide the drill point and to resist the cutting forces. The hole will be out of round and jagged.

One way to overcome this problem is to use a trepanning cutter. Instead of cutting away all the metal in the hole as swarf, the trepanning cutter removes a thin disc of metal. This leaves a clean cut hole in the stock, and a disc of metal slightly smaller than the hole. The principle of trepanning is shown in Fig. 12.12(a) on page 246.

The simplest type of trepanning cutter is the traditional tank cutter shown in Fig. 12.12(b). This has a number of disadvantages, and the type of cutter shown in Fig. 12.12(c) is better when a number of holes of the same size have to be cut.

Countersinking

Figure 12.13(a) shows a typical rose-bit used for countersinking. Since the bit is conical in form, it is self-centring, and does not require a pilot to ensure axial alignment with the hole being countersunk (see page 246).

Countersinking is used for the following purposes.
1 To provide a hole for the head of a

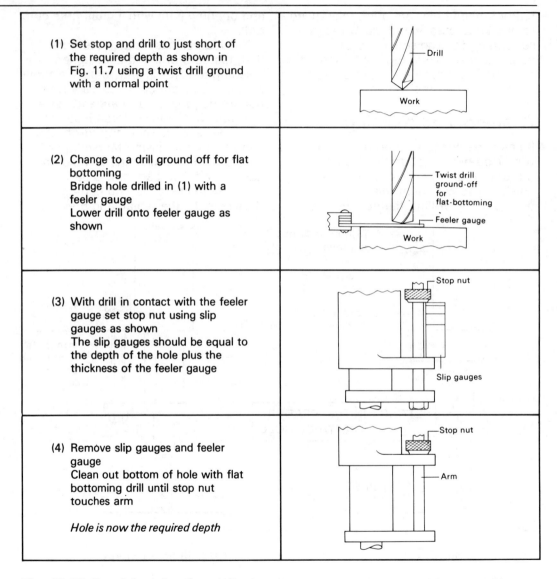

Fig. 12.10 Precision depth setting

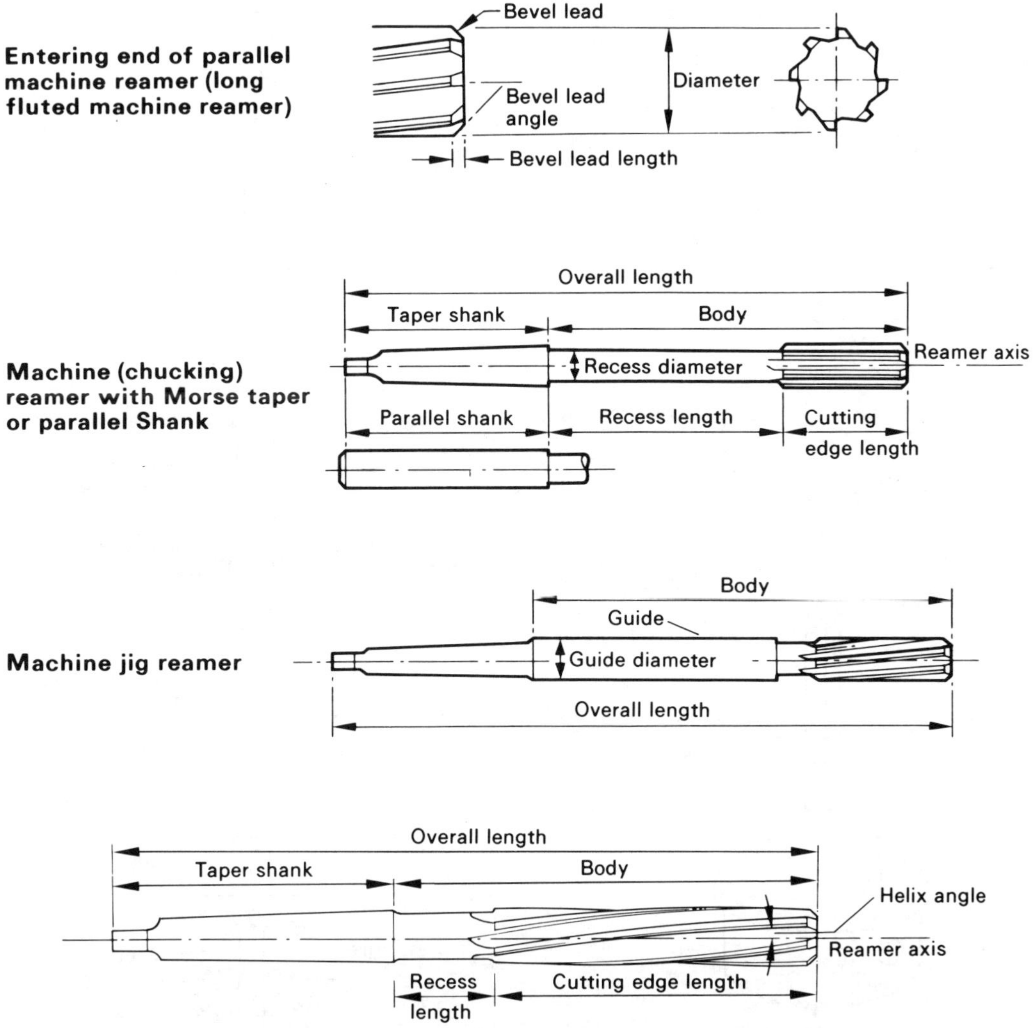

Entering end of parallel machine reamer (long fluted machine reamer)

Machine (chucking) reamer with Morse taper or parallel Shank

Machine jig reamer

Long fluted machine reamer with Morse taper shank, right-hand cutting with left-hand helical flutes

Fig. 12.11 Types of machine reamer

DRILLS, DRILLING MACHINES AND DRILLING

countersunk screw so that a flush surface is left after the screw is inserted.
2 To deburr a hole after drilling. Burred holes are dangerous to handle, and mating components with burred holes will not join together correctly.
3 To chamfer sharp corners in order to make the component safer to handle and less likely to crack when hardened.

Counterboring

Figure 12.13(b) shows a typical counterboring cutter. It is similar in design to an end-mill but is fitted with a pilot to ensure axial alignment with the hole being counterbored.

Counterboring is used to provide a hole to accept the head of a cheese-head or a cap-head screw so that a flush surface is left after the screw is inserted. Screws that are left 'proud' of the surface (standing above the surface) are dangerous. Whenever possible, screw heads and nuts should be sunk into the job by countersinking or counterboring.

Spot facing

Figure 12.13(c) shows a typical spot facing cutter. It provides a locally machined, flat seating for nuts or bolt-heads that are pulled down on to otherwise rough castings or forgings.

Basic alignments of the drilling machine

Figure 12.14 shows the basic alignments of the spindle axis and workpiece. The geometry of the drilling machine is

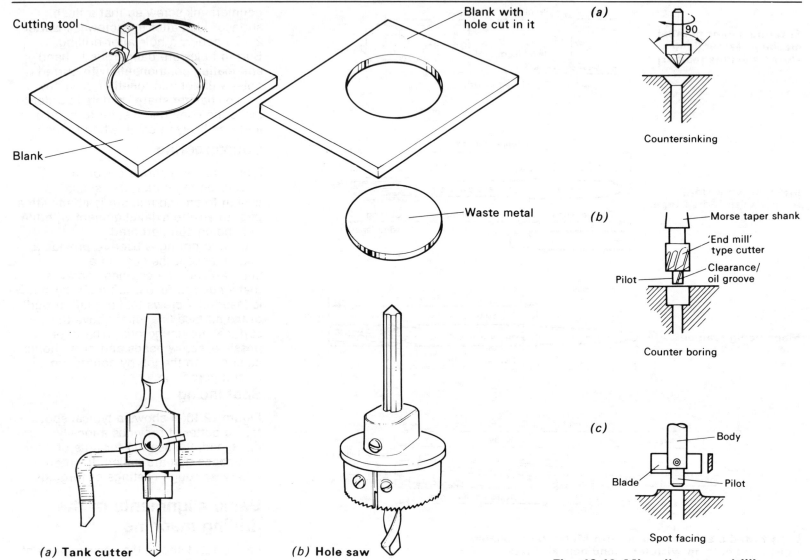

(a) Tank cutter *(b)* Hole saw

Fig. 12.12 Trepanning large holes

Fig. 12.13 Miscellaneous drilling operations

DRILLS, DRILLING MACHINES AND DRILLING

designed to keep these alignments.

The spindle locates and rotates the drill and is located in precision bearings in a sleeve. The sleeve can move in the body of the drilling machine so that it travels to or from the workpiece in a path parallel to the axis of the spindle. The combined spindle and sleeve assembly is known as the *'quill'*.

Reference to Fig. 12.14 shows that the spindle axis is perpendicular to the surface of the workpiece. It must, therefore, be perpendicular to the surface of the machine worktable. This table is adjustable up and down a precision ground column so that work of various thickness can be accommodated. To preserve the table alignment, the axis of the spindle and the axis of the column must be mutually parallel. Further, the axis of the column is perpendicular to the machine base.

The bench drilling machine

The simplest type of drilling machine is the bench drilling machine shown in Fig. 12.15(a). It takes drills up to 12·5 mm diameter, either in a chuck or directly mounted in the taper nose of the spindle. The spindle speed is varied by altering the belt position on the stepped pulleys (page 248).

For normal drilling operations the spindle axis must be at right angles to the working surface of the table. However, if the hole is to be drilled at an angle, the table can be tilted as shown in Fig. 12.15(b).

The feed is operated by hand through

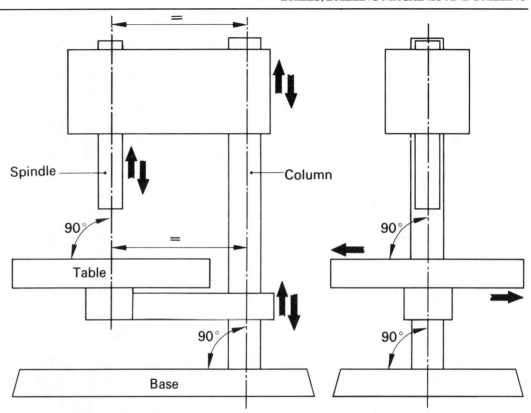

Fig. 12.14 The drilling machine – basic geometry

a rack and pinion as shown in Fig. 12.16. This type of feed mechanism enables the operator to 'feel' the progress of the drill through the material being cut. Hence the name 'sensitive feed' (page 248).

The pillar drilling machine

Basically, this is an enlarged version of the 'sensitive bench' machine described previously. It is floor-mounted and much more heavily constructed. The spindle is driven by a more powerful electric motor and the spindle speed is varied by a gearbox. Sensitive rack and pinion feed is provided for setting up and starting the drill. Power feed is provided for the actual drilling operation, the rate of feed being controlled by an extra *(a)* **Bench drilling machine**

(b) **Table tilted**

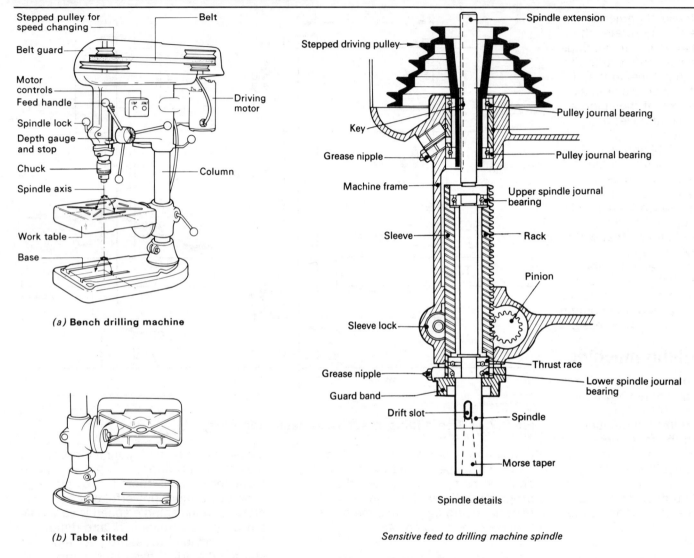

Fig. 12.15 Sensitive bench drilling machine

Spindle details

Sensitive feed to drilling machine spindle

Fig. 12.16 Sensitive feed mechanism

gearbox. The spindle is bored to a Morse taper and takes drills inserted directly into the spindle, as well as drill chucks. Holes up to 50 mm diameter can be drilled from the solid on the larger machines.

A typical pillar drilling machine is shown in Fig 12.17(a).

From Fig. 12.17(b) it will be seen that the machine table can be swung about the pillar as well as rotated about its own axis. By a combination of these movements, any point on the table can be brought under the drill. Thus all the holes can be drilled in a component without removing it from the machine

The column type drilling machine

This is similar to the pillar drilling machine except that the machine elements are mounted on a cast, box-type column as shown in Fig. 12.18(a). This has the advantage that the worktable may be raised or lowered without loss of axial alignment, as shown in Fig. 12.18(b) (see page 250).

Column type machines are often equipped with a compound table to enable the work to be positioned under the drill easily. When the table lock is released, the table is free to move on ball bearing slides to and from the column and from side to side. An example of a compound table is shown in Fig. 12.18(c).

The radial arm drilling machine

For heavy work, it is often more

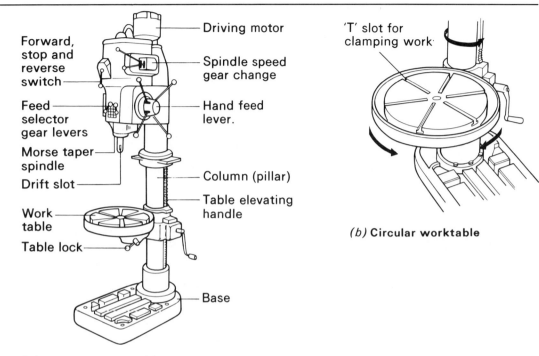

(a) Pillar drilling machine

(b) Circular worktable

Fig. 12.17 Pillar drilling machine

convenient to move the drilling head over the work than to move the work. The radial arm drilling machine can do this and an example is shown in Fig. 12.19(a). Drilling machines such as this represent the most powerful machines available: they can drill holes up to 75 mm diameter from the solid. Powerful drive motors are geared directly into the head of the machine and a wide range of power feeds is provided. Sensitive and geared manual feeds are also available. The arm is raised and lowered by a separate motor mounted on the column. The arm can be swung from side to side round the column and locked in position. The drilling head can be run back and forth along the arm by a large hand wheel operating a rack and pinion mechanism. The spindle motor is reversible so that power tapping attachments can be used. Figure 12.19(b) shows the range of movements of such a machine.

MECHANICAL ENGINEERING CRAFT THEORY VOLUME 1

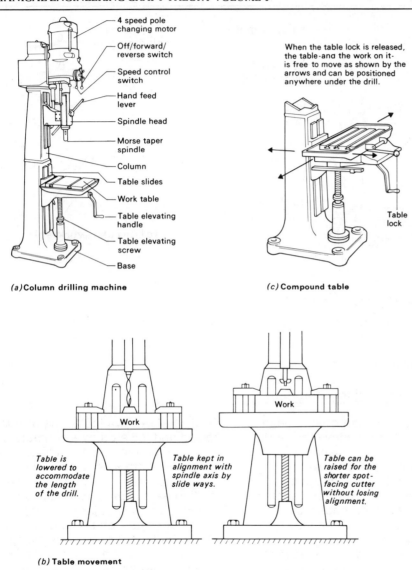

Fig. 12.18 Column type drilling machine

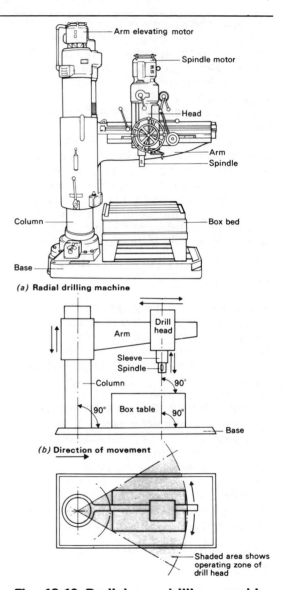

Fig. 12.19 Radial arm drilling machine

Holding the drill in the drilling machine

To drill a hole in a component so that it is correctly positioned, four basic conditions must be satisfied.
1 The drill must be placed (located) so that its axis coincides with the axis of the drilling machine spindle.
2 The drill and the spindle must rotate together without slipping. That is, the drill must be restrained by the spindle.
3 The workpiece must be located so that the centre lines of the hole to be drilled are in alignment with the spindle axis, as shown in Fig. 12.20.
4 The workpiece must be restrained so that it is not dragged round by the drill.

It will be seen from Fig. 12.21 that a taper location can compensate for variations in size due to manufacturing tolerances and reasonable wear. However, even a small amount of dirt in the taper can cause considerable misalignment, as shown in Fig. 12.21(c) (page 252). Therefore, before the drill is inserted in the spindle, both the drill shank and the spindle bore should be wiped clean. This also prevents undue wear and damage to the spindle due to the drill slipping. The narrow angle of taper of the drill shank causes it to wedge in the spindle of the drilling machine. This provides sufficient restraint to prevent the drill dropping out of the spindle, and to prevent slip between the drill and the spindle as they rotate. If the drill 'digs in' to the workpiece, or the drill seizes in the hole,

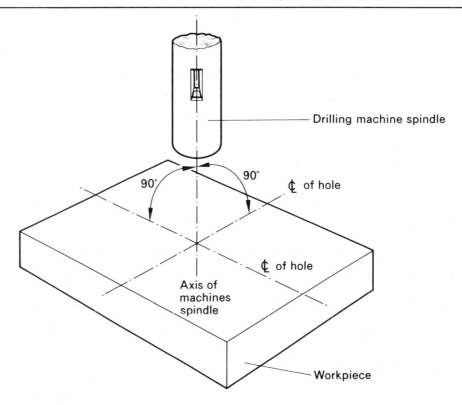

Fig. 12.20 Basic drilling alignments

there is not enough frictional restraint and slip occurs. This results in the spindle bore and the drill shank becoming scored so that proper location and restraint of the drill becomes impossible.

Straight shank drills and other small cutting tools are often held in self-centring chucks. The principle of the drill chuck as a device for locating and restraining small drills is shown in Fig. 12.22. It will be seen that the chuck and its arbor rely upon a system of concentric tapers to create axial alignment (page 252).

Work holding

The same principles of location and restraint can be applied to the workpiece. Figure 12.23(a) shows the restraints acting on a simple component

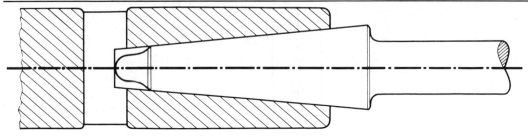
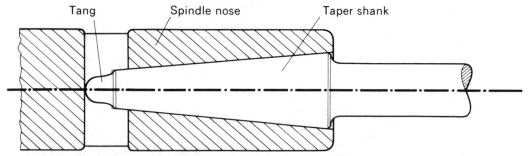
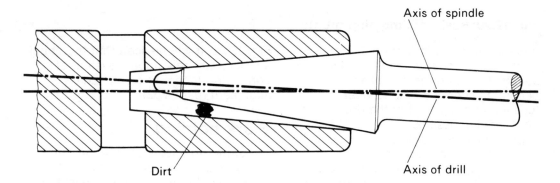

Fig. 12.21 Taper location – alignment error due to dirt

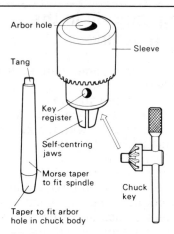

(a) **Typical drill chuck and accessories**

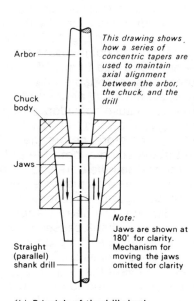

(b) **Principle of the drill chuck**

Fig. 12.22 The drill chuck

DRILLS, DRILLING MACHINES AND DRILLING

held in a machine vice. The geometric alignments necessary to place the component correctly, relative to the axis of the drilling machine spindle, are shown in Fig. 12.23(b). Components that are too large to be held in a machine vice are usually clamped directly to the machine table.

Cylindrical components are more difficult to hold as only line contact between flat and round surfaces is possible. It is advisable to insert a vee block between a cylindrical component and the fixed jaw of the vice to provide a three-point location.

The vee block, or a pair of matched vee blocks, are also used to locate a cylindrical component when its axis lies in the horizontal plane. Figure 12.24(a) shows the restraints acting on a cylindrical component supported on vee blocks. The geometrical alignments necessary to locate the component correctly, relative to the drilling machine spindle, are shown in Fig. 12.24(b).

Jigs are also used for locating components under the drill in a drilling machine. Usually they are used where a large number of holes are to be drilled and it would be a waste of time and money to mark out each component and centre punch each hole. A jig not only locates and restrains the workpiece, it also guides the drill. Figure 12.25 shows a jig for drilling a cross hole in a shaft. By locating the shaft in a vee, variations in the diameter of the shaft will not affect its position under the drill. The bush guides the drill and prevents it from wandering off centre. The curved

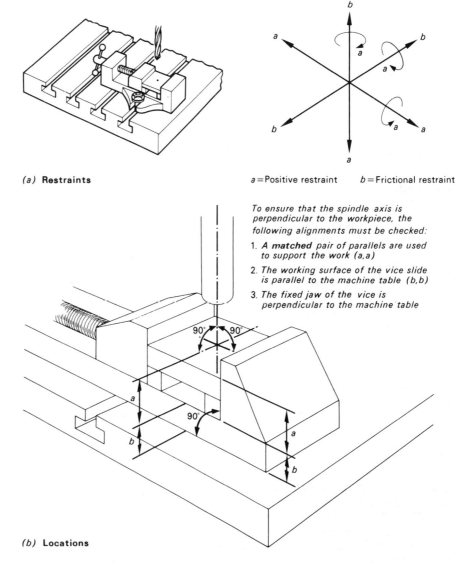

(a) **Restraints**

a = Positive restraint b = Frictional restraint

To ensure that the spindle axis is perpendicular to the workpiece, the following alignments must be checked:

1. *A matched* pair of parallels are used to support the work (a,a)
2. The working surface of the vice slide is parallel to the machine table (b,b)
3. The fixed jaw of the vice is perpendicular to the machine table

(b) **Locations**

Fig. 12.23 Work holding in the machine vice

surface of the shaft would probably cause the drill to wander if there was no bush. If the hole has to be reamed, a removable bush located in a liner sleeve is used as shown in Fig. 12.26. The bush is used to drill the pilot hole. The bush is then removed and the taper lead on the end of the reamer causes it to align with the pilot hole. The liner offers no guidance as there is clearance between it and the reamer (see page 256).

Drilling thin plate

For a hole of reasonable form to be produced, the drill must be cutting its full diameter before the point breaks through. This is because at the moment of breakthrough, the point ceases to locate the drill and the body lands have to take over, as shown in Fig. 12.27(a). When drilling sheet and thin plate, the drill breaks through too soon and grabs, forming a lobed hole. This effect is shown in Fig. 12.27(b). Not only is an out-of-shape hole produced, but the resulting ragged edges are very dangerous. Further, when small drills grab, they are often broken. When large drills grab, they may twist up the workpiece, pulling it clear of its clamps, and causing it to spin round dangerously (see page 257).

To overcome these problems, the drill point has to be ground to a very obtuse point as shown in Fig. 12.27(c). This enables the body to enter the hole before the point breaks through. The actual point angle will depend on the drill diameter and the thickness of the

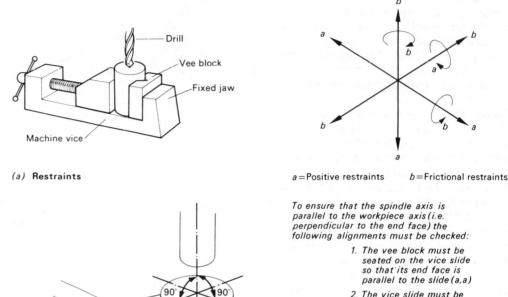

(a) Restraints

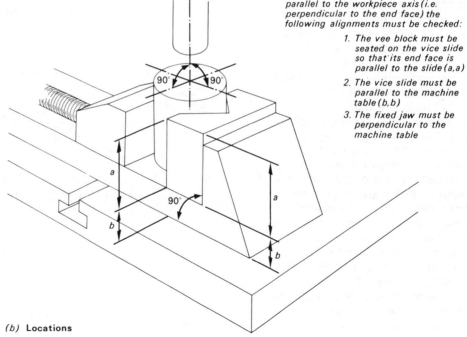

(b) Locations

a = Positive restraints b = Frictional restraints

To ensure that the spindle axis is parallel to the workpiece axis (i.e. perpendicular to the end face) the following alignments must be checked:

1. *The vee block must be seated on the vice slide so that its end face is parallel to the slide (a,a)*
2. *The vice slide must be parallel to the machine table (b,b)*
3. *The fixed jaw must be perpendicular to the machine table*

Fig. 12.24 Work holding cylindrical work

plate. It must be remembered that the efficiency of the drill decreases as the point angle becomes flatter.

To increase the efficiency of an obtuse angled drill, and reduce the axial cutting force, the point should be thinned to reduce the length of the chisel point as shown in Fig. 12.27(d).

The drill can also be ground with a pilot point as shown in Fig. 12.27(e). This is much more difficult to produce, but it enables large holes to be produced in thin plate.

When drilling plate, it is essential that it is supported right up to the cutting edge. Components should be supported on a wood block as shown in Fig. 12.27(f).

Drilling plastic materials

The difficulties of drilling plastic materials are completely different from those of drilling metals. The situation is further complicated by the fact that the difficulties of drilling thermosetting plastics are different from those of drilling thermoplastic materials. And within these main groups, there are hundreds of individual material specifications, each requiring special consideration. Then, each individual component being drilled introduces its own special problems just as it would if made from metal. thus, practically every situation requires its own treatment; drilling plastic components is more an art than a science.

The following notes, therefore, are a generalisation of the main problems and

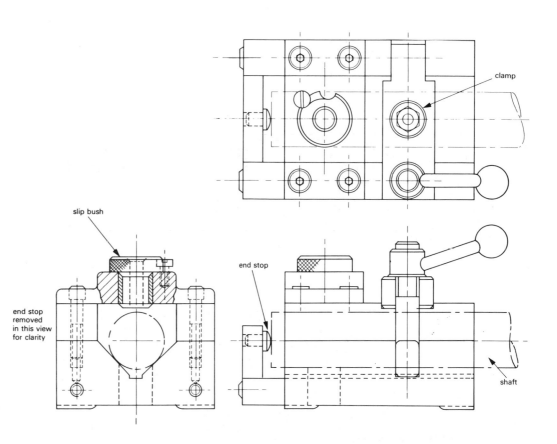

Fig. 12.25 Drill jig

255

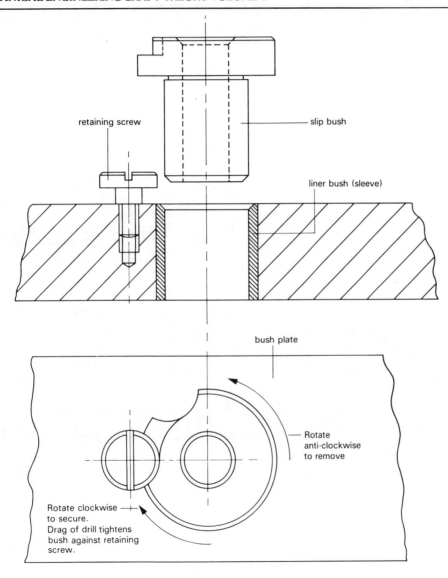

Fig. 12.26 Removable bush and liner sleeve

their solutions within broad material groupings.

Thermosetting plastics

Thermosetting plastics will not soften when they have been moulded. They tend to be rigid and rather brittle. Bakelite is a thermosetting plastic.

Heating effects When drilling metal components, much of the heat generated when cutting is conducted away through the body of the component (metals are conductors of heat). Plastic materials are heat insulators, therefore the heat generated is trapped in the hole and can only be conducted away through the drill. This results in the drill overheating and the component burning. Coolant cannot be used as in metal cutting, but an air blast is useful in cooling the drill and the component. It also blows the swarf towards the extractor inlet as shown in Fig. 12.28 on page 258.

Shrinkage However much care is taken, heat is generated in the hole whilst drilling. This causes the component to expand and shrink again on cooling. This effect is so pronounced that oversize drills have to be used to produce the required size of hole. For example:
2 BA tapping size drill
steel   − 3·7 mm
thermo-setting plastic   − 3·9 mm

Feed Two problems affect the rate of feed. First, the heating effect already mentioned, and second the tendency for the swarf to clog in the flutes of the drill. To overcome these, the drill is fed into the workpiece with a 'woodpecker' action. That is, instead of a continuous uniform rate of feed as usually employed when drilling metals, the drill is fed in quite rapidly and then momentarily withdrawn so that the plastic can 'breathe'. This allows the air blast to cool the drill, and eject the swarf. The hole tends to shrink in size and is cleared as the drill is given its next increment of feed. This prevents the hole closing on the body of the drill as well as preventing the drill and workpiece overheating. This method of feeding is shown in Fig. 12.29 (page 259).

Abrasion Thermo-setting plastics, especially those with mineral fillers such as asbestos and mica, are highly abrasive and wear out high-speed steel drills very rapidly. Therefore carbide-tipped drills are generally used. Usually an ordinary 'masonry' drill is adequate as it tends to drill oversize and this allows for the shrinkage after drilling. Where a precision hole is required, precision ground carbide tipped drills are used. The specially designed plastic drill has a slow spiral, an 80° point angle, wide flutes to prevent clogging and a generous clearance angle so that it cuts freely. It will also have a thin web to reduce the axial force (feed force) on the workpiece. Often the flutes are polished to help prevent clogging. The general point angle of 118° is suitable for opening up cored holes, but the 80° angle is preferable for drilling from the solid as it helps to prevent chipping the moulding as the drill breaks through, as

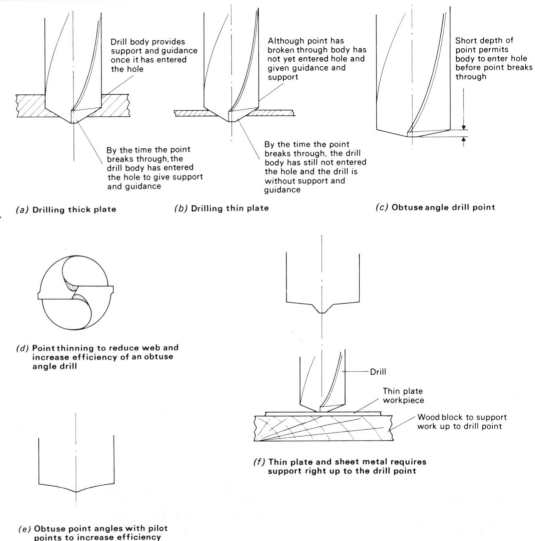

Fig. 12.27 Point grinding of twist drills for thin plate

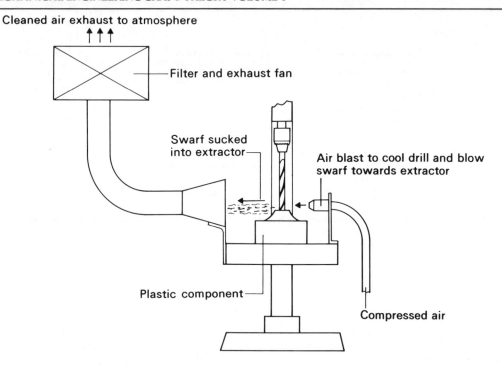

Fig. 12.28 Air blast and extraction

well as reducing the feed force.

Cutting speed This tends to be kept to a fairly low value to reduce the heating effect and wear from abrasion. For holes up to 12 mm diameter, the cutting speed is in the range of 35 m/min to 45 m/min depending on the type of plastic being drilled and the filler used.

Workholding Components made from thermosetting plastics tend to be brittle and care has to be taken in clamping to avoid cracking them by using too much force or distorting them.

Thermoplastic materials

Thermoplastic materials soften every time they are heated. Nylon, P.V.C. and polystyrene are examples of this group of plastic materials.

Thermoplastic materials are not drilled as often as thermosetting plastics. This is because it is much easier to core the holes into components made from thermoplastic materials during the moulding process. There are more thermoplastic materials than there are thermosetting plastic materials and the properties vary much more widely between each sub-group of materials. Therefore it is only possible to generalise in the space available in this chapter. However, the following notes give some indication of the main problems and their solution.

Heating effects As with thermosetting plastics, heat generated when cutting cannot be conducted away through the components. This causes the material to overheat rapidly, and soften and weld itself to the drill. As softening occurs at temperatures only a little above the boiling point of water, overheating only affects the component. The temperature is too low to affect the temper of an ordinary high-speed steel drill. Coolant cannot be used but an air blast can. (See Fig. 12.28.)

Shrinkage This effect is even more acute than with thermosetting plastics. Allowance has to be made when selecting drill sizes if the diameter of the finished hole is critical. There is also the problem of the material closing on the body of the drill. The additional friction this causes results in premature overheating and complete clogging of the drill flutes. This results in either a ruined component, or a broken drill, or both.

Feed The importance of using a 'woodpecker' feed action to allow the hole to 'breathe' was fully discussed on page 257. This action needs to be even more exaggerated when drilling thermoplastics. The drill is run much faster and each feed increment is very

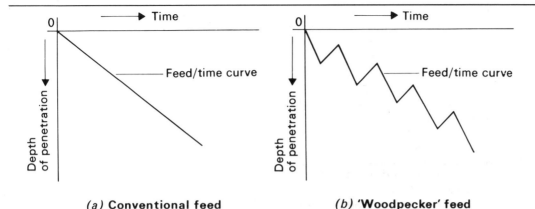

Fig. 12.29 'Woodpecker' feed action

coarse, resulting in a 'bodging' action. The required amount of material is removed before the temperature can build up to the softening point for the plastic concerned. The special high-speed drills that have been marketed for drilling thermoplastic materials are generally used. These drills have slow helix angles, very wide flutes, thin webs and acute points. The flutes are polished to reduce clogging. They are ground with a generous clearance angle and are given a keen cutting edge. The total geometry of the drill is designed to enable it to cut as freely as possible and to eject the swarf rapidly. This prevents the generation of too much heat.

Abrasion With a few exceptions, thermoplastic materials do not contain abrasive fillers and high-speed steel cutting tools perform satisfactorily. 'High-speed' cutting tools are more economical to use than carbide-tipped tools and they are easier to service and provide with the keen cutting edge necessary to ensure free cutting without overheating.

The notable exception is the drilling of glass-reinforced-polyester materials (GRP). The glass fibre is very abrasive and high-speed steel tooling is worn undersize almost immediately. Even carbide-tipped tools are not satisfactory as the steel body of the drill is rapidly worn down. The only satisfactory way to drill GRP components on a production basis is to use solid carbide drills. These are very expensive and very fragile and require careful and expert handling. All the previous drills shown for plastic materials have slow helixes to prevent them from being drawn into the workpiece, but drills designed for GRP have a quick helix to help eject the swarf rapidly. The material offers sufficient resistance to cutting to prevent the drill from being drawn in, and rapid removal of the swarf helps to reduce the wear of the drill body due to abrasion.

Cutting speed As most thermoplastic materials are not abrasive, they can be cut with a much higher speed than thermosetting materials. For holes up to 12 mm diameter, the cutting speed is in the range of 200 m/min to 250 m/min with a fine feed for carbide tooling, and 80 m/min with a coarse feed for high-speed steel drills. The acute 'woodpecker' feed action prevents the heat build-up normally associated with high cutting speed.

These cutting speeds and this feed action give an economic production rate and prevent the temperature from rising to the softening point of the plastic.

When drilling GRP components, the cutting speed is dropped to the lower range because GRP is so abrasive. With the lower cutting speed, care must be taken to avoid overfeeding the fragile, solid carbide drill as it will break.

Workholding Components made from thermoplastic materials are less brittle than those made from thermosetting plastics and are less liable to crack when clamped. However, they tend to be easily distorted because they are inflexible. Where holes are only being opened up to size, after being cored, it is quite normal to 'hand-hold' the component in a simple fixture. The cutting forces are sufficiently low as not to endanger the operator.

Exercises

1. Sketch, in good proportion, a taper shank twist drill, and label the following features: tang; shank; body; flute; chisel point.
2. Calculate the spindle speed in rev/min for a high speed steel twist drill 14 mm in diameter if the cutting speed is 33 m/min ($\pi = 22/7$).
3. Calculate the cutting speed for a 3·5 mm diameter twist drill if the spindle speed is 3000 rev/min.
4. Calculate the time taken for a twist drill to penetrate 15 mm into a steel plate if the spindle speed is 600 rev/min and the feed is 0·3 mm/rev ($\pi = 3·14$).
5. Show, by means of a sketch, the effect of grinding a drill point with unequal lip lengths.
6. Suggest possible causes for the following drill faults:
   a) the chisel point is chipped
   b) excessive force is required to make the drill bite into the work
   c) the corners of the lips become 'blued'
   d) the tang has been twisted off
   e) the shank is scored
7. A reamer is used to correct a drilled hole. Which of the following hole faults *cannot* be corrected by a reamer?
   a) poor finish
   b) axial position
   c) out of roundness
   d) oversize diameter
8. a) State *two* differences between hand and machine reamers.
   b) Describe briefly the difference between a reamer with a fluted cutting action and a reamer with a rose cutting action.
9. Show, by means of sketches, the following operations that can be performed on a drilling machine.
   a) countersinking
   b) counterboring
   c) spot-facing
10. a) Explain why a bench drilling machine is said to have a 'sensitive' feed.
    b) Describe two methods by which the drill may be held in a drilling machine.

13. The centre lathe and turning

Construction features

The centre lathe is a machine tool designed to produce cylindrical, conical and plane (flat) surfaces using a single point tool. It also produces screw threads. These surfaces and threads may be external or internal to the component. Figure 13.1 shows a typical, modern centre lathe and names the more important features. It will be seen that it is built up from a number of basic units, which are accurately aligned during manufacture in order that precision turned components may be produced.

The bed

A typical lathe bed is a strong, bridge-like member, made of high grade cast iron and it is heavily ribbed to give it rigidity. Its upper surface carries the main slideways. Since these slideways locate, directly or indirectly, most of the remaining units, they are responsible for the fundamental alignments of the machine. For this reason the bed slideways must be manufactured to high dimensional and geometrical tolerances. Further, the lathe must be installed with care in order to avoid distortion of the bed.

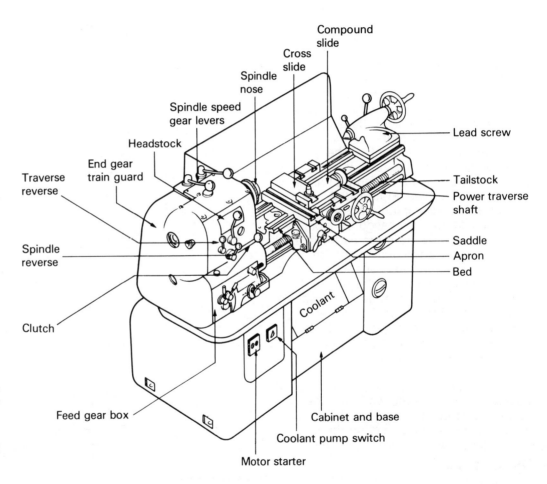

Fig. 13.1 The centre lathe

The headstock

The headstock, or 'fast-head' as it is sometimes called, is a box-like casting supporting the spindle. It contains a gearbox, so the spindle may be rotated at various speeds.

The spindle is machined from a massive, hollow, alloy-steel forging and it carries and rotates the various work-holding devices and the work itself. The spindle is hollow to accept bar stock and its nose is bored internally to a Morse taper to accept the adaptor sleeve. The sleeve accepts the Morse taper shank of the live centre. The periphery of the spindle nose is machined to provide a mounting for the work-holding devices. Figure 13.2 shows three typical spindle nose mountings. Mountings based on taper locations are to be preferred as these are self-aligning and compensate for normal wear without loss of accuracy.

The spindle is located in strong and accurate bearings so that its axis, and the axis of the work-holding devices mounted upon it, are parallel to the bed slideways of the machine both in the horizontal and vertical planes. The spindle, its bearings and the headstock castings must be sufficiently rigid to prevent the mass of the work and the work-holding device, together with the cutting forces, from deflecting the spindle axis from its normal alignment.

The tailstock

The tailstock, or 'loose-head' as it is sometimes called, is located at the

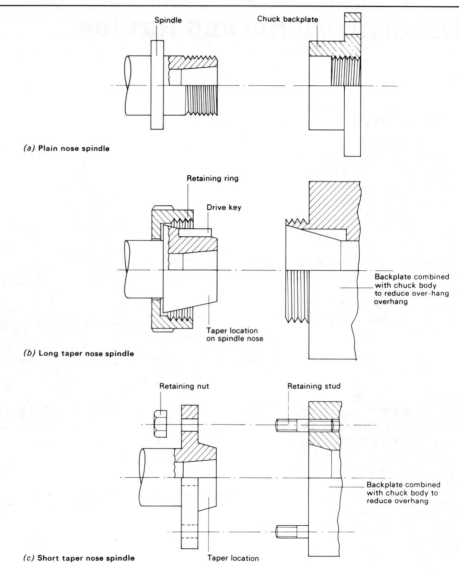

Fig. 13.2 Spindle nose mountings

THE CENTRE LATHE AND TURNING

opposite end of the bed to the headstock. It is free to move back and forth along the bed slideways and can be securely clamped in any convenient position. It consists of a cast iron body in which is located the barrel or poppet. The barrel is hollow and is bored with a Morse taper. This taper locates the taper shank of a dead centre and it also locates taper shank drills, drill chucks, die holders, etc. The bore is co-axial with the spindle. That is, they have a common axis and this is a basic alignment of the lathe.

The barrel of the tailstock is given longitudinal movement within the tailstock body by means of a screw and handwheel. The screw also acts as an ejector for devices inserted in the barrel. The barrel can also be locked in any convenient position.

The body of the tailstock is mounted on a base with adjusting screws to provide lateral movement. Figure 13.3 shows a section through the tailstock.

The carriage

This controls the movement of the cutting tool. It consists of the saddle which spans the bed of the lathe; the apron which hangs down in front of the saddle and carries the controls; the cross-slide which controls the in-feed of the tool, and the compound slide which can control angular movement of the tool.

The carriage may be moved back and forth along the bed slideways using either the traverse handwheel (manual operation) or the power traverse. Figure

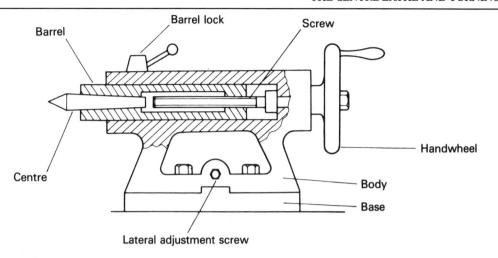

Fig. 13.3 Centre lathe tail stock

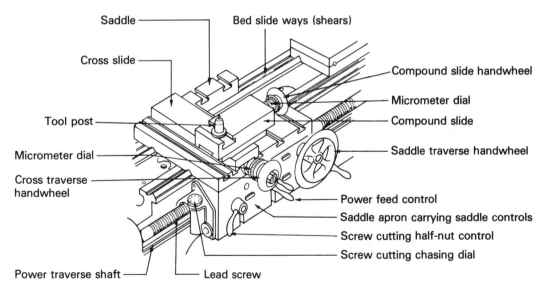

Fig. 13.4 Carriage

263

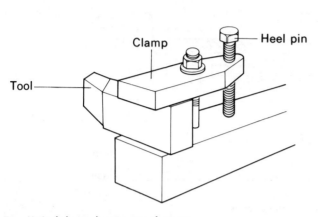

(a) **English (clamp) type tool post**

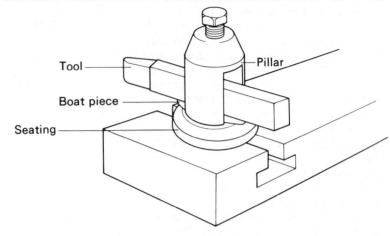

(b) **American (pillar) type tool post**

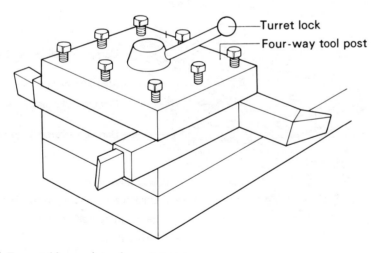

(c) **Turret (4-way) tool post type**

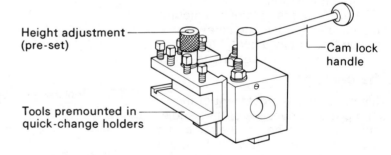

(d) **Quick-release type tool post**

Fig. 13.5 Centre lathe tool posts

THE CENTRE LATHE AND TURNING

13.4 shows the carriage of a lathe in greater detail than Fig. 13.1.

The tool post

The tool post is mounted on the compound slide and carries the cutting tool. Figure 13.5 shows the four types most commonly used.

The type shown in Fig. 13.5(a) is simple and robust, but suffers from several disadvantages. The height of the tool can only be adjusted by the tedious process of adding or subtracting packing and shims until the tool is the correct height and in line with the spindle axis. This has to be repeated every time the tool is changed. Further, only one tool is carried at a time. When machining a small batch of complex components, rapid tool changing is not possible.

The type shown in Fig. 13.5(b) is commonly used for light duty lathes. The tool height is quickly and easily adjusted by rocking the boat piece in its spherical seating. Unfortunately, this type of tool post lacks rigidity due to the overhang of the tool. Further, adjustment of the boat piece alters the effective cutting angles.

The four-way turret type tool post shown in Fig. 13.5(c) saves tool changing when making a batch of components, each tool being swung into position as required. The limitation of this arrangement is that the number of tools is restricted to four, and the vertical adjustment is made by inserting packing under the tool. The shank size of the tool is also restricted.

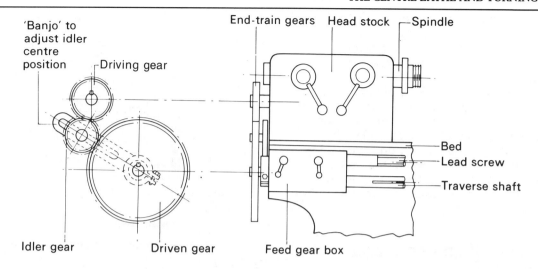

Fig. 13.6 Centre lathe end train gears

The quick-release tool post shown in Fig. 13.5(d) is now increasingly used. An unlimited number of tools may be pre-set in the holders ready for use. Tool height is quickly and easily adjusted by means of a screw, and can be pre-set for each tool away from the lathe.

The feed gearbox

This is driven from the spindle by the end train gears as shown in Fig. 13.6. The reason for driving the feed gearbox from the spindle is that the tool movement per revolution of the spindle must remain constant even if the spindle speed is changed. The feed gearbox has three functions.
1 To control the speed at which the saddle is driven along the bed when power traversing.
2 To control the speed at which the cross slide moves across the saddle when power cross-traversing.
3 To control the speed of the lead screw when cutting screw threads, and thus control the lead of the screw being cut.
Note: Power traverse is provided by the traverse shaft and the lead screw should only be used when screw cutting to preserve its accuracy.

Many lathes are provided with a slipping clutch, or a shear pin, in the traverse shaft drive to prevent damage to the gearbox if too heavy a cut is taken.

The lead screw is usually provided with a dog-clutch so that it can be

265

disconnected when not in use to prevent wear. Figure 13.7 shows a typical, Norton-type feed gearbox.

Principle of the Norton-type gear box.

The roller gear (R), which is driven by the input shaft, can be engaged with any station (1–9) on the cluster cone gear by means of the tumbler gear (T). The tumbler gear is carried on a movable yoke which is located in the gearbox casing by a peg in the spring-loaded handle. The peg locates in holes in the gear box casing.

Basic alignments and movement

Figure 13.8(a) shows the basic alignment of the headstock, tailstock, spindle and bed slideways. It will be seen that the common spindle and tailstock axis is parallel to the bed slideways in both the vertical and horizontal planes. This is the basic alignment of the lathe and all other alignments are referred to it.

The movement of the carriage alone is shown in Fig. 13.8(b). It will be seen that it moves the cutting tool in a path parallel to the spindle axis and this produces cylindrical surfaces.

The cross-slide on top of the carriage is aligned at 90° to the spindle axis as shown in Fig. 13.8(c). Since this slide moves the tool in a path at right angles to the spindle axis, it is used for producing plane surfaces. This operation is called 'facing' and is used

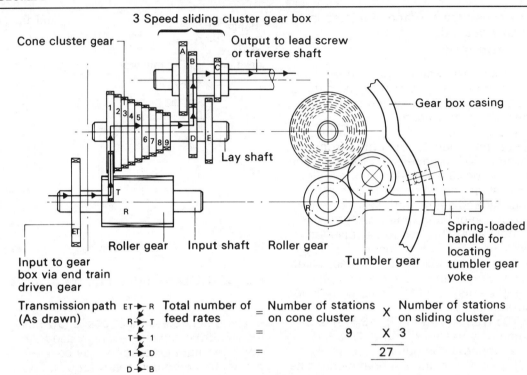

Principle of the Norton-type gear box

The Roller Gear (R), which is driven by the input shaft, can be engaged with any station (1–9) on the cluster cone gear by means of the tumbler gear (T). The tumbler gear is carried on a movable yoke which is located in the gearbox casing by a peg in the spring-loaded handle. The peg locates in holes in the gear box casing.

Fig. 13.7 Centre lathe feed gear box

to machine the flat ends of components. The cross-slide is also used to control the depth of cut, or in-feed, of the cutting tool, and for this purpose the handwheel is fitted with a micrometer dial.

The top or compound-slide is located on top of the cross-slide and can be set at an angle to the spindle axis as shown in Fig. 13.8(d). Since it moves the tool in a path that is at an angle to the spindle axis, it is used to produce conical or

THE CENTRE LATHE AND TURNING

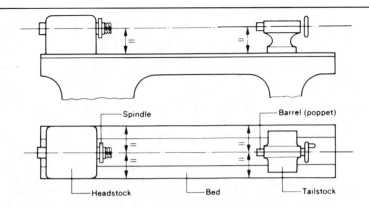

(a) Basic alignment

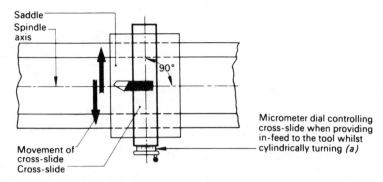

(c) The cross-slide

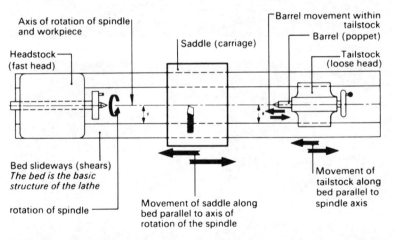

(b) The carriage or saddle provides the basic movement of the cutting tool parallel to the work axis

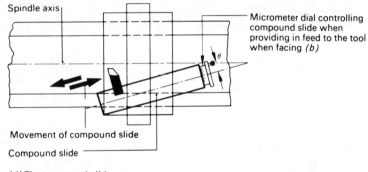

(d) The compound slide

Fig. 13.8 Centre lathe – basic geometry

(a) Taper turning

(b) Screw-cutting

(c) Cylindrical (parallel) turning

(d) Facing (surfacing)

Fig. 13.9 Turned surfaces

THE CENTRE LATHE AND TURNING

tapered components. Taper turning is considered more fully in *Mechanical Engineering Craft Theory and Related Subjects: Volume 2*. When set parallel to the spindle axis, the compound slide can be used for controlling the in-feed of the cutting tool when facing the component from the cross-slide. For this purpose the handwheel of the compound-slide is fitted with a micrometer dial.

The surfaces produced by these basic alignments and movements are summarised in Fig. 13.9. As these surfaces depend upon the movements and geometrical alignments of the slideways for their production, and are independent of the shape of the cutting tool, they are said to be generated.

Work-holding on the centre lathe

The general requirement of lathe work is that all diameters should be concentric or, if eccentricity is required, that the degree of offset should be accurately controlled. The most satisfactory way of achieving concentricity is to turn all diameters at one setting. This is not always possible and a range of work-holding techniques and devices have been designed. These enable a wide variety of components to be set and re-set to achieve the accuracy of concentricity desired.

These work-holding devices must be capable of:
1 locating the work relative to the spindle axis;
2 rotating the work at the correct speed without slip;
3 preventing the work being deflected by the cutting forces. Some slender work requires additional support;
4 holding the work sufficiently rigidly so that it will not spin out of the machine or be ejected by the cutting forces. At the same time it must not be crushed or distorted by the work-holding device.

The following are the normal methods of work-holding on the centre lathe. They exclude special turning fixtures.

Between centres

This is the traditional method of work-holding from which the centre lathe gets its name, and is shown in Fig. 13.10(a). It will be seen that the component is located between the centres and is driven by the catchplate and carrier. Since the driving mechanism can 'float', it has no influence on the accuracy of location of the workpiece. The centres have Morse taper shanks and are located in taper sockets in the spindle and tailstock barrel. The use of taper locations ensures axial alignment irrespective of variations due to manufacturing tolerance and wear. Figure 13.10(b) shows the restraints acting upon a component held between centres. The advantages and limitations of this method of workholding are listed in Table 13.1 on page 270.

For parallel turning, the axis of the spindle centre and the axis of the tailstock centre must be coincident with each other and parallel to the main bed slideways. The tailstock is provided with lateral (sideways) adjustment to achieve this.

When turning between centres, a trial cut should be taken along the component. It is then checked at each end with a micrometer caliper. If the readings are the same, then the component is a true cylinder and the roughing and finishing cuts may be taken. If the readings are different, then the tailstock has to be adjusted as shown in Fig. 13.11(a). Further trial cuts may be taken until the diameter is constant along the length of the component (page 271).

A more convenient method of bringing the axis into alignment by lateral adjustment is shown in Fig. 13.11(b). This can only be done if a parallel test bar is available. Note that a mandrel cannot be used as it has a built-in taper and would give false readings. (See page 271). Care must be taken in the preparation of the centre hole and the way the component is mounted between the centres. Figure 13.12 shows a section through the component. It will be seen that the conical hole in the compound locates on the flanks of the centre. The point of the centre takes no part in the location of the component. Figure 13.12(b) shows two typical faults that can occur when the centre hole is incorrectly drilled. The work will only run true on the centre if the centre hole is undamaged. Therefore where components have to be taken in and out

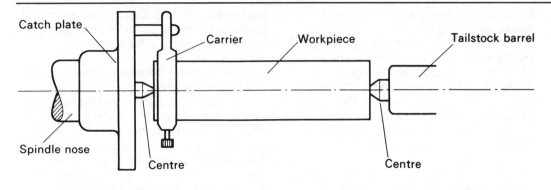

Table 13.1 Work-holding between centres

ADVANTAGES

1. Work can be easily reversed without loss of concentricity
2. Work can be taken from the machine for inspection and easily re-set without loss of concentricity
3. Work can be transferred between machines (e.g. lathe and cylindrical grinder) without loss of concentricity
4. Long work (full length of bed) can be accommodated

LIMITATIONS

1. Centre holes have to be drilled before work can be set up
2. Only limited work can be performed on the end of the bar
3. Boring operations cannot be performed
4. There is lack of rigidity
5. Cutting speeds are limited unless a revolving centre is used. This reduces accuracy and accessibility
6. Skill in setting is required to obtain the correct fit between centres and work

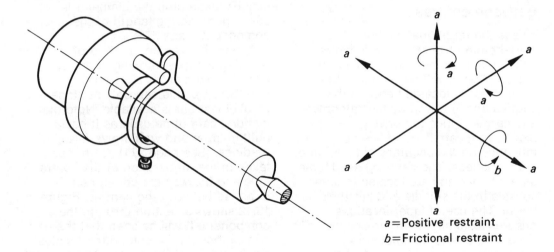

a = Positive restraint
b = Frictional restraint

Fig. 13.10 Work holding between centres

of the centres frequently, the centre hole should be *recessed* or *protected* as shown in Fig. 13.12(c) (see page 272).

The taper mandrel

If the diameter of a hole is small, it is difficult to make the boring tool sufficiently rigid to true up the previously drilled hole. Under these conditions, it is better to rough out the external diameters and then drill and ream the bore to provide a round hole of good finish. Mount the component on a mandrel as shown in Fig. 13.13(a) and finish turn the external diameters, which will then be true with the mandrel axis. A mandrel press for mounting and dismounting the component is shown in Fig. 13.13(b) on page 272.

The mandrel is tapered so that the further the component is forced on, the more firmly it is held in place. Therefore, the direction of cutting should always be towards the 'plus end' of the mandrel.

Figure 13.14 shows the restraints acting on a component mounted on a mandrel. The restraints shown are those relative to the mandrel. The restraints acting on the mandrel itself are the same as for any component mounted between centres. Table 13.2 lists the advantages and limitations of this method of workholding (page 273).

The self-centring chuck

Figure 13.15(a) shows the construction of a typical three-jaw chuck. It will be seen that the scroll not only clamps the component in place, but it locates the

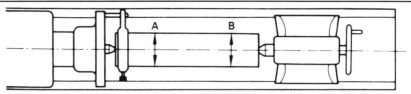

For parallel cylindrical turning the axis of the headstock spindle must be in alignment with the tailstock barrel. If this is so, then the diameter of the component at 'A' will be the same as the diameter at 'B'

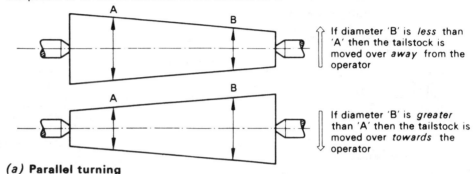

If diameter 'B' is *less* than 'A' then the tailstock is moved over *away* from the operator

If diameter 'B' is *greater* than 'A' then the tailstock is moved over *towards* the operator

(a) **Parallel turning**

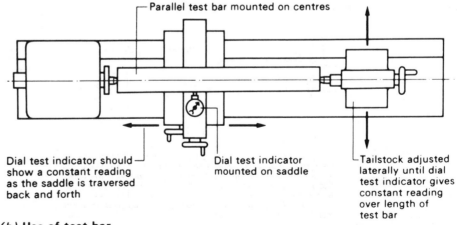

(b) **Use of test bar**

Fig. 13.11 Parallel turning – setting the tailstock

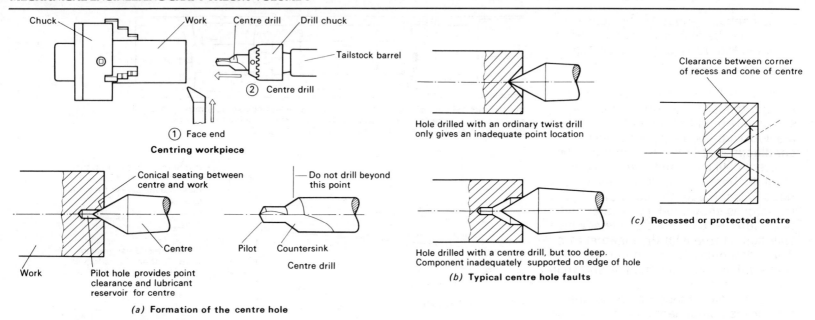

Fig. 13.12 The centre hole

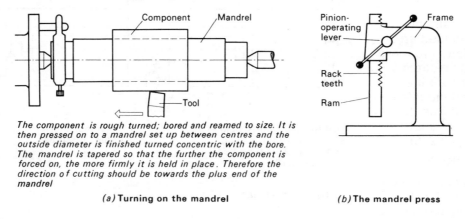

Fig. 13.13 Mandrel work

THE CENTRE LATHE AND TURNING

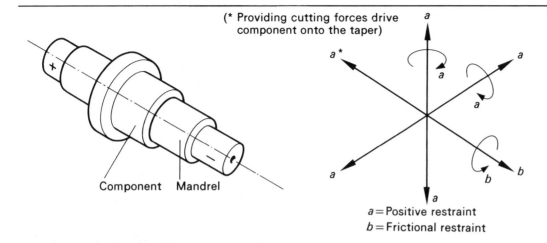

Fig. 13.14 The mandrel – restraints

Table 13.2 Work-holding on the mandrel

ADVANTAGES	LIMITATIONS
1 Small-bore components can be turned with the bore and outside diameters concentric 2 Batch production is possible without loss of concentricity or lengthy set-up time 3 The advantages of turning between centres apply (see Table 12.1)	1 Bore must be a standard size to fit a taper mandrel. Adjustable mandrels are available but these tend to lack rigidity and accuracy 2 Cuts should only be taken towards the 'plus' end of the mandrel 3 Only friction drive available, and this limits size of cut that can be taken 4 Special mandrels can be made but this is not economical for one-off jobs 5 Items 2 to 5 of the limitations in Table 12.1 apply

component as well (page 274). This is fundamentally bad practice, as any wear in the scroll and/or the jaws, impairs the accuracy of location. Further, there is no means of adjustment possible to compensate for this wear.

The jaws of this type of chuck are not reversible and separate internal and external jaws have to be used as shown in Fig. 13.15(b). When changing jaws, the following precautions should be observed:

1 check that each jaw in the set carries the same serial number and that this serial number is the same as that on the chuck body;
2 insert the jaws sequentially: number 1 jaw in number 1 slot, etc.

When new, self-centring chucks are quite accurate. To preserve this accuracy, never:

1 try to hammer the work true;
2 hold on an untrue surface such as hot rolled (black) bar;
3 hold on the tips of the jaws.

The restraints acting on a component held in a three-jaw, self-centring chuck are shown in Fig. 13.15(c). The advantages and limitations of this method of workholding are listed in Table 13.3 on page 274.

The four-jaw independent chuck

This type of chuck, which is shown in Fig. 13.16, is much more heavily constructed than the self-centring chuck and has much greater holding power. Each jaw is moved independently by a square thread screw and is reversible. These chucks are used

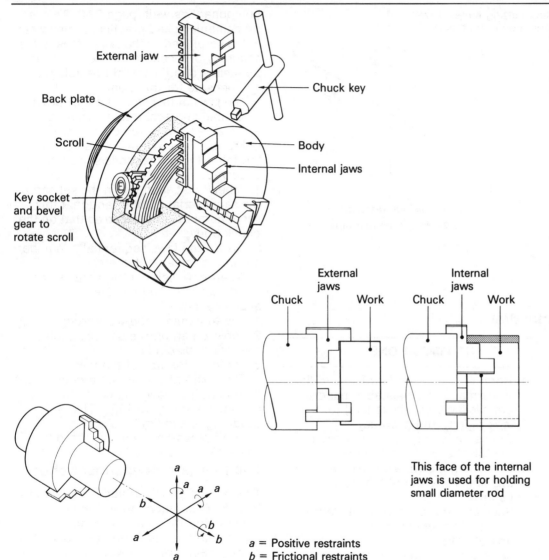

Fig. 13.15 The three-jaw, self centring chuck

Table 13.3 The self-centring chuck

ADVANTAGES

1. Ease of work setting
2. A wide range of cylindrical and hexagonal work can be held
3. Internal and external jaws are available
4. Work can be readily performed on the end face of the job
5. The work can be bored

LIMITATIONS

1. Accuracy decreases as chuck becomes worn
2. Accuracy of concentricity is limited when work is reversed in the chuck
3. 'Run out' cannot be corrected
4. Soft jaws can be turned up for second operation work, but this is seldom economical for one-off jobs
5. Only round and hexagonal components can be held

THE CENTRE LATHE AND TURNING

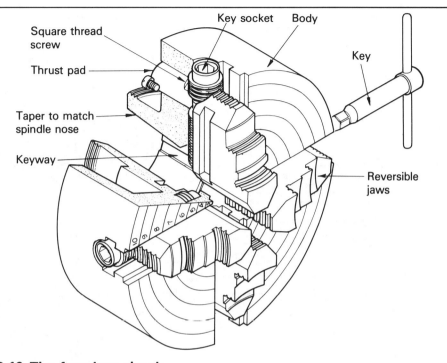

Fig. 13.16 The four-jaw chuck

for holding:
1 irregularly shaped work;
2 work that must be trued up to run concentrically;
3 work that must be deliberately offset to run eccentrically.

Eccentrically mounted work must be balanced when using the four-jaw chuck.

The jaws of the four-jaw chuck can be reversed for holding externally on the workpiece and so separate internal and external jaws are not required. (See page 271.) As the jaws are moved independently in this type of chuck, the component has to be set to run concentrically with the spindle axis. If a smooth or previously machined surface is available, a dial test indicator (DTI) may be used as shown in Fig. 13.17(a). Alternatively, if a centre point is to be picked up for drilling and boring, a floating centre and dial test indicator may be used as shown in Fig. 13.17(b). Rough work may be set as shown in Fig. 13.17(c) (page 276).

The restraints acting on a component held in a four-jaw independent chuck are shown in Fig. 13.18. The advantages and limitations of this method of workholding are considered in Table 13.4 on page 277.

Concentricity

When a component is being turned, it is usual to try to keep the various diameters concentric, that is, with the same axis. The meaning of concentricity and eccentricity is shown in Fig. 13.19.

In Fig. 13.19(a) the two diameters A and B are concentric; they have the same centre of rotation and lie on the same axis. For example, if diameter B was rotated in a vee block and a dial test indicator was in contact with diameter A, then the dial test indicator would show a constant reading.

In Fig. 13.19(b) the two diameters A and B are eccentric; they have different centres of rotation and do not lie on a common axis. The distance E between the centres of rotation is the amount of 'offset' or eccentricity. In this example, if the diameter B was rotated in a vee block and a dial test indicator was in contact with diameter A, then it would show a variation in reading equal to 2E. This variation between the maximum and minimum readings of the dial test indicator is called the *throw*.

Throw = 2 × Eccentricity = 2E

The easiest way to ensure concentricity is to turn as many diameters as possible at the same setting without removing the component from the lathe, as shown in Fig. 13.20. If the work does have to be

275

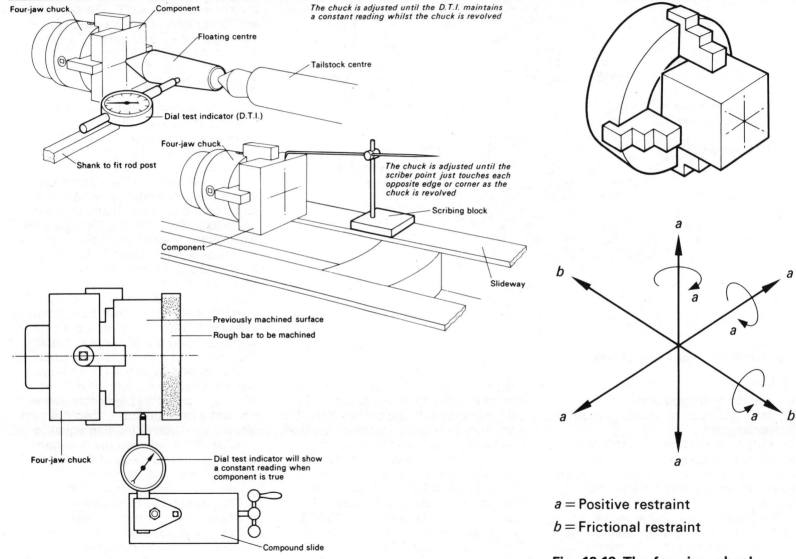

Fig. 13.17 The four-jaw chuck – work setting

a = Positive restraint
b = Frictional restraint

Fig. 13.18 The four-jaw chuck – restraints

Table 13.4 The four-jaw chuck

ADVANTAGES

1. A wide range of regular and irregular shapes can be held
2. Work can be set to run concentrically, or eccentrically at will
3. Considerable gripping power. Heavy cuts can be taken
4. Jaws are reversible for internal and external work
5. Work can readily be performed on the end face of the job
6. The work can be bored
7. There is no loss of accuracy as the chuck becomes worn

LIMITATIONS

1. Chuck is heavy to handle on to the lathe
2. Chuck is slow to set up. A dial test indicator (DTI) has to be used for accurate setting
3. Chuck is bulky
4. The gripping power is so great that fine work can be easily damaged during setting

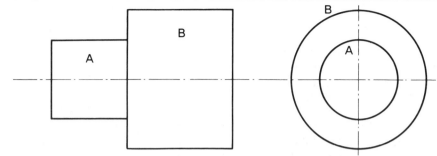

(a) **Concentric diameters** (both diameters have the same centres)

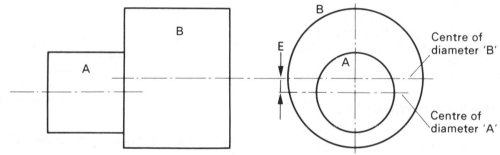

(b) **Eccentric diameters** (each diameter has a different centre)

Fig. 13.19 Concentricity and eccentricity

removed from the chuck and turned round, then it should be mounted in a four-jaw chuck and trued up as shown in Fig. 13.17. If, of course, only limited accuracy of concentricity is required, the component may be reversed in the self-centring chuck.

Tool height

Although a tool may be ground to the correct cutting angles, these can be destroyed by mounting the tool off-centre. Figure 13.21 shows why it is essential to mount the tool at the centre height of the workpiece. As well as altering the effective cutting angles, mounting the tool off-centre can also distort the profile of the component when taper turning, screw cutting or forming (see page 278).

1. Figure 13.21(a) shows the tool

correctly set. It will be seen that the effective cutting angles are the same as those ground on the tool.

2   When the tool point is set below the centre height of the job, as shown in Fig. 13.21(b), the effective rake angle is decreased and the effective clearance angle is increased.

3   When the tool point is set above the centre height of the job, as shown in Fig. 13.21(c), the effective rake angle is increased and the effective clearance angle is decreased.

Figure 13.22 shows the effect of setting a boring tool above and below centre. It will be seen that the changes in the effective cutting angles are the reverse of those shown in Fig. 13.21.

Types of turning tool

The lathe uses single-point cutting tools based on the principles discussed in Chapter 9. As well as being ground to the correct cutting angles, the lathe tool must also have the correct plan view (profile) according to the operation being performed. Figure 13.23 shows some typical tool profiles and their applications.

Some of the tools shown are cutting orthogonally and some obliquely. These terms are explained in Fig. 13.24. It is easier to re-grind an orthogonal tool to the correct cutting angles, but an oblique tool generally cuts more easily. An oblique tool reduces the chip thickness, and the load on the tool, for any given value of metal removed per revolution (page 280).

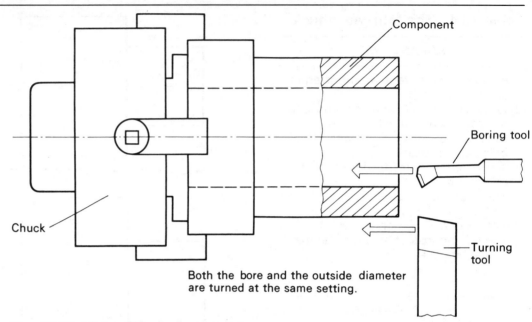

Both the bore and the outside diameter are turned at the same setting.

Fig. 13.20 Maintaining concentricity

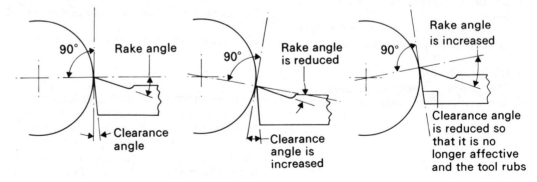

(a) **Tool set correctly on centre height**

(b) **Tool set below centre height**

(c) **Tool set above centre height**

Fig. 13.21 Effect of tool height on turning tool angles

THE CENTRE LATHE AND TURNING

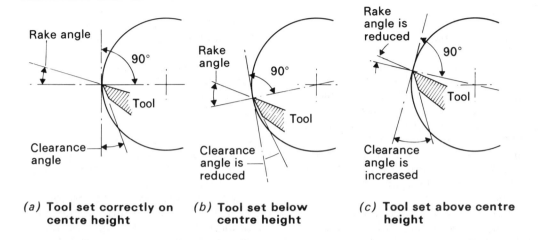

(a) **Tool set correctly on centre height**

(b) **Tool set below centre height**

(c) **Tool set above centre height**

Fig. 13.22 Effect of tool height on boring tool angles

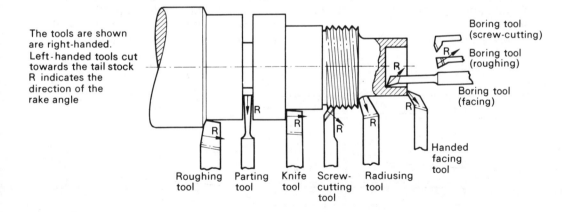

Fig. 13.23 Lathe tool profits

Boring on the lathe

Hollow as well as solid components have to be produced on the lathe. Holes concentric with the spindle axis, may be produced by:
1. drilling;
2. reaming;
3. boring;
4. a combination of the above.

The technique, or combination of techniques, chosen will depend upon the size of the hole and its depth/diameter ratio, the accuracy required, and whether a 'through' or 'blind' hole is required.

Drilling

Unless the bore is only a shallow recess, it is usual to rough out the hole with a twist drill held in the tailstock. A start is made for the twist drill by using a centre drill in exactly the same way as when preparing a component for turning between centres. As the feed force available from the tailstock barrel screw is limited, it is usual – when drilling large holes – to drill a pilot bore first, and then open it up with successively larger drills. The limitations of a drilled hole were discussed earlier. They are:
1. poor finish compared with boring or reaming;
2. lack of dimensional accuracy;
3. lack of 'roundness' or geometrical accuracy;
4. lack of positional accuracy as the drill tends to 'wander', especially when drilling deep holes in soft materials such as brass.

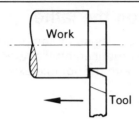

(a) **Orthogonal cutting**

The cutting edge is perpendicular to the direction of feed. Useful for producing a square shoulder at the end of a roughing cut

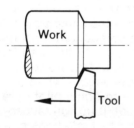

(b) **Oblique cutting**

The cutting edge is inclined to the direction of feed. Most efficient form for rapid metal removal

Fig. 13.24 Orthogonal and oblique cutting

Reaming

The quality of the hole is greatly improved if it is drilled slightly undersize and finished with a reamer (Fig. 12.7). The reamer should be held in a 'floating' holder so that it can follow the drilled hole without flexing. This prevents ovality and bell-mouthing. Figure 13.25 shows a typical reamer holder. The reamed hole has a good finish and a high degree of roundness. However, a reamed hole has the following limitations.

1   There is a lack of positional accuracy as the reamer follows the axis of the original drilled hole, and reproduces any 'wander' that is present;

2   Unless the quantity of components being produced warrants special tooling, only holes with diameters the same as standard reamer sizes can be produced.

Where a hole is too small to bore accurately, it is usual to drill and ream the hole to size, and then turn the outside diameter true with the bore while the workpiece is mounted on a mandrel (see page 271). In this case the initial 'wander' of the drilled hole is unimportant.

Boring

Figure 13.26 shows a solid boring tool used for small holes and a boring bar with an inserted tool-bit for larger holes. It also shows the necessity for secondary clearance on a boring tool to prevent the heel of the tool fouling on small diameter holes. Because of the overhang of the tool point from the tool post and the slender shank of the tool, boring tools are prone to chatter and the cut is liable to run off due to deflection of the shank. This makes boring a highly skilful operation compared with external turning, and great care is required in grinding the

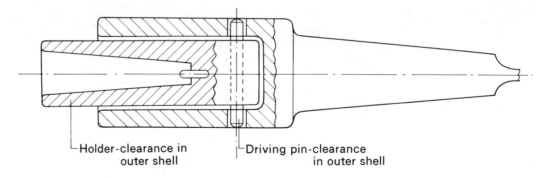

Fig. 13.25 Floating reamer holder

THE CENTRE LATHE AND TURNING

tool and selecting appropriate feeds and speeds.

If a standard size hole is required, it is often preferable to drill, then bore slightly under size to remove any 'wander' in the hole axis, and ream to size. The reamer will give a better finish and a truer hole than a small boring tool.

Whilst boring is the only possible means of removing 'wander' and giving a high degree of positional accuracy, it has the following limitations:
1 chatter and poor surface finish, especially on small diameter holes where only a slender tool can be used;
2 the hole tends to be oval and bell mouthed due to deflection of the boring tool shank. These defects become less severe as the hole diameter increases, thus allowing an increasingly more rigid boring tool.

Speeds and feeds

To keep the cost of production as low as possible during a machining process, the waste material must be removed as rapidly as possible. Unfortunately, high rates of material removal usually result in a poor finish and relatively low dimensional accuracy. For example, a hole is quickly roughed out with a twist drill, but if a high degree of accuracy and finish is required, the hole must be finished with a reamer which only removes a small volume of material.

The factors controlling the rate of material removal are:
1 the finish required;

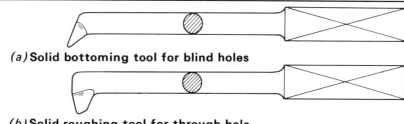

(a) Solid bottoming tool for blind holes

(b) Solid roughing tool for through hole

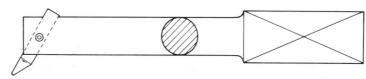

(c) Boring bar with inserted tool bit for bottoming a blind hole

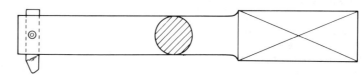

(d) Boring bar with inserted tool bit for roughing a through hole

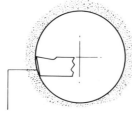 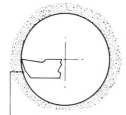

Primary clearance only, causes heel of tool to rub. Increasing clearance weakens the tool

secondary clearance prevents heel of tool rubbing, but permits a small primary clearance to be used to give strength to the tool

(e) **Need for secondary clearance**

Fig. 13.26 Centre lathe – boring tools

281

2 the depth of cut;
3 the tool geometry;
4 the properties and rigidity of the cutting tool and its mounting;
5 the properties of the workpiece material;
6 the rigidity of the workpiece;
7 the power and rigidity of the machine tool.

In a machining operation, the same rate of material removal may be achieved by using:
1 A high rate of feed and a shallow cut as shown in Fig. 13.27(a). Unfortunately this not only leads to a rough finish, but imposes a greater load on the cutting tool, as shown in Fig. 13.27(b).
2 A low rate of feed and a deep cut as shown in Fig. 13.28(a). This gives a better finish and, if the size is correct, avoids having to take a finishing cut. It also reduces the load on the cutting tool, as shown in Fig. 13.28(b). Unfortunately, a deep cut is liable to cause excessive chatter.

Therefore a compromise between depth of cut and rate of feed has to be found. However, it is usually advisable, for the reasons given above, to use the deepest cut possible for any given set of conditions.

Table 13.5 gives suitable speeds and feeds for turning operations on a centre lathe using high-speed steel tools. These are only a guide and the actual rates used may be increased or decreased, as experience dictates, for any particular set up.

Example 13.1 Calculate the spindle speed, to the nearest rev/min for turning a 25 mm diameter bar at a cutting speed of 30 m/min (take π as 3·14).

Solution

$$N = \frac{1000S}{\pi D}$$

where: N = spindle speed

S = 30 m/min
π = 3·14
D = 25 mm

Therefore:

$$N = \frac{1000 \times 30}{3 \cdot 14 \times 25}$$

$$= 382 \text{ rev/min}$$

(to the nearest rev/min)

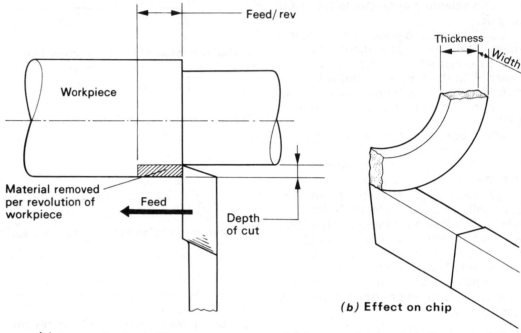

(a) Coarse feed: shallow cut

(b) Effect on chip

With coarse feed and shallow cut, the chip is bent across its deepest section. The bending force increases as the cube of the depth of the chip, i.e. doubling the depth of the chip increases the bending force eight times

Fig. 13.27 Effect of high feed rates

THE CENTRE LATHE AND TURNING

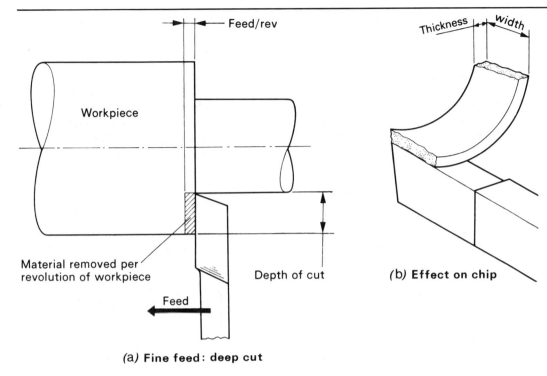

(a) Fine feed: deep cut

(b) Effect on chip

Fig. 13.28 Effect of deep cuts

Table 13.5 Cutting speeds and feeds for HSS turning tools

MATERIAL BEING TURNED	FEED (mm/rev)	CUTTING SPEED (m/min)
Aluminium	0·2–1·00	70–100
Brass (alpha) (ductile)	0·2–1·00	50–80
Brass (free-cutting)	0·2–1·5	70–100
Bronze (phosphor)	0·2–1·0	35–70
Cast iron (grey)	0·15–0·7	25–40
Copper	0·2–1·00	35–70
Steel (mild)	0·2–1·00	35–50
Steel (medium carbon)	0·15–0·7	30–35
Steel (alloy-high tensile)	0·08–0·3	5–10
Thermo-setting plastic (low speed due to abrasive properties)	0·2–1·0	35–50

Notes:
1. The above feeds and speeds are for ordinary H.S.S. cutters. For *super* H.S.S. cutters the feeds would remain the same, but the cutting speeds could be increased by 15% to 20%.
2. The *lower* speed range is suitable for heavy, roughing cuts.
   The *higher* speed range is suitable for light, finishing cuts.
3. The feed is selected to give the required surface finish and rate of metal removal.

Example 13.2 Calculate the time taken to turn a brass component 49 mm in diameter by 70 mm in length if the cutting speed is 44 m/min and the feed is 0·5 mm/revolution. Only one cut is taken (take π as $22/7$).

Solution

$$N = \frac{1000S}{\pi D}$$

where: N = spindle speed
S = 44 m/min
π = $22/7$
D = 49 mm

$$N = \frac{1000 \times 44 \times 7}{22 \times 49}$$
$$= 286 \text{ rev/min}$$

Rate of feed = 0·5 mm/rev
= 0·5 × 286 mm/min
= 143 mm/min

Time taken to traverse 70 mm = $\frac{70}{143}$ min
= $\frac{70 \times 60}{143}$ s
= $\underline{29\cdot37 \text{ s}}$

Exercises

1. Sketch and describe the following types of lathe tool post, paying particular attention to their advantages and limitations.
   a) pillar (American) type tool post
   b) four-way turret type tool post
2. Describe a possible cause for a workpiece being tapered when turned between centres on a centre lathe. Describe how this fault may be corrected.
3. When turning a long component between centres, why:
   a) is the tailstock centre 'eased' from time to time?
   b) is a revolving centre sometimes used?
   c) can a soft centre be used in the headstock spindle?
4. a) By means of a simple line diagram, show a typical component being turned between centres on a taper mandrel. Why is the mandrel in the lathe with its 'plus' end towards the headstock?
   b) Describe the advantages in turning the component selected on a mandrel.
5. Describe how the jaws of a self-centring chuck are changed from internal to external, and include any precautions that must be taken to ensure concentricity.
6. By means of simple line diagrams show *two* methods of setting work concentric in a four-jaw independent chuck.
7. a) Sketch the following types of turning tool:
      (i) straight nosed roughing tool
      (ii) bar (knife) turning tool
      (iii) left-hand facing tool
      (iv) parting-off tool
   b) Show, by means of a sketch, the effect on the rake angle and on the clearance angle of setting a lathe tool *above* centre.
8. a) A tool bit of 9 mm square section is to be held in a boring bar to bore a blind hole of 55 mm in diameter. Show by a neat, well proportioned sketch, how the tool bit is ground and held for this operation.
   b) State why it is sometimes necessary to provide a *secondary clearance* for a

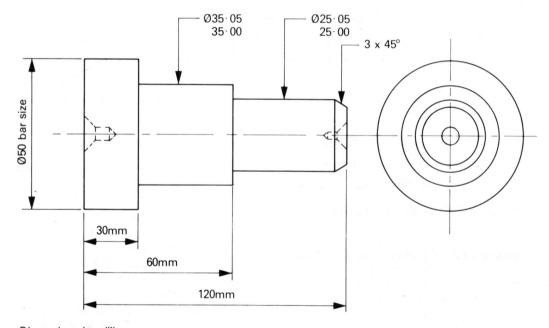

Dimensions in millimetres
Untolerance dimensions ± 0·5mm
Blank size Ø50 x 130
Material: free cutting mild steel
Projection: 3rd angle

Fig. 13.29

boring tool.
(*WAEC* 1974)

9. a) Calculate the spindle speed, to the nearest rev/min, for turning a 50 mm diameter bar at a cutting speed of 40 m/min (take π as 3:14).
   b) Calculate the time taken to turn the above component if the feed is 0:2 mm. Only one cut is taken.

10. a) With reference to the component shown in Fig. 13.29, describe with the aid of sketches how:
    (i) the ends of the blank are faced and centred
    (ii) the blank is mounted between centres ready for turning
    b) Draw up a simple operation schedule for producing the component shown in Fig. 13.29, using the following headings.

Operation no	Description of operation	Tools used

14. The shaping machine and shaping

Generation of a plane surface

The purpose of a shaping machine is to generate flat (plane) surfaces by means of a single point tool similar to a lathe tool. As shown in Fig. 14.1, these surfaces may be parallel, perpendicular, or inclined to the working surface of the machine table.

To understand how this machine generates a plane surface, it is easiest to consider the surface parallel to the machine table. The ram of the shaping machine moves the cutting tool backwards and forwards in a straight line as shown in Fig. 14.2(a). Each time the tool moves forward it cuts a sliver of metal from the workpiece. Each time the tool moves backward the tool lifts clear of the workpiece and the workpiece moves across in a path perpendicular to the tool movement as shown in Fig. 14.2(a). The work remains stationary during the forward (cutting) stroke of the tool, and only moves across by one cross-traverse increment during the return (non-cutting) stroke. The appearance of the machined surface is of a succession of closely spaced, straight line cuts. For this reason it is often referred to as a ruled surface. The method by which the surface is generated is shown in Fig. 14.2(b).

From the foregoing explanation of the generation of a plane surface by 'ruling', it should be apparent that the geometrical relationship between the ram (and therefore the cutting tool) movement and the work table movement is fundamental to the flatness of the surface generated. The geometrical alignments of the machine elements are considered on page 290.

Construction of the shaping machine

Figure 14.3 shows a modern shaping machine and identifies the more important features and controls (page 288). The more important elements of the machine will now be considered in detail.

The column

The column or body of a shaping machine is a ribbed casting of cellular construction and is very rigid. The top of the column carries the ram slideways, while the table slideways are machined on the front of the casting. These slideways are fundamental to all the other machine alignments and are prepared with great care. The crank and slotted link mechanism that drives the ram is contained within the column. The driving motor and variable speed

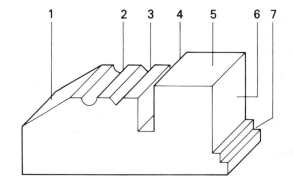

1. Inclined surface
2. } Grooved surface
3. }
4. Slotted surface
5. Horizontal plain surface
6. Vertical plain surface
7. Stepped surface

Fig. 14.1 Surfaces produced on a shaping machine

gearbox are mounted on the rear of the casting. The motor drives the gearbox input shaft by vee-belts and multiple sheave pulleys. The output shaft of the gearbox carries a pinion gear that engages, and drives, the stroke or 'bull' wheel that carries the crank. (See page 291.)

The ram

This is a rigidly braced casting that is located on top of the machine column. The slotted link (page 291) drives the ram back and forth in its slides all the time the machine is operating. The ram is supported in *dovetail* slides. Care must be taken to ensure that the slides are not over-tightened so that the ram cannot slide freely. Figure 14.4 shows a section through the ram and column slideways. It will be seen that the slideway on one side of the column is adjustable to compensate for the wear that occurs as the ram moves back and forth (page 289).

The ram head

This consists of three basic elements: the *tool slide*, the *clapper box* and the *tool post*.

The *tool slide* controls the in-feed of the cutting tool into the workpiece; that is, it controls the depth of cut and is adjusted by a lead screw fitted with a micrometer dial. A slide clamp is often provided so that the tool slide can be locked after it has been set so that the depth of cut cannot alter. The vibration of cutting tends to move the screw. It also removes the cutting forces from the

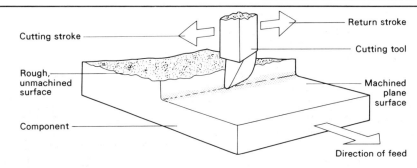

(a) Cutting action of the shaping machine

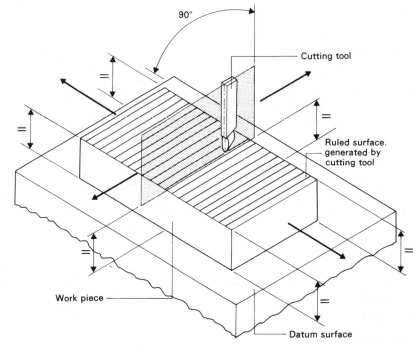

(b) Generation of a plain surface by ruling

Fig. 14.2 Generation of a plane surface

screw and nut, thus preserving their accuracy. The tool slide can also be tilted for machining inclined surfaces that are short and steep. For this purpose a protractor scale is provided. Many larger, modern machines are provided with an intermittent power feed to the tool slide screw. The slide and its movements are shown in Fig. 14.5.

The clapper box allows the cutting tool to lift on the return stroke, as shown in Fig. 14.6. If the tool was rigidly fixed to the tool slide, it would be dragged back through the uncut workpiece as the workpiece moved over ready for the next cut. This would damage the workpiece and the cutting edge would be rubbed away or even broken off the cutting tool. When cutting a surface parallel to the worktable, the clapper box is centralised.

The tool post carries the cutting tool in the same way as it does on the lathe. Details of a typical shaping machine tool post are shown in Fig. 14.7(a). Heavy duty machines often carry a double tool post assembly as shown in Fig. 14.7(b). In this case the tool posts are mounted in tee-slots so that they can be moved out of vertical alignment when the tool is set over at an angle as shown in Fig. 14.7(c) (page 290).

The cross rail

This carries the horizontal table slideways and is mounted on the vertical slideways of the column or body. The cross rail can be raised and lowered by

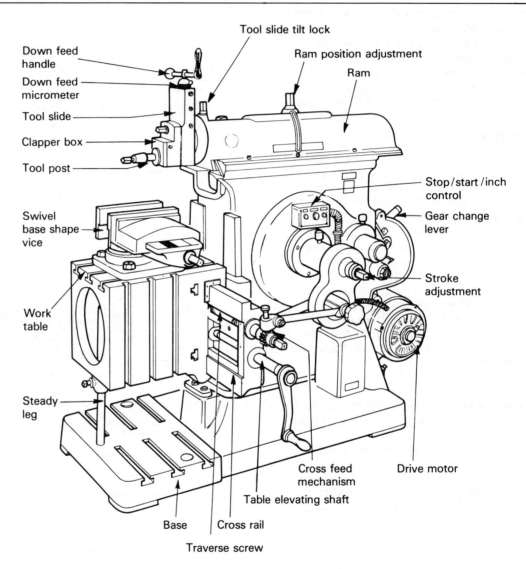

Fig. 14.3 The shaping machine

THE SHAPING MACHINE AND SHAPING

The adjusting screw is tightened to increase force F_N thus increasing component forces F_V and F_H. These latter two forces combine to resist the forces show at (a) and (b) of this figure, i.e. those forces tending to displace the ram. Note: F_N must NOT be increased to the point where the ram becomes stiff to slide back and forth

The dovetail slide

Fig. 14.4 The ram slide

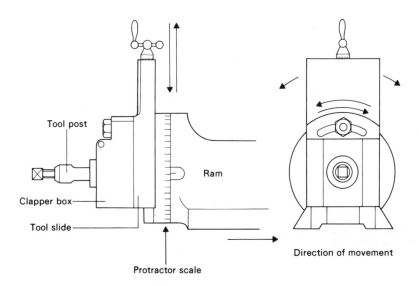

Fig. 14.5 The ram head assembly

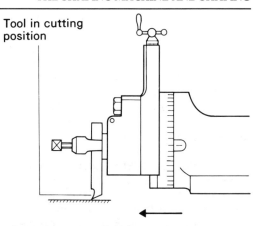

During the forward (cutting) stroke the forces on the tool keep the clapper box shut

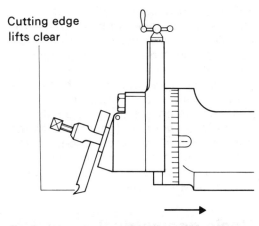

During the return stroke the clapper box is free to lift this allows the tool to ride over the work without wear or damage to the cutting edge of the tool.

Fig. 14.6 Action of the clapper box

means of an elevating screw in order to compensate for different thicknesses of work. On some shaping machines a power drive is provided to the elevating screw and nut. This is to provide a powered vertical traverse to the worktable when machining surfaces perpendicular to the worktable. The general arrangement of the 'cross rail' is shown in Fig. 14.8(a).

The cross rail casting also carries the table traverse lead screw together with the pawl and ratchet intermittent drive mechanism. Details of this mechanism are shown in Fig. 14.8(b). The complete table feed system is considered more fully on page 295.

The work table

This is a box-shaped casting with tee-slots in its upper surface and down one side as shown in Fig. 14.9(a). It also has a vee machine in the vertical side to carry cylindrical work, as shown in Fig. 14.9(b). The upper surface of the table is machined after assembly in the workshop to ensure that it is parallel to the surface swept out (generated) by the combination of ram and cross-traverse movements. This ensures that the working surface of the table is a true datum for work setting.

Basic geometrical alignments

To produce surfaces that are flat (plane) and parallel to the horizontal working surface of the machine table, the

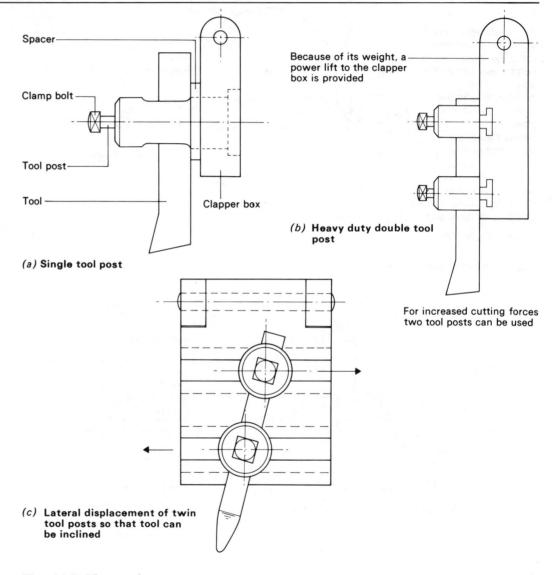

Fig. 14.7 The tool post

THE SHAPING MACHINE AND SHAPING

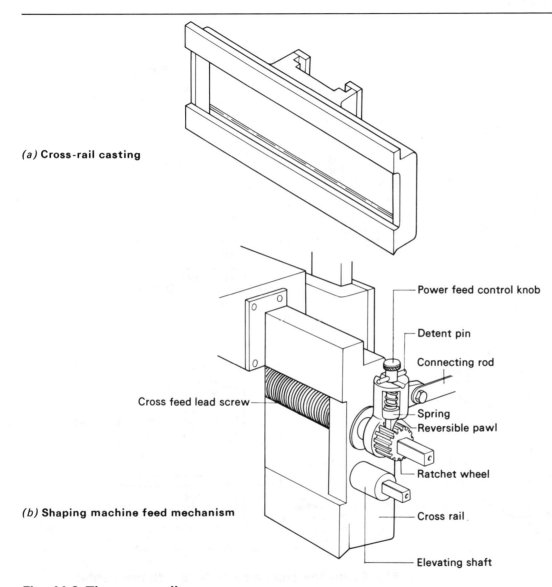

Fig. 14.8 The cross rail

movement of the ram must be parallel to the table over all its area.

To produce surfaces that are flat (plane) and parallel to the vertical working surface of the machine table, the movement of the ram must also be parallel to the side of the table over all its area.

Figure 14.10 shows the basic geometrical relationships and the arrangement of the slideways and movements found in a modern shaping machine.

Slotted link quick return mechanism

This is the drive mechanism found in most mechanical shaping machines. Its purpose is to convert the rotary motion of the driving motor and gearbox into the reciprocating motion of the ram. As well as being simple and compact, it has the advantage of giving the ram a higher velocity during its return (non-cutting) stroke than during its forward (cutting) stroke, thus reducing the wasted time that occurs on the return stroke.

Figure 14.11(a) shows the basic elements of a slotted link mechanism. The *pinion* is mounted on the output shaft of the gearbox and engages the *stroke wheel* which it drives. The stroke wheel is also sometimes called the *bull wheel*. The stroke wheel carries a *crank pin* which engages the *die block*. The die block is free to rotate about the crank pin and to slide in the slot in the link casting. This is the *slotted link* from

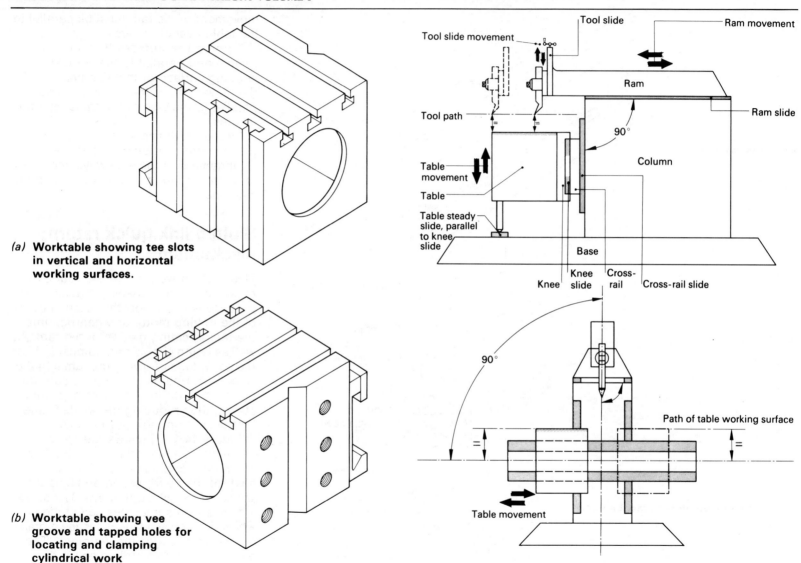

(a) Worktable showing tee slots in vertical and horizontal working surfaces.

(b) Worktable showing vee groove and tapped holes for locating and clamping cylindrical work

Fig. 14.9 The work table

Fig. 14.10 The shaping machine – fundamental alignments

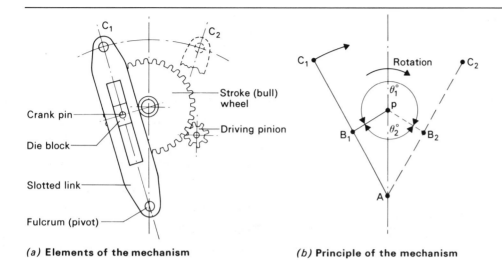

(a) Elements of the mechanism

(b) Principle of the mechanism

Fig. 14.11 Slotted link quick return mechanism – principle

which this mechanism gets its name. The slotted link is restrained at its lower end by the *fulcrum pin*, about which it is free to pivot. When the stroke wheel rotates, the free end of the link moves back and forth. (From C_1 to C_2).

Referring to Fig. 14.11(b), the line ABC represents the slotted link. It is driven by the crank pin B and is restrained at its lower end by the fulcrum pin A. The crank pin B rotates with uniform velocity about P.

Forward stroke (cutting)

The crank pin moves from B_1 to B_2 through $\theta_1°$ as the link moves from C_1 to C_2.

Return stroke

The crank pin continues to move from B_2 to B_1 through $\theta_2°$, as the link returns from C_2 to C_1.

Since the crank pin B is rotating with uniform velocity, it takes a longer time to travel the greater distance represented by $\theta_2°$ of arc than it takes to travel the shorter distance represented by $\theta_1°$ of arc. Thus:

$$\frac{\text{Cutting time}}{\text{Return time}} = \frac{\theta_1°}{\theta_2°}$$

Note: The longer the stroke, the greater the difference between $\theta_1°$ and $\theta_2°$. Hence the slotted link quick-return mechanism is more effective when it is set to a long stroke than when it is set to a short stroke.

A typical ram velocity/displacement graph is shown in Fig. 14.12(a) for one complete cycle, or double stroke, of the ram; that is, for one complete revolution of the stroke wheel. It will be seen from the graph that the velocity varies from zero at the start and finish of each stroke to a maximum at the mid-stroke position (page 294).

Apart from the obvious waste of time and energy when 'cutting fresh air', it is important to match the stroke length to the length of the workpiece. Figure 14.12(b) shows what happens when the stroke is too long.

1 The tool hits the work with a high velocity and this results in:
(a) the cutting edge being chipped;
(b) the work being displaced.
2 The tool leaves the work with a high velocity and this results in:
(a) chips flying off the machine in a dangerous manner;
(b) the edge of the job crumbling and the scribed line disappearing.
This occurs particularly when shaping cast iron.
3 The continual shock loading on the transmission and the sudden release of the load at the end of each stroke results in excessive wear to the machine.

Figure 14.12(c) shows how these problems can be avoided by setting the stroke length correctly:
1 the tool takes up the cutting load relatively gently;
2 there is less chance of chipping the tool and displacing the workpiece;
3 there is no sudden shock load on the transmission;
4 the tool leaves the cut equally gently;

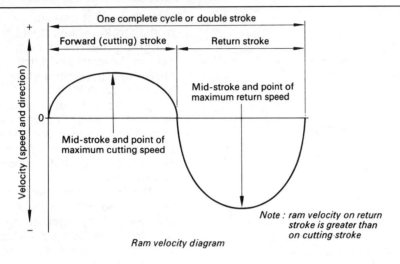

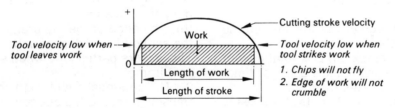

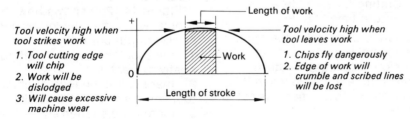

Fig. 14.12 Displacement/velocity diagram

5 the edge of the workpiece does not crumble;
6 the chips drop just in front of the workpiece and are not thrown all over the workshop.

Ram position

To adjust the position of the ram and cutting tool relative to the workpiece, unlock the clamp and move the ram back and forth until it is in the required position. Then relock the clamp. This recouples the ram to the drive mechanism.

Stroke length

The crank pin is not fixed to the stroke wheel in a set position, but is mounted in slideways so that it can be adjusted to or from the centre of rotation. The further it is moved outwards from the centre of rotation, the greater becomes its throw, and the longer becomes the stroke of the ram. This movement of the crank pin in its slides is controlled by a lead screw and nut. The lead screw is rotated by a pair of bevel gears which take the drive through the centre of the stroke wheel shaft to the outside of the machine. A locking ring on the outside of the machine is released and the squared end shaft is rotated by a removable handle until the desired stroke length is achieved. The handle is removed and the locking ring tightened before the machine is re-started.

The fact that the tool of a shaping machine does not have a constant velocity when cutting (Fig. 14.12) presents a special problem when attempting to calculate the cutting speed in strokes per minute. In the workshop, a simple formula working on the average velocity of the tool is used.

cycles/minute (double strokes) = $\dfrac{1000S}{2L}$

where: S = cutting speed in m/min
L = length of stroke in mm

Example 14.1 Calculate the number of cycles (double strokes) per minute for shaping cast iron at a cutting speed of 25 m/min, if the stroke length is 250 mm.

Solution

cycles/minute = $\dfrac{1000S}{2L}$

where: S = 25 m/min
L = 250 mm

= $\dfrac{1000 \times 25}{2 \times 250}$

= 50 cycles/min

Table feed mechanism

The final pawl and ratchet drive to the table lead screw has already been shown in Fig. 14.8(b). In this section the complete feed system is considered.
Note: The pawl and ratchet change the reciprocating motion of the rocker arm into an intermittent rotary motion for the lead screw.

The pawl and ratchet convert the continual and uniform rocking motion of the pawl carrier bracket into the intermittent rotary motion of the table traverse lead screw. This intermittent movement of the screw is essential to ensure that the table only moves on the return stroke and remains stationary on the forward stroke.

The rate of traverse is controlled by the amplitude of the rocking motion of the pawl carrier bracket. The slowest (finest) rate of traverse is when the pawl is set to move the ratchet wheel – and the lead screw – through an increment of only one tooth at a time. The fastest (coarsest) rate of traverse is when the pawl is set to move through an increment of several ratchet wheel teeth at a time. With this type of feed mechanism, five teeth is generally the coarsest setting possible without the mechanism jamming.

Traverse rate (mm/double stroke)
= $\dfrac{\text{Lead of traverse screw}}{\text{Number of teeth on ratchet wheel}} \times \dfrac{\text{increment per double stroke}}{}$

Example 14.2 Calculate the traverse rate for a shaping machine equipped with a 6 mm lead traverse screw and a 30-tooth ratchet wheel, when set to an increment of three teeth per double stroke. If the machine is running at 50 double strokes/min, calculate the time taken to traverse 24 mm.

Solution

Traverse rate = $\dfrac{6 \text{ mm}}{30 \text{ teeth}} \times 3$ teeth

= 0·6 mm/double stroke

Time taken to traverse 24 mm at 50 double strokes/min:

Time taken = $\dfrac{\text{width of component}}{\text{traverse rate} \times \text{number of double strokes/min}}$

= $\dfrac{24}{0·6 \times 50}$

= 48 seconds

Work holding

The method by which the shaping machine generates a plane surface has already been shown in Fig. 14.2. It will be seen that the component has to be restrained to resist the thrust of the cutting tool, and located so that the plane surface generated is in correct geometrical relationship with the chosen datum.

There are several ways of holding the workpiece on a shaping machine. The most usual is to use a swivel base vice as shown in Fig. 14.13(a). In order to produce accurate work, it is essential that the fixed jaw and upper surfaces of the slides of the vice are accurately aligned with the machine worktable. After the vice has been positioned for a particular job, it should be checked for alignment as shown in Fig. 14.13(b).

Usually it is good practice to cut against the fixed jaw of a vice so that the cutting forces are resisted by a solid abutment. Figure 14.14(a) shows the restraints that apply when work is set in this manner. However, this is not possible on a shaping machine when long components are being machined unless the machine is set as shown in Fig. 14.14(a). Nevertheless, the shaping machine works more efficiently when set to a long stroke, so the arrangement shown in Fig. 14.14(b) is often used on this machine. It will be seen that the main cutting force is only restrained by friction, and care must be taken in setting the work to prevent it being dislodged.

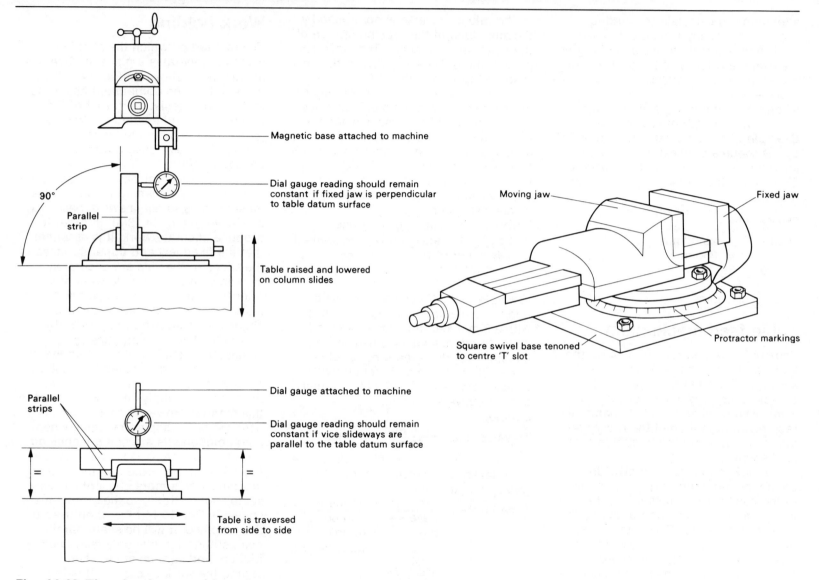

Fig. 14.13 The shaping machine vice

THE SHAPING MACHINE AND SHAPING

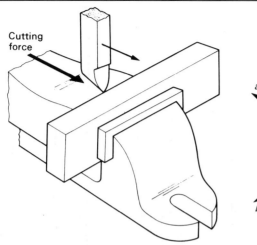

(a) Cutting force perpendicular to fixed jaw

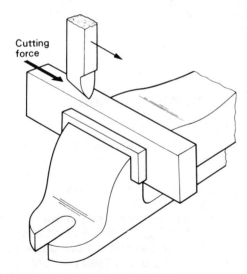

(b) Cutting force parallel to fixed jaw

Fig. 14.14 Machine vice – restraints

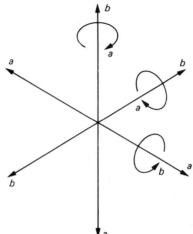

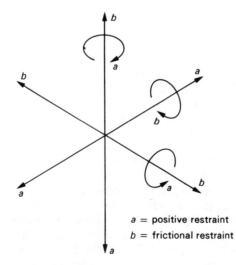

a = positive restraint
b = frictional restraint

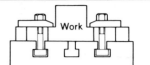

Work clamped to machine table

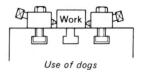

Use of dogs

(a) Large work can be fastened directly to the shaping machine table

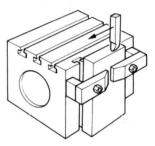

(b) Large work can be fastened directly to the side of the shaping machine table for squaring up the ends

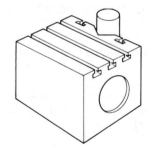

(c) Large cylindrical work can also be fastened into the vee slot on the side of the shaping machine table

Fig. 14.15 Alternative methods of work holding

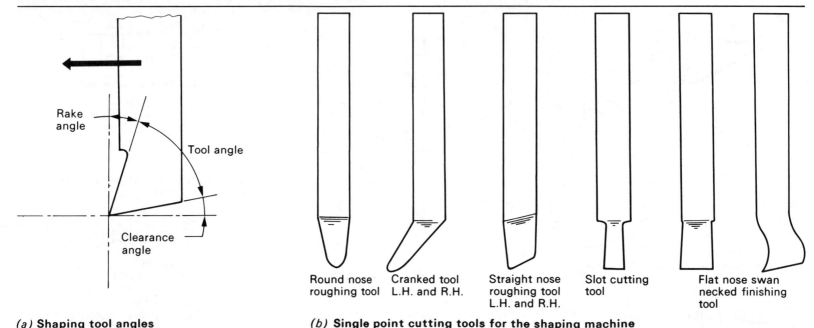

(a) Shaping tool angles

(b) Single point cutting tools for the shaping machine

Fig. 14.16 Shaping tools

Large jobs may be mounted directly on the machine table using clamps or dogs as shown in Fig. 14.15(a). Surfaces may be machined perpendicular to each other using the side of the table, as shown in Fig. 14.15(b). The side of the table is often provided with a 'vee' for holding cylindrical work as shown in Fig. 14.15(c).

Tools and tool-holding

One of the great advantages of the shaping machine for jobbing-shop work is the fact that it uses cheap, single point tools similar to lathe tools. Further, these tools can be ground off-hand when it is necessary to change their shape to suit a particular job, or to re-sharpen them. Some typical shaping machine tools are shown in Fig. 14.16, in which the similarity to lathe tools is evident.

The shaping machine tool is held in a tool post similar to that used on the lathe. Figure 14.17(a) shows the forces acting on the tool and the tool holder, whilst Fig. 14.17(b) shows the restraints acting on a shaping tool held in a simple, single-tool post.

Shaping machine application

Figure 14.18(a) shows a blank sawn from a hot-rolled mild steel bar. Figure 14.18(b) shows the dimensions to which the blank is to be squared up on a shaping machine.

The correct sequence of operations is set out in Fig. 14.19. It will be seen that the top surface of the moving jaw slides, and the face of the fixed jaw, provide the datum surfaces. It is essential that they are square to each other and in correct relationship to the work table surface.

THE SHAPING MACHINE AND SHAPING

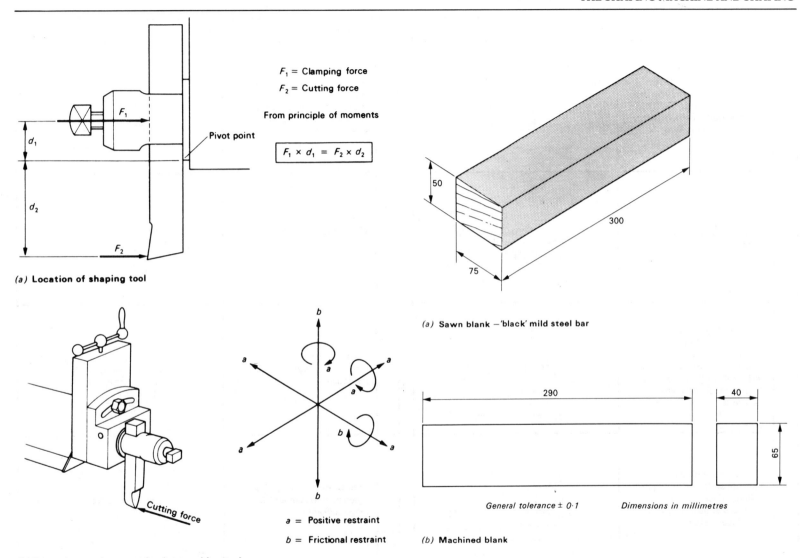

F_1 = Clamping force
F_2 = Cutting force

From principle of moments

$$F_1 \times d_1 = F_2 \times d_2$$

(a) Location of shaping tool

(a) Sawn blank – 'black' mild steel bar

a = Positive restraint
b = Frictional restraint

(b) Restraints acting on a shaping machine tool

(b) Machined blank

General tolerance ± 0.1   Dimensions in millimetres

Fig. 14.17 Shaping machine – tool holding

Fig. 14.18 Blank to be machined

Op.	Description	Set up
1	Set vice jaws parallel to ram using a D.T.I. mounted in the tool post. When vice is correctly set the D.T.I. reading should be constant as it travels along the parallel strip	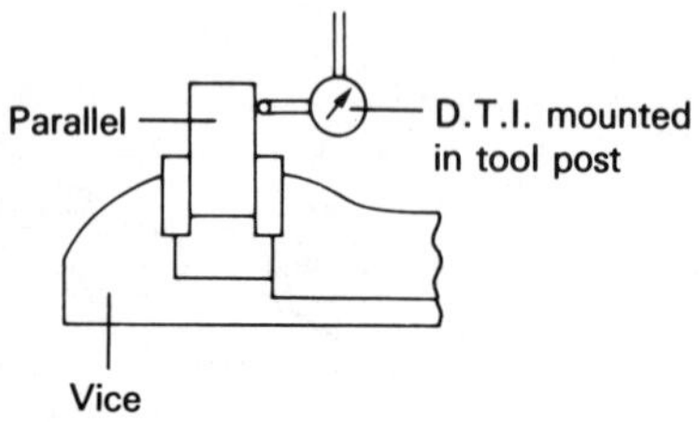
2	Set sawn blank in vice using grips. Machine upper surface A	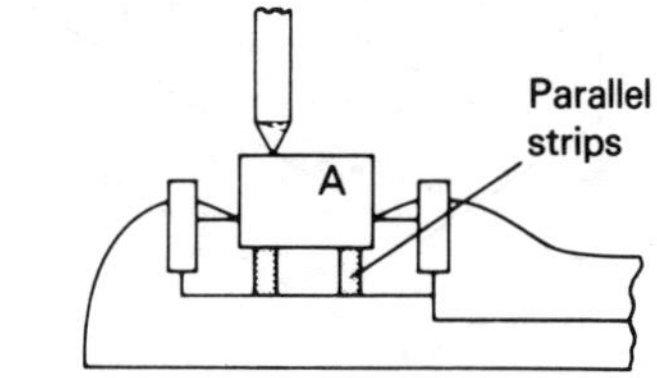
3	Turn job through 90° so that previously machined surface is against fixed jaw of vice. This ensures that surface A and B will be perpendicular to each other. Machine surface B	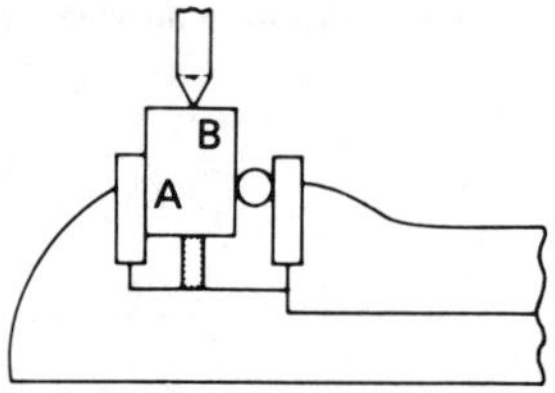
4	Turn job through 90° and machine surface C until job is 40mm thick. Check thickness at each end to ensure parallelism	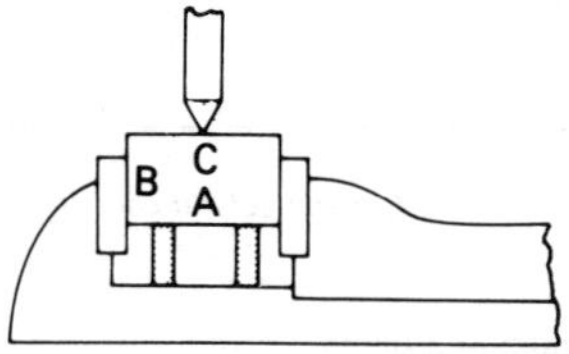

Op.	Description	Set up
5	Turn job through 90° again and machine surface D until job is 65mm wide. Check thickness at each end to ensure parallelism	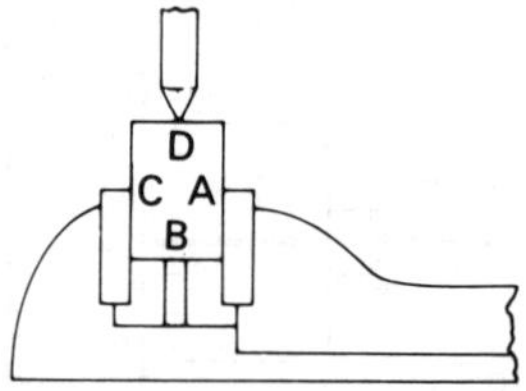
6	Turn vice through 90° and check with D.T.I. Set clapper box as shown in Fig.9.31	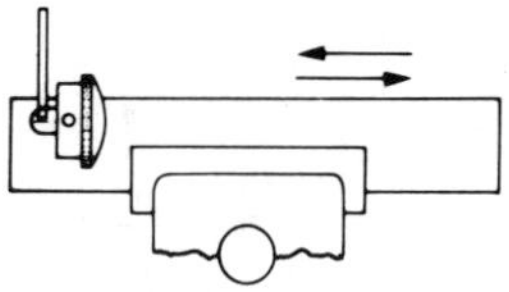
7	Machine end of blank. Check for squareness with try-square	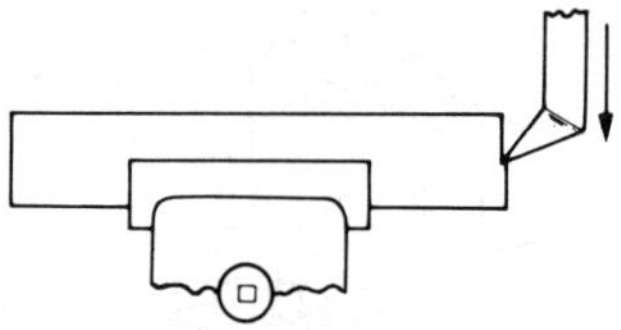
8	Turn blank end for end and machine opposite end to length (290mm)	as for 7 above

Fig. 14.19 Machining a blank to size on the shaping machine

Exercises

1. With the aid of a line diagram, show how a shaping machine generates a plain surface, and explain why this surface is often referred to as a 'ruled' surface.
2. With the aid of line diagrams, show how the clapper box functions and explain how it protects the tool and the work on the return stroke.
3. Explain, with the aid of clear sketches, the basic principles of the slotted link quick return mechanism as applied to the shaping machine.
4. Explain why:
   a) the stroke of the shaping machine ram should be set so that it is only *slightly* longer than the workpiece.
   b) the work piece should be positioned so that, wherever possible, the tool cuts along the workpiece and not across it.
5. With the aid of sketches, show the sequence of operations for *squaring up* a blank on a shaping machine while the blank is held in the machine vice.
6. a) Show how work may be held in the machine vice so that it is kept flat against the fixed jaw with no tendency to lift as the vice is tightened up.
   b) Show how *grips* can be used to hold thin components in the machine vice.
7. With the aid of a line diagram, show how the cutting tool is held on a shaping machine.
8. Calculate the number of cycles (double strokes) per minute for shaping a metal blank at 30 m/min if the stroke length is 360 mm.
9. a) Calculate the traverse rate for a shaping machine equipped with a 6 mm lead traverse screw and a 40-tooth ratchet wheel, when set to an increment of two teeth per double stroke.
   b) If the machine is running at 80 double strokes/min, calculate the time taken to traverse 60 mm.
10. A flat horizontal surface 50 mm wide and 120 mm long is to be machined on a shaping machine.
    a) State a suitable length of stroke for the cutting tool.
    b) What would be the effect on the surface being cut if a stiff hinge prevented the clapper box from operating properly?
    c) Why is the shaping machine head sometimes tilted at one angle?
    (*WAEC* 1974)

15. The milling machine and milling

Types of milling machine

The milling machine produces plane (flat) surfaces that may be parallel, perpendicular or at an angle to the work table as shown in Fig. 15.1. Unlike the shaping machine and the lathe, the milling machine uses a *multi-tooth cutter*. Since the cutter has a number of cutting edges it can remove metal more rapidly than the single-point tools discussed so far. Milling cutters will be discussed on page 304 of this chapter and their cutting action will be discussed more deeply in *Mechanical Engineering Craft Theory and Related Subjects: Volume 2*.

Figure 15.2 shows two basic types of milling machine. There are other types of machine for heavy duty, manufacturing purposes. Figure 15.2(a) shows a *vertical milling machine*. It derives its name from the fact that its spindle axis is arranged in a vertical plane. Figure 15.2(b) shows a *horizontal milling machine*. This machine derives its name from the fact that its spindle axis lies in a horizontal plane.

The geometrical movements and alignments of the vertical milling machine are shown in Fig. 15.3(a). Basically, the movements and alignments required are the location

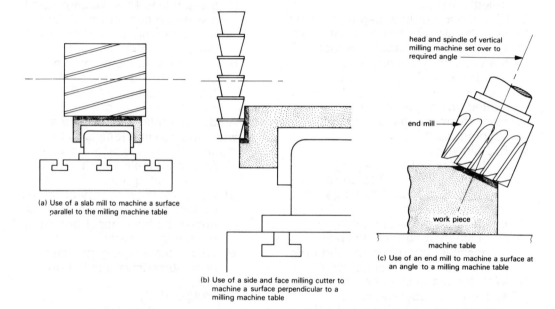

(a) Use of a slab mill to machine a surface parallel to the milling machine table

(b) Use of a side and face milling cutter to machine a surface perpendicular to a milling machine table

(c) Use of an end mill to machine a surface at an angle to a milling machine table

Fig. 15.1 Milled surfaces

and rotation of a cutter by a spindle so that the axis of the cutter is perpendicular to the work table, or at a desired and controlled angle to the work table. The work table provides the datum surface from which the work is set as well as supporting the workpiece. Therefore the working surface of the work table must lie in a horizontal plane beneath the cutter and perpendicular to the cutter axis.

It is also necessary to be able to move the work table in a direction at right angles to the longitudinal traverse, and it is necessary to be able to raise and lower the table in order to feed the work into the cutter and to compensate for different thicknesses of work. All these

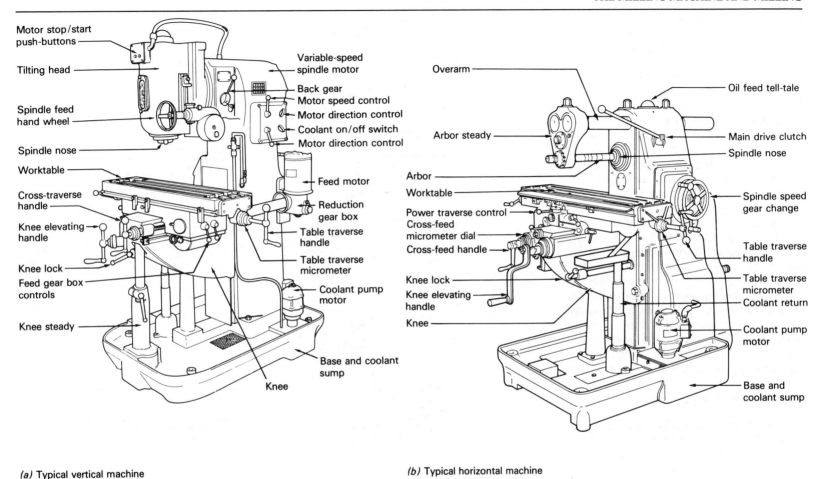

(a) Typical vertical machine

(b) Typical horizontal machine

Fig. 15.2 Milling machines

movements are controlled by lead screws fitted with micrometer dials so that the table can be accurately positioned under the cutter.

Figure 15.3(b) shows the geometrical movements and alignments of a horizontal milling machine. This time the basic movements and alignments required are the location and movement of the workpiece by the work table in a plane beneath the cutter that is parallel to the spindle and cutter axis. The spindle must have a horizontal axis.

As in the vertical milling machine, it is necessary to be able to move the work table in a direction at right angles to the direction of longitudinal traverse. It is also necessary to be able to raise and lower the work table in order to feed the work into the cutter and to compensate for different thicknesses of work. Again, the table movements are controlled by lead screws fitted with micrometer dials so that the table and workpiece can be accurately positioned under the cutter.

Milling cutters

The geometry of a milling cutter is rather different from that of the single point tools previously discussed. Figure 15.4(a) shows why the milling cutter tooth has to have a secondary clearance angle to prevent the heel of the tooth *interfering* with the machined surface of the workpiece. Provision also has to be made for swarf clearance to prevent the cutter jamming when working in a slot. It will be seen that the tooth form can be made up of a series of straight lines, or

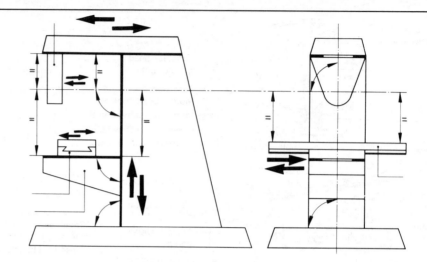

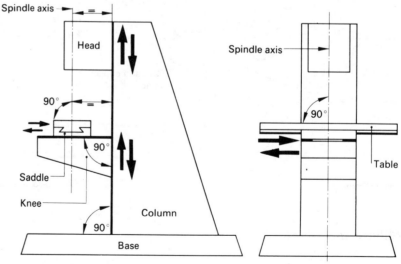

(B) VERTICAL MILLING MACHINE

Fig. 15.3 Milling machine – movements and alignment

it can be given a curved profile as shown in Fig. 15.4(b).

The rake angle of a milling cutter tooth is controlled by the degree of *offset* given to the tooth when the cutter is manufactured. The rake angle cannot be altered subsequently. The rake angle of a milling cutter tooth is measured relative to a series of radial lines struck from the centre of the cutter as shown in Fig. 15.5. In Fig. 15.5(a) the rake face of the tool lies on the radial line and this gives a zero rake angle. If the tooth is offset from a radial line as shown in Fig. 15.5(b) and 15.5(c) then positive and negative angles of rake respectively are created at the point of cutting (page 306).

The principles of orthogonal and oblique cutting discussed in Chapter 13 also apply to the milling cutter. That is, the straight tooth cutter shown in Fig. 15.6(a) cuts orthogonally and the helical tooth cutter shown in Fig. 15.6(b) cuts obliquely (page 306).

As in a single point tool, the straight tooth that cuts orthogonally is the easiest to design, manufacture and maintain. However, the helical tooth form that cuts obliquely reduces the cutting forces by producing a thinner chip and smooths out the load on the machine by producing a more constant cutting action. That is, there is always more than one tooth in contact with the workpiece at a time, and this prevents the intermittent cutting action associated with straight tooth cutters. This intermittant action can cause chatter and a poor surface finish as well as creating wear in the machine gear

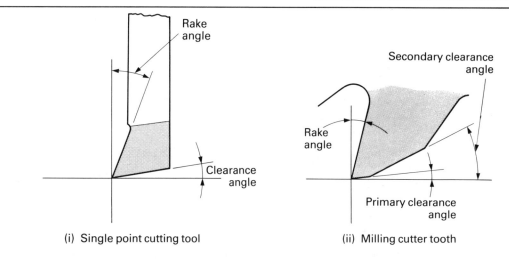

(i) Single point cutting tool   (ii) Milling cutter tooth

(a) Comparison of cutter angles

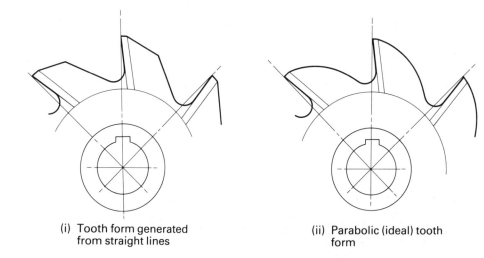

(i) Tooth form generated from straight lines   (ii) Parabolic (ideal) tooth form

(b) Tooth profiles

Fig. 15.4 Basic cutter geometry

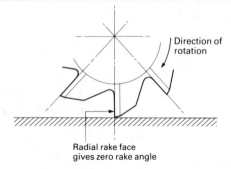

(a) Radial milling cutter teeth – zero rake angle

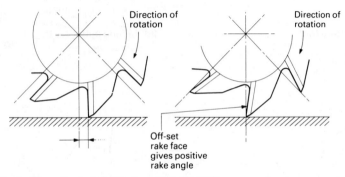

(b) Off-set milling cutter teeth (trailing) – positive rake angle

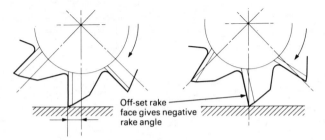

(c) Off-set milling cutter teeth (leading) – negative rake angle

Fig. 15.5 Milling cutter – rake angle

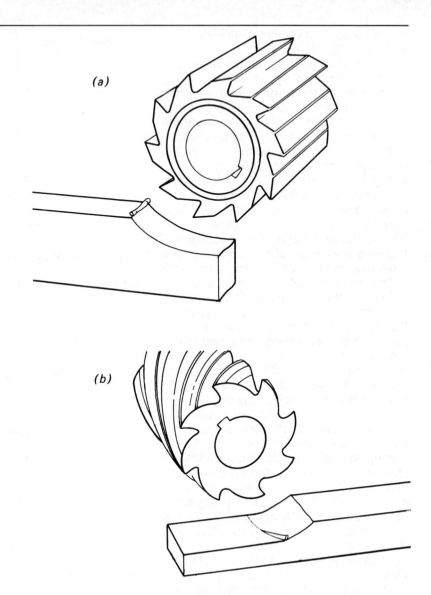

Fig. 15.6 Milling cutter – helix angle

THE MILLING MACHINE AND MILLING

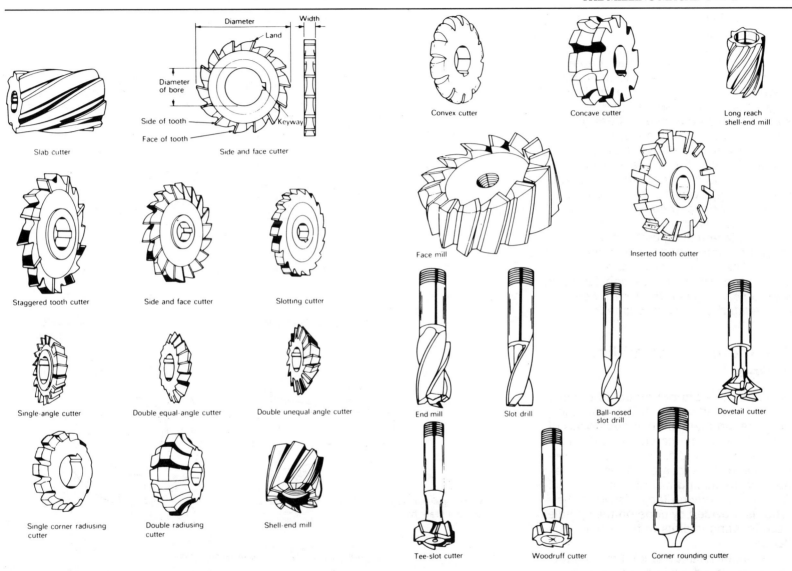

Fig. 15.7 Typical milling cutters

box and spindle bearings.

Unlike single point tools, such as lathe and shaping machine tools, the milling cutter cannot be readily adapted to new shapes to suit a particular job. Therefore milling cutters are made in a large range of standard shapes and sizes. When a component is designed, care must be taken to ensure that it can be made with one of the standard cutters. Figure 15.7 shows a few of the large range of standard cutters that are commercially available. In this chapter, we are only concerned with the more basic cutters such as the slab mill, the side and face milling cutter, the face milling cutting and the end milling cutter. The more complex and specialised cutters will be considered in *Mechanical Engineering Craft Theory and Related Subjects: Volume 2.*

The mounting of milling cutters

Milling cutters are not mounted directly on to the spindle of a milling machine. They are mounted on to various types of *arbor* designed to match the cutter to the machine spindle. Figure 15.8 shows how the arbor is located in the spindle nose of the milling machine by a special, non-driving taper. Drive to the arbor is provided by *dogs* on the spindle nose locating in slots in the arbor flange.

The taper location is kept in contact by means of a draw bolt that passes through the whole length of the spindle

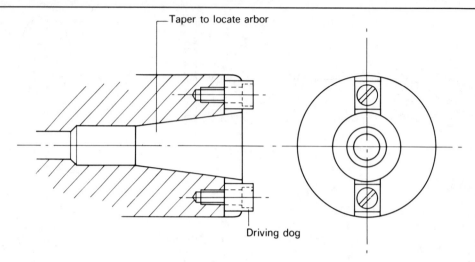

Milling machine spindle nose

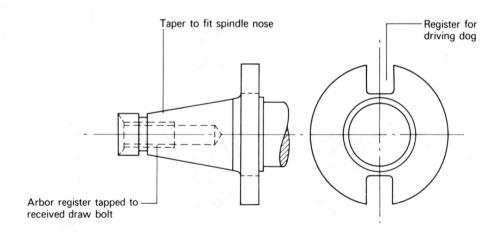

Taper register of arbor to fit spindle nose

Fig. 15.8 Milling machine spindle nose details

THE MILLING MACHINE AND MILLING

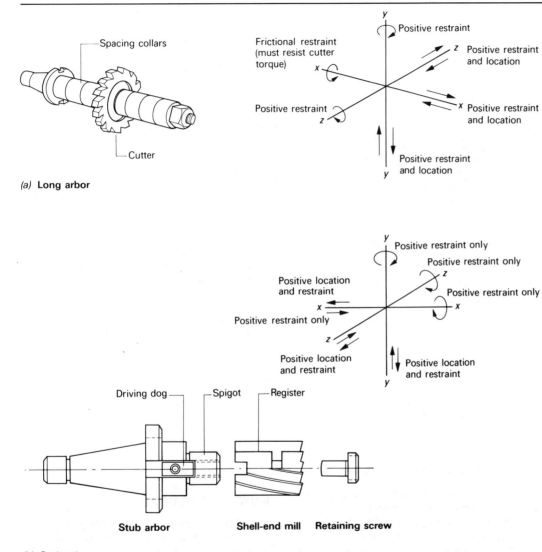

Fig. 15.9 Mounting of arbors and cutters

and screws into the end of the arbor. Upon tightening up the draw bolt, the arbor taper is drawn tightly into the spindle taper. To ensure concentricity and true running of the arbor, both tapers must be carefully cleaned before assembling the arbor into the spindle.

The *long arbor* usually associated with the horizontal milling machine and its cutters is shown in Fig. 15.9(a). In the example shown, the cutter is driven by friction alone. This is sufficient for the majority of jobbing applications, but for heavy production cutting it is usual to key the cutter to the arbor to provide a positive drive.

Large end mills (shell end mills) and face milling cutters are usually mounted on *stub arbors* as shown in Fig. 15.9(b).

Small end mills are usually held in a special chuck. The chuck is mounted in the spindle of the machine and there is no arbor. Figure 15.10 shows a typical chuck mounting for screwed shank, solid end mills (page 310).

The forces acting on a milling cutter, removing metal rapidly, are very great. Therefore the cutter arbor must be adequately supported, and the cutter correctly mounted, to avoid inaccuracies and chatter. The correct method of cutter mounting is shown in Fig. 15.11 on page 311.

In Fig. 15.11(a) the cutter is incorrectly mounted: there is excessive overhang from the point of support allowing the arbor to flex. This causes inaccuracy, chatter and poor surface finish. In extreme cases, the arbor may be permanently bent and the cutter teeth may be chipped. The replacement of both arbor and cutter is very expensive.

In Fig. 15.11.(b) the overarm and steady bearing have been slid back over the arbor to provide support as close to the spindle as possible. This reduces the overhang to a minimum and supports the cutter with the maximum possible rigidity.

Sometimes the shape and size of the work itself prevents the cutter from being mounted close to the spindle nose. Figure 15.11(c) shows how an additional, intermediate steady can be placed on the overarm to support the arbor behind the cutter, and again reduce the effective overhang to a minimum.

The cutting action

Figure 15.12 shows the difference between up-cut milling and down-cut milling.

Up-cut milling

This is the traditional method. It has the great advantage of not tending to drag the work into the cutter. Therefore, it can be used on worn and cheap machines lacking in rigidity. However, it has a number of disadvantages.
1 The cutter tends to rub before it bites into the metal, resulting in cutter wear and poor finish.
2 The cutting forces are at a maximum as the chip leaves the workpiece. This results in transmission bounce and the traditional milling machine 'rumble'.

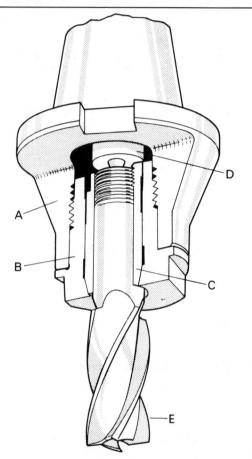

Fig. 15.10 Mounting of screwed shank, solid end mills

This leads to heavy machine and cutter wear and poor surface finish.
3 The cutting forces tend to lift the component off the work table.
4 The feed mechanism must drive the workpiece against the full thrust of the cutter.

A **The main body of the Clarkson AUTOLOCK Chuck**, which houses the precision-made, self-locking parts of the chuck.
A wide range of tapers is offered from stock, and special fittings can be made to order

B **The locking sleeve.**
A precision fit, positions the collet and mates with the taper nose of the collet

C **The collet.**
Is of split construction and internally threaded at the rear end

D **The male centre.**
Hardened and ground, it serves to centre the cutter and anchors the extreme end to ensure rigidity and true running

E **The AUTOLOCK cutter.**
Any tendency of the cutter to turn in the chuck during operation increases the grip of the collet on the shank of the cutter, thus ensuring maximum feeds and speeds.
The cutter cannot push up or pull down during operation

Down-cut milling

This has a number of advantages.
1 The cutter bites into the workpiece immediately and the load is eased off the tooth gradually. This leads to smooth operating conditions resulting

THE MILLING MACHINE AND MILLING

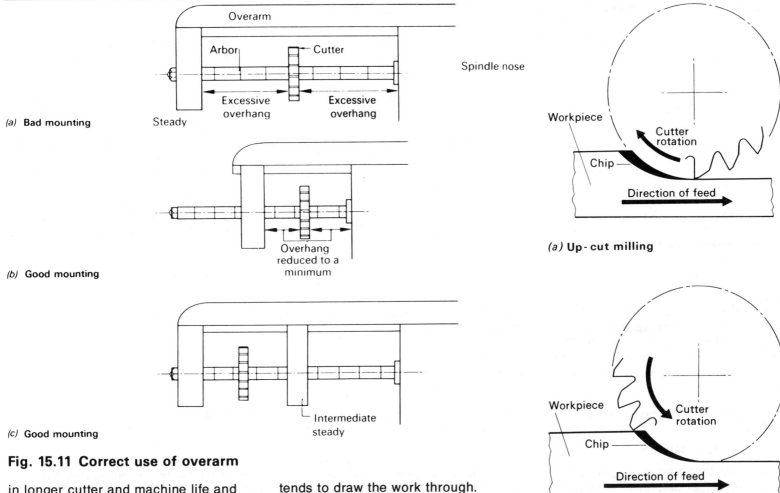

Fig. 15.11 Correct use of overarm

(a) Up-cut milling

(b) Down-cut milling

Fig. 15.12 Up-cut and down-cut milling

in longer cutter and machine life and good surface finish.
2 The cutting forces press the workpiece down on to the table, giving maximum rigidity.
3 The feed mechanism only has to control the rate of feed as the cutter tends to draw the work through.
   There is one major disadvantage to this technique. It must only be used on a modern machine in good condition and fitted with a *back-lash eliminator*.
   Never use down-cut milling unless you know for sure that the machine is

311

Table 15.1 Cutting speeds and feeds for H.S.S. milling cutters

MATERIAL BEING MILLED	CUTTING SPEED m/min	FEED PER TOOTH (CHIP THICKNESS) (Millimetres)					
		Face mill	Slab mill	Side & face	Slotting cutter	Slitting saw	End mill
Aluminium	70–100	0·2–0·8	0·2–0·6	0·15–0·4	0·1–0·2	0·05–0·1	0·1–0·4
Brass (alpha) (ductile)	35–50	0·15–0·6	0·15–0·5	0·1–0·3	0·07–0·15	0·035–0·075	0·07–0·3
Brass (free-cutting)	50–70	0·2–0·8	0·2–0·6	0·15–0·4	0·1–0·2	0·05–0·1	0·1–0·4
Bronze (phosphor)	20–35	0·07–0·3	0·07–0·25	0·05–0·15	0·04–0·07	0·02–0·04	0·04–0·15
Cast Iron (grey)	25–40	0·1–0·4	0·1–0·3	0·07–0·2	0·05–0·1	0·025–0·05	0·05–0·2
Copper	35–45	0·1–0·4	0·1–0·3	0·07–0·2	0·05–0·1	0·025–0·05	0·05–0·2
Steel (mild)	30–40	0·1–0·4	0·1–0·3	0·07–0·2	0·05–0·1	0·025–0·05	0·05–0·2
Steel (medium carbon)	20–30	0·07–0·3	0·07–0·25	0·05–0·15	0·04–0·07	0·02–0·04	0·04–0·15
Steel (alloy-high tensile)	5–8	0·05–0·2	0·05–0·15	0·035–0·1	0·025–0·05	0·015–0·025	0·025–0·1
Thermo-setting plastic (low speed due to abrasive properties)	20–30	0·15–0·6	0·15–0·5	0·1–0·3	0·07–0·15	0·035–0·075	0·07–0·3

Notes:
[1] The above feeds and speeds are for ordinary H.S.S. cutters. For *super* H.S.S. cutters the feeds would remain the same, but the cutting speeds could be increased by 10% to 15%.
[2] The *lower* speed range is suitable for heavy, roughing cuts.
The *higher* speed range is suitable for light, finishing cuts.
[3] The feed is selected to give the required surface finish and rate of metal removal.

designed for this technique and is in good condition.

Speeds and feeds

Calculations involving milling cutters are treated rather differently from those considered for lathes and drilling machines because the milling cutter is a multi-tooth cutter. When milling, the feed is given as a rate per tooth, not as a rate per revolution as on a centre lathe. Milling cutters are more difficult to re-grind than single point tools, and greater care must be taken to avoid overloading and overheating the teeth.

The speed and feed values given by cutter manufacturers are only an approximate guide. As in all machining operations, the actual rates chosen will depend upon such factors as:
1. surface finish;
2. material strength;
3. rigidity of work and cutter;
4. breadth of cut;
5. depth of cut;
6. cutter tooth form;
7. type of cutter;
8. coolant.

Some typical feeds and speeds for milling a range of materials with high speed steel cutters are given in Table 15.1.

Example 15.1 Calculate the spindle speed in rev/min for a milling cutter 125 mm in diameter, operating at a cutting speed of 30 m/min (take π as 3).

THE MILLING MACHINE AND MILLING

Solution

$$N = \frac{1000S}{\pi D}$$

where: N = spindle speed
S = 30 m/min
π = 3
D = 125 mm

Thus: $N = \dfrac{1000 \times 30}{3 \times 125}$

= $\underline{80 \text{ rev/min}}$

Example 15.2 Calculate the table feed in mm/min for a 12 tooth cutter revolving at 80 rev/min when the feed per tooth is 0·1 mm.

Solution

Feed/rev = feed/tooth × number of teeth
= 0·1 × 12
= 1·2 mm/rev

Table feed = feed/rev × rev/min
= 1·2 × 80
= $\underline{96 \text{ mm/min}}$

Example 15.3 Using the following data, calculate the time taken to complete a 270 mm long cut using a slab mill (take π as 3).

Solution

Diameter of cutter = 125 mm
Numbr of teeth = 6
Feed/tooth = 0·05 mm
Cutting speed = 45 m/min

$$N = \frac{1000S}{\pi D}$$

where: N = spindle speed
S = 45 m/min
π = 3
D = 125 mm

Thus: $N = \dfrac{1000 \times 45}{3 \times 125}$

= $\underline{120 \text{ rev/min}}$ .... (1)

Feed/rev = feed/tooth × number of teeth
= 0·05 × 6
= 0·3 mm/rev

Table feed/min = feed/rev × rev/min (from (1))
= 0·3 × 120
= $\underline{36 \text{ mm/min}}$ .... (2)

Time to complete a 270 mm cut

$= \dfrac{\text{length of cut}}{\text{table feed/min (from (2))}}$

$= \dfrac{270}{36}$

$= \underline{7\cdot 5 \text{ min}}$

Milling applications

A few simple applications will now be described in which the geometric relationships of the milling machine movements will be exploited. These geometrical relationships were discussed on page 302.

All the examples considered in this section require the work to be held in a machine vice. More complex applications involving alternative methods of work holding will be considered in *Mechanical Engineering Craft Theory and Related Subjects: Part 2*.

Squaring up a blank on a horizontal milling machine

Figure 15.13(a) shows a blank sawn from hot-rolled (black) mild steel bar. This blank is to be squared up all over to the dimensions shown in Fig. 15.13(b) on a horizontal milling machine. The cutters that will be used are shown in Fig. 15.13(c). The roller or slab mill will be used to square up the sides A, B, C and D, while a staggered tooth side and face mill will be used to square up the ends of the blank after the vice has been swung through 90°.

The correct sequence of operations is set out in Fig. 15.14. It will be seen that the top surface of the moving jaw slide of the vice, and the face of the fixed jaw, provide the datum surface for this operation. It is essential, therefore, to check the relationship of these surfaces to the machine table and machine movements. A dial test indicator is used to make these checks before machining the blank.

When mounting the cutter on the arbor, it is also essential to clean the arbor, the spacing collars and the cutter so that it runs true. A cutter that is running out through careless mounting will leave a poor finish as well as cutting oversize.

Squaring up a blank on a vertical milling machine

The blank shown in Fig. 15.13 can also be squared up on a vertical milling machine using the cutters shown in Fig. 15.15. The face mill shown in Fig. 15.15(a) should be large enough to span the width of the work. Care must be taken to check that the spindle of the machine is perpendicular to the machine table, or the surface cut by the face mill will be hollow. If the machine is fitted with an inclinable head, a test arbor should be inserted in the spindle nose and its axis checked with a dial test indicator so that any error can be corrected before the cutter is mounted in place. The face mill is used to square up sides A, B, C and D in the same sequence of operations (Fig. 15.14).

A long reach shell end mill is used to square up the ends of the blank, as shown in Fig. 15.15(b). There is no need to rotate the vice through 90° and re-set it when using a vertical milling machine. Use of the cross-feed motion and slides will ensure perpendicularity of the ends to the sides of the blank.

Generation of perpendicular surfaces on a horizontal milling machine

The use of a side and face milling cutter to produce a surface perpendicular to the work table of the horizontal milling machine, has already been introduced. (Figures 15.13 and 15.14). It will be seen that the distance from the periphery of the cutter to the spacing collars limits the size of the work that can be machined.

Alternatively a shell-end mill or a face mill mounted on a stud arbor can be fitted to a horizontal milling machine as shown in Fig. 15.16. Since the spindle axis of a horizontal milling machine is parallel to the table working surface, it follows that the surface cut by a face mill mounted on a stub arbor will be perpendicular to the work table. This technique, as shown in Fig. 15.16, is frequently used for facing up large rectangular components.

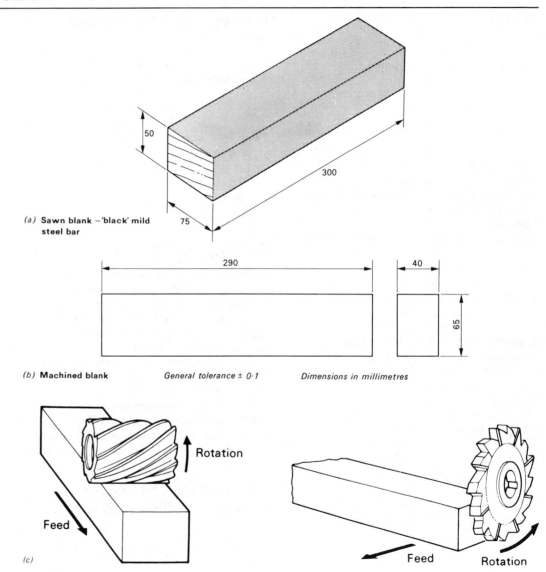

Fig. 15.13 Blank to be machined

THE MILLING MACHINE AND MILLING

Op.	Description	Set up
1	Set vice jaws parallel to table using a DTI. When vice is correctly set the DTI reading should be constant as it travels along the parallel strip.	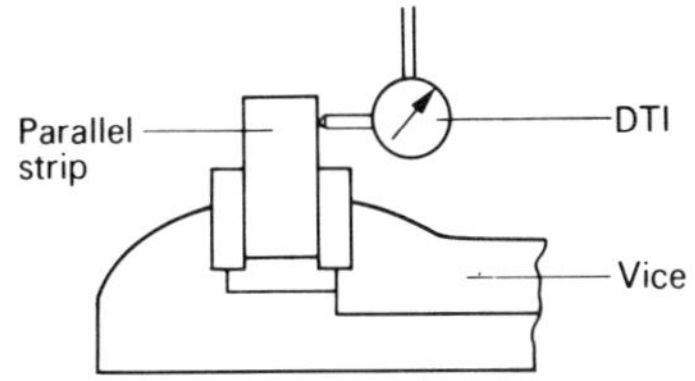
2	Set sawn blank in vice using grips. Mill surface 'A' using a slab (roller) mill.	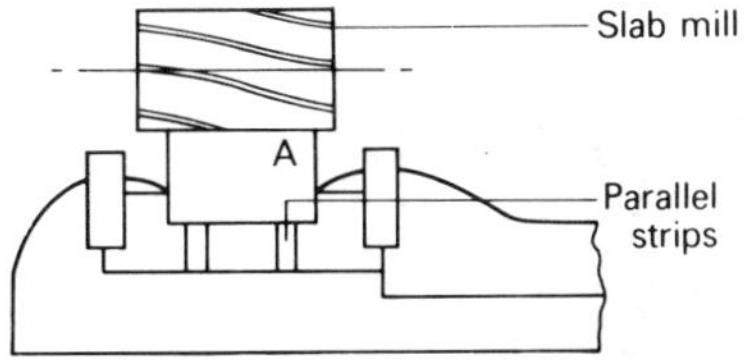
3	Turn job through 90° so that previously machined surface (A) is against fixed jaw of vice. This ensures surface (A) and (B) are perpendicular to each other. Machine surface 'B'.	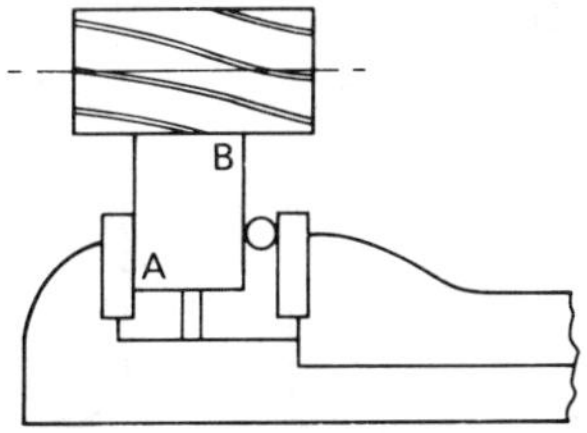
4	Turn job through 90° and machine surface 'C' until 40mm thick. Check thickness at each end of job to ensure parallelism.	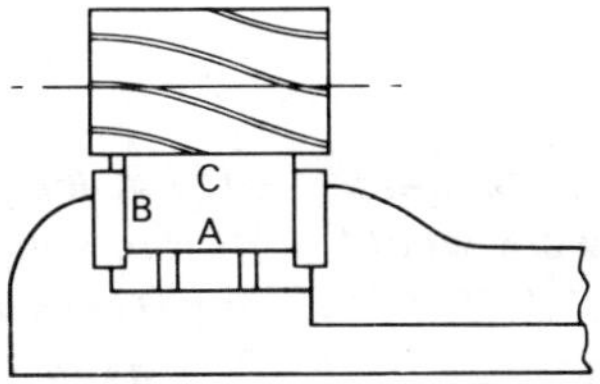

Op.	Description	Set-up
5	Turn job through 90° again and machine surface 'D' until job is 65mm wide. Check width at each end to ensure parallelism.	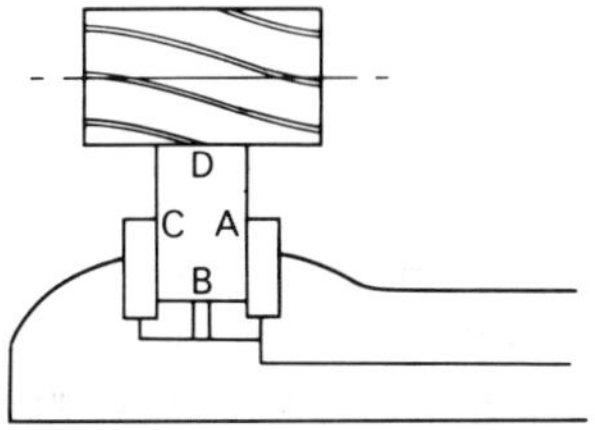
6	Turn vice through 90° and check with DTI parallel to spindle axis.	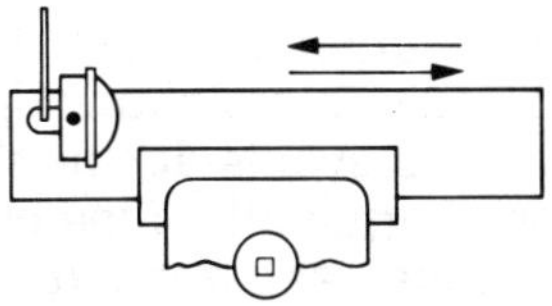
7	Use side and face milling cutter to machine end square.	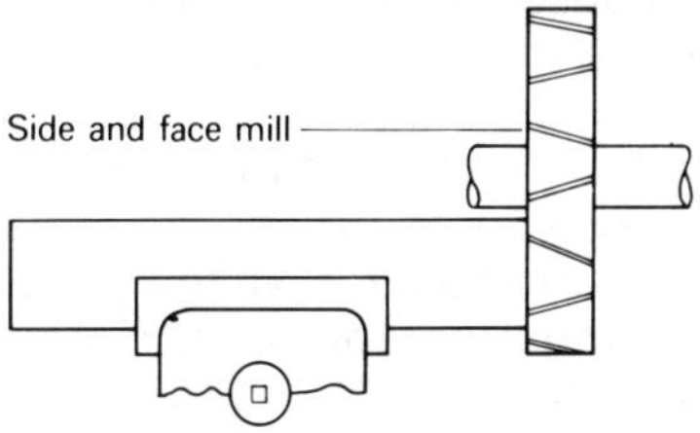
8	Wind table across and machine to length. Check length with vernier caliper.	As 7 above

Fig. 15.14 Operation sequence to square up a blank on a horizontal milling machine

Safety

The milling machine is the most dangerous machine in the workshop.
1. It must never be used without permission and without careful instruction in the use of its controls.
2. *Guards* must always be in position when the cutters are revolving. Two types of guards are shown in Fig. 15.17. The guard prevents accidental contact with the sharp teeth of the cutter, which can produce deep and extensive cuts. It also prevents clothing from becoming snagged in the revolving cutter, which can cause the operator to be dragged into the machine. If the operator is dragged into the cutter, the result is inevitably partial or total loss of a limb.
3. Never try to brush away swarf or wipe away coolant while the cutter is revolving. If the brush or cloth becomes caught in the cutter, serious injury to the operator can result (see 2).
4. Stop the machine and wind the work clear of the cutting zone before taking measurements.
5. Isolate the machine when setting up, changing cutters, and cleaning down, to prevent the machine being started up accidentally.
6. Milling machine swarf is in the form of needle like chips. For this reason use a swarf rake; *never* remove swarf with your fingers.

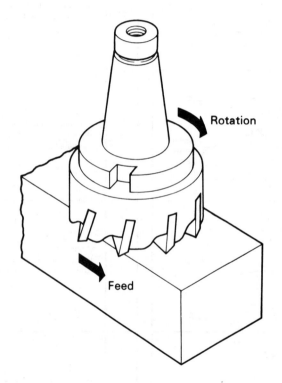

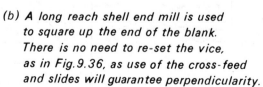

(a) *A face mill large enough in diameter to span the width of the work would be used to square up sides A, B, C and D in the same sequences as described in Fig 9.30*

(b) *A long reach shell end mill is used to square up the end of the blank. There is no need to re-set the vice, as in Fig. 9.36, as use of the cross-feed and slides will guarantee perpendicularity.*

Fig. 15.15 Cutters to square up a blank (vertical milling machine)

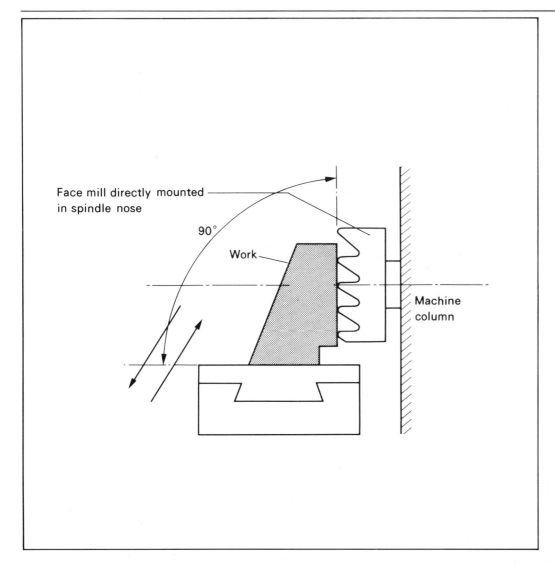

Fig. 15.16 Generation of perpendicular surfaces on a horizontal milling machine

Fig. 15.17 Milling cutter guards

Exercises

1. With the aid of sketches, show a typical job for which:
   a) a horizontal milling machine would be most suitable
   b) a vertical milling machine would be most suitable
2. Name *three* milling cutters and state a type of work for which *each* would be suitable
   (*WAEC* 1974)
3. With the aid of sketches show:
   a) why a milling cutter tooth requires secondary clearance
   b) how a milling cutter tooth is given a rake angle by offsetting the tooth from the centre line of the cutter.
4. What precautions must be taken when mounting a milling cutter on the arbor of a horizontal milling machine to avoid bending the arbor and 'run out' of the cutter?
5. During a cut on a horizontal milling machine, there is excessive vibration and 'chatter'. State *three* possible causes of the vibration.
   (*WAEC* 1974)
6. State *two* safety precautions that should be taken when setting up a milling machine, and *two* safety precautions that should be taken when operating a milling machine.
7. Calculate the spindle speed in rev/min for a milling cutter 140 mm in diameter operating at a cutting speed of 44 m/min ($\pi = {}^{22}/_{7}$).
8. Calculate the table feed in mm/min for a 15 tooth cutter revolving at 60 rev/min when the feed per tooth is 0·15 mm.
9. Explain, with the aid of sketches, the difference between *up-cut* and *down-cut* milling, and list the advantages and limitations of each process.
10. Draw up an operation schedule, using the headings shown below, for milling the component shown in Fig. 15.18 from a blank that has already been squared up to size. Either a horizontal or a vertical machine may be used.

Operation no	Operation	Sketch of set-up

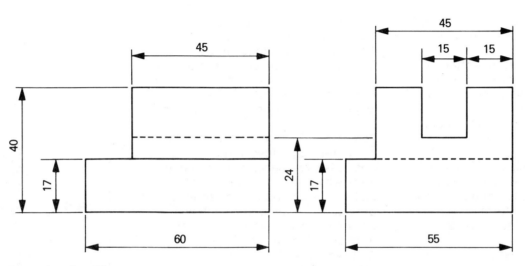

Dimensions in millimetres
General tolerance ± 0.2
Material: mild steel
Blank size 60 x 55 x 40 ready machined
Projection: 3rd angle

Fig. 15.18

Glossary

Ammeter. An instrument for measuring the flow of electric current. (Unit of current = the ampere)
Annealing. The process of softening a metal by heating it above a critical temperature (depending upon the metal) and cooling it slowly.
Arbor. A spindle upon which cutters are mounted.

Bick iron. A device similar in shape to a blacksmith's anvil, but much smaller and lighter, that can be mounted on a bench. Sheet metal is formed over it.
Bossing. (as in bossing or panel beating heads). The process of indenting (raising) a pattern in sheet metal to give it stiffness.
Burr. The ragged corner or edge left on metal when it is cut. It should always be removed with a file before handling as it can cause bad cuts.

Calipers. (for measuring). Devices used for transferring the distance between surfaces to a rule or other measuring scale.
See: inside caliper, outside caliper, vernier caliper, micrometer caliper, (refer to text as appropriate).
Clearance angle. The angle ground on a cutting tool so as to prevent the face of the tool behind the cutting edge from rubbing on the work piece.
Note: This is defined with diagrams in the text. Refer as appropriate.
Coefficient. (of linear expansion). The amount by which unit lengths of a metal expand for each 1°C increase in temperature. It varies from metal to metal.
Compress. To reduce the size of a component by squeezing it.
Compressive. Descriptive of a load or force which reduces the size of a material or component by squeezing it.
Conductor. A material which will transmit (carry) heat and/or electricity from one place to another.
Counterboring. The process of enlarging the end of a hole to form a recess. (See Fig. G.1.)
Countersinking. The process of forming a conical recess at the start of a hole to receive the head of a screw. (See Fig. G.2.)

Datum. A common point, line, or surface from which measurements are taken.
Dogs. Small, protruding blocks of metal attached to a moving part of a machine which engage in slots in an adjacent component causing it to move also.
Draughting. The process of producing technical drawings.

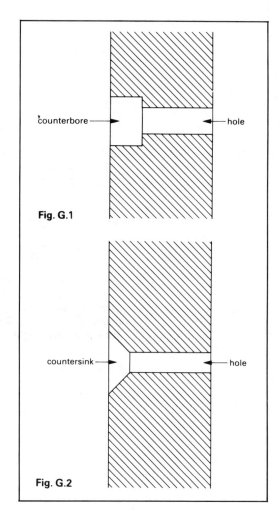

Fig. G.1

Fig. G.2

Draughtsman. A person who produces technical drawings of components for the craftsman to make.

Ductile. The property of a material that allows it to be bent or stretched without springing back to its original size and shape or without breaking.

Electro-magnetic waves. Invisible waves caused by rapidly varying electrical and magnetic fields. The basis of radio waves, light waves etc.

Facet. A small flat surface or 'face'.

Feed (as applied to a drill). The distance the drill moves into the work piece for each complete revolution. The act of driving the drill into the work piece.

Fitting. Assembling together the parts of a mechanism. This often involves making small adjustments to the size and shape of the parts using hand tools.

Flute. The grooves found in a twist drill, reamer, tap etc., which allow the chips to escape from the cutting zone.

Flux. A fluid or paste used when hard and soft soldering. It reacts with the metals being joined to ensure:
  i) chemical cleanliness
  ii) lack of oxidation resulting from the heat of the process
  iii) even flow of the solder over the faces being joined.

Force. That which moves or tends to move a body. That which distorts or tends to distort a body.

Forging. The process of hammering red-hot metal to shape.

Form-relieved. The gradual reduction in size of a form cutter tooth to prevent it rubbing on the freshly cut surface.

Frequency. The number of complete vibrations that a wave makes every second. (Unit = the Hertz (Hz) e.g. 6Hz = 6 complete vibrations every second. Particularly applied to electro-magnetic and accoustical waves.

Fulcrum. A hinge or pivot point. A point of balance.

Galvanometer. A very sensitive instrument for detecting the presence of very small electric currents.

Grain (of a metal). The individual crystals and particles that make up a metal.

Hygroscopic. Absorbs water from the atmosphere.

Infra-red. Electro-magnetic waves whose frequency (Hz) is less than that of visible red light, but greater than radio waves. e.g. heat radiation.

Insulator. A material that is a very poor conductor of electricity. In a good insulator the passage of current is negligible.

Jennying. The process of using a sheet metal working machine fitted with small, interchangeable rollers for forming metal to a desired shape.

Joule. (J) Unit of energy or work. e.g. 1 joule of work is done, or energy is used, when a force of 1 newton moves through a distance of 1 metre in the direction of application of the force.

Leverage. The magnification of a force by the use of a lever. In this instance the distance between the tool and the vice is the 'leverage distance' and the work piece is the 'lever'. The greater the leverage distance, the greater the force at the vice causing the metal to bend.

Mandrel. A short stiff spindle upon which a cutter or a work piece may be mounted and rotated.

Marking out. The process of drawing on metal with a sharp pointed instrument (scriber) to show the shape to which the metal is to be cut and to show the size and position of any holes to be cut in the metal.

Mass. The quantity of matter in a body that is acted upon by the 'force of gravity' to give a body its weight. *Note*: A body has the same *mass* no matter where it is, but it would weigh less on the moon that on the earth because the moon's force of gravity is weaker.

Medium (through which waves travel). A substance capable of being disturbed by the waves and aiding their transmission.

Melting point. The point on a temperature scale at which a substance changes from the solid state to a liquid state.

Micrometer. Any measuring device that uses the relationship between the rotation and the axial movement of a screw and nut.

Moment (of force). The turning effect of a force.

(the) **newton (N)** The ISO unit of force. (The average gravitational attraction (on earth) on a mass of 1kg is 9·81 newtons.)

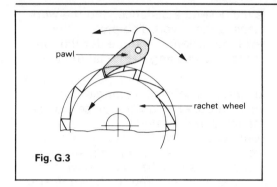

Fig. G.3

Orthographic (projection). The technique of drawing three dimensional solids on a plain surface for technical purposes.

Pawl. The claw that engages a ratchet wheel so as to impart intermittent rotation. (See Fig. G.3)

Perpendicular. At right angles (normal) to, e.g. AB is perpendicular to CD in Fig. G.4.

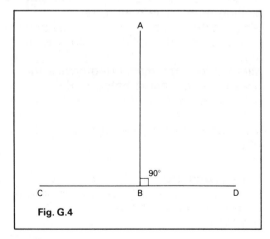

Fig. G.4

Projection. The convention which controls the relationship between the position of the 'views' is an orthographic drawing.
The act of transferring the outline of a three dimensional solid on to a plane (surface).

Property. That quality of a material which controls its behaviour with respect to its environment and working conditions.

Pyrometer. A device used for measuring high temperatures beyond the range of simple thermometers.

Quenching. Rapid cooling from high temperatures as in the hardening of medium and high carbon content steels.

Quill. The complete assembly of a spindle and its bearings in a cylindrical housing.

Radiation. The transmission of heat by electro-magnetic (infra-red) waves.

Rake angle. The slope of the cutting face of a cutting tool.

Reamer. A cutting tool that opens up an undersize hole and provides it with a good surface finish and accurate geometrical roundness.

Serrated, serration. Shallow, vee-shaped ridges on the surface of a shaft which run parallel to the axis of the shaft.

Shim steel. Bright-rolled, spring grade, steel foil used for fine packing in precision assemblies.

Solder. A low melting point alloy, used for joining metals and sealing joints that are mechanically interlocked.

Spectrum. Range: particularly of frequencies of electro-magnetic waves.

Spindle. The rotating member of a machine tool to which the cutters or, in the case of the lathes, the work holding devices are attached.

Swaging. A forging process for changing the cross-sectional shape of work piece from square, hexagonal, etc., to round.

Swarf. The scrap material removed by a cutting tool when machining. Also called 'chips' when more finely divided.

Tang (of a file). The portion of a hand tool that is inserted into a wooden handle. Since the tang is pointed, it is very dangerous to use a hand tool without a correctly fitted handle.

Taper. A progressive reduction in cross-section along the length of a component.

Tempering. A heat treatment process that reduces the brittleness and increases the roughness of a quench hardened steel cutting tool. It is accompanied by some loss of hardness.

Tensile (strength). Ability of a material to resist a *pulling* force without breaking.

Tensile (force). A *pulling* force as compared to a compressive or *squashing* force.

Thermocouple. A pair of dissimilar metals, joined at one end, which produce an electrical potential difference (voltage) across their open ends when heated. A device which exploits this phenomenen in a temperature measuring instrument.

Thermostat. A temperature sensitive switch or valve used to control electric currents or fluids.

Tinning. The process of coating ferrous or non-ferrous metals and alloys with a thin coating of molten solder (tin/lead alloy).

Tolerance. The numerical difference between the upper and lower limits of a dimension.

Tool angle. The angle between the rake and clearance faces of a cutting tool.

Torque. Alternative name for *turning moment*. The turning effect of a force. The product of the force and the perpendicular distance between the point of action of the force and the point of rotation. (unit = Nm)

Torsion. A force which twists or tends to twist a shaft or spindle.

Trepanning. A process for producing large circular holes in thin material by cutting an annular groove and removing a thin disc of metal.

Wavelength. The distance between corresponding points on adjacent waves, particularly electro-magnetic and accoustical waves. See Fig. G.5.

Web (as part of a drill). A narrow, interconnecting strip of metal. See Fig. G.6.

Weight. The effect of gravitational acceleration (force of gravity) on the *mass* of a body
Weight = Mass × Gravity
($9.81 N = 1$ kg $\times 9.81$ ms^{-2})

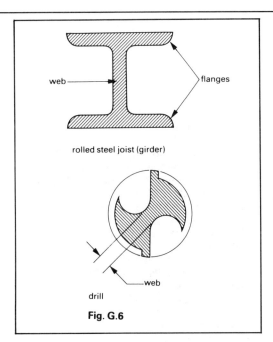

Fig. G.6

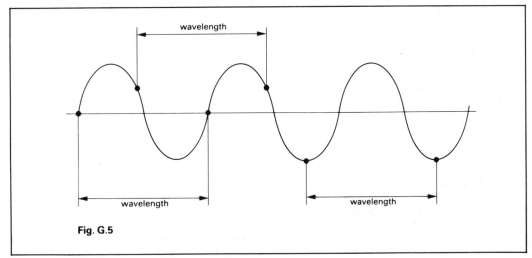

Fig. G.5

Index

aluminium. *See* materials
angles. *See* calculations
annealing. *See* heat treatment
anvil. *See* forging
averages. *See* calculations

bench shears. *See* sheet metal working
bend allowance. *See* sheet metal working
blind holes, drilling of, 240, 242–3
boring. *See* centre lathe
brass. *See* materials
bronze. *See* materials
built-up edge. *See* metal cutting

calculations
    angular conversion, 18, 20
    angular measurement, 16–17
    angular notation, 15–16, 19
    averages, 10
    cancelling, 3
    formulae, 13
    formulae, transposition of, 14–15
    fractions (decimal), 5–6
    fractions (vulgar), 1–3
    percentages, 6
    proportion, 10, 12
    ratio, 10–11
    right-angled triangle, 23–4
    square roots, use of tables of, 21–2
    squares and square roots, 18, 20
    squares, use of tables of, 21
case hardening. *See* heat treatment
cast iron. *See* materials
centre lathe
    alignments and movements of the, 266–9
    bed, 261
    boring of the, 279–81
    carriage, 263
    centres, work holding between, 269–70
    chuck, independent 4 jaw, 273, 275, 277
    chuck, self-centring 3 jaw, 271, 273–4
    concentricity, 275–8
    constructional features, 261 *et seq*.
    drilling on the, 279
    feed gear box, 265–6
    headstock, 262
    reaming on the, 280–1
    speeds and feeds for the, 281–3
    tailstock, 262–3
    taper mandrel, 271–3
    tool height, 277–9
    tool posts, 278–9
    turning tools, 264–5
    work holding on the, 269 *et seq*.
chip formation. *See* metal cutting
chisel. *See* metal cutting *and* hand tools
clearance angle. *See* metal cutting
compression strength. *See* materials, properties of
conduction. *See* heat
conductivity. *See* materials, properties of
convection. *See* heat
copper. *See* materials
corrosion resistance. *See* materials, properties of
counter-boring, 245–6
countersinking, 244
cutting fluids. *See* metal cutting
cutting speeds. *See* metal cutting *and* individual processes

datum lines and edges. *See* marking out

decimal fractions. *See* calculations
development. *See* geometrical drawing
dimensioning. *See* engineering drawing
dividers. *See* marking out
drilling machine
    basic alignment, 245–6
    bench type, 247–8
    column type, 249–50
    drill holding, 251–2
    pillar type, 247, 249
    radial arm type, 249–50
    work holding, 251, 253–4
drilling
    plastic materials, 255–9
    thin plate, 254–5, 257
drills, types of, 234. *See also* twist drills
ductility. *See* materials, properties of

elasticity. *See* materials, properties of
engineering drawing
    abbreviations, 56
    conventions for, 50–5
    dimensioning, 57–8, 61–3
    dimensioning from a datum, 59
    dimensions, 64–5
    dimensions (auxiliary), 59, 63
    dimensions, duplication and selection of, 68
    first angle projection, 51, 56–8
    isometric projection, 49
    oblique projection, 49
    orthographic projection, 49–50
    perspective, 48
    redundant views, 60
    rivets, 76, 78–9
    screw threads, 74–7

sectioning, 65, 70–3
sketching, 84, 86–8
tolerancing, 64, 69
expansion. *See* heat

file. *See* hand tools *and* metal cutting
fitter's bench, 194
fitter's vice, 195
fitting
    locking devices, 208–9
    screw thread tables, 213–14
    screw thread taps and dies, 211–13
    screwed fastenings, 206–10
    spanners and keys, 209–11
    tools. *See* hand tools
first angle projection. *See* engineering drawing
force, 39, 40
    effects of, 40
    levers, 45
    moment of a, 42–3
    principle of moments, 44, 46
    stress and strain, 40–2
forge welding, 172
forging
    anvil, 166
    basic operations, 170 *et seq.*
    cutting off, 171
    forming tools for, 168–9
    hammers for, 166–7
    hearth, 165–6
    principles of, 163
    work holding, 166–7
formulae. *See* calculations
fractions. *See* calculations
fusibility. *See* materials, properties of

gauges
    caliper (snap), 143, 145
    plug, 143, 145
    ring, 145
gauging, 142 *et seq.*
geometric drawing
    construction of plane figures, 82–3

development, 82, 84–5
division of lines, 79–80
setting out angles, 80–2
grinding, off-hand. *See* metal cutting
guillotine shear. *See* sheet metal working

hacksaw. *See* metal cutting *and* hand tools
hand shears. *See* sheet metal working
hand tools
    cold chisel, 196–7. *See also* metal cutting
    files, 197–201. *See also* metal cutting
    hacksaw, 199, 211–12. *See also* metal cutting
    use of, 203–6
hardness. *See* materials, properties of
headstock. *See* centre lathe
hearth. *See* forging
heat
    conduction of, 29
    convection of, 29
    expansion of metals, 27–8
    latent, 29–30, 32
    quantity of, 29
    radiation of, 29
    sensible, 29–30, 32
    specific heat capacity, 30–1, 33
heat treatment, 108 *et seq.*
    annealing (ferrous), 115
    annealing (non-ferrous), 116
    case hardening, 113–15
    hardening faults, 117–18
    normalising, 116
    quench hardening, 108, 111–12
    tempering, 112, 114
high carbon steel. *See* materials
high speed steel. *See* materials
hole punching. *See* sheet metal working

impact strength. *See* materials, properties of
isometric projection. *See* engineering drawing

latent heat. *See* heat
lathe. *See* centre lathe

locking devices. *See* fitting

malleability. *See* materials, properties of
mandrel (taper). *See* centre lathe
marking out
    cumulative error, 153, 155
    datum (centre-line), 153–4
    datum (edge), 154
    datum (surface), 154–5
    need for, 147
    preparation for, 147–8
    scribed line, 148–50
    scribing instruments, 148–50
    setting scribing instruments, 151–2
    sharpening scribing instruments, 151
    templates, use of, 152
    vee blocks, use of, 156, 158
materials
    aluminium, 107, 110
    brasses, 107, 109
    cast irons (alloy), 106–7
    cast irons (grey), 102, 104
    cast irons (malleable), 102, 105
    cast irons (spheroidal graphite), 102, 105–6
    casting of, 96, 98
    common forms of supply, 97
    copper, 107, 110
    engineering, 95
    ferrous, 97, 99
    hot and cold working of, 95–6
    non-ferrous alloys, 107 *et seq.*
    non-ferrous metals, 106
    properties of, 91–5
    steel (high carbon), 101, 104
    steel (high speed), 101–2
    steel (medium carbon), 100–1, 103
    steel (mild), 100–1
    tin bronze, 107, 109
    working of, 96–8
    workshop identification of, 107, 111
    wrought iron, 97, 100
measurement
    angles, 138, 142. *See also* calculations

calipers, 131, 133
feeler gauges, 142–3
micrometer caliper, 132, 134–5
radius gauges, 142, 144
standards of length, 129
steel rule, 130, 132
surface plate, 139
try-square, 138–40
vernier caliper, 135–8
medium carbon steel. *See* materials
metal cutting
    built up edge, 177–8
    chip breaker, 178–9
    chip continuous, 177
    chip discontinuous, 176–7
    chip formation, 176
    chisel, cutting angles and, 179–80
    chisel, resharpening, 189, 191
    clearance angle, 174
    cutting fluid, 184–6
    cutting speed, 184
    file, cutting angles and, 179, 181
    grinding, off-hand, 188–90
    hacksaw, cutting angles and, 181–2
    lathe tools, cutting angles and, 182, 185
    scraper, cutting angles and, 181, 183
    shaping tools, cutting angles and, 188–90
    sheet metal, 185–9
    single point tools, resharpening, 190, 192
    thread cutting taps and dies, cutting angles and, 182–3
    tool angle, 174–5
    tool life, 184
    twist drills, cutting angles and, 182, 184
    twist drills, re-sharpening, 189, 191
micrometer caliper. *See* measurement
mild steel. *See* materials
milling
    applications of, 313–15
    cutter mounting, 308–10
    cutter types, 304–7
    downcut (climb), 310–11
    perpendicular surfaces, 314, 316–17
    safety, 316–17
    speeds and feeds, 312–13
    surface types, 302
    up-cut, 310–11
milling machine
    horizontal, 302–4
    vertical, 302–4
moment of a force. *See* force

non-ferrous metals. *See* materials
normalising. *See* heat-treatment

oblique projection. *See* engineering drawing
orthographic projection. *See* engineering drawing

percentage. *See* calculations
principle of moments. *See* force
proportions. *See* calculations

quench hardening. *See* heat-treatment
quick-return mechanism. *See* shaping machine

radiation. *See* heat
ratio. *See* calculations
reamers (and reaming), 243, 245
riveted joints. *See* sheet metal working
rivets. *See* engineering drawing

safety
    accidents, causes of, 120
    behaviour in the workshop, 122
    drilling, 125, 127
    grinding, 127
    hand tools, 122, 124
    legislation, 121
    milling, 126–7
    need for, 120
    personal, 122
    portable power tools, 125
    turning, 127
    welding, 128
screw threads. *See* engineering drawing

screw thread taps and dies. *See* fitting *and* metal cutting
screwed fastening. *See* fitting
scriber. *See* marking out
sectioning. *See* engineering drawing
self-secured joints. *See* sheet metal working
sensible heat. *See* heat
shaping machine
    alignments, 290, 292
    applications, 298–300
    clapper box, 287–9
    construction of the, 286 *et seq*.
    cross rail, 288, 291
    generation of a plane surface, 286–7
    quick-return mechanism (slotted link), 291, 293–4
    ram, 287, 289
    table feed mechanism, 295
    tool holding, 296–7
    tool post, 290
    tool types, 298
    work-holding, 295–8
    work-table, 290, 292
shear strength. *See* materials, properties of
sheet metal working
    bend allowance, 222, 224
    cutting tools, 215–17. *See also* metal cutting
    development, 220–1. *See also* geometrical drawing
    forming tools, 218–20
    handforming tools, 217–18
    hole punching, 216–17
    riveted joints, 224–6
    riveted joints, defects in, 227–8
    rivets, types of, 226–7. *See also* engineering drawing
    self-secured joints, 222–3, 225
    soft soldering, 227, 229
    soldering fluxes, 229
    soldered joints, types of, 230–2
    solder, types of, 229
soldering. *See* sheet metal working
spanners and keys. *See* fitting

specific heat capacity. *See* heat
spot-facing, 245–6
squares and square roots. *See* calculations
steel rule. *See* measurement
stress and strain. *See* force

tailstock. *See* centre lathe
temperature, 31–2
    associated with forging, 36–7
    associated with heat-treatment, 36, 38
    associated with soldering, 39
    melting point of common metals, 39
    workshop estimation of, 35–6, 38

temperature measurement
    optical pyrometer, 35
    radiation pyrometer, 34–5
    thermocouple pyrometer, 34
tempering. *See* heat-treatment
template. *See* marking out
tensile strength. *See* materials, properties of
tool angle. *See* metal cutting
tool life. *See* metal cutting
toughness. *See* materials, properties of
trepanning, 243–4, 246
triangular. *See* calculations
try-square. *See* measurement

twist drill, 234 *et seq.*
    cutting angles, 235–8. *See also* metal cutting
    cutting speeds and feeds, 236–8
    failures and faults, 240–2
    types of, 239, 240

units, basic scientific, 26

vernier caliper. *See* measurement

wrought iron. *See* materials